The Descent of Political Theory

The Descent of Political Theory

The Genealogy of an American Vocation

John G. Gunnell

The University of Chicago Press
Chicago and London

John G. Gunnell is professor of political science at the State University of New York, Albany.

The University of Chicago Press, Chicago 60637
The University of Chicago Press, Ltd., London
© 1993 by The University of Chicago
All rights reserved. Published 1993
Printed in the United States of America

02 01 00 99 98 97 96 95 94 93   5 4 3 2 1

ISBN (cloth): 0-226-31080-9
ISBN (paper): 0-226-31081-7

Library of Congress Cataloging-in-Publication Data

Gunnell, John G.
    The descent of political theory: the genealogy of an American
vocation / John G. Gunnell.
        p.   cm.
    Includes bibliographical references (p.   ) and index.
    ISBN 0-226-31080-9—ISBN 0-226-31081-7 (pbk.)
    1. Political science—United States—History.   I. Title.
JA84.UG78   1993
320'.0973—dc20   93-519
                                                            CIP

For Jennifer Anne and Daniel Thomas

This antinomy between scientific truth *and political* reality *is something quite new.*

Paul Valéry

Contents

Preface

This study had its inception in 1982 when I served as program chair for the political theory section of the annual meeting of the American Political Science Association and, at the same time, wrote an essay on political theory for a volume on the "state of the discipline" which was the theme for the meeting.[1] I approached this as a historical project and soon found that I was uncovering considerably more material than could be incorporated in the essay. One of the reviewers of the draft manuscript, Norman Jacobson, to whom I owe more than one intellectual inspiration, suggested that I think about presenting the material in a still more extended form.

The research and writing have occupied a significant portion of my time during the last decade. Even when I have been engaged in various other endeavors, it has remained in the background and found its way into a number of collateral projects. Although much of the original impetus behind the project was critical, in that I wished to provide a historical dimension to some of my more deconstructive analyses of contemporary academic political theory, it soon began to take on a different character. This was in part because I became fascinated with the material and with the very process of excavating the past of political theory. I also found that intellectual archaeology evokes understanding and sympathy. It is difficult to penetrate the sites of dead cultures and take on the task of digging up the earnestly fashioned artifacts with an instrumental and hostile purpose.

As my friend Gene Poschman has so aptly put it, there are two kinds of academic activity—dredging and polishing. Most political theorists are polishers—even when producing what they sometimes purvey as history. Although I have attempted, given my past life as a polisher, to impart a certain sheen to the form in which this material is presented, the research has been definitely a dredging operation. Although I have taken into account and benefited from the extensive secondary literature that is relevant to this study, I have often been exploring unsurveyed terrain. One of my first digs involved reading the twenty or more oral histories randomly collected, and largely forgotten, by the American Political Science Association and buried in the archives of the Helen Dwight Reid Foundation in Washington, D.C. Since that time, the APSA oral history project has been resurrected, and as part of that project, as well as in conjunction with my own work, I conducted an extensive oral history of David Easton.[2]

One of the characteristics of dredging is that vast amounts of material are sifted in order to extract small nuggets. Much of my effort involved extensive personal interviews, perusing countless volumes of academic journals, reading and scanning hundreds of political science books, examining what often seemed to be endless boxes of musty personal papers and archival material, and listening to many hours of cassette tapes. And it is in this regard that I will begin to acknowledge at least a few of the many debts that I have incurred while writing this book.

The library at the State University of New York at Albany contains, through the prodigious and nearly single-handed efforts of John Spalek, professor of German, what is probably the world's largest single source of material on German émigré scholars and artists. The German Intellectual Émigré Collection includes the personal papers of more than seventy-five individuals, and it is supplemented by more than one hundred oral history tapes as well as by the records of such organizations as the Emergency Rescue Committee and the American Council for Émigrés in the Professions. Among the papers most useful for my work were those of Arnold Brecht, Henry Ehrmann, John Herz, Erich Hula, Erich Kahler, Otto Kirchheimer, Emil Lederer, Henry Pachter, Hermann Rauschning, and Hans Speier.

The library of Bowdoin College in Brunswick, Maine, near where I have spent a large portion of my life, proved to be a rich source for nineteenth-century books and journals and various fugitive items of the period. Although I visited the library at the University of Chicago for only a short time, the papers of Charles Merriam that I consulted were meticulously cataloged and organized. The Daniel Coit Gilman collection at the University of California at Berkeley was valuable for pursuing certain aspects of the work of Francis Lieber as well as Gilman's own career.

In the course of this study, Gene Poschman has provided me with dialogue as well as bibliographic resources. Even though I have attempted to acknowledge his insights into the history and historiography of political science, I probably have simply appropriated and embellished many without attribution. He is as generous with his ideas as he is with his wine cellar.

The study of the history of political and social science has, in recent

years, become an identifiable research specialization, and I have profited from the work of, and conversations with, a number of individuals
both in this country and abroad. Among those on the Continent, I
should mention Erkki Berndtson, Björn Wittrock, and Peter Wagner.
In the United States, I have gained much from my association with
Raymond Seidelman and James Farr and, more recently, John Dryzek
and Stephen Leonard. We have argued and exchanged information
about the history of political science, and their intellectual seriousness,
academic integrity, political commitment, and personal good humor
deserve recognition. My colleague at Albany, Peter Breiner, has been a
great help with my work on Weimar and the émigrés.

There is one area of secondary literature that I would single out for
special recognition, not only because of its intrinsic merit but because of
the general insights that I gained from it in threading my way through
what at times seemed to be the impossible labyrinth of the Weimar conversation. This is the work that David Kettler, Volker Meja, and Nico
Stehr have done on Karl Mannheim.

I found in the course of my investigations that there were some individuals who did not want the burial sites of political theory disturbed. In
some instances, they may have been suspicious of my motives, while in
other cases they did not want their past opinions disinterred. Among
those, however, who were personally open and provided valuable information, either in interviews or correspondence, were Sheldon Wolin,
Norman Jacobson, John Hallowell, Dwight Waldo, Herbert Simon, and
Gabriel Almond. Sheldon's dedication to the vocation of political theory has for many years provided an intellectual touchstone for my
work, and he is a distinct presence in this book. Although this work has
led to more than one new friendship, I must single out my association
with David Easton.

Since I spent a large part of twenty years of my academic career questioning the philosophical assumptions about science and theory represented in the behavioral movement in political science, I repeatedly
found myself critically involved with the arguments of the movement's
most significant theoretician and most articulate representative. It was
not until 1985, however, that I actually met David. In 1986, I interviewed him twice in connection with my research, and this eventually
led to a series of extended taping sessions for the APSA oral history and
to our mutual involvement in an international study group on the comparative history of political science. David is a person of profoundly
generous intellectual spirit, and from our meetings, I not only learned a
great deal about him and his work, and gained a deeper appreciation of
its character and motivation, but derived a knowledge of the develop-

ment of political science from the 1940s through the 1960s that could not be elicited from any other source. His late wife Sylvia added much to our discussions and to my sense of what it means to combine grace with deep social commitment.

For twenty-five years, George Kateb has been constant in his personal and professional support. Terry Ball and John Nelson have repeatedly helped sustain my work. John Tryneski encouraged and nurtured this project for several years before it reached a fully intelligible form. Released time for the final stages of writing and revision has been generously provided by a university fellowship from the National Endowment for the Humanities.

Finally, to Dede, as always, after thirty-six years.

Introduction

. . . only that which has no history is definable.

Nietzsche

Although there may be suspicions about what the title of this work is intended to convey, the only senses that I will admit to are Darwinian and Platonic. This study is, quite literally, a reconstruction of the hereditary derivation and ancestral extraction of the enterprise of academic political theory—as well as the self-images and images of its subject matter that were generated in the course of its evolution. And it focuses on political theory's trepidation and ambivalence with respect to entering the cave of politics. Most narrowly construed, this is an intellectual history of academic political theory in the United States. Most broadly conceived, it is an exercise in the history of the social sciences. In at least two respects, it is a contribution to the history of political science. First, the principal focus is on the period, from the late nineteenth century through the 1960s, in which political theory was largely identified with the discipline of political science. Second, not only was the discipline the primary context of political theory, but debates in and about theory were at the heart of disciplinary controversy and transformation and the search for professional identity. The subfield of political theory has characteristically been the locus of self-reflection about the state of political science, its past, and its future prospects.

The basic intention of this work is to reconstruct accurately the evolution of political theory as a discursive practice and trace the changes that have most fundamentally determined its current structure and content. The purpose is twofold. The first is internal to the field. It is to provide a historical dimension to reflection on the enterprise of political theory. Although the project might be adequately justified on the grounds of historical antiquarianism, the motivating assumption is that a critical examination of the field requires an appreciation of its genealogy. Both graduate students and professional scholars characteristically find themselves thrown into a universe of discourse, and its parochial variants, in terms of which they define themselves intellectually but

1

with only a dim or mythical patrimonial awareness of its form and content. There is little sense of the degree to which controversies about such matters as liberalism and the relationship between political theory and political practice, which today structure and animate the field, are, despite their contemporary character, the discursive legacy of a past which has receded from consciousness.

Although there is a general problem about the relationship between political science as a whole and its increasingly specialized subfields, the situation is much more acute with respect to political theory and cannot be adequately explained in terms of normal trends in disciplinary differentiation. During the course of the behavioral revolution in political science during the 1950s, and the intellectual and professional hegemony achieved by the behavioral movement in the 1960s, the relationship between political theory and political science, as well as the constitution of each, was permanently changed. Although in many ways still institutionally linked to political science, political theory increasingly came to understand itself, and to be understood, as a distinct enterprise. During the last two decades, political theory, despite its continued position as a subfield of political science, has emerged as a relatively autonomous endeavor with a distinct professional identity. Political theory, as a subfield of political science, is today little more than an outpost of the wider interdisciplinary field and has little to say to or about political science, while much of the literature of political theory is of marginal interest and intelligibility to political scientists. This estrangement is rooted in an old quarrel, and a principal reason for undertaking this study is to recover the original terms of that quarrel.

One of the difficulties in writing about the history of political theory as an academic field is that it has in large measure understood itself as the heir to a great tradition of political thought constituted by the canon of classic texts from Plato to Marx, which it has, at the same time, posited as its subject matter and designated as the history of political theory. I have argued that this tradition, as characteristically conceived, is little more than a reified analytical and retrospectively constituted construct.[1] What I am investigating here is what I take to be the "real history of political theory," that is, the history of the academic practice that created the image of the great tradition and projected it as its past. But this also suggests a more general problem.

Many of the images of political theory that have populated the field and held its practitioners captive, images of theory as both a subject matter and form of inquiry and as both a product and activity, have a mythical character. They have been generated within, and have little sense and reference outside, this academic practice. They include not

only attempting to endow political theory with world-historical significance by attaching it to the great tradition but urging the notion that it is
a tributary of theory in the natural sciences, claiming that it is the source
of knowledge that holds the promise of a reformation of society, suggesting that it is the reflective dimension of political life, or even that it
is, itself, a higher form of political discourse and a mode of political action. These images cannot withstand much scrutiny, but untangling
them from the real history of the field is difficult. Not only does each
image carry with it its own version of the past, but the story of their generation constitutes a large part of that history. Furthermore, these images represent something more than a series of internal disciplinary
crises of identity. They reflect the congenital problem of the relationship of political theory to politics, the problem of the authority of
knowledge vis-à-vis political authority.

Although I assume that this study is of intrinsic interest to professional political and social scientists, political theorists, and political philosophers, my basic concern is neither simply the scholarly one of
providing an account of the history of a particular academic field nor
the critical one of forcing some self-reflection on the members of an intellectual community regarding the sources of its identity and the nature of its regulative assumptions. The second, and more external,
purpose of this study is to explore a dimension, and present a case
study, of the relationship between academic and public discourse in the
United States—and maybe even to suggest something universal about
the more general perennial issue of theory and practice.

Political science, of all the social sciences, is, as Bernard Crick so
forcefully argued, a peculiarly American enterprise with respect to
both its origins and historical constitution. This fact has been a point of
departure for both praise and blame, but it is important to understand
exactly what kind of claim is being asserted. It is not that the study of
politics, generically conceived, is an American phenomenon or that this
particular discipline has not, for better or worse, been exported and
transformed in new settings. It is also, especially, not to say that this academic institution has not been profoundly affected by exogenous intellectual influences. It is to say only that, among the social sciences, it
manifests a special relationship to American politics and exemplifies
most sharply the relationship between the American academy and public life. But if political science is an American invention, even more so is
political theory.

This is not a claim about a generic or stipulative concept (such as political reflection or political thought) but about a specific academic practice with a distinct historical career. If political science was embedded in

American culture and the American university, political theory was embedded in political science. Political theory is a peculiarly American institution and its history has manifested in a special way the problem of the relationship between academic and public discourse in the United States. This issue is not an abstract and externally imposed narrative theme. There are few commentators on the history of political science who have failed to note that the dilemma of theory and practice and the tension between professional and political commitments have been self-conscious and constitutive issues in the discourse of the discipline, and the history of political theory reveals the fate of the aspirations that have defined American social science as well as some of the latent or recessive characteristics of that enterprise. This is not a general study of intellectuals and politics but rather of academicians who have pursued an image of engagement in terms of theoretical intervention. While some commentators have lamented the retreat of public intellectuals into the academy, this is a story of those scholars who have attempted to reach beyond the confines of the university and touch political life.[2]

It is not, in some respects, so much the proximity of political theory to American politics but its distance from it that makes it a felicitous vehicle for exploring the relationship between academic and public discourse. As I attempt to demonstrate in the first two chapters, an important dimension of the origin of the social sciences in the United States was practical—both in terms of location and purpose. Yet, despite the relative success of someone such as Francis Lieber in bridging theory and practice in the mid-nineteenth century, there was, early on, a problem in bringing knowledge to bear on power. Paradoxically, as I have attempted to demonstrate in the case of Max Weber in Germany after the turn of the century, the solution seemed to require the separation of the two. This strategy was also endemic to the American experience. Politics was a dangerous game—not only to play but to observe, comment upon, and confront. Like T. S. Eliot's image of the anthropologist studying cannibals, there was, in a triple sense, a fear of being consumed by the object—the possibility not only of becoming a menu item but of gaining a taste for the cuisine as well as a concern that participatory observation might lead to a loss of credibility from the perspective of both actors and peers.[3] Politics was inherently fascinating but also distasteful and a source of anxiety. Purity and contamination were at issue, and often the goal was not only to understand the subject matter but ultimately to abolish or transform it. From the beginning, distance was indicated but the question was how, at the same time, to gain authority and affect political life.

In chapter 2, I explore the manner in which political science found in the idea of the state not only a substitute for politics but something which both distinguished the discipline as a field and lent a sense of scientific significance to its endeavor. The search for the state had a yet deeper meaning, but the most immediate problem was one of distance—both overcoming it and maintaining it. The answer to this seemed to be science and the university. Here was, simultaneously, the cloak of academic freedom and scientific authority. Yet the answer was disappointing. It was not simply that the university was not safe from politics—neither internally nor externally. First of all, after the Civil War, the American university, unlike that of Germany and England, had no clear authoritative role in, or structural relationship to, politics and public life. In a highly pluralistic society, the authority of knowledge seemed to require speaking with a neutral voice grounded in scientific values and facts. Again, science and society required, as a matter of principle, separation in order, as a matter of practice, to get them together. In exactly what manner this was to be achieved, however, became the persistent problem of social science after the turn of the century, and it was particularly the problem of political science, which from its earliest beginnings had been understood both as a discipline with an end in action and as an institution that must avoid direct political action. This issue became the special province of political theory. To a large extent, then, the problem of the relationship between academic and public discourse in the United States was a problem of the relationship of the university to politics. It was not only the lack of a definite public role for the university in general but the fact that academic life created its own demands, both intellectual and material, that made the engagement of political life very difficult.

My concern is not to investigate, in any detail, the actual intercourse between political science and politics but rather to follow the path of the conversation about this issue. I do not want to say merely that this is a study of the history of academic political theory from this perspective, since my claim is the stronger one that the dialogue on this issue has been definitive with respect to the nature of that history. It was within the discourse of political theory that the agony of political science's relationship to politics was played out. This is, however, less a study of the successes and failures of these inhabitants of the university in their attempts to explain and transform politics, and of the manner in which they were affected by it, than an analysis of the image of the relationship between these realms that has been embraced and propagated, with various degrees of reflection, by political theorists in the course of conducting and rationalizing their activity. It is in part a story of how a certain kind of claim to social knowledge has, in the search for identity and legitimacy, attempted to provide itself with an authoritative past and a philosophically compelling self-image.

This means, almost inevitably, that the discussion has critical implications, since that self-image has seldom been realistic or realizable. As Thomas Kuhn has noted, history can be an antidote to the images by which we are possessed. But although I view this study as necessary background for a critical examination of the field of political theory and for thinking about its present and future, my concern here is more with a dilemma than a failure. The purpose is less one of demonstrating the often hyperbolic character of political theory's understanding of, and hopes for, its activity than of describing the pathos inherent in its position and, more generally, in the situation of political philosophy, or what might be called philosophical politics, in a liberal society.

Although institutionalized political studies began in the nineteenth century, this period, treated in the first two chapters, might well be considered the prehistory of both political science and political theory—no matter how determinative this past may have been. It was with the establishment of the American Political Science Association, and the subfield of political theory—with the creation of a professional as well as a discursive identity—that the conversation which I am reconstructing commences in a fully differentiated manner. Chapters 3–6 tell the story of the maturation of political theory as an intellectual enterprise and its relationship to the vision of American liberalism. Although the scientism associated with the work of Charles Merriam and the Chicago School is often, and quite correctly, viewed as constituting an important transformation in political science and political theory, my emphasis is on the often neglected continuities with the previous generation. Despite growing distinctions between theory as science and theory as history, as each evolved during this period, they continued to be understood as complementary, if not integrally related. The unraveling of this relationship began only in the 1940s.

The crux of this study is the account, in chapters 7–9, of the impact of the German émigré scholars on political science and political theory. This influence was so crucial, during the 1940s and 1950s, that in some respects it would not be an exaggeration to suggest that political theory, as it is understood today, was reinvented during the dialogue which was precipitated by this intellectual migration and the transplantation of the Weimar conversation. To interpret this period requires reconstructing the intellectual world from which the émigrés exited as well as the manner through which they entered and transformed the American dialogue. Much of the story of the refugee intellectuals has been thoroughly and comprehensively documented, and there are detailed studies of, and autobiographical reflections on, the life and work of particular individuals such as Hannah Arendt, Leo Strauss, Eric Voegelin, and those, such as Theodor Adorno and Herbert Marcuse, who were associated with the Frankfurt school. My concern is not to recapitulate this material but only to construct a composite image and emphasize selectively certain dimensions and contours of the transition to American political science and American society.

Despite my emphasis on the American identity of political theory, the implication is not that the field has been insulated from decisive external influences. Much of the first two chapters are devoted to exploring its nineteenth-century German roots and the transfer of ideas through the work of individuals such as Lieber and John W. Burgess. Even during the first three decades of the twentieth century, particularly after World War I, which might be considered as a period representing the Americanization of political science, Merriam, his student Harold Lasswell, and others continued to find sustenance in European ideas. In the case of the émigrés, then, it was not the European influence that was novel but rather the particular vision that sprung from the Weimar experience and which conflicted so starkly with the basic values of American political science—values such as liberalism, scientism, relativism, and historical optimism—and which resisted assimilation. Although I do not want to depreciate the changes in the practice of political science effected during the behavioral revolution of the 1950s and the behavioral movement of the 1960s, this was a peculiarly conservative revolution. It was in large part fought to preserve and realize the basic political and intellectual values of the discipline—to sustain the liberal science of politics.

Although the immediate designated opponent may have been what was characterized as endemic stagnating forces within the field, it was to a large extent the insinuation of the ideas of the European Right and Left into the discourse of the field and the emerging intellectual ambience created by these ideas that gave form and meaning to behavioralism. The Europeans, however, did not come to this country as political theorists but adopted, and adapted to, that identity—and to the vessel of the field of political theory into which they poured new content. One of the ironies of this story is that behavioralists, in distancing themselves from this literature, and in their search for an articulate and defensible notion of science and theoretical identity, ultimately attached themselves to another body of émigré literature—the philosophy of logical positivism and empiricism. By the end of the 1960s, both mainstream political science and political theory were mortgaged to realms of discourse that were in many ways alien to their experience of both science and politics. What the Europeans and Americans shared was the problem of theory and practice, but despite considerable moralizing, this issue, and concerns about concrete political issues, were increasingly sublimated in the legitimating philosophies that characterized the polarized debates of the period. Political theory, as a subfield, was estranged from political science, and two distinct images of theory emerged: one as a normative/historical project and one as the core of an empirical political science. Although the "policy turn" and the announcement of a "postbehavioral revolution" in mainstream political science at the end of the 1960s served to soften the dichotomy, political theory was well on the way to becoming an intellectually, if not professionally, autonomous field with tenuous links to political science as well as an increasingly problematical understanding of its relationship to politics.

Since I have actively participated in the critical discussion of a wide range of issues in the field of political theory during the last twenty-five years and addressed the state of the field as a whole, the portion of the last chapter dealing with the period after the 1960s is brief.[4] I am certainly too close, in both time and concern, to these matters to be the historian of this portion of the dialogue. Although my perspective on these issues had much to do with the initiation of this study, my account of the history of the field, despite the somewhat more judgmental character of the concluding discussion, has not been designed to justify my animadversions. Such a claim, however, inevitably raises contentious historiographical issues which I will identify and briefly address but which I do not want to overshadow the substantive claims in this work.

Although this study might be most fruitfully read against a broader background of work on the history of social and political science, I have attempted to construct the narrative in a manner that allows it to stand on its own and be intelligible to a broad audience and yet not duplicate previous research. But I also want to distance myself to some degree from past work in this area. My particular approach is in part a reflection of the subject matter as well as a function of the particular problems posed, but it is also prompted by a general dissatisfaction with much of contemporary intellectual history and especially that relating to the history of the social sciences in general and political science in particular.[5] This study represents a conscious attempt to put into practice some of the general prescriptions about interpretation and intellectual history that I have advanced and to avoid some of the problems that I have singled out for criticism.[6]

My designation of this work as genealogical and methodologically archaeological, and as a study of discourse and discursive evolution, should not be construed as seeking to locate it within the intellectual ambience derived from Foucault and representatives of postmodernism. Although I am not unsympathetic to some dimensions of this body of thought and although I cannot say with certainty that I would have picked up these particular concepts had they not been floating so conspicuously on the contemporary currents of academia, the literal meaning of the terms more accurately conveys my sense of what I am doing. My deployment is in many ways more a challenge to current conventional images of intellectual genealogy than an appropriation, and it reflects some very distinct theoretical claims about interpretation, its object, and its objective.

This is not, except incidentally, a history of an institutional structure, profession, or discipline. Neither is it a history of the work of particular individuals—even though the identification of the actors and their place in the discourse is a matter of importance. Some individuals, and texts, that are less well known have been given special attention, while no attempt has been made to deal with the vast secondary literature that has been devoted to individuals such as Strauss and Arendt. What is being examined here is, quite literally, the evolution of the form and content of a concrete and discrete conversation reconstructed in detail from primary sources. It is a reconstruction of political theory as a discursive practice—and of all the accidents as well as conscious choices that have driven the conversation forward.

What I am doing here I call *internal* history in order to differentiate it from a variety of projects that I label *external* history. One kind of the latter is the "presentist" accounts that have characterized much of the history of the social sciences, that is, histories designed as vehicles of disciplinary legitimation and critique in which rhetorical purpose governs method and interpretation. My concern is less to condemn such efforts, which often provide valuable information and insights about both the past and present, than to differentiate them from my project.[7] I have little patience with the simplistic claim that since historical re-"Basic" search always involves theoretical assumptions, problem and data selection, interpretation, and various valorizing premises, there is no point in talking about objectivity—any more than I see much to be said for philosophical claims about what constitutes true objectivity. Objectivity is a practical issue to be argued in contexts where there are criteria for the application of the concept. Intellectual history may not be paradigmatic of such a situation, but it is not lacking a structure of discussion about such matters.

A quite different type of external history is represented by the current emphasis on contextual explanations, that is, understanding

books, authors, or conceptual change by locating them in their historical contexts. Some of the best research in recent years has been the
product of such approaches, but they are not without problems and alternatives.[8] My point is not that contextualism is inherently defective or
that the sociology of knowledge, for example, cannot be a valid enterprise but rather that many examples of this genre suffer from a number
of specific difficulties.

First of all, they often, in fact, have little to say in depth about what is
to be interpreted while devoting much effort to an account of what is to
be taken as the explanatory context. Second, the putative context is
often uncritically presented as a given and less systematically linked to
what is being studied than juxtaposed to it, with often little more than
allusive connections. Third, while the context is presented as a kind
of independent variable, it often is not logically equivalent to what is
being explained but rather is a composite image derived from a colla-
tion of secondary works—themselves in need of interpretation and
burdened by their own historiographical problems. Fourth, what is offered as a context is frequently a sociological abstraction, again often
dependent on secondary sources, to which concrete texts and intellectual developments are either functionally linked or characterized as responses. Finally, contextualism often tends toward rationalization and
determinism, that is, it is urged that, given the context, things necessarily happened in the manner that they did. The consequence is a failure to explore internal developments. The emphasis on contexts often
involves not only losing sight of the evolutionary dimension of discourse but neglecting the extent to which the immediate context comes
too late to explain many already formed dimensions of the object of inquiry. The real issue, however, is not so much one of context versus non-
context as one of appropriate context.

My claim is that the proper context for understanding the history of
political theory is the disciplinary and professional world in which it resided. Although certain assumptions are made about external political
and social factors and their relationship to political theory and political
science, they are not offered here as an explanation of the character of
the discourse under examination. The connections that are traced are
ones involving claims and arguments between participants in a conventional discursive practice rather than between that practice and its milieu or environment—even though the images of that environment
held by the agents involved are very much at issue. We would be well
served by a history of political science that explored systematically the
conditions (social, political, economic, etc.) surrounding its development. But while there may be a need for such an external history, or

what might be called a history of relevant contexts, contemporary intellectual historians are in danger of leaning too far in the direction of Lysenko and believing that texts and the activities to which they belong are functions of environment. Internal history is an attempt to provide a theoretic corrective to past research efforts, to inject a little Mendelian thinking and focus on discursive evolution.

Some of the reasons for pursuing internal history are, however, more pragmatic and relate to the particular subject and its historical location. The idea of writing an internal intellectual history of political science in, for example, Poland after World War II, where it was a branch of the ministry of propaganda, might seem ludicrous. On the other hand, as much as one might agree that American political science has been an *American* science of politics and as much as its history has been governed by its concern about its relationship to politics, the fact is that its career has been a quite differentiated one. Its development is in many ways much more convincingly explained by its internal conceptual and institutional dynamics than by its reference to its political and social environment—an environment from which it was often quite insulated. This point can be made more concrete by considering one of the foci of this study which is a perennial problem in the history of political science.

Histories of political science almost invariably seek to explain the rise of behavioralism, and post–World War II scientism in general, in terms of such contextual factors as the new emphasis on natural science and technology, the Cold War and McCarthyism, the conservatism of the dominant liberal ideology, and increasing demands for specialization in the academic world and society. Furthermore, it is usually presented as a rather drastic change, a new paradigm which is hard to square with what is often characterized as the long history of institutional and normative studies. Thus we are pressed more than ever to seek the influences in the environment that brought it about, and since it seemed to perform certain functions in the total social complex, these functions are transformed into explanations of its origin. But it is just such assumptions that have led to an almost total neglect of the decade that preceded what is usually designated as the behavioral era. This decade, the 1940s, as I attempt to demonstrate, has much to do with understanding behavioralism and the controversies surrounding it which, in turn, shaped the subsequent development of political science and political theory.

By calling this a discursive history, I am saying that it is an account of the evolution of the discourse of political theory in the context of a formal academic practice. But, in a somewhat more literal sense, it is a discursive history in terms of the approach. In tracing the conversation and threads of argument, it moves back and forth between various literary forms and contexts, between arguments and rejoinders to those arguments. Although I have at times made reference to certain secondary sources for those interested in further exploration, I have rarely relied on such sources except for certain basic information. And no attempt has been made to attach to this study an excessive bibliographical apparatus. It is sometimes difficult not to become overwhelmed by the minutiae and permutations that are uncovered in such a study, and at a certain point, it was necessary to make choices about what constituted the core of the conversation and about where its boundaries lay. There is a difference between a reconstruction of a conversation and a stenographic record.

My claim is that at a quite accurately specifiable time and place a self-conscious conversation about political theory as an activity, subject matter, and concept was initiated. Only a few definite hypotheses initially informed the archaeological venture of sifting through the discursive artifacts and uncovering successive strata. First, I assumed that some of the paradigmatic beliefs that had defined the field, such as the assumption about the existence and character of a great tradition comprising the canon of classical texts, were explained less by looking at the extent to which such a tradition in fact existed than by following the evolution of this notion in the development of the field. Second, it seemed clear from the beginning that the abiding concern of political theory, which governed its self-understanding, was its relationship to politics. Third, the emergence of political theory as a somewhat intellectually and professionally autonomous field in the 1970s had been accompanied by a dispersion and pluralization of the field and by an inversion of its original relationship to political science whereby the subfield had become largely a microcosm of the wider interdisciplinary endeavor.

These issues, it seemed, could not be fully explored without digging deeper into the past. What became clear was that despite the continuity in the conversation about political theory, there had been conceptual transformations that had very fundamentally changed the contours of the activity and its conception of itself—so much so that at certain points, such as in the 1940s, the conversation was held together more by form than any basic mutual understanding. Some of the strata appeared so discontinuous—such as those between the 1930s and 1950s—that I was reminded of the catastrophism propounded by nineteenth-century biologists and geologists. But even in instances of radical disjunction, the changes could be followed in more detail than the gross record initially indicated. The general process was one of working back, or down, through the literature until traces of political theory as a concept and practice petered out—and then working forward and reconstructing the development. Again, what is under investigation here is not political theory in some functional, categorical, or analytically and retrospectively defined sense. If someone should ask if the term "theory" is really crucial for identifying what I am talking about, the answer is affirmative. This is the history of a practice in which the very word "theory" has been essentially contested, and the evolution of its meaning is of decisive importance.

Finally, although my general assessment of how the evolution of the discourse of political theory has informed the present character of the conversation is inherent in the form and content of this study, I have largely confined my analysis to a reconstruction of the conversation and its meaning and refrained from editorializing about its contemporary significance. I have occasionally explicitly suggested the manner in which certain concrete phases in the evolution of political theory pointed forward to later aspects of the discourse, but, for the most part, I have left the issue of the presence of the past to the reader.

1

The Practice of Theory:
End and Beginning

I am, indeed, not one of those who believe that every institution here is incomprehensible to all human beings except the natives of this country.

Francis Lieber

In 1969, Sheldon Wolin, professor of Political Science at the University of California, Berkeley, writing in the *American Political Science Review,* identified "political theory as a vocation" and sought to reawaken, among contemporary scholars, a sense of what that venerable calling, manifest in the "achievements of the long line of thinkers from Plato to Marx," had involved. He argued, however, that the vocation now attached less to the activity "by which theories are created" than to "teaching about past theories" and transmitting that tradition to the present—a task that belonged, he suggested, to the academic scholar and teacher. This vocation was demanded as an antidote, or at least a complement, to the scientism that had come to characterize the discipline of political science. Its "historyless" posture and eschewal of evaluative concerns in favor of the pursuit of pure science had resulted in "complacency" and withdrawal from a concern with public relevance. For Wolin, the *trahison de clercs* was not, as for Julien Benda, the surrender of the contemplative attitude to political passion, but the displacement of the latter in "methodism." Political theory, Wolin argued, was not only the locus of "wisdom" or "tacit knowledge" required for practical political judgment in a time of modern social crisis but even a source of "scientific imagination" so sorely lacking in the contemporary field.[1]

In speaking of political theory as a vocation, Wolin was clearly playing upon Max Weber's disquisitions on science and politics and addressing the problem of the tension between the commitment to science and the commitment to public life, but he was also giving voice to, and accentuating, a sentiment that permeated the academic community of political theory. That sentiment, however, the idea that political theory was something that could be construed as an autonomous enterprise,

15

was, despite Wolin's implication to the contrary, more a product of the evolution of the discipline of political science than something indigenous to the literature conventionally construed as constituting the great tradition of political theory. Although Wolin's argument was cast in dramatic world-historical terms, it had a more mundane significance. His statement reflected more than two decades of increasing tension between mainstream political science and a large part of the subfield of political theory with respect to the nature and purpose of political inquiry. And the issue was not simply an intellectual one. It was a matter of professional autonomy in an era of academic specialization.

The article, published in the leading journal of political science, was derived from Wolin's 1968 address to the inaugural panel of the interdisciplinary Conference for the Study of Political Thought—what was officially called an "unaffiliated" organization, consisting primarily of political scientists specializing in political theory, which held its meetings in conjunction with the annual convention of the American Political Science Association (APSA). This organization was created largely to counteract what was perceived as the depreciated status of normative and historical political theory. However exalted the image of political theory evoked by Wolin, it was offered to academic political theorists as a vision of their subfield or, maybe more pointedly, as a vision of a separate professional identity to which they might aspire. This identity was articulated on the threshold of political theory's emergence, in the 1970s, as a somewhat autonomous field of study. The Conference became one of the principal organizational vehicles for the constitution of political theory as an intellectually distinct field that would evolve and flourish during the next decade.

At yet another level, however, Wolin was also addressing a problem and echoing a faith that had in large measure defined the discourse of social science in the United States from the beginning and which especially characterized the discipline of political science. The concern about social science's relationship to politics was hardly an invention of the newly discovered vocation of political theory. The late 1960s also marked the beginning of the "policy turn" in American political science which in motif harked back to the earlier years of the field. The discipline, as a whole, began to qualify the commitment to science that it had fought so hard to establish as part of its identity during the years of the behavioral movement. In the same issue of the *APSR* that Wolin's article was published, David Easton, of the University of Chicago, who more than anyone else had articulated the values and agenda of the behavioral revolution, sharply turned away from the discipline's dedication to pure science. In this version of his 1969 presidential address to the

APSA, Easton announced a "new revolution," a "post-behavioral revolution" that consisted of "a deep dissatisfaction with political research and teaching, especially of the kind that is striving to convert the study of politics into a more rigorously scientific discipline modeled on the methodology of the natural sciences." Its "credo of relevance" would "reverse" the earlier priorities regarding the relationship between basic theoretical empirical science and problem-oriented research and "put whatever knowledge we have to immediate use" in order "to respond to the abnormal urgency of the present crises."

Although Easton argued that the long-term goal of basic research and the "discovery of demonstrable basic truths about politics" would not be abandoned, it was necessary to address the "problems of the day to obtain quick, short-run answers with the tools and generalizations currently available." It was also morally necessary, as recognized in the "tradition inherited from such diverse sources as Greek classical philosophy, Karl Marx, John Dewey, and modern existentialism," for knowledge to bear the "responsibility for acting," and to once again join theory and practice. Finally, the new revolution would, first, recognize that despite all the past concern with objectivity and value-freedom, social research always "rests on certain value assumptions," and, second, it would, like "the great political theorists of the past," begin once more the task of "speculative theorizing" and "construct new and often radically different conceptions of future possible kinds of political relationships."[2]

These essays reflected, and shared, a concern about what was perceived by many in the late 1960s as the disengagement of political science from substantive political issues and as a crisis in the university's relationship to public life. Wolin's vision of the vocation of political theory and Easton's image of a new revolution implied, however, a connection between academic and public discourse that was belied by the actual role of the discipline, including political theory, in political life. But this connection was one to which social science in general had traditionally aspired and one that it had attempted at times not only to reconcile with academic professionalism but to achieve through that very medium. If, then, this concern about the public role of political science was a common property, what, exactly, was it that had so estranged what had come conventionally to be called "scientific" and "traditional" political theory? Easton's address symbolized the beginning of the end of two decades of conflict between mainstream political science and the subfield of political theory, but it did not signal a reconciliation.

Wolin's evocation of the vocation closely followed, temporally and conceptually, his more prosaic but equally critical analysis in the *Inter-*

national Encyclopedia of the Social Sciences. Here "Political Theory" received a separate entry to which Wolin contributed a section on "Trends and Goals." The other section, on "Approaches," was authored by Arnold Brecht. Brecht's contribution largely reflected a volume he had written nearly a decade earlier and represented concerns that he, as a German émigré, had brought to this country just prior to World War II. But political theory was also extensively discussed in the subsection "Methods and Theory" under the entry for "Political Science" written by Easton. These three statements were, in effect, the residue of a long historical development and represented central strands in the evolution of political theory as an academic discourse. Easton's treatment was a quintessential statement of the conception of theory embraced by the behavioral movement in its quarrel with other images of theory. And it represented the position against which Wolin wished to contrast his image of political theory as a vocation. There was little disagreement between Easton and Wolin with regard to what had taken place in the field and about the past of political theory, but their assessments of its current status and fate differed considerably.

Easton claimed that "by the 1960s the methods of modern science had made deep inroads into political research, under the rubric of the study of political behavior," and that this "full reception of scientific method" had brought about a sharp break with former modes of theorizing and involved "casting aside the last remnants of the classical heritage." Empiricism in political science had produced a wealth of data which required a "new theoretical coherence" that was "forced upon the field with a sense of self-preservation." This development led to "a strong inclination to pose questions in a sharply different manner" and "tended to drive political science away from a prescriptive, problem-directed discipline" and toward a "growing acceptance of the difference between factual and evaluative statements."[3] Wolin, on the other hand, set out to define concretely and historically the classical heritage from which, he suggested, contemporary empirical theory in political science had consciously broken away.

He claimed that the "classic form of political theory took shape in fifth-century Athens and was largely the work of Socrates and his circle" which was in turn "consolidated by Plato and Aristotle." This "truly classical paradigm" determined the "methods and objectives" for the next several centuries and was the basis on which all "later alternatives" must be understood. Despite historical changes, "the practice of theorizing" consisted of "fairly well-defined conventions relating to methods of inquiry, the constitution of the subject matter, and the purposes of inquiry." According to Wolin, this paradigm came under siege in the seventeenth century with the "quest for scientific political theory," but even in the work of Hobbes, "who was the first to launch a systematic attack against the classical notion that there was a natural structure appropriate to every political form," the "state of political theory" was still marked by "moral and political motives." It was "only during the past half century" that political science, in a manner that could be taken as "disingenuous," had "sought to disentangle itself from moral and political concerns" and had "altered the character of theorizing in several significant ways." In the pursuit of scientism, "the alliance with philosophy" had been rejected, the attempt to "formulate synoptic pictures" of politics and political reality had been relinquished, the idea of an "underlying 'nature' to political phenomena" had been abandoned, and the "critical function" of political theory had been surrendered. This turn toward "purely empirical theory" was marked, Wolin claimed, by "arrogance" and "naive positivist assumptions" that distorted even the real character of natural science. He argued that "one would be hard-pressed to concoct a better solution for the sterilization of political theory," since it produced a narrow vision that made it impossible "to speak meaningfully to the quandaries of political existence."[4]

These conflicting renditions had never been more starkly enunciated, yet these images of theory and the tension between them were not antique. They would have been hardly intelligible a generation earlier. Both, in important respects, were the product of the impact of the immigration of ideas from the Continent beginning in the late 1930s. Brecht's discussion of political theory represented a perspective that, conceptually, stood somewhere between those of Easton and Wolin and that, historically, cast a shadow over each. His thematic focus was on social scientific theory and what he perceived as the dilemma created by its inability to arbitrate between values. Brecht treated political theory somewhat generically in terms associated more prominently with European philosophy than with the traditional discourse of American political science. The discussion, however, reflected issues that had become increasingly prominent and that had contributed significantly to shaping the intellectual structure of political theory in recent years.

The previous edition of the *Encyclopaedia,* written in the 1930s, neither devoted a section to political theory nor recognized it as a division under the entry for political science. There are a number of factors that are relevant in explaining this omission, not the least of which was the fact that the publication was to a large extent the product of European authors. The section on "Political Science" was written by Hermann Heller, a German émigré at the University of Madrid. Political theory was a distinctively American concept that belonged to the history of American political science. Heller's perspective was still a variation of the traditional German *Staatslehre,* and he had only a vague grasp of the development of the field of political science. Heller claimed that there was a tradition of political studies reaching from antiquity to the present, and he located political science as a branch that differed from the theory of the state that had developed in Germany. Although it was distinguished by a concern with government, legislation, and the question of power, he concluded that the term "political science" had "no fixed connotation." He found it "impossible . . . to formulate any precise definition of either the content or the method," since it was lacking both any definite "set of problems" or "prescribed methodology."[5] There was no focused discussion of political science in the United States, and Merriam who, beginning in the 1920s, had become the leading spokesperson for the field and its scientific identity, was prominently mentioned, but in terms of his first academic incarnation—as a historian of political ideas. To the extent that it was identifiable, political science, in Heller's view, represented a trend, since the Renaissance, toward the exclusion of "logical and ethical speculation." In the modern period, there was also a danger from "the radical relativization of life" represented in the work of individuals such as Nietzsche and Bergson which not only threatened political practice but which "must lead to the self-destruction of political science."[6] This discussion adumbrated a kind of argument that would not find full expression in the United States for at least another decade but that would profoundly transform the discourse of political science.

It was not, however, simply the European orientation that was reflected in the lack of attention to political theory. Although political theory had existed in the United States as a concept, a body of literature, and a subfield within political science for at least fifty years, the notion of political theory represented by Wolin simply had not been invented. Any tension, or even distinction, between political science and political theory would have been difficult to locate, and to the extent that there was a distinction between theory as "history" and theory as "science," the two were perceived as complementary. There was actually limited reflection about what political theory was, or should be, prior to the formation of the APSA in 1903. Political science, as a professional association, was born with a subfield of political theory, because political theory as a subject matter had become a conventional aspect of the nineteenth-century university curriculum. Subsequent attempts to define it and locate its place in the discipline were in no small measure responses to this institutional fact, but its origins had left a structural and conceptual imprint that was more determinative for the evolution of the field than many would imagine—or care to acknowledge.

Theory was not a concept that had a great deal of currency in the nineteenth century. Its presence in the field of political science, by the late 1800s, was one of the most prominent manifestations and hardly a matter of simply borrowing from more established uses. To the extent that the term "theory" did appear in the literature of the era, its use was often somewhat pejorative and carried the sense of claims that were less than scientifically, or empirically, credible. James Mill had taken pains to point out that he would have termed his study of the human mind a "theory" if the term had not been "perverted" and divested of its "original and literal meaning, that is, viewing and observing," and associated with speculation and hypothesis.[7] Darwin, for example, influenced by Lyell's account of geology and various empiricist, inductivist accounts of science, claimed that he "worked on true Baconian principles, and without any theory collected facts."[8] Auguste Comte, whose work became so influential in both England and the United States, had stressed the experiential basis of positive science and maintained the ultimate subordination of imagination to factual observation but nevertheless claimed that "no real observation of any kind of phenomenon is possible, except in as far as it is first directed, and finally interpreted, by some theory."[9] However, despite Comte's impact on John Stuart Mill, the term "theory" scarcely appeared in the latter's attempt to reconstruct the logic of science. Mill tended to reserve the term for talking generically about abstraction and speculation.[10] Questions about the status of theory in relation to facts were passed off in William Whewell's 1840 treatise on the inductive sciences by suggesting that theories are merely unconfirmed facts while facts are confirmed theories.[11]

A general book on government, published in 1853, was titled *Theory of Politics,* but the concept was never actually employed in the text.[12] There was, however, at least one widely available work of the period in the English-speaking world that did focus on the concept of theory and which, after the turn of the century, became an occasional resource for American political science. George Cornwall Lewis, editor of the *Edinburgh Review* and author of several works dealing with political analysis, was influenced by his more illustrious contemporary Mill, as well as Comte and Whewell and what he took to be the arguments of Bacon. In a two-volume treatise published in 1851, he spoke of theories of politics which he divided into two types—causal (or "positive") and normative ("universal jurisprudence").[13] In seeking to extend "to politics those methods of observation and reasoning which experience has proven to be most effectual, and which are employed with success in other departments of knowledge," his goal was increased certainty for the purpose of social control, or what he termed the "denaturalization" of the forces affecting civilization.[14]

While notions of theory as a component of empirical science were, then, not absent from nineteenth-century discourse, this was not the main channel through which the concept of theory and the notion of political theory as a subject matter and field of study initially entered the discipline. The sedimentation of the concept of political theory in the language of political science was the product of two converging tributaries: the study of ethics in the traditional college curriculum and, more significantly, the literature on the theory of the state which was so important in the evolution of political studies in the United States.

"Theory of the state" was not a very literal, or altogether felicitous, translation of *Staatslehre,* and it had no clear historical precedent in American literature. Although the term "state" was not entirely absent from American political discourse or from discourses about politics before the middle of the nineteenth century, it was a word that was neither frequently nor systematically employed apart from references to the American states. Its formal use was synonymous with the Europeanization, and particularly Gemanization, of political studies. Even by the end of the century, statements about political science, politics, and the state in an authoritative encyclopedia were all written by European authors. Paul Janet, from France, the author of a text on the history of political science and its relationship to moral principles, presented an outline of political thought from ancient to contemporary times. He discussed "theoretical," as opposed to "applied," political science and characterized it as that part of social science that deals with the "foundation of the state and of the principles of government." The task, as he saw it, was to establish "general laws, which it draws either from experience or from reason, and which are as much the generalized expression of facts as the pure conception of an ideal more or less possible of realization."[15] Johann Caspar Bluntschli, of Heidelberg, was assigned the section on politics, which he defined as the "art and science of the state" (praising Bismarck and the Prussian style), as well as the section on the state itself. Even though he maintained that there was a moral law above the state, he stressed that the latter was the institution that held society together, represented the "moral unity of the nation," and provided "solidarity, duration, and permanence." It was nothing less than "the living personification of the fatherland, the instrument of its strength at home and abroad, the author and enforcer of the law, the supreme arbiter of interests, judge of peace and war, the protector of the weak, the representative of all that is general in the wants of society, the organ of the common reason and the collective force of society: such is the state in all its power and majesty."[16]

This kind of "state-talk" was quite far removed from the actual political discourse of the day, and it might very well be asked why the state, rather than, for example, politics, in the more ordinary sense of the term, became the object of political inquiry. The most immediate explanation lies in the historical circumstances that accounted for the appropriation of the German tradition as the source of an emerging disciplinary language, but for a discipline seeking identity, autonomy, and authority, a claim of access to the mystery of the state, something deeper and more transcendental than mere politics, was appealing. Politics and government were hardly adequately sublime. In the German tradition, the attitude of the professoriate toward politics as parties, interests, and the like was little more than contemptuous. Those aspects of political science that were rooted in the English tradition were still influenced by utilitarian philosophy and the attitudes of the Augustan age, which treated politics as somewhat unseemly and springing from aspects of human being that it hoped society would repress.

Crick has suggested that the concern of political scientists for political reform during the Progressive Era reflected a deeper motivation—"they were in revolt against politics itself, full of a deep disgust at the dirt of politics that led to an aspiration for objectivity, dignity and the authority of science."[17] But the attitude was hardly confined to this phase of the discipline. The flight of nineteenth-century social science from politics—the fear and trembling with respect to both retribution and contamination—is an important part of the story of the evolution of these disciplines. Sociology and political economy found it somewhat easier to depoliticize themselves and their subject matter, but political science also found ways—conceptual, methodological, and institutional—to distance itself from politics and make its subject matter apolitical. Studying the state was surely one. Yet, paradoxically, the goal was political change.

The dilemma of American social science and the university in the nineteenth century has been well documented.[18] Social science in many of its basic dimensions began as a reform movement. Lacking political authority, it sought purchase in the authority of knowledge which in turn led to specialization, differentiation, and gravitation toward the university to ensure its claim to science. Once social science was academically institutionalized, professionalization created demands that not only competed with political commitment but contradicted it, and protecting academic status from political encroachment and defilement became a continuing problem. The case of Frank Blackmar at the University of Kansas is representative and instructive. Like so many of those who established the early departments of history and political science, he was trained (1889) at the Johns Hopkins University. Recruited by the Kansas regents, he proposed a department of "History and Politics," but he was told that "the people of Kansas would not tolerate a Department of Politics within the University, as they had enough politics within the state already." His second proposal for a department of "History and Political Science" was also rejected, and he settled for "History and Sociology."[19] Fear of politics was, however, even more deeply rooted.

George Beard, one of the founders of psychoanalysis in the United States, attributed the ubiquity of mental illness or "American nervousness" to politics and religion.[20] This sociologically induced "neurasthenia" was, he claimed, exacerbated by the unsettling conditions of late nineteenth-century political life in the United States which included class conflict and constant striving for social and material advancement. Beard warned his patients of the particular stress involved, and the amount of "nerve-force" expended, in political pursuits. He suggested that "there are two institutions that are almost distinctively American—political elections and religious revivals" and that they "appeal mostly to the emotional nature of men, and have little to do with the intellect."[21] One of the reasons that he advanced for the creation of a "national association for the protection of the insane" was the "cost in brain and nerve" caused by the "excitement and disappointment" associated with politics, for "it is the very essence of politics to disappoint those who have to do with it." Even if every other putative cause of American nervousness were discredited, the spectacle of election politics would be enough to explain it. Beard argued that "the experiment attempted on this continent of making every man, every child, and every woman an expert in politics and theology is one of the costliest experiments with living human beings."[22] He recommended political apathy as a source of mental health.

Many years earlier, Lieber, when still a "stranger in America" and observing American democracy, had asked "how does . . . our system of politics affect the mind? Are the frequent excitements, which penetrate into the smallest arteries of our whole political system, not productive of much evil in this very particular? Aristotle, even in his time, observed the great problem of insanity among politicians. . . . Do then our politics not lead, with many individuals, to an alienation of the mind?"[23] In the end, Lieber concluded that, at least as a "final cause," elections and other aspects of democratic politics and its "disappointments" were less responsible for the "appalling frequency of alienation of the mind" than "religious excitement" and "a diseased anxiety to be equal to the wealthiest."[24] Lieber was more deeply involved in public life than any academic of the century, but from his perspective there was no doubt that politics was an unsettling business. Both conceptually and existentially, his approach to politics, like that of those who succeeded him, was circumspect.

Lieber was the founder of systematic political studies in the United States, even though there were indigenous works which might be considered as antedating his efforts.[25] Nathaniel Chipman, for example, had in the late eighteenth century set out to give an account of the "social nature of man" and, relating himself to a philosophical tradition of writing about "the subject of government" that reached back to Plato and Aristotle, sought to "derive the principles, that might be pursued in civil institutions."[26] For a period of nearly three decades, however, Lieber's work was the principal matrix for the conversation about political inquiry. He was continuously sensitive to the dangers of politics, while attracted by it, as both an activity and object of analysis, but what is most striking is that he, the first American theorist of the state, was the last to be intimately, or maybe successfully, involved in public life.

The extent of Lieber's association with the public figures of his time is truly astounding: in Germany with the founder of the gymnasium movement and later with his early mentor, the historian of Rome and ambassador to the Vatican, Barthold Niebuhr; his postexile involvement in England with Mill, Austin, and Bentham; the mutually influential association with Tocqueville and Beaumont; and his contacts and relationships with public figures in the United States such as Judge Joseph Story, Chancellor James Kent, John C. Calhoun, Presidents Jackson, Lincoln, Johnson, and Garfield, Governor Marcy of New York, Henry Clay, Charles Sumner, Daniel Webster, Poe, Longfellow, and leading military men such as Winfield Scott, U. S. Grant, and John Fremont. There may, then, have been some justification for his announcing in a letter to his wife that "the two highest statesmanlike political philosophers now living are De Tocqueville and Lieber."

For a person of his time, his professional life as an academician began at a relatively late age (35). He thought of himself, probably quite accurately, as both a political philosopher and a "publicist," and he saw his mission in part as perpetuating a class of individuals who could articulate these roles. Lieber's early years, before emigration, were deeply involved in patriotic causes. His family was dedicated to Prussian nationalism, and these attitudes were reinforced at the University of Berlin by his exposure to Wilhelm von Humboldt, Johann Gottlieb Fichte, and Frederick Schleiermacher. Lieber came to maturity at the point of a fundamental transformation in the German university, and this had much to do with his vision of political studies. Although there had been reforms in Germany during the eighteenth century and increased support from both the nobility and middle class, the universities, largely Protestant, state-controlled institutions, remained as a whole weak. They had a limited social base and were alienated from such intellectual movements as the *Aufklärung*. Education was basically a state function. After the death of Frederick the Great (1786), academic freedom was sharply restricted. The Prussian diplomat von Humboldt reacted by writing a book on the limits of government in 1792, and Kant, reprimanded under a royal edict protecting orthodoxy, responded with a tract defending the freedom and authority of philosophy (1798). The French Revolution and the Napoleonic Wars, however, brought profound changes.

The university became the seat of a new nationalistic political consciousness and resistance—as well as source of increased state concern with respect to political attitudes. This was complemented, and facilitated, by the reforms initiated at institutions such as Berlin which attempted to move the university away from religious and utilitarian perspectives and toward a neohumanistic education that would train a bureaucratic professional elite. The University of Berlin, created in 1810 by von Humboldt during his short tenure as secretary of the Department of Education and Religion, was conceived not only to resurrect German higher education after the wars but to reconstitute the political order as a *Rechtsstaat* or liberal regime that rejected absolutism but stopped short of democracy. This university, which recruited Hegel (1818) and Ranke (1825), was consciously designed to produce the governmental and political leaders of the new order and to sustain its values. It was precisely this model of a national university that Lieber championed in the United States in his propagation of American nationalism.

After the defeat of Napoleon, the universities continued to develop, but there was also a strong reactionary movement against the liberal tendencies of faculty and students. The Carlsbad Decrees of 1819 imposed censorship on the faculty and restrictions on student organization. Many were persecuted and imprisoned, and many, like Lieber, fled abroad. Lieber's relatives had fought in the war of liberation (1813–14), and he himself was wounded at Waterloo. After his army service, his nationalism was transformed into radicalism in response to the weakness and repressiveness of Frederick William III and Metternich. His deep involvement in the nationalist movement led to his arrest and denial of entrance into the university. Although he eventually matriculated at Jena and gained a doctorate in 1820, he was banned from teaching and further study because of his continued agitation. After going off to fight for the liberation of Greece, Lieber's views were moderated by disillusionment and by his subsequent association with Niebuhr in Rome. Upon returning to Germany in 1823, first to Berlin and then Bonn, he was still under surveillance as a subversive and imprisoned for a time before escaping to England in 1826. Utilitarian friends aided him in securing a position as a gymnasium instructor and swimming coach in the United States, and he emigrated in 1827, settling in Boston.

He became a correspondent for a German newspaper, but for the next five years, he dedicated himself principally to translating portions of a German encyclopedia and creating an American version (thirteen volumes) which became an authoritative publication and gave him a measure of financial security. It was in the *Encyclopedia Americana* that the state, as the organizing concept of political inquiry, was first introduced in the United States. "As the idea of *politics* depends on that of the *state*, a definition of the latter will easily mark out the whole province of the political sciences. . . . This idea of the state is the basis of a class of sciences, and gives them a distinct character as belongs to the various classes of history, philosophy, theological, medical &c., sciences."[27] The state, he claimed, was the "natural condition of man, because essential to the full development of his faculties," and it was something quite distinct from "the form of government" which was "merely a means of obtaining the great objects of the state."[28] Lieber also presented the distinction, so basic to the German curriculum and eventually to American categories, between the "*abstract,* or purely philosophical, and the *historical* and *practical,*" study of politics. And he suggested twelve more specific divisions: natural law, abstract or theoretical consideration of the state and literature on this subject from Plato to the present, political economy, police science, practical politics (administration), history of politics, history of the European and American states, statistics, public (constitutional) law, international law, diplomacy, and political practice.[29]

Lieber, naturalized in 1832, was actively seeking more regularized employment, either in government or academia, during the years that he worked on the *Encyclopedia*. Although his efforts were frustrated, he made influential friends and persisted in the task of applying European concepts to the analysis of American institutions. His association with Tocqueville, initially through a common interest in prison reform, was important in this respect, but Tocqueville took much from both the *Encyclopedia* and his discussions with Lieber. Lieber moved easily between academic and governmental circles while seeking a position and dealing with various reform issues. His political views and associations were, in American terms, basically conservative. He was, for example, certainly against slavery but avoided the abolitionist movement. He worried about immigration policies that threatened racial purity, and arguments for feminist rights were an anathema.

It is difficult to ascribe precisely the beginning of autonomous political studies in the United States. At Princeton University, the president, the Reverend John Witherspoon, lectured on "politics" and "civil society" and his son-in-law, the Reverend Samuel Stanhope Smith, taught "moral and political science." But such studies were typically an aspect of moral philosophy. In 1819, Thomas Jefferson, seeking a more secular approach to the study of government, had sponsored Thomas Cooper, a utilitarian political economist from England, at the University of Virgina. But his secularism prompted him to move, within a year, to South Carolina College where he served in a variety of capacities from president to professor of political economy. Lieber succeeded Cooper at Carolina. Although it was here that Lieber wrote his major treatises, this was not his preferred location, and he never failed to view the twenty years he spent at this institution as a form of cultural and political exile.

The two volumes of Lieber's *Manual of Political Ethics* (1838–39), which he later described as an exercise in enlightened patriotism, were conceived much along the lines of the public aspects of moral philosophy taught in American colleges. But despite its practical purpose of political education, and tempering political "excitement," it was the first example in American literature of a systematic treatment of government, politics, and law. It was specifically designed to compete with, or supersede, classic works in moral and political philosophy written from the English/Scottish perspective such as that of William Paley and to apply European concepts to the analysis of American politics.[30] Above all, *it was the first study of the state in America and the first study of America as a state.* A stylistically ponderous and exhaustingly comprehensive work (although touchy subjects such as slavery were conspicuously missing), it was a studied attempt, following the path of German scholars of the period, to meld philosophy and history, dealing with everything from the metaphysics of the state to smuggling. Foremost among its goals was to distinguish the state from the family, the church, and other social entities and to establish the primacy of the state—and by implication that of the field devoted to studying it.

Lieber presented an extended theoretical discussion of the state as a "*jural* society," which referred to a moral relationship founded on right and justice and prior to positive law. The state was natural, or "aboriginal with man," and existed by necessity. While yet a means, and not superseding the individual, it was the highest form of society, "the glory of man," and its purpose was to obtain the highest ends of humanity.[31] Central to his position was, again, the notion that the state was prior to government. The truly legitimate state, the "hamarchy," was a sovereign organism, exemplified in the United States and England and the evolutionary path leading to their appearance (through Christianity, the rise of the Teutonic world, and the advent of representative government and capitalism).[32] He emphasized the reciprocity of rights and duties, but stressed the latter. He rejected contractarian theories yet held on to a notion of natural rights and the priority of individual liberty. He attacked socialism and defended the sanctity of property as an extension of the individual. The Gallic disease that he feared was democratic absolutism, which, he believed, always manifested an element of communism. His answer was "institutional liberty" created through representative government and the system of checks and balances characteristic of the *Federalist* with its image of decentered and limited governmental power.

The *Manual* had little impact in the decade following its publication, and neither his study of political and legal hermeneutics nor a tract on property and labor succeeded in gaining him the position in the North that he consistently coveted. Although he even considered returning to Germany, the publication of *Civil Liberty and Self-Government* (1853), which focused on American government, gained him a larger academic and political audience. Lieber again promoted his vision of the state as a natural and necessary organic "sovereign society" with "an indelible character of individuality." Although ultimately an instrument of the individual and the social collectivity, the state was prior to and acted through government—which was only "a contrivance which holds the power of the whole."[33] Whether or not his assessment of his own role was accurate, his hopes and ambitions were clear: "Aristotle taught a royal youth and a future conqueror, and the Athenians indeed, but at a period when the sun of Greece was setting, while my lot has been to instruct the future law-makers of a vast and growing commonwealth in the noblest branches that can be imparted to the minds of youth preparing themselves for the citizenship of a great republic."[34]

Lieber resigned from Carolina in 1855 and finally, in 1857, was appointed to a chair at Columbia that he asked be designated as History and Political Science. His repressed concerns became manifest in a militant nationalism and Republicanism. Through the period of the Civil War and its aftermath, he was consistently involved in affairs in Washington and wrote tracts on guerrilla warfare, international law, and the governance of armies in the field. In the classroom, he attacked contract theory as an intellectual basis of the South's position and defended the North in terms of the organic image of the state as the "proper destiny" of man as a "political being."[35]

In his inaugural address at Columbia (1858), on the necessity of studying history and political science in "free countries," Lieber argued the "need of a national university." This would not be a governmental institution but would function in "spirit" and "effect" like the Prussian university that even under foreign rule had contributed to "quickening and raising German nationality" and, within a short time, making the state a great power. Although there was constant danger of governmental centralization, the United States also required a greater sense of nationality and patriotism, since only nations could represent the "great commonwealth of our race which extends over Europe and America."[36] In this address, Lieber also presented the most systematic exposition of his image of political science or "political philosophy." He argued that people are born into society, an organic entity which was not the product of artifice but grounded in "love and instinct of association." "History" and "statistik" were but respective modes for studying the past and contemporary, continuous and static, dimensions of social relations. And in approach, he stressed a middle road between the "so-called historical school," which valorized the past, and the "philosophical school," which postulated necessary laws of social evolution. But primarily Lieber wished to identify the domain of political science with the state. Political science, he claimed, "treats man in his most important earthly phase; the state is the institution which has to protect or to check all his endeavors, and, in turn, reflects them." And, in the end, the history of the state was nothing less than the history of civilization from primitive society in Africa to "Anglican self-government and liberty."[37]

Political economy was, he suggested, a branch of political science, but man as a producing and exchanging animal was not as significant as the study of man as a "jural being—as citizen." Such work was particularly important in a country where there was a great deal of liberty and political action, since "nowhere is the calming effect of an earnest treatment of politics more necessary." Here there was a need for "what might be called political physiology and political pathology."[38] Political science "ought to be taught not only in college." These "fundamental truths," from the matters dealing with the origins of society up to "the greatest of institutions—the state," ought to be "ingrained in the minds of every one that helps to crowd your public schools."[39] One branch was "political ethics," and another involved the "science of government," which included both a historical account of forms of government and "a survey of all political literature as represented by its prominent authors, from Aristotle and Plato" to the present as well as "those model states which political philosophers have from time to time imagined and which we now call Utopias." Next the political philosopher should deal with "our own polity and political existence" and finally with that "branch which is the glory of our race"—international law.[40]

Lieber, then, set out the nascent format for the field that would become known as political theory, and he indicated the purpose of such studies. In an introduction to a course of lectures at the law school (1859), dealing with "the ancient and the modern teacher of politics," he maintained that "I belong to no party while teaching," but at the same time he continued to stress the practical dimension of political science and the authority of its claims.[41] While the state had historically been central to the development of civilization, many thinkers in the past, such as Aristotle, had lived at the nadir of their culture and were only able to summarize and lament. Although Lieber claimed that he was forced to teach "the science of public affairs at a period of depressed public mind" and at a time when too much of life was drawn into the political realm, the modern thinker, he maintained, lived, on the whole, in a period of progress in the development of the state and could contribute and play an active role. During the founding of the American state, "political literature" (Montesquieu, etc.) had been influential, and political science was still as necessary to the statesman as "the medical book to the physician."[42] He did, however, wish to correct one of the problems that stood in the way of the influence of political literature. This was its tendency, from Plato to modern communism, to develop extravagant schemes. This had contributed to the belief that political speculation was connected with fanaticism. Lieber wished to demonstrate that political studies could play a more conservative role and to affirm that the "faithful teacher of politics ought to be a manly and profound observer and construer" and stay away from "fantastic theories."[43]

By the advent of the Civil War, Lieber pursued the theory of the state in support of the Union and argued that the American state, with its population of European immigrants, represented the latest stage in the history of the Teutonic state and "in the history of the cis-Caucasian spreading over the globe."[44] He spent his last years at Columbia in the law school after President Barnard, who had come from Mississippi, attempted to have him dismissed altogether (on the avowed basis that his approach was not needed in an undergraduate college). He continued to be involved in public affairs at the national, state, and city level and in circles of higher education until he died in 1872. Not only did he set the stage for the development of the graduate program at Columbia, but he had a profound effect on individuals such as Daniel Coit Gilman, the first president of Hopkins and sponsor of political studies at that institution, and on Theodore Woolsey at Yale. But there was another important connection which was central to the development of the ideas introduced by Lieber.

In a posthumous tribute to Lieber, Bluntschli noted that "from 1860 to 1870, Francis Lieber, in New York, Edward Laboulaye, in Paris, and I in Heidelberg, formed what Lieber used to call a 'scientific clover-leaf,' in which three men, devoting themselves especially to political science, and at the same time uniting the historical and philosophical methods, combining theory with practical politics," maintained close intellectual contact.[45] Although Bluntschli's work would not be available in translation until 1885, when it became a popular text, many of the Americans who studied in Germany during the previous decade were influenced by his ideas. Herbert B. Adams, the principal organizer of studies in history and political science at Hopkins, studied with Bluntschli (as well as with Johann Droysen, Heinrich von Treitschke, and Karl Knies) in 1876 and secured his academic appointment on the basis of Bluntschli's recommendation. The Bluntschli library was eventually bought and presented to the university by the German citizens of Baltimore, along with papers contributed by his family. President Gilman also secured the papers of Lieber and Laboulaye and recognized their common theoretical and ideological position in his dedication.[46]

Bluntschli, while a Munich law professor, edited the *Staatswörterbuch* which carried on the tradition of the *Staatslexikon* that had represented liberal German political thought. His *Allgemeine Staatslehre* was published in 1851 and translated as *The Theory of the State*.[47] He took this to be the first division of political science *(die Staatswissenschaft)* which also included *Staatsrecht* (public law) and *Politik* (politics). Bluntschli examined the conception of the state, its historical basis, forms, external conditions, principal elements and divisions, functions, ends, and the character of sovereignty—all of which he considered essential for any more specialized study of law and politics. His analysis was informed by Aristotle as well as by Hegel and German idealism in general, but it was not simply reducible to such influences.

He conceived his work as a scientific study, and proper scientific method, in his view, required the complementary approaches of "philosophy" and "history" which he wished to distinguish from the perversions of "abstract ideology" and "mere empiricism." The French Revolution was an example of the "fever" created by abstract ideology, and crude empiricism lacked a critical attitude and tended to "servilely honor" existing institutions. For Bluntschli, the state had an ideal side or a moral and spiritual element, but this rested on, and resided in, real material form and fact. A truly philosophical method recognized this and, as opposed to "mere abstract speculation" (to which Hegel tended to succumb with his treatment of the state as a "logical abstraction"), employed "concrete thinking." This entailed uniting idea and object by penetrating beneath outward events to "knowledge of the human mind" and the "elevation of the spirit of man in history."[48]

According to Bluntschli, the genius of Aristotle and Cicero, as opposed to the ideas of Plato and Bentham who tended to fall into the trap of "mere ideology," resided in the unification of these two aspects of scientific method. He understood the contemporary period as representing the end "of the old strife between the philosophical and historical school" and his own work as weaving the two together in the tradition of Tocqueville and Mill.[49] By talking about a general teaching regarding the state, Bluntschli was suggesting that the concern was less with particular states than with "a universal conception of the State" that must precede such specialized studies.[50] Such a conception required looking at universal history and the rise of the modern form of the state which, he believed, had been realized by the Aryan or Indo-Germanic race, just as the modern form of religion was the product of the Semitic race. Through a study of the organic development of the state, it was possible to grasp the "common political consciousness of civilized mankind" and the "fundamental ideas and essentially common institutions" that would make it possible to find the general in the particular.[51] The development was not simply natural. It was a product of free will and human action, from Alexander to Napoleon, but it was rooted in a common human nature which implied the need for a universal state.

Bluntschli distinguished between the "conception" of the state and the "idea" of the state. While the former had to do with the nature and characteristics of actual states, the latter was an ideal, the "splendor of imaginary perfection," not yet realized. It was something to be discovered by philosophy rather than history.[52] The state, as conceived by Bluntschli, was indeed an interesting entity. It was a "moral and spiritual organism," masculine in personality, as distinguished from the feminine church, which began with the "appearance of the white races, the children of light, who are the bearers of the history of the world." He conceded that, like the evolution of human beings, there was a bodily history represented by the inferior races which was the material cause and preceded "proper history" as the "pigments and brushes" do "the work of the artist."[53] Although Bluntschli opposed slavery, which he argued was contrary to human nature and "vicious" in its American manifestation, later editions of his work noted that even though "North America seems disposed to give the negro full political rights," there was some question of whether this could be sustained, since a "naturally inferior race" was involved and "political right presupposes political capacity."[54]

His politics were in the German liberal tradition. He rejected both what he called the legal state, which was limited to the protection of rights, as well as the police state. It was necessary to take account of both justice and public welfare, and this was what he believed was happening in an age in which modern national states were being formed. He had no doubt that communism was in conflict "with the nature of man as created by God" and that even though socialism was "more temperate and humane," it was "equally absurd." The state had "no absolute power over private property which lay "outside the range of public law" even though it was necessary to recognize the limits of private property and the need for res publicae.[55] In his view, the idea of a social contract, however, was as unhistorical, illogical, and dangerous as the idea of divine right or of might making right. The state arose from the social impulse of human nature and passed from unconscious to conscious stages of development. Bluntschli saw himself, and individuals such as Lieber as reflecting, and even adumbrating, in theory what was being realized in practice in the modern age, and he believed that representative democracy, originating in America, pointed toward the historical completion of the state.

It was this first wave of German influence represented by Lieber and Bluntschli that constituted one of the distinct elements in the origin of the American form of political studies and political theory, but this blended with, or was grafted onto, a more indigenous source. From the mid-seventeenth century, the study of ethics in the American university had included much of the literature that would eventually be understood as constituting the field of political theory.[56] Emerging political science was very much a program of civic education, and this was grounded both in the moral philosophy and religion that had largely defined the traditional university curriculum. The education of citizens and statesmen in the ways of general political morality and the entailed rights and duties of American government and politics was the goal, and the classic texts from Plato to the *Federalist* were understood as an important contribution to this practical body of wisdom.[57] Both the historical study of the state as well as the study of the history of political ideas were easily accommodated to this curriculum. The traditional curriculum and the theory of the state were fused in the work of Theodore Woolsey.

Herbert Adams claimed that "the great northern and the great southern tributaries to American political science were brought together when Woolsey edited, in 1874, a revision of Lieber's *Civil Liberty and Self-Government*."[58] Woolsey was the first of the major native American theorists of the state to be educated abroad (at Bonn and Paris), and he reinforced the general pattern of analysis advanced by Lieber and Bluntschli. After graduating from Yale in 1820, Woolsey studied law and theology (training as a Presbyterian minister). He returned to the university as a professor of Greek in 1830 and served as president from 1846 until 1870. Writing on subjects as diverse as international relations and divorce, he was much influenced by Lieber. He taught "Political Philosophy" which at Yale, as well as elsewhere, tended to be a generic designation encompassing political science, the Constitution, economics, and related subjects. And he later specialized in teaching international law. In addition to publishing a collection of his sermons on religion delivered at Yale, his work on political science and the state appeared in 1878 and became an influential text.[59]

Derived from his lectures at Yale during the years 1846–71, the work considered human rights, the theory of the state, and the operation of the state or practical politics (which basically followed the German classification of *Naturrecht, Staatslehre,* and *Politik*). He rejected the English idea of natural rights and contract theory in favor of an image of justice that connected rights with God and the ends of humanity. He stressed the extent to which the state was a natural entity that was not merely a protector but creator of rights, and he warned against the extremes of communism and socialism and the conditions of modernity that gave rise to them. Most of the work, however, was devoted to an encyclopedic discussion of various aspects of the history and current practice of politics and political ethics.

There were certain other works which had some currency during the period and which bore a resemblance to the kinds of subjects that would characterize research and teaching in what came to be called political theory. Among these were Frederick Grimke's *Considerations upon the Nature and Tendency of Free Institutions* (1848) and F. P. G. Guizot's *History of the Origins of Representative Government* (1852). By the middle of the century, "political philosophy" had emerged as a conventional element in the curriculum at schools such as Yale, Amherst, William and Mary, Dartmouth, Columbia, and Rutgers. Although within this broad field a literature called "political theory" was less than well defined, it was, by the early 1880s, gaining a distinct place in the curriculum, as the theory of the state and the history of political thought. The department of History and Political Science at the University of California at Berkeley, under Bernard Moses, a graduate of Heidelberg and a student of the historical economist Knies, emphasized "a knowledge of the fundamental principles of theoretical politics." Moses coauthored a text devoted to the study of the state and divided, along German lines, between the analytical study of the structure and evolution of the state as an organism and politics or the practical dimension of state action.[60] Berkeley was the first, at least among the major universities, to offer a course specifically titled "political theory" (History of Political Theories, 1883). Cornell offered a course in "Theoretical Politics" (the philosophy of the state) in 1880, and Michigan began a course in the "History of Political Ideas" in 1881.[61]

By the time the major graduate programs in political science began to appear at institutions such as Columbia and Hopkins in the 1880s, the theory of the state, as advanced by Lieber, Bluntschli, and Woolsey, constituted, both substantively and methodologically, a distinct and influential paradigm. And it would be further sedimented by the new generation of scholars who were trained in Germany and France and who were most influential in institutionalizing graduate education in political science during the last quarter of the century. It was, however, principally through the work of John W. Burgess at Columbia that political theory emerged as a definite intellectual field, and its emergence had much to do with the discipline's concern about its relationship to political power.

2

State and University

We must submit to be called radical, I suppose; for that is a name attached to everybody attempting reform, and Social Science is emphatically a science of reform.
Samuel Eliot

Is it not possible for man, a being of reason, created in the image of God, to solve the problems of his existence by the power of reason?
John W. Burgess

The vision of political science that developed in the American university was one that united the field with history and combined civic education and leadership training with a general commitment to the scientific rationalization of society, and the goal was an articulation of government and university.[1]

One of Woolsey's students at Yale was Andrew D. White, who grafted systematic political studies on the base of moral science at Michigan (1857), and who, a decade later, established a school of political science at Cornell where he was also the first president. White also studied at the Sorbonne and College de France, where he worked under Laboulaye, and at Berlin with Ranke. Charles K. Adams was White's student and succeeded him at Michigan, where in 1881 he introduced the German model of studies, which he had observed at Bonn, Berlin, and Leipzig. He then followed White as president of Cornell (and later became president of Wisconsin). Although Herbert Adams and Burgess were the most crucial figures in the development of graduate political science and its image of the relationship between academic and public discourse, one other individual and institution deserves particular mention.

Although not a principal author himself, Julius Seelye, professor of "mental and moral philosophy" at Amherst College, revised in 1880 Laurens Hickok's popular textbook on moral philosophy.[2] His interests were eclectic, but in his revision of Hickok, he extended the discussion of the state and particular aspects of state authority, law, and politics. Government (divine, civil, and parental) was already a principal focus of the book, which emphasized the continuity of moral and public duty, obedience to government, natural law, the organic character of the state as a body of citizens, and the notion of government as an agent of the sovereign state. Burgess and Adams, as well as many of the colleagues and students they recruited, came from Amherst under the tutelage of Seelye.

Gilman, who did so much to further the professionalization of the social sciences, recruited Herbert Adams and supported his department of History, Politics, and Economics (beginning in the late 1870s) at Hopkins. Gilman had also studied abroad and was committed to the creation of graduate research universities based on the European model. He taught at Yale (geography) before becoming president of the University of California. When his notion of graduate education was resisted at Berkeley, he accepted the first presidency at Hopkins on the basis of the trustees' strong commitment to allow the implementation of his plan. Although for Adams the dominant category was history, he was concerned that it not be narrowly construed. It was, in his view, as for those who preceded him, virtually indistinguishable from political science, since the subject matter was the state. Edward Freeman's aphorism "History is past Politics and Politics present History" appeared frequently in his work and even as a sign in his seminar room.[3]

Adams's own specialty was local history and government.[4] He believed that this subject connected a student's own community "not only with the origin and growth of the State and Nation, but with the mother-country, with the German fatherland, with villages and communities throughout the Aryan world."[5] What connected history with political science was not simply unity of the subject matter but the idea that history had meaning, that the facts were part of a story with universal and philosophical significance as well as immediate political relevance. Political institutions were grounded in something deeper than the short history of the United States, and understanding past continuities was viewed as the key to future progress.

The Teutonic theory of the state, and the kind of vision associated with Bluntschli and Lieber, was central to the course of study, but it was an extensive and diverse curriculum which included such advanced subjects as studies in socialism (Marx, nihilism, etc.) as part of the program in political economy. The graduate seminar began in 1881 and included not only resident faculty but visitors from abroad such as James Bryce. Adams maintained that it was neither "slavishly following foreign methods nor establishing in this country a German university," but even though it may have been in many ways "pre-eminently American," the form and content unmistakably reflected Adams's image of

German education.[6] The Historical and Political Science Association, created in 1877 by Henry Carter Adams as an extension of the seminary and designed to draw in lawyers and others from the community, was described by Herbert Adams as "a kind of Staatswissenschaftlicher Verein . . . like that in Heidelberg University."[7]

What Adams hoped for was the establishment of a school of politics whose curriculum and expertise would command the attention of national government, and this vision of the articulation of university and state was embraced by his students. An impressive group was trained at Hopkins, and many did seminal research and institutional work in the emerging, yet often not clearly defined, social scientific disciplines at major graduate institutions: Albion Small (sociology, Chicago), E. A. Ross (sociology, Stanford and Wisconsin), John Commons (economics, Syracuse and Wisconsin), Edward Bemis (economics and sociology, Chicago and Kansas), Henry Carter Adams (political economy, Cornell and Michigan), John Dewey (philosophy and education, Michigan, Chicago, and Columbia), Frederick Turner (history, Wisconsin), Thomas Woodrow Wilson (history, political economy, jurisprudence, Wesleyan, Bryn Mawr, and Princeton). A group of these students, including Ross, Commons, Adams, and Bemis, were also the principals in some of the most notorious academic freedom cases of the late nineteenth century. What in part was manifest in these cases were the problems of reconciling academic and political commitment and of defining the relationship between the university and politics. While Herbert Adams and Burgess were relatively secure, but maybe less than realistic, in their vision of the public role of the private university, their students were forced to deal more directly with the practical dimensions of the problem. Cases like that of Ross, fired from Stanford, and Bemis, dismissed from Chicago, did much to dispel the idea that direct political advocacy was the answer to social science as an agent of reform.

The highly professionalized research university such as those which developed at Hopkins and Columbia raised, however, new issues about the relationship between academic and public discourse. At Columbia, as well as Hopkins, the practical mission of political science tended to give way to the demands of scholarship. Government did not seek out academic experts, and the scholars did not seek out government. Exactly how education itself would be an active force in social affairs would remain vague. It is common to view Adams and Burgess primarily in terms of their conservative elitist, nationalist, and antidemocratic sentiments.[8] This perspective, however, fails to account for the ideological positions that emerged from the Hopkins and Columbia schools. An emphasis on their particular political attitudes obscures the more general, and immediate, issue which was shared across the ideological spectrum—the problem of the university and politics. For Burgess, Adams, and others who studied in Germany, it was not merely the concept of the state and *Staatswissenschaft* that they adopted but images of the relationship between theory and practice. These images may have been partial, or less than accurate, representations of the actual, and complex, situation in Germany, but there were some general features of the relationship between the state and university that were attractive to American scholars.

By the time that this generation of Americans went to study in Germany, the German university had become a principal actor in public life. It was the basic source of governmental and professional elites—the training ground of the *Bildungsbürgertum*, and its ties to political power were unique among European nations. While in the early years, and again before 1848, it had harbored dissidents, it was, despite some tolerated opposition, now a source of strong nationalist sentiment and at the same time, notwithstanding its traditional rights and immunities, under the bureaucratic control of the state. The triumph of Prussia in the Wars of Unification entailed, by 1870, the dominance of the Prussian university which supported the Bismarckian Reich and the German empire. As the middle class gained advantage within society, most of the tension between the state and university subsided, and oppositional forces all but disappeared.[9] The German scholars were united in their attachment to some form of an idealist vision of history and the evolution of the state. Nationalism overrode particular political differences, and individuals as diverse in some respects as Otto von Gierke and Treitschke were joined in the sanctification of national power and an organic and communal vision of political life.

They were committed to German unification and found justification for this position in the idea of the state as an organic metaphysical world-historical entity reconciling authority and freedom or power and right. They believed that liberal values were to be realized within the framework of a *Rechtstaat* which they conceived as embodied in Bismarck's reformed Prussian nation. Although someone such as Droysen, like Lieber and Burgess, emphasized the limited sphere of state competence internally, he stressed the state as representing the ethical community of the nation, giving identity to the individual, and as serving as the vehicle of historical progress exemplifying God's providence and the spirit of reason. The "mandarins" were a special class which not only legitimized the state theoretically but traditionally accepted its authority and perceived their role as organically tied to the sphere of state action.[10] They were a distinctive elite who were held in high esteem and deeply tied to various forms of state power through the system of examinations that provided entrance into the bureaucracy and other privileged ranks of state service. The professional autonomy of the university faculty and its attachment to the value of *Lernfreiheit* and independent scholarly research were mitigated by the assumption that it was in very large measure a functionary of the state and a social class deeply integrated into the structure of state power.

It would be a mistake to assume that the mandarins were a monolithic group or that their situation did not undergo considerable change during the last quarter of the century. What is important is, again, less whether Americans such as Adams and Burgess accurately construed the situation in Germany than how they interpreted it.[11] The models that they appropriated did not easily apply to the American context where the role of the emerging university and its relationship to politics was far from settled. One of the things that most distinguished the American academy (as opposed to those in Germany, England, and France) was the lack of any definite institutional tie to political power and authority. Academic and political elites were often far removed from one another—even when ideologically attuned. While the work of Adams and Burgess reflected one perspective on the German context, and the one that most clearly came to inform the discipline of political science, other notions about the relationship between academic professionalism and public life were derived from the experience of those who studied in Germany. And to understand political science, it is necessary to understand the path that the discipline, as a whole, did not take.

There were two distinct but complementary and converging dimensions to the development of social science in the United States. One reflected the differentiation and specialization of the traditional nineteenth-century university curriculum, while the other involved the institutionalization, and eventual academization, of social reform movements. The schools of history and political science founded at Hopkins and Columbia, as well as the American Historical Association (1884) and the American Political Science Association (1903), were in part defections from the American Social Science Association (ASSA) and its program for social change, but there were other paths and visions exiting from the association. The story of the rise and demise of the ASSA has been told as both tragedy and progress, but whatever the perspective, it is clear that the ideals of reform and pure science "did not dwell in peace."[12] What has not been sufficiently recognized is the extent to which the development of academic professionalism was tied up with the Germanization of social theory which in various ways drew social scientists away from the Anglo-American roots of the ASSA. The development of political science, and the work of individuals like Burgess, however, both resembled and diverged from the vision initially represented by the American Economic Association, which was the second professional organization to break away (1885) from the parent ASSA.

Although the American social science movement was, through its membership and its concerns, consistently tied to the world of higher education, its roots were more practical than academic. It was born of a concern with political and economic reform and was initially inspired by the British Social Science Association which had been devoted to the amelioration of the conditions of the working class. The ASSA long held John Stuart Mill as one of its heroes.[13] It would be too simple to suggest that social science succeeded religion as a vehicle of social reform, but many of the founders of American social science, both those, such as Richard Ely, committed to the state-sponsored control of capitalism and the elimination of political corruption and his laissez-faire opponent, William Graham Sumner, came from evangelical backgrounds and viewed their efforts as a continuation of their religious goals.[14] For individuals like Samuel Eliot, the association sought people who "love their Saviour" and want "to follow him" in the relief of suffering and the aid of the infirm and needy represented in the laboring classes and women and children.[15] Society was taken to be a divine institution, and individuals were viewed in terms of their place in the social organism. Social science was the pursuit of facts, the dissemination of principles, and the application of a unified body of knowledge to uplifting the general welfare.

The ASSA (originally the American Association for the Promotion of Social Science) was closely related to earlier organizations which were even more explicitly action-oriented. The concept of social science had from the first been associated with the advocacy of social change, and it was not primarily a concept that developed within the university.[16] It was particularly associated with utopian schemes of socialism and associationism such as that promoted in the journal *Phalanx* which was established in 1843. The Society for the Advancement of Social Science had been founded in New York in 1862 and began publishing the *New York Social Science Review* in 1865. It declined advocacy of partisan policy, but it was clearly hostile to government centralization and largely reflected the program of Herbert Spencer. The goal of the ASSA was to link systematic social knowledge and reform. Although the membership was diverse, including individuals such as Lieber and Woodrow Wilson, Frank B. Sanborn typified the spirit of the ASSA—or at least one dimension of what, from the beginning, was an inherently contradictory spirit. While he was the organization's general secretary for most of its vital life, from its foundation in 1865 to the turn of the century, the titular heads were characteristically university presidents whose vision of social science was increasingly less congenial to the activism represented by Sanborn.

This New England Unitarian and transcendentalist, who early in his life had been one of the financial organizers of John Brown's raid, held steadfastly to the vision of scientific reform embracing the three-fold objective of education, administration, and "agitation and indoctrination."[17] He believed in the possibility of mediating the extremes of theory and practice through an amateur but organized form of social inquiry. It was to be devoted to social change, carry intellectual and moral authority, and put the best and the brightest into positions of social responsibility. The association began its formal annual meetings in 1868. Its organ, the *Journal of Social Science*, stressed, in the first issue, that "social science is not socialism," since the latter pulls down rather than pulls up, but rather "radicalism" devoted to the conservation of good and the uplifting of society through a science that derived general laws from the facts and applied this knowledge to issues of health, economics, education, and jurisprudence.[18] Some of the efforts on behalf of goals such as civil service reform, part of the "purification of politics," were notable, but attention to such general issues as charity and delinquency was accompanied by studies of county coroners, occupational health and ventilation, Texas cattle disease, and numerous other more restricted problems.[19]

Within a few years, Sanborn was less than sanguine about the success of the association. He believed that as "disciples and missionaries" of social science they had overestimated their effectiveness, and he suggested that it might be necessary to emphasize the development of general knowledge more than immediate and practical goals.[20] But he held on to the hope that social science was "coming forward to supremacy" and that a vision reaching from the ancients to Hobbes, Vico, Comte, and Adam Smith was being realized. What Sanborn projected was an image of social science as institutionalized prophecy that could detect "infallible omens" of social change and solve conflicts such as that between labor and capital by "missionary" work based on the "wholesome truth."

It is the main advantage of Associations like ours, that they train observers to know when the hour has struck; they maintain signal stations by which the fullness of time is announced in advance, as we foretell the weather in one place by hearing what it was yesterday in another place. Distant out-looks are thus made from towers and mountain-tops,—or else the ear is laid to the ground, and the announcement of coming change is heard in tremblings of the earth, a low vibration in the air.[21]

By the turn of the century, the organization was largely moribund, but its failure was not rooted simply in its inability to shape public policy. It was also a function of the fact that social science had professionalized, specialized, differentiated, and moved toward the university. As one observer noted, the ASSA was the now "enfeebled mother" of associations who had "once dwelt alone in her omniscient interest" but was now "impoverished by the very activity" of her progeny.[22] To some extent the impetus toward reform was dulled by the demands of the university and the temperament of scholars, but others who had seen the university as a basis for pitting the authority of knowledge against political authority were to be disappointed. Ever after, social science would to some extent represent a kind of disembodied political discourse.

The creation of the American Political Science Association (1903) and the American Sociological Association (1905) in effect brought the ASSA to an end. The APSA significantly drained the organization of both members and leaders while at the same time explicitly rejecting the vision of social science as agitation. Sanborn, looking backward over the struggle, noted that there had been much misunderstanding of who they were and what they wanted to do, and he lamented "the little that has been permanently effected by all our activities and by the thousand kindred efforts to improve mankind." He claimed that "what we really meant, most of us, was to apply the methods of research and reasoning to those institutions and necessities of society which we saw daily treated unreasonably or merely by tradition." But still he held on to his belief that "the mission of Social Science is to promote the temporal regeneration of depraved societies, as the spiritual regeneration of evil and ignorant souls is wrought by divine grace."[23] It might be fair to say that the ASSA died from its own logic. The analogy between individual redemption through evangelical Christianity and the redemption of society by social science was difficult to sustain in either theory or practice. And the attempt to solve social problems through the application, and on the basis of the authority, of expert knowledge inevitably moved the enterprise in the direction of the university and professionalism.

Despite the attempts of some to advance the idea of the university as a force in social reform, the original membership of the ASSA was hardly one in which academics predominated. Sanborn was never at east in an academic setting. Although Andrew White, then president of Cornell and still enthusiastic advocate of the civilizing forces of science (over superstition, religion, etc.),[24] persuaded him to do a stint at teaching something like sociology, he remained, at best, suspicious of professional academia. He was not attuned to what he called the "effusive omniscience which is the mark of the college professor of the present era,—especially in New York, New Haven, and Harvard."[25] The failure to join the ASSA to an institutionalized academic order was symbolic of the failure to find an accommodation between "agitation and investigation." Just as Sanborn represented the vision of social science as social action, Gilman represented the demand for professionalization.

In his 1880 presidential address to the ASSA, Gilman took the position that "the Association is not a society for the promotion of reform, or an assembly whose object is charity; but its object is the promotion of science, the ascertainment of principles and laws" by the same methods as the natural sciences.[26] The idea was not to withdraw from social concern but to substitute the authority of knowledge for direct political action. Sanborn continued to be wary of university affiliation, and Gilman's rejection of an effort to merge the ASSA with Hopkins doomed the organization. What made the university a poor place for agitation was not simply the demands and allure of professionalism and the fact that the authority of the university rested on its claim to scientific objectivity. The university was, at the same time and somewhat ironically, too closely tied to society and various interests and values—particularly those of business and industry. The belief of individuals like Ely that it could serve as a base for authoritative claims about social change was, in addition to personal hubris and an image of the university professor as biblical prophet, based on a less than clear understanding of certain aspects of German academia as well as naiveté about the American university.

The social science that first took distinctive shape within the university was economics, and by the mid-1880s, it had something of that aura of hard science which it has managed to retain ever since. Although many of the economists were content to remain within the ASSA, they moved away from the role of reform and adopted the stance of experts who spoke for various points of view. Prominence as an economist, however, usually meant an allegiance to the methodology of classical economics—represented by Sumner at Yale and Charles F. Dunbar at Harvard. It was in this context that the radical Ely, who had been one of the founders of the American Institute of Christian Sociology, pushed for the creation of the American Economic Association (AEA) and for what might be understood as the professionalization of radicalism.[27]

The son of a minister, but, maybe significantly, Puritan rather than Anglican, he set out, armed with an image of himself as a righteous messenger, to fulfill his ethical obligations to society as a scholar and

Christian humanist. Suspended from Dartmouth for leading a student strike against the trustees, he transferred to Columbia and received his doctorate at Heidelberg in 1879. He took it upon himself, teaching at Hopkins and heading the political economy program (1881), to lead the opposition to classical conservative economics. Sumner accused Ely, quite accurately, of politicizing the discipline, just as Ely pointed out, also accurately, that it was already politicized. But Ely believed that effective opposition required creating a more academic and professional organization as both a counter to the entrenched position and as an authoritative base for his brand of political advocacy. But Ely's organization had hardly begun (1885) before the forces of professional conservatism and conservative professionalism in the university inhibited the AEA as an instrument of advocacy.

Ely was not, even in his earliest writings, an advocate of anything approaching revolutionary socialism, but he did envision the "harmonious action of the State, Church, and individual moving in the light of true science." He argued that the remedy for the "evils of socialism, nihilism, and anarchism is a better education in political, social, and economic science" and that the "three chief agencies through which we must work for the amelioration of the working class, as well as of all classes in society . . . are Science, the State, and the Church." The state was "legally organized society" and "the product of the same God-given instincts which led to the establishment of the Church and Family."[28] He was, however, perceived as advocating socialist reform and, in terms of both his demeanor and arguments, became an embarrassment to his colleagues in the AEA. As they began to value professional status and security more than the commitment to social change, Ely lost his post as executive secretary. By 1894, he had written two books on socialism, and at Wisconsin, where he moved when he was not promoted to full professor at Hopkins, he was charged with being a "college anarchist." Specifically, the issue was social agitation with respect to his work on behalf of the labor movement and corrupting the politics of the students. When he went on "trial," there was little support from his peers. Although he might have mounted a defense on the basis of academic freedom, and was in fact encouraged by the president of the university to do so, he instead denied the charges and allowed, in a public statement read at Chautauqua, that if the allegations were true, he would be unfit for his position. This man who had spent his honeymoon studying the "feudal society" at the Pullman factory tried in later years to identify himself as a conservative and friend of the wealthy rather than a democratic radical and was eventually elected president of the AEA, which by the early 1890s was bereft of its original vision and had become professionally acceptable to establishment economists.

The idea behind the AEA had been most clearly enunciated by Ely, but it was in many ways shared by individuals such as Edmund J. James of the University of Pennsylvania (whom Ely first met in Germany and who was the founder of the American Academy of Political and Social Science [AAPSS] in 1890). James was at least as radical as Ely but also eventually became more conservative and entered academic administration. The idea behind the AAPSS was to bring together elites from business, religion, government, and education in order to discuss current issues and popularize social science. It eventually led to the creation of the National Municipal League (1894)—a "good government" organization sponsored by James, Frank Goodnow (at Columbia), and A. Lawrence Lowell (of Harvard) which was devoted to separating politics from administration and, where possible, substituting the latter for the former.

For Ely, and many of those who joined in his efforts, the AEA represented an attempt to create an organization that would play a role similar to what was perceived as that of the *Verein für Sozialpolitik,* which had been established in Germany in 1872 and served as a largely academic forum for discussing and influencing state policy. The charter of the AEA stated that "We regard the state as an agency whose positive assistance is one of the indispensable conditions of human progress." Ely had studied economics (and minored in political studies under Bluntschli), and the focus of his subsequent research at Hopkins was the crisis in the American labor movement. In Germany, he was impressed at once both by freedom of learning and "the idea of relativity as opposed to absolutism" and by "the insistence upon exact and positive thought."[29] He affirmed, "I found my master in Karl Knies" and "tasted the new and living economics" which went against the orthodoxy by regarding society as an evolving organism and "the state as an agency whose positive assistance is one of the indispensable conditions of human progress."[30]

He believed that the German professors had adopted the name "'Historical' in order to ally themselves with the great reformers in Politics, in Jurisprudence, and in Theology" and that it represented not only a different methodology (inductive rather than a priori) but "the grand principle of common sense and Christian precept." He claimed that it led to "no *doctrinaire* extremes," and even if an adherent believed in socialism, he would advocate a "slow approach." Most of all, it no longer permitted "science to be used as a tool in the hands of the greedy and the avaricious for keeping down and oppressing the laboring classes. It does not acknowledge *laissez-faire* as an excuse for doing nothing while people starve, nor allow the all-sufficiency of competition as a plea for grinding the poor."[31] But Ely also came to a new vision of the relationship between the university and politics.

"In Germany, I had seen that they had developed their economics out of German life, and the German professors were part of this life" with "public and administrative positions." He saw the "close connection between the state and the universities" and the "importance of linking book knowledge" and "practical experience" in a manner that he believed would not be dissimilar from the relationship between the American military academies and the armed forces.[32] It may be fair to accept his view, like that of Adams, that the ideas were ultimately "American" and that the German experience was only a "midwife," but it is also true that there was little basis in the American experience for the kind of academic practice that Ely envisioned or for the type of state action that he propagated.[33] And even his image of the role of the *Verein* was probably based on a limited understanding of its history. Ely's exposure to the German historical economists such as Wilhelm Roscher and Knies, whose work dominated the field during the last half of the nineteenth century, contributed to his image of economic science as both a reform science and a mode of historical inquiry.[34] These economists emphasized the role of the state in social reform and rejected the position of the classical school of English economists. They viewed the economy as an evolving organism bound to the career of the nation-state. Economic science was conceived as an empirical, nominalistic, historical form of inquiry that sought comparative descriptive generalizations that reflected natural laws of economic development and that could serve as a basis of social policy. These were the values that inspired the formation of the *Verein*.[35]

The *Verein* never adopted a revolutionary socialist or Marxist position. Leaders such as Gustav Schmoller (Berlin) and Lujo Brentano (Munich) attempted to bring theory to practice by supporting social reform through a mild state socialism. The history of the *Verein* was a stormy one which involved considerable ideological conflict as well as controversy about the relationship between politics and academic inquiry. It eventually gave rise to the famous *Methodenstreit* within the social sciences which began as a dispute between historical and classical economics, and more immediately with Carl Menger's 1883 critique of the historical school and Schmoller (its generally acknowledged leader and chairman of the executive committee of the *Verein*). Schmoller was the most influential of the so-called *Kathedersozialisten*. These academic or professional "socialists," so dubbed because of their concern with state-sponsored reform, were severely criticized by more conservative professors and attacked as anarchists and social democrats by Treitschke. Although threatened by the Prussian ministry, they were loyal to the monarchy and not far removed from the kind of social legislation supported by Bismarck.

Even in the German context, however, the *Verein* was less than successful in finding a solution to the increasingly complex problem of the relationship between the university and politics. But as significant as the problem of the relationship between academic intellectuals and the state may have been in Germany, it was still greater in the United States where there was little in the way of institutional connection between the two realms. Burgess, much more than Adams, was clearly worried about the views that individuals such as Ely were importing from Germany and about their implications for the direction of political science as a discipline. The concerns were partly ideological, but they also involved a different image of the articulation of academic and public discourse. Although few did as much as Burgess to adapt European ideas and forms of education to the American context, he saw some notions, such as those hovering around socialism, as distinctly "foreign." He noted at one point that "it is notorious that nearly all Americans who have studied political economy in Germany during the last decade, have returned to this country with a more or less pronounced leaning toward State Socialism. This evil is in process of remedy by the development of American schools of political science."[36]

As disparate as the ideologies of individuals such as Ely and Burgess may have been, however, and no matter how much they may have differed with respect to the strategies for the public role of social science, they both left Germany believing that history and science were one, that political progress was in some way historically immanent, that the state was something on the order of a divine entity and the bearer of social progress, that normal politics was not an adequate source of public virtue, and that academic knowledge could in principle and practice be applied to the conduct of public affairs. By the early 1880s, however, it was still far from clear what, exactly, political science was all about or where it fitted into the university curriculum. Sheldon Amos's call for and justification of a science of politics (published in a series of scientific treatises dealing with fungi, fermenting vegetable molds, etc.) covered everything from marriage to the history of political parties in Australasia.[37] It was in Burgess's work and his organization of political studies at Columbia that the field, as is still recognizable today, took shape.

Few individuals have described their intellectual position as succinctly as Lieber's successor at Columbia in the course of characterizing his magnum opus:

I would say that the book represents the Teutonic nations—the English, French, Lombards, Scandinavians, Germans and North Americans—as the great modern nation builders, that it represents the national State, that is, the self-conscious democracy, as the ultima Thule of political history; that it justifies the temporary imposition of Teutonic order on unorganized, disorganized, or savage people for the sake of their own civilization and their incorporation in the world society; that it, therefore justifies the colonial system of the British Empire especially; that it favors federal government, and, finally, that it extols above everything the system of individual immunity against governmental power formulated in the Constitution of the United States and upheld and protected by the independent judiciary.[38]

Burgess, born in Tennessee in 1844 to a family of Unionist slave owners, was on the scene of American political science until 1931. He had served with the Union army and was a passionate American nationalist, but if Sanborn was a supporter of John Brown, Burgess, despite his view that the Civil War was the objective manifestation of the human spirit working toward the perfection of the union and the modern state, saw the raid as a precipitous crime of passion that violated the plan of providence and reason.[39] Burgess had been an undergraduate at Amherst, from 1863 to 1867, but he had been dissatisfied with the curriculum in history and political science. Attracted by Lieber, he attended Columbia Law School for a time, but, after contracting typhoid, finished his studies as an apprentice in Springfield, Massachusetts. Rather than practicing law, however, he took a post teaching history and political economy at Knox College. After two years, he went, in 1871 on the advice of the American (Hegelian) historian George Bancroft, to Germany. He studied, until 1873, at Göttingen, Berlin, and Leipzig.

In this post-Hegelian and post-Rankean atmosphere, he worked under figures such as Theodor Mommsen, Roscher, Droysen, and Treitschke.[40] He became firmly attached to both the philosophy and practice of the German state and to, at least his image of, German education and its relationship to politics. His favorite teacher was Roscher, but he was less ideologically attuned to his work, since "whether conscious of it or not, he was laying the groundwork for state socialism." Burgess expressed "reverence for Mommsen" who "was Nietzsche's conception of a superman" and who was dedicated to the collaboration of Germany, England, and the United States.[41] But he noted that "the teacher, however, who led me in the line of the work to which my subsequent professional life was devoted was Rudolf von Gneist, the chief professor of public law and the counsel to Bismarck on all legal matters." Burgess believed that while studying in Germany, he "practically saw the German Empire constituted."[42]

It was this vision of the unity of academic study and public policy that Burgess brought back to the United States—a vision that was reinforced by his image of the career of his predecessor at Columbia. But Burgess's efforts, much more than those of Lieber, were single-mindedly directed toward the goal of creating a systematic science of politics and a curriculum to support it. Although the German model was consistently paramount, he also had in mind the Sorbonne, College de France, and particularly the École Libre which, through its independence from government control, he believed had exercised a sane and conservative influence. His goal was to establish a private institution with a public purpose. Through vehicles such as the *Political Science Quarterly (PSQ)* (a journal founded in 1885 and devoted both to the promotion of science and to practical political issues) and a professional political science association, he hoped "to create a school of American political philosophy and distinct American literature" that would reflect the "progressive development of truth through free research."[43] Burgess came to Columbia in 1876 with a dual appointment in the School of Arts (history and political science) and the School of Law. He had failed, during the previous two years, despite the encouragement and aid of Seelye, to create a program of graduate education on the German model at Amherst College. More specifically, he noted that "the conscious object of my work at Amherst was to establish a school of political thought."[44] But the idea of a scientific study of politics did not appeal to an Amherst establishment that still saw higher education primarily as theological training.

In 1880, the Columbia trustees invited him to formulate a plan. His proposal called for a faculty of political science, composed of individuals in a variety of fields from both the School of Arts and the School of Law, which would offer graduate instruction in history, political economy, public law, and political philosophy.[45] The proposal was accepted, and the trustees resolved to create "a school designed to prepare young men for the duties of public life, to be entitled a School of Political Science," and to offer a curriculum "embracing the History of Philosophy; the History of the Literature of the Political Sciences" and a number of other areas touching upon comparative public law and political institutions. The "purpose" was "to give a complete general view of all the subjects both of internal and external public polity, from the threefold standpoint of History, Law, and Philosophy," and the "prime aim," announced in the college catalog of the academic year 1880, was "the development of all the branches of the political sciences" with the "secondary aim" of preparing "young men for all the political branches of public service."[46]

There is little basis for quarreling with Burgess's own assessment that, during the decade between 1890 and 1900, the school became the leading graduate faculty in political science in the country.[47] But in this endeavor, the primary aim of creating professional political science increasingly overshadowed the secondary aim of preparation for public service. And as it did so, the question that became more pressing was how the practical purpose of political science was to be realized. Burgess's claim, however, was that the primary aim was essential to the secondary one, a thesis which would persist among those who followed him during the next century. He argued that "unless a sounder political wisdom and a better political practice be attained, the republican system may become but a form, and republican institutions but a deception." This required "a higher political education" that would provide "the elements of the political sciences with their literature and with the methods of a sound political logic."[48]

By 1891, the school was divided into departments which included History and Political Philosophy. The key to the entire program was the "historical method" and the teaching of substantive history which Burgess maintained was the foundation of "a true and valuable public law and political science. Theory and speculation in politics must be regulated by historic fact." There was an undergraduate department of History and Political Science which employed the "gymnastic method" of drill and recitation and which brought students by the end of the third year to the beginning level of the School of Political Science, which included courses in "history, philosophy, economy, public law, jurisprudence, diplomacy, and sociology" and which moved the student in the direction of independent scholarly research involving primary sources.[49] The method of graduate study continued to be one that in Burgess's view, much like that of Bluntschli, was designed "to escape the dangers of a barren empiricism on the one side, and of a baseless speculation." Here the curriculum was organized around the "history of *institutions*, the origin and development of the State through its several phases of *political organization* down to the modern constitutional form," and this included "the history of the philosophic theories of the state." The next phase was a study of "the existing actual and legal relations of the State," and the culmination was to "seek finally through comprehensive comparison to generalize the ultimate principles of our political philosophy."[50]

Burgess understood his endeavor in the most comprehensive sense as founding "a School of Political Thought," and part of this institution was the Academy of Political Sciences, an association of scholars drawn from the faculties and graduates of the Schools of Law and Political Science. Burgess considered this as the "central point of our whole system" and as "a permanent body of growing scholars" devoted to original research and publication in political science.[51] He had little to say about how the scholarly organization of the School of Political Science would

concretely relate to the world of public affairs. This problem was bequeathed to his students. Herbert Adams praised the "alliance of History and Political Science" that began with Lieber and which was
building under Burgess during the 1880s. "Political science is the application of this historical experience to the existing problems of an ever
progressive society. History and politics are as inseparable as past and
present. This view is justified by the best historical and political opinion
of our time: Ranke, Droysen, Bluntschli, Knies, Roscher, Nietzsche,
Freeman, Seeley."[52] And he praised the special library, which was another example of the "best of German training," as well as the new general library administration under Melvil Dewey which, "like the School
of Political Science, has been grafted from young Amherst college upon
the sturdy trunk of old Columbia." Here, he noted, resources "can be
massed upon any given point with the precision and certainty of a Prussian army corps, in the execution of a military manoeuvre."[53]

Burgess was persistent in his attachment to the idea of the superiority of "the three great branches of the Teutonic stock" represented in
Germany, Great Britain, and the United States, and he could never reconcile himself to the American entrance into World War I and the estrangement from Germany.[54] Western imperialism, manifest destiny as
a basis for the expansion of the United States, anti-Catholicism, and
bans on immigration were all essential elements of his position. "It is
evident," he argued in an early speech, "that Uncle Sam does not want
such rabble [as Czechs, Hungarians, and South Italians] for citizens."[55]
Yet it is a mistake to allow these aspects of his position to obscure the fact
that Burgess surrounded himself with people of diverse political persuasion, dedicated to social change and reform through the application
of knowledge. His colleagues, as well as most of those involved in
founding the discipline of political science, reflected in word and deed
the kind of goals that were characteristic of the ASSA and were dedicated to social change and the uplifting of society through knowledge.
He noted that his student Theodore Roosevelt might have made a
mark as a scholar but took up "practical politics" and was "destined for
greater things."[56]

Although he conceived the state as the locus of unlimited sovereignty
and the ultimate source of law, Burgess, like Lieber, was intent on distinguishing it from government and particularly from the legislative
branch which, like the *Federalist*, he saw as a source of caprice and
danger, particularly in the form of economic regulation, to the liberty
and property of the people and nation. Burgess was intent on finding
not only a sovereign national community but on putting limits on
government—and particularly the state governments. In the first issue

of the *PSQ*, he stated that he wanted to "excite skepticism" about the "dogma that our political system is an indestructible union of immutable states"—an idea that he claimed had no basis in either history or current fact. If this was in any way implied in the Constitution, it was necessary, he claimed, to remember that this document was only an attempt to *"express"* something and was not the "creator" of anything. The State was neither government nor the Constitution. It was a "nationality"— a people with a common language residing in a specific territory. It was based on "geography and ethnography, the womb of constitutions." This was the source of all legal right.[57]

Burgess, as a strong nationalist, had been against slavery but in part because it involved the introduction of an "inferior race" into what he wished to conceive of as a homogeneous people and threatened, along with what he perceived as an array of various other aberrations—such as Mongols, Mormons, and silver mines—to bring about national decay. He also developed an extraordinary version of American political history. The American "states," according to his account, were not properly States at all but "commonwealths." He argued that the original colonies, as grants from the English crown, developed, over time, a national unity and sentiment which, as expressed through the Continental Congress, constituted a sovereign claim to independence. The Articles of Confederation, which set up separate and independent states, amounted however, as he believed Hamilton had understood, to an act that "usurped the sovereignty of the *people of the nation.*" The ratification of the Constitution signified, in turn, nothing less than a "revolution against usurpation," and it issued in a national government as the representative of the people. While local governments represented the "natural" communities that together formed the nation whose will was expressed through the federal government, the "states" were bastard entities which were little more than "a meddlesome intruder in both spheres—the tool of the stronger interest, the oppressor of the individual."[58]

Thus, Burgess argued, the State is the national community, and the government is the agent of the State. The American state, however, had a longer genealogy and a "transcendent mission." It was rooted historically in a "predominant Teutonic nationality," and it was destined to be "the perfection of the Aryan genius for political civilization."[59] This meant that it was essential neither to "sectionalize" it into states nor to "pollute" it with non-Aryan elements, but it was equally important not to allow the intrusion of paternalism and socialism, such as that sometimes advocated in contemporary Germany and imported to the United States. This, he believed, was the greatest danger now that the

Civil War was over, and he saw the judiciary as the guardian of the rights of human beings to property and association in the face of government interference at various levels. He was not, however, an advocate of natural rights or contract theory. Rights were created by the state in the course of its evolution and protected by the Supreme Court from politicians and mass majorities represented in institutions such as labor unions which might extend government in a socialist direction. It was in part his distrust of government that led him to conclude that "the American university must therefore be a private institution" even while serving a public purpose.[60]

No one propagated the Teutonic theory of state and the Hegelian image of history as long and as assiduously as Burgess, and no one did more to make the state the object of political science. History was the objective record of "the progressive revelations of the human reason" and "spirit" and "its advance toward its own perfection." Thus political science was a historical science focusing on the evolution of the state and the development of liberty and sovereignty, from classical democracy through modern representative governments and projected toward an eventual world state wherein politics and political science would be complete. What Burgess designated as "the doctrines of political science" were understood as objectively embodied in constitutional law. Although consciousness of "the political idea" and the state first arose in "post-Roman Europe," it was not until modern times that "philosophical reflection" attained a level that allowed the formulation of propositions that could be "arranged into a body of science."[61]

Burgess understood himself as applying the methods of natural science to politics and law.[62] Political science, he argued, was not merely history, or the compilation and recounting of facts, but the selective ordering of facts "in the forms and conclusions of science" which raised history to "a higher plane." And in an important way it also went beyond the facts altogether. Following Bluntschli, Burgess distinguished between the "concept" of the state, which was a product of empirical science and the historical examination of actual states, and the "idea" of the state, which was an ideal construct which pointed toward perfection. Inquiry involved "philosophical speculation" which was the "forerunner of history" and awakened "ideals" that in "the form of propositions" were, like generalizations from facts, also "principles of political science" which could inform political practice. Such speculation should not go unregulated and depart from a "constant, truthful and vital connection with the historical component," but "it lights the way of progress, and directs human experience toward its ultimate purpose." Although history and political science, as modes of inquiry, were not identical, "the two spheres so lap over one another and interpenetrate each other that they cannot be distinctly separated. Political science must be studied historically and history must be studied politically. . . . Separate them, and the one becomes a cripple, if not a corpse, the other a will-o'-wisp."[63]

Political theorists after the turn of the century would find functional predecessors in the literature of other countries, with whom they would both identify and disagree as they defined their projects, but political theory, as the theory of the state and the history of political ideas, was a distinctly American product. It evolved in the context of emerging political science which was itself an American social science, and it reflected the problems of the relationship between public and academic discourse as they were structured and defined in the American context. The first issue of the *PSQ* defined the "domain of political science" as the historical and comparative study of the state.[64] By the early 1890s, political theory continued to differentiate into two relatively distinct but related components—the theory of the state and the history of political ideas. These reflected, in a general way, what Burgess and the German analysts had understood as the idea of the state, on the one hand, and the concept and history of the state, on the other hand. The boundaries and content of these divisions would undergo considerable transformation in subsequent years, but they would still resonate nearly a century later in distinctions such as that between historical and empirical political theory.

The first course at Columbia that was distinctly a history of political theories was taught by Archibald Alexander, head of the philosophy section. Sometimes, such as at the University of Pennsylvania and the University of Wisconsin, the history and philosophy of the state were combined in a single course, but Princeton and Harvard added courses strictly on the history of political theory. At Hopkins, Adams offered a course on "Historical Politics," and Westel Woodbury Willoughby, first at Stanford and later at Hopkins, was teaching both the theory of the state and political philosophy by 1895. Although the core ideas were distinctly German, there were certain works from England which reinforced the basic pattern.

Frederick Pollock's textbook helped to popularize one way in which the history of political theory would be perceived—the pedigree of political science. He argued that Aristotle was the "founder of political science" and that it was possible "to follow the fortunes and growth of this science" which Pollock regarded as "sufficiently well marked off from others." The evolution was not "continuous and rapid," since there had been "much wild speculation" and "many grave mistakes" as well as "what has been put forward under the name of science by social and political agitation." But, on the whole, he counted the history as constituting a "real advance" and claimed that "political science must and does exist, if it were only for the refutation of absurd political theories and projects."[65] Pollock wished to make a definite distinction between political science and political prudence or between what he called "theoretical politics," which included the general theory of the state as well as the theory of government, and "applied politics," which was the practical counterpart and object of these spheres of knowledge. He also suggested that the "theory of politics," unlike much of moral philosophy, had practical implications and considerable direct influence in public affairs but that such claims must be submitted to "scientific criticism."[66]

The English science of politics of this period, like the American, pursued the historical-comparative method and sought to integrate science, philosophy, and practical judgment.[67] Pollock built on the formulations of Sir Henry Maine as did the work of others, such as J. R. Seeley, Henry Sidgwick, Walter Bagehot, E. A. Freeman, and Bryce, which was in varying degrees complementary with, and often utilized in, the American curriculum. Bryce's *American Commonwealth* (1888), one of the few works since Tocqueville to focus concretely on American political institutions, was a popular text, and Bagehot's *Physics and Politics* (1873) reinforced the evolutionary scientific perspective.

The 1890s marked the apotheosis of the idea of the state. A student of Seelye and Burgess offered, in his popular textbook, one of the most extravagant, but by no means idiosyncratic, statements of the period. He spoke of the state as representing the two "great truths" of the "individuality of man and the organic unity of the race" and accorded to it attributes worthy of deity: "one and universal," "manifold," and "supreme." The "true State" was nothing less than the sovereign people in their "organic capacity" and the source of all rights. As such it was "the greatest of all earthly institutions" and, as it expanded "its sway over the earth," it ushered in a world of "righteousness and peace."[68] Although Woodrow Wilson claimed that there was "no model" for his study of the state and that there had been nothing like it before, it still reflected the basic idea of Aryan development promulgated by his teachers at Hopkins.[69] It traced the comparative history of government (authorized organized force) from earliest times to the contemporary world. Wilson had nothing specifically to say about political theory, but another member of the second generation at Hopkins was more concerned with the identity of political theory and its place among the elements of political science. Westel Woodbury Willoughby was the last grand theorist of the state.

He argued that the domain of political science was constituted by the state which was to be studied descriptively and historically in its various forms and in terms of administration, or the art of government. He considered his work as falling within the realm of political theory or political philosophy, which was a "philosophical examination of the various concepts upon which the whole science of politics rests." He understood this as an analytical (Austinian) endeavor concerned with the "general postulates of Political Science, and incidentally with the History of Political Theories."[70] With respect to both his notion of political theory and his conception of sovereignty, Willoughby set himself apart from Burgess and the Columbia school. First of all, like Wilson, he demystified the idea of the state and identified it with political institutions. He argued that while total sovereignty was located in the state, this meant basically the authorized organization of government. Second, he emphasized the distinction between political science and politics, which he believed was blurred in the work of individuals such as Burgess. He claimed that the extent of the state's actions and the establishment of rights was a matter belonging to "politics or the Art of Government, and not within the domain of political theory" and political science.[71]

The concept of the state, as anything more than a synonym for government, had not been a common indigenous element of American political discourse. It primarily belonged to, and developed within, the specialized vocabulary of the discipline of political science. The emphasis on the state and the attending constitution of political theory was most immediately the product of the German origins of the systematic study of politics in the United States and the German education of the second generation of American scholars. The concept functioned in a number of ways in the emerging discipline. It defined the domain of political science as an autonomous field, and, as a supervenient vision of political reality, it served to underwrite the legitimacy and authority of political science vis-à-vis politics. It was, for many, a secular substitute for the mystery and social bond of religion. It offered a way for political science to talk about its subject matter in a manner that distanced the discipline from the perceived dangers and baseness of political life. As esoteric and metaphysical as the language of the state may have been, it reflected practical purposes ranging from the propagation of nationalism to the defense of conservative and radical ideologies. Progressive political scientists after the turn of the century would hold on to the idea of the state, because it offered an instrumentality for social control and change and a substitute for politics. Yet there was still something else involved, a theoretical concern with important practical purpose.

It is not sufficient to look back on the idea of the state, as some of its detractors would soon do, as simply an archaic vision of political reality that supported a formalistic, legalistic, institutionalist mode of analysis. On the contrary, it was the first of many attempts in political science to find an organic coherency in American political life that went beyond legal and constitutional structures and formal institutions and to posit a homogeneity that lay beneath the often intractable but dynamic and proliferating pluralism of social and governmental forms. It was, in short, a search for the nation and for a political community—a search for something that was strangely missing in the *Federalist* and other documents of the founding generation but that had been assumed in the concept of a people that fought a revolution and constituted a new democratic society. It was surely in part ideology and narrow circumstantial concerns that led nineteenth-century theorists to press the distinction between the state and the government, but it was also part of a search for the people as something more than an abstraction from individuals or a reference to the sum of factions and interests. The idea of the state was at the core of the nineteenth-century vision of popular government, and its failure as a vision of political reality entailed a fundamental recasting of the theory of liberal democracy.

3

The Institutionalization of Theory

History and Political Science, now and forever, two and inseparable.
William Archibald Dunning

It would be some time before the sentiment of Dunning's toast at the organizational meeting creating the APSA would be directly questioned. What Americans had brought back from Germany, and a curriculum dominated by the arguments of Ranke, Hegel, and their successors, was a sense of the identity of history, philosophy, and science as well as a critical spirit that focused on ideas and forms of consciousness as the fundamental political data.[1] It was Dunning who most explicitly defined political theory in these terms within the Columbia school. Although Burgess's voice in the conversation about political science and political theory receded dramatically after the turn of the century, it is a mistake to conclude that he "contributed little to what became its dominant techniques and concerns" or that he "left no disciples."[2] Despite the continuing assumption that the increased emphasis on scientism and the ideological changes that characterized the next generation represented a fundamental epistemic break,[3] the continuities, from Burgess to Merriam, may be more important than the changes in understanding subsequent developments.

Expelled from Dartmouth College while a freshman for a reprisal against sophomore hazing, Dunning transferred to Columbia where he eventually received his doctorate in 1885. Except for a period of study in Berlin with Treitschke, he remained at Columbia until 1922 when he died as president-elect of the APSA. He was a member of the editorial board of the *PSQ* for over thirty years and editor for a decade, and he was one of the founders as well as a president (1915) of the American Historical Association (AHA). He was appointed Lieber Professor of History and Political Philosophy in 1913.

Nothing in the early career of academic political theory was as important as the publication of the first volume of Dunning's trilogy on *A History of Political Theories* (1902). This work and the succeeding volumes

(1905, 1920), more than any other contribution of the period, established political theory as a distinct genre and provided a form that dominated teaching and research for at least half a century. It was a study of political ideas, from Socrates through Herbert Spencer, viewed in terms of their historical context and as a tradition which illuminated modern thought and institutions. Although he conceived political theory as a generalized consciousness embedded in political life and institutions, the core of this organic development, which culminated in nineteenth-century ideas of politics and society, he understood as represented in the classic texts from Aristotle onward. In a volume of contributions by former students of Dunning, which was in part intended as an extension of his studies to more "recent times," Charles Merriam noted that his texts "quickly superseded the earlier work of Bluntschli and Janet, and became the standard histories of the evolution of political thought, the indispensable guide for all serious students of formal political philosophy."[4] It also constituted the full Americanization of the history of political theory.

There is some irony, and accident, in the fact of Dunning's formative influence. He was never primarily committed to the study of the history of political theory. It remained for him a sideline that grew out of his teaching role in Burgess's school in which he created a course in the "History of Political Theories." His principal scholarly concern was Southern political history and, particularly, the Reconstruction period. As Merriam noted, he never devoted himself "exclusively to the gods of pure political theory," and he maintained a "certain reluctance to throw his entire weight upon the side of political philosophy."[5] By the time he had completed the final volume, he admitted that his interest in "the silly mass of political theory that I have been engaged in . . . has dwindled to the vanishing point."[6]

Among those at Columbia, Dunning was singularly uninterested in making contact with political practice and took pride in detachment. Merriam, for whom Dunning had given a special research course in political philosophy and who had taught Dunning's courses when the latter was on sabbatical, concluded that he had "two aversions"—"contact with political affairs" and "the development of systematic or dogmatic political philosophy."[7] His view of the university was distant from that of both Burgess and other colleagues such as Smith and Goodnow, as well as many of the students, such as Charles Beard and Merriam, who would emerge from the Columbia school. As one student noted, Dunning always stressed the "incapacity of political theory to exact any influence whatever upon political movements and institutions. It was purely a luxury discipline."[8] He believed that at best the role of the uni-

versity was "to imbue a certain element of the community with the apti-
tude for application of reason to the definition and the attainment of
social and individual ends." Since in life in general it was really emotion
and "feelings" that determined "ends," while reason related to "means,"
the university could help in some degree to "guide and restrain the
course of humanity by the light of reason." Yet those "idealists" who advocated "agitation, uplift, and reform" might, he suggested, be more
appropriately associated with the institution that preceded Columbia—
The Bloomingdale Asylum for the Insane.[9]

Although he never directly criticized Burgess, to whom he dedicated
his first volume, for having "so powerfully stimulated the study of both
history and political theory in America," he was adamant about the
dangers of nationalism and imperialism in America, England, and Germany. The United States, in the "era of the new imperialism," was, despite the rhetoric of altruism, no longer seeking "internal perfection"
over "external dominion."[10] He also applauded the appearance of
Harold Laski's work and its contribution to the demise of the hold that
Austin's theory of sovereignty had long maintained on certain dimensions of political inquiry.[11] He personally praised Beard's critical account of the American founders but also continually stressed the role of
belief over interest in historical explanation and was archly critical of
new trends such as realism and revisionism that "put the hiss in history."
He claimed that the dogmas of political science had become liberty,
equality, popular sovereignty, and self-determination without adequate
regard for the fact that "authority is what makes any form of human
society possible."[12] Yet Dunning was instrumental in recruiting James
Harvey Robinson (1895) whose "new History" represented the pragmatic spirit and the rejection of history "for its own sake."

Dunning argued that the "critical spirit" in history that had developed during the nineteenth century in the work of Hegel and others
had produced changes as profound as those achieved in natural science. Historical explanation was a matter of discovering the "objective
actualities—the occurrences that impressed the senses of men" and
then of determining "the causal nexus between them." History was a
"stream of causation." But for Dunning, "beliefs" were the principal
subject matter of history and the "most powerful factor in the chain of
causation."[13] The purpose of historical research was to recover past
ideas, and he ended his own attempt to recount the history of political
ideas at 1880, in part, because he did not believe that it was possible to
gain the distance required for objectivity with respect to more recent
events. Although he was committed to the idea of history as progress,
he was equally dedicated to the notion that the truth of political ideas,

or what he usually referred to as "doctrines" and "dogmas," is relative. The historian's judgments must be tempered by the realization that "whatever a given age or people believes to be true *is* true for that age and that people." What the historian seeks is basically the "scope and content" of "the ideas which underlay the activities of men" and the reasons for which they "did things."[14] But it was his assumption of progress and a common human nature that made possible an attitude of tolerance toward the past and hope for the future.

Even though he believed that the English and American character explained why "comprehensive systems of political theory should never have had much vogue" in those countries, he found it difficult to understand, given the emphasis on historical studies and their boast to "the possession and application of eminently just ideas of government," why "the history of political theories has attracted but little attention." His intention was to make the first serious attempt to "trace out, in origin and development, the life of these ideas in the broad field of the world's progress" and chronicle "the successive transformations through which the political consciousness of men has passed from early antiquity to modern times." And he claimed that "no history of political theories of just the character indicated . . . has ever been published."[15] Dunning recognized a Continental literature of which his work was at least generically or functionally the lineage, but his sense of engaging in a novel enterprise was clear.[16] There were at least two English authors whose work was relevant to his enterprise—one of whom he discussed.

H. S. Tremenheere, in the first edition of his work, set out to bring the "ancient wisdom" of classical political thought to bear on the "formation of public opinion," and in a later enlarged volume, he extended this "manual of the principles of government" to "modern times" and a discussion of thinkers from Machiavelli to Mill.[17] The wisdom that he wished to convey largely involved a Burkean concern about the French Revolution and the emergence of mass democracy. Robert Blakey had treated the "history of political literature" as the study of the evolution of "political truth" which, "like all other truth, expands and develops itself as time rolls on" and which was in turn the "direct and tangible expression of politics" and represented "progressive steps or landmarks, in the general framework of European thought, on legislation and general government."[18] Although Blakey's somewhat idiosyncratic and encyclopedic work can in retrospect be construed as containing features that would characterize the history of political theory by the turn of the century, there is little direct connection between his endeavor and the field as it appeared in the United States.

Dunning emphasized that he was not writing a history of either political science or political literature and that his project was much more extensive than that of those who had focused on specialized topics such as jurisprudence. He praised Janet's work as a "magnificent creation" and believed that it came the nearest to the kind of undertaking in which he was engaged. Dismissing von Mohl's work as little more than a "classified bibliography of politics," he noted that "in the German literature the lack of a history of political theories is surprising." He believed that Hildenbrand's volume on Greece and Rome, although incomplete, recognized the "importance of objective history in determining the lines of political theory" as well as the link between "juristic and purely political philosophy." Bluntschli's "prolific" work was "solid and respectable" but geographically and temporally limited.[19] Blakey, he claimed, represented the only attempt in English to do the kind of thing he had in mind, but even though Blakey gave "full weight to the influence of institutions on political science," his concern was "with literature alone," and the volumes in general were "crude, scrappy, and superficial, and abound in errors of simple fact." A "promise" was sounded in Pollock's work, but it was a "light sketch" and too much occupied with jurisprudence.[20]

Dunning wanted to be much more "comprehensive," "systematic," and "accurate," but above all he wanted to trace the "evolution of political consciousness" and provide "an interpretation of political theory in its relation to political fact."[21] He believed that there was a "pretty definite and clearly discernible relationship between any given author's work and the current of institutional development," and "the only path to the accurate apprehension of political philosophy is through political history."[22] What Dunning understood himself as writing about was the history of ideas about authority. As civilization develops, "man seeks some explanation of the phenomenon of authority," and this was the "material for the history of political theories." He believed that politics and political theory had a distinct historical career beginning in classical Greece—"primitive political theory is not political at all, but purely sociological." The "existence of political consciousness" and "the idea of the state" was something which belonged to "advanced communities and which marked a "high stage of intellectual development."[23] Dunning was carving out not only the province of political theory but that of political science in general among the social sciences.

For Dunning, the history of political theory was "in a large sense merely an account of the progress" represented in the differentiation of political philosophy from law, theology, and ethics. "Where for any reason progress in this direction ceases, the history of political theory ceases." This differentiation, however, pertained to the "European

Aryan peoples" who were "the only peoples to whom the term 'political' may be properly applied." He noted the continuity of this position with Burgess's work, but he stressed that he was dealing with it as a fact and not a claim of racial superiority.[24] It was necessary to go back further than the existence of the study of politics to explore the theory of politics, since the former was as much a "result" as a "cause" of "objective political history." And although he believed that it was inevitable that such a history would be closely tied to the perspectives of ethics and jurisprudence, he stressed the autonomy of "political theory proper" as the subject of his history.[25]

Merriam clearly worried about a certain dismay and "form of pessimism" that emerged in the last volume of Dunning's work and which, he believed, was linked to its "dispassionate and objective quality, its detached point of view."[26] But although this may have been part of Dunning's growing weariness with the enterprise, it was also a reflection of Merriam's uneasiness with Dunning's vision for political science. What Merriam was referring to was Dunning's claim that the history of political theories indicated that "the movement of thought had but swung full circle."[27] The sense of a certain kind of immanence of political ideas had, however, always been present in his work—such as his claim, in the first volume, for the seminal and universal character of Greek thought and the idea that "the great thinkers of Hellas explored the entire height and depth of human political capacity and outlined the principles which at all times and in all circumstances must determine the general features of political life."[28] But there was little indication that Dunning relinquished his faith in progress. He praised the sociology of Comte as ranking with "the greatest achievements of the human mind in generalizing from the past the elements of progress in civilization" and in "specifying the method and utility of history." And he stressed "the importance of societarian speculation in the history of political theory," including the closely linked "dogmas" of socialism and sociology. He finally asked, however, in his last chapter, whether the twenty-three centuries of political doctrines added up to "progressive change in a uniform direction" or to "a series of haphazard and never ending transformations."[29]

With respect to ideas about the "forms and agencies" of political control, he saw, as in the case of slavery, "progressive modification in theory." As far as the classification and analysis of governmental forms, he could discern little advance, and with regard to the theory of political change, "when one compares the a priori and fanciful teachings of Plato with those of Rousseau and the Saint-Simonians" or "the more sober and scientific treatment of the same subject by Aristotle and

Polybius with that of Vico and Comte, it will require much hardihood to pronounce that the moderns manifest a great progress in the philosophy of government." On the other hand, the evolution of the idea of representative government, the separation of state and society, and the doctrine of sovereignty were clear examples of progress and "advance in political speculation."[30] Finally, in terms of the constant problem of resolving the dilemma of authority and freedom, he saw the issues and solutions as perennial. Anarchism, constitutionalism, nationalism, and societarianism had persisted from the Greeks to the present.

Dunning believed that the first few years of the twentieth century had "brought to light much literary evidence of lively interest in political theory." He saw the "historical method" as dominating in the United States, Great Britain, and France while the "constructive method" was more characteristic of Germany and Southern Europe. He found progress in the decline of speculative ideas and the lack of a distinctly American political philosophy. He shared the view, that bridged the nineteenth and twentieth centuries, that the study of political theory served to undercut irresponsible speculation. Speculative philosophy was more prevalent in unsettled countries, while ones that were stable and advanced in the ways of constitutional democracy, tended to give up normative claims in favor of factual and causal problems relating to the development of the state.[31] This same point of view was echoed by individuals such as Albert Bushnell Hart (at Harvard) and Beard, and it indicated the affinity between the historicism of Dunning and the scientific realism of progressives such as Beard and Merriam. Their image of science was still rooted in the nineteenth-century idea of critical history and its emphasis on facts. For Beard, "speculative theorists" were a danger to realism and reform. The purpose of political science was to illuminate political fact and undercut dogma, and he specifically noted how Dunning's approach pointed up the manner in which political philosophy grew out of political circumstances.[32] Hart's famous statement was that "the most distinctive American theory of Government is not to theorize."[33]

Although Dunning had established political theory as a subject matter and field of scholarship, he had little to say about its contemporary character and how it fitted into the discipline of political science. In the early issues of the *American Political Science Review (APSR),* which began publication in 1906, most of the literature entries in the bibliographical section under "political theory" were European. What constituted American political theory, whether in political science or elsewhere, was far from entirely clear. As something more than a historical artifact and a general, and not very well circumscribed, literature category, the concept of political theory was still quite unformed. Just as Dunning gave concrete meaning to political theory in the context of the Columbia school, Willoughby did so at Hopkins. He agreed that American politics was largely nonideological, and he set out to address the question of political theory as a scholarly activity and an aspect of political inquiry. More than anyone else of the period, Willoughby, in a series of pieces after the turn of the century, began to define and defend the domain of political theory.

Willoughby had taken his degree in history at Hopkins (1891) with no specific work in political science. He studied and practiced law, and taught at the University of California for a period, before returning to Hopkins in 1905 as a reader in political science, and he remained there until he retired in 1933. His book on the state was followed by *Social Justice* (1900), and he wrote extensively on the American constitutional system as well as acting as a political consultant, particularly in matters relating to China. Willoughby, first of all, wished to dispel the characteristic distrust of speculation and theory, such as that present in Dunning's work, and to demonstrate that theory had historically been of value in practical affairs and that it was important in scientific inquiry. Although the terms "theory" and "philosophy" might evoke images of metaphysics and other intellectual misadventures, he argued that speculation was a positive good and insisted on the "value of political philosophy" as the basis of systematic political inquiry. It supplied theoretical principles, offered a critical perspective, aided in defining terms, and provided a key to interpreting the past and, particularly, understanding European politics.[34]

To appreciate Willoughby's concerns, it is necessary to understand the context of the creation of the APSA. Despite the practical orientation of political science, it, like sociology, emerged as a relatively conservative profession in that it distanced itself from direct political involvement and stressed expert knowledge as the bridge between academic and public discourse. Public law and public administration were the principal foci, and often municipal reform was the main concern. Goodnow, the first president of the APSA, a leading student of Burgess, and the founder of public administration in the Columbia school, was an active urban progressive.[35] In the same year that he became president of the APSA, he was appointed to the Eaton Professorship of Public Law and Municipal Government which was endowed by a civil service reformer who had become concerned with nonpartisan municipal reform through better administration. Many of the individuals such as Goodnow who were instrumental in establishing political science as a profession were involved in some phase of practical governmental re-

form and actually participated in administration at home or in the foreign territories.

Action began in 1902 at a meeting sponsored by an organizing committee from universities and governmental agencies (and that included
Burgess, Goodnow, Melvil Dewey, and Smith) that called for an American Society for Comparative Legislation but that issued in the creation
of a fifteen person committee to assess the demand for a separate association. The committee (which included Willoughby but no one from
Columbia) found that there was, indeed, great demand for an association "to take the scientific lead in all matters of political interest" and
"advance the scientific study of politics."[36] The foundational meeting
was held at a joint session of the AEA and AHA in December 1903 at
New Orleans. Although it was deemed "impossible" and "undesirable"
to separate the interests of history, political science, and political economy, it was decided that the field of political science could be "clearly
distinguished" as a way of treating common phenomena from a different "standpoint." Woodrow Wilson was elected vice-president and
Willoughby secretary-treasurer of the new association, and a committee was established for each subfield or section. One of the sections was
"Politics and Political Theory" and the first theory committee consisted
of Willoughby, Dunning, and Merriam.[37] The purpose of the APSA
was to "embrace the whole field of Political Science," and from the beginning, political theory was understood as the core of the field.

The APSA was devoted to "advancing the scientific study of politics,"
and its charter explicitly stated that it would not "assume a partisan position upon any question of practical politics, nor commit its members
to any position thereupon." Yet Henry Jones Ford (at Hopkins and,
later, Princeton) argued, at the time of the creation of the *APSR,* that
the discipline must be put on "an objective basis" and "experience the
reconstruction which the general body of science has undergone at the
hands of inductive philosophy" in order to "bring political science to a
position of authority as regards practical politics." The purpose was to
go beyond the study of particular forms of authority and seek universal
principles for the "guidance of statecraft," and this required general
laws that were neither spatially nor temporally "parochial."[38] The history of the discipline would be one of attempting to reconcile these
propositions, but from the beginning the idea was that only by establishing itself as scientifically detached could it hope to influence politics.
Some individuals such as Jesse Macy at Grinnell, who was a close friend
of Ely and came from an abolitionist Quaker background, had tried to
revive the more radical spirit of social science as president of the short-
lived Political Science Association in the mid-1890s. But though on the

executive council of the APSA, he could do little to change the overwhelming disposition in the field, and he himself did not directly engage in political activity.

In his presidential address, Goodnow emphasized that the business of political science was to study the state and concern itself with the "various operations necessary to the realization of the State will." And he stressed the extent to which political theory was involved in this pursuit. Like constitutional law, it was concerned with the "organization of authorities which express the state's will" and as such was itself a "special discipline" that studied phenomena that were "peculiarly subjects of political science to which any association devoted to the scientific study of Political Science should address itself." Although Goodnow's realism and practical concerns made him wary of "philosophical speculation," he noted that no matter how "contemptuous may be one's belief in the practical value of the study of political theory, it is none the less true that every governmental system is based on some more or less well defined political theory."[39]

In the introduction to his work on *The Political Theories of the Ancient World*, Willoughby attempted to allay fears about the study of political theory by linking science to history and both to practical life. He defended "political speculation" as part of the philosophical search for the essential truth of human phenomena and, apart from any "practical results," as important in itself and as "enticing by giving play to our highest intellectual faculties." It had attracted "the greatest thinkers of all times," and thus the study of the history of political theories not only brings us into contact with one of the most important subjects of human thought but provides "an insight into the logic and significance of political history." Theories "have been evoked by particular objective conditions" and "reflect the thought, and serve to interpret the actuating motives, at the root of the most important political movements" as well as the general "'intellectual climate' of their times." Historical study, in general, he argued, was a way of better understanding "conceptions and problems," particularly in the case of "abstract political philosophy." And the "value of the historical method in all fields of investigation is now so well recognized."[40]

He claimed that an objective knowledge of past theories was the best way to begin the formulation of a "true" theory of one's own, but, at the same time, some prior notion of a valid philosophy was necessary for describing and critically analyzing earlier ideas. He believed that in his own work he had provided such a logically coherent philosophy and developed "a correct and fairly complete outline of political theory." From this perspective, he hoped to eventually cover "the entire history of political philosophy." He claimed that he did not limit himself to the "written word" but included among his sources political practice and speculative thought. This was necessary because "political speculations are almost necessarily the outcome of existing objective political conditions" and are designed to solve problems "born of the concrete facts of contemporaneous life." He believed that his project resembled "a philosophy of history," since a "true history" should link "political theory and fact" and "exhibit a continuous movement, a logical development from point to point, from cause to consequence" that would explain why certain ideas were accepted or rejected and how they were logically linked to the political conditions of the time.[41]

The book, published the year following Dunning's first volume, was intended to be part of a largely parallel, and somewhat rival, project. Willoughby, much like Dunning, tried to establish the uniqueness of his undertaking. He claimed that no one writing in English, apart from Pollock's "little book," had tried to encompass the "whole history of political philosophy," and although Janet was the "best work that we have," histories in other languages (mostly German) were far from "completely satisfactory." Although he believed that Dunning's work had "conspicuous merits," it focused too exclusively on "political theories as they were to be found crystallized and explicitly stated in literature" and failed to elicit the theories immanent in the "objective facts" and institutions. He concluded that his and Dunning's work more "supplement" than duplicate one another.[42]

The place of political theory in political science was, however, far from settled, and it was this issue to which Willoughby continued to devote much attention in these early years. In his 1904 article on the newly formed APSA, he reaffirmed the autonomy of political science as a discipline and its place in the "new period of scientific study and teaching of matters political in the United States." He claimed that the field of political science, which was devoted to studying "men effectively organized under a supreme authority for the maintenance of an orderly and progressive existence," consisted of three basic parts. The first was the "province of political theory and philosophy" which was devoted to "the analysis and exact definition of the concepts employed in political thinking, and which thus includes the consideration of the essential nature of the state, its right to be, its ends, its proper functions and its relation to its own citizens, and the nature of law."[43]

Political theory, however, was still largely a category and subject matter designation. The 1906 section on political theory at the annual meeting of the APSA included, for example, both a paper (by Merriam) on Hobbes's state of nature and observations on methods of amending state constitutions. The most elaborate analysis of political theory in the first decade of the twentieth century was a symposium on "Political Theory and National Administration" at the World's Fair in St. Louis in 1904. Speakers included Bryce, and Merriam served as secretary, but here Willoughby, soon to be managing editor of the *APSR,* attempted to provide a systematic discussion of "political philosophy" or "political theory" and its relationship to other fields. It is worth noting the transformation in semantic force between the common reference to political "theories" and the discussion of "political theory." The latter usage was a step away from the idea of political theory as simply a variety or class of phenomena and a move toward the notion of political theory as a distinct—albeit still largely generic—activity and product.

For Willoughby, "political," as usual, meant the "state," but he rejected "cosmic" and "metaphysical" notions of "philosophy" and equated the term with "theoretical discussion of the essential characteristics of the material and phenomena with which science has to deal." Theory was "abstract" only in that it was concerned with "generalizations" and "essential and fundamental qualities" rather than with "particulars" and "accidental and unessential characteristics." He claimed that there were two "sides" to political philosophy—the "scientific or analytical" which deals with the state as it "is" and the "teleological or ideal" which deals with the ends of the state. The former is what makes it possible to approach the state as a universal phenomenon and unite "into a harmonious whole that multitude of phenomena which, in appearance, is so confused and confusing." It is this which makes possible a "terminology" and set of "definitions" in political science.[44] He claimed that until recently the analytical dimension had received almost no attention. Emphasis on theological and metaphysical, or ethical and ideal, matters characterized by natural law teaching had prevented "the creation of a true and useful science of politics." But now, "in both ethical and political speculation the absolute has given way to the relative." Although politics could be subjected to "utilitarian" criticism and although it was still necessary to discover an ethical basis for the existence of political authority in general and for any particular government, political philosophy was not concerned with universal utopian claims. According to Willoughby, "rigid political analysis has rendered possible the creation of a true political science" or one based on "exact observation" and "the formulation of exact definitions and classifications."[45]

In attempting to delimit the province of political theory, Willoughby devoted a great deal of attention to distinguishing, and demonstrating the relationship between, political theory and various fields such as metaphysics, ethics, theology, political economy, sociology, history, and law. He noted that many of the great political philosophers, from Plato to T. H. Green, had also been philosophers in the general sense and concerned with such metaphysical issues as human nature. The relationship between political and ethical theories had been even more intimate. For Willoughby, this indicated a logical relationship between theoretical and practical ethics or between the ethicist and politician. Despite the fact that political philosophy and theology had been historically linked, there was, he believed, no logical connection, and at least in modern times economics was only tangentially concerned with things political. Willoughby was also particularly concerned with demonstrating that, contrary to the claims of many sociologists, political science was not logically subordinate to sociology and that political organizations were not in some fundamental way derivative from "lower" social units. One field that Willoughby did not distinguish from political theory was psychology, and he wanted to demonstrate that sociology had no particular hold on psychological explanations.

Willoughby reaffirmed the basic unity of political science, political theory, and history. Political theories were the product of "objective conditions" at various times and, simultaneously, "influenced" the course of history. Thus political theory made it possible to "determine the thoughts and intentions of men of the past," and a history of the development of political theories provided the basis of historical explanation.[46] In the end, Willoughby believed that speculative inquiry could be basically divided into metaphysics, ethics, and political philosophy. The first addressed questions about men as "rational moral beings," the second derived principles for action, and the third was concerned with the realization of these principles. The three were logically connected and practically interdependent. But despite the scientific and practical reasons for engaging in political philosophy, Willoughby again wished to insist that "the greatest incentive to the study of political theory is that pure intellectual delight which is to be obtained from the pursuit of any speculative inquiry" and which springs from the "mind's insatiable demand" for understanding the whence, how, and what of "human phenomena" and particularly the nature of "the corporative control" that is essential and universal and the basis of civilized life.[47]

There was a sense in which political theory was understood as requiring legitimation. Since speculation was not favored in general, and its role in science was even more suspect, individuals such as Willoughby were determined to identify theory and give it a place in scientific political inquiry. And this to a large degree also entailed demonstrating its practical use. In the same World's Fair symposium, George Grafton Wilson of Brown University, a specialist in international law, defended the study of political theory and its "right" to exist. Wilson noted that "critics" often saw little justification for political science let alone political theory specifically. But he argued that even though political practice and the state existed long before political speculation, theory revealed the nature of phenomena and made them amenable to control. Also political theories had strongly influenced political activity, and political actors had been guided by theories. Thus they were necessary aspects of the explanation of politics. Some theories may have been wrong or harmful, but that was all the more reason for attempting to develop correct ones, particularly in an era of expanding state activity.

The subject matter of political theory was, however, Wilson suggested, a considerable problem. What, for example, exactly is political and what is nonpolitical in human association and what was the proper "method" for studying political phenomena. Wilson distinguished three types: "static" analysis using the method of "pure logic;" the still more "positive" method, characteristic of economics, of deductive reasoning from definitions and axioms; and the historical-comparative approach which he believed was less narrow and more empirical. But he recommended caution in employing analogies, such as those with biology, in such studies. Although the "state" was the conventional object of political inquiry, Wilson suggested that more attention be devoted to the "efficiency" of the state than to questions of its past and present form. Speculation about the origin and basis of the state was important, but he stressed the need to specify what the state is as a subject of political theory. He concluded that all these issues really revolved around the question of the "end or ideal for which the state exists"—the question that has informed political inquiry from Plato to the present.[48]

Behind these extended attempts by Willoughby and Wilson to define the domain of political theory were some very concrete concerns both about the status of political science, and the place of theory in the discipline, and about the limits of state interference and the authority of national as opposed to state governments. Although Willoughby was quite willing to see close connections between political science and other disciplines, he continued to insist that the discipline "has been marked off as a study which by its methods and subjects of inquiry requires for its successful study separation from the other social sciences, and especially from History and Economics." Thus, he claimed that the establishment of the APSA was "undoubtedly the most important event that has occurred in the history of the scientific study of politics in this country." And the general study of government was descriptive in character and different from political theory which was concerned with "the essential nature of the state." "The value of this purely abstract study, which unfortunately has been too much neglected in this country, it is difficult to overestimate."[49]

Since, in his view, earlier work in political theory had been "subjective" and concerned with such things as natural rights without regard for "conditions of time and place," it was of little "scientific value." But now, he claimed, political theory was "analytical" and able to provide "the propaedeutic of a true political science" for application by the jurist or statesman for the resolution of such practical issues as the sovereignty of the states.[50] Willoughby admitted that "political science may never hope to produce an art of statesmanship which will furnish the citizen and the public official with the exact guidance that the chemist, the physicist, or the mathematician furnishes to those in the technological trades, but it may and does furnish information of extensive value." It may not be a substitute for practical experience, but it provides the knowledge that allows one to use that experience. Political science, employing methods both historical and comparative, provided "a surfeit of material awaiting scholarly, scientific treatment" that has not been available since the time of Aristotle.[51]

Although Willoughby was concerned with the practical mission of political science, it was also clear that he believed that this required, at the same time, a distinct separation not only between "teleological or ideal" and "scientific and analytic" political theory but between political science as a whole and politics. On these, and other, grounds he was pointedly critical of Burgess and the influence of Bluntschli. He continued to disagree with Burgess's formulation of sovereignty as something prior to and above the government and with his notion that "real" states were not realized outside the West. And he attacked the mystical idea of a universal state which Burgess had warned "the scientific mind must not approach too closely." He believed that Burgess, with his "absolutist reasoning," his racism and Teutonic views, his hypernationalism, and his willingness to take on the "political destinies of the entire world" had entered the realm of "Politics and Statesmanship" and "overstepped the boundaries" of the "proper field of pure political theory." He had become more of a "constitutional lawyer" than a political theorist. Willoughby argued that rather than deducing principles of "political expediency or morality," political theory should concern itself with the nature of the state and with "a rigid examination of the concepts and terms employed in political thinking" in order to "construct a scientific system of thought."[52]

Despite these pointed discussions *about* theory and studies *of* it, much of the substantive contemporary literature designated as political theory continued to be of foreign origin. Individuals such as Dunning and

Merriam contributed articles on the work of particular past thinkers such as Locke and Jefferson, and this type of work in the history of political thought remained the state of the art through the first two decades of the century. Merriam, for example, in a volume dedicated to Dunning, examined the "political philosophy of John C. Calhoun" and represented it as an element in the "general movement of political theory."[53] The pattern of scholarship set by Dunning was soon evident in other work. One of the early volumes that exemplified the emerging paradigm was the Carlyles' study of medieval political theory. Gierke's treatise on the "political theories" *(publiscistischen Lehren)* of the Middle Ages, which was part of a projected specialized study of state and corporation in Germany *(Das deutsche Genossenschaftrecht)*, was translated in 1900, but the Carlyles possessed a more general idea of the enterprise.[54] Their work set out to demonstrate that there was no great "gulf" between ancient and modern thought, because there was a "living and active political theory" during the Middle Ages out of which modern political theory "has arisen by a slow process of development." The image was one of political theory as "continuous, changing in form, modified in content, but still the same in fundamental principles." And they accepted the prevailing notion that political principles, conscious and unconscious, were "reflected in the nature of public life" and "that theory never moves very far away from the actual condition of public life."[55]

Early work in the history of political thought continued to view political theory, and the study of it, in practical terms. John Neville Figgis saw political ideas as having limited literary value and philosophical depth. Truth, he noted, has little to do with politics, and "political thought is very pragmatist." Yet the material was important because "the actual world is the result of men's thoughts" as much as it is a product of their material interests, and in the long run the "theorist" contributes to shaping the political universe. Figgis repeatedly apologized for the fact that the material was really quite dull stuff on its face, but it was necessary "if we would understand the common facts of to-day." It was not an exercise in "antiquarianism," and the purpose was "not to revive the corpse of past erudition" but "to make more vivid the life of to-day, and to help us to envisage its problems with a more accurate perspective." Figgis claimed that "no subject illustrates more luminously the unity of history than the record of political ideas," and in studying that record, "we seek to see our own day as from a watch-tower." To understand that past required never losing sight of the "connection between theory and practice" and the need to study political theories in terms of the political conditions in which they arose. And just as past ideas and circumstances must be seen in terms of their interaction, the study of this past and the penetration of these thoughts and ideas constituted, in effect, the "embryology of modern politics." Figgis put it dramatically: "Mariana planted, Althusius watered, and Robespierre reaped the increase."[56]

Some, such as Bryce, who was elected president of the APSA in 1909, pursued the theme that political science, as a historical science, was not an exact science with laws similar to those in natural science. He argued that calling it a science referred only to the possibility of discerning uniformities in human nature and generalizing to some extent about the causes of actions in politics. But as uncertain as it might be in certain respects, it could be put in the service of statesmen and citizens. For Bryce the state was still conceived as an organism, and the environment was the key to understanding its evolution.[57] Others, such as Lowell, who succeeded his friend Bryce as president of the APSA, believed like Ford that a truly scientific "physiology" of politics was possible and that the province of political science was to study the actual process of government, "to discover the principles that govern the political relations of mankind, and to teach those principles to the men who are in a position to give them effect hereafter."[58] He noted that Bentham had not served in Parliament. Despite variations on the themes, these individuals were at one in their beliefs that political science must be separate from politics but gain authority over it, that there was a kind of uniformity to human nature that provided a basis for some kind of universal understanding of both past and present, that history had intrinsic meaning, that science, historical or otherwise, was a matter of placing things in context, and that administration should override "normal" politics.

James Garner, in his 1910 textbook, attempted to trace the development of the science of politics from Aristotle to the present and to justify the notion of a comprehensive form of inquiry that encompassed, but was more than, what had sometimes been understood as the particular political sciences (such as public law).[59] In the course of his discussion, he attempted to sort out some conventional distinctions and locate political theory in political science. He noted, first of all, the nineteenth-century tradition (for example, Lewis and Pollock) of distinguishing between theoretical and applied politics or between the science and art of politics. And he concluded, accurately, that this was a distinction between political science and politics rather than between theoretical and applied knowledge within political science. He also noted that Pollock accepted the German division between the study of the general concept of the state (including its origin, types, nature of sovereignty, etc.) and an examination of specific existing forms, as well as between the idea of the state as an artificial person and the manifestation of that personage in historical acts such as war. Finally, he suggested that while a distinction between political theory or philosophy (*Staatslehre*) and political science (*Staatswissenschaft*) was generally observed, it was difficult to make. Garner perceived that these distinctions were in some way related to one another and to current notions of political theory and political science, but he was less than clear about their evolution during the past century.

The concerns of political theory inevitably pushed it beyond the boundaries of the social sciences. George Sabine, a Cornell alumnus and assistant professor of philosophy at Stanford, entered the conversation for the first time. He stressed the practical character of not only the human sciences and the extent to which history reflected the "evolution of value" but the normative basis of all science. He argued that the "traditional distinction between descriptive and normative science will not hold," since ethics needs facts, and cognition cannot be separated from purpose and valuation. Although he saw some advance in the Hegelian revision of liberalism, such as that represented in the work of T. H. Green, he worried about idealist logic and its theory of the state and its tendency to substitute the "social organization" for the individual. Individualism, he believed, must remain at the core of liberalism, and the latter was the only basis of moral and social reform.[60]

The concept of political theory, however, remained tied to the idea, and celebration, of the state and its evolution—whether viewed from the perspective of German philosophy or in terms of the belief that it was "a corollary of the Darwinian theory that the state has a natural history." Ford looked to a "natural history" of the state and sought to extract "the foundations of political science from the naturalistic point of view established by Darwin's *Origin of the Species*." On this basis, he concluded that the "state was absolute and unconditioned" and that "Man did not make the State; the State made Man."[61] For Ford, the state was still an "organism" that stood behind government and from which all rights and liberty flowed. There was a close tie between the notion of political knowledge as a directive social force and the idea of the state as the vehicle of its application.[62] In 1914, R. G. Gettell (at Amherst College) offered an extended analysis of the nature and scope of political theory that generally reflected, and synthesized, the dominant views in the discipline.

Gettell affirmed that political theory was concerned with the "subjective" phase of the state. The state was one of the basic forms of institutions that emerged as human beings evolved from nature and created their own environment, and it was only natural that they would think and debate about it. Such thought was both cause and effect—theories both reflected and influenced politics and could be understood only in terms of the political conditions of the time. Political theory, he argued, was "relative in its nature" and was hardly the repository of "ultimate truth." He believed, however, that "at the present time political theory is of particular interest and importance." The modern state, he argued, was just fully taking shape and settling upon the "first principles" that would direct its growth and govern the scope of its activities. The contemporary tendencies toward the expansion of the function of the state held great possibilities for good and evil, and it was necessary to reflect on the past and analyze the present in making and understanding choices.[63]

He claimed that "a fundamental change of mental attitude is now revolutionizing political theory." Heretofore political theory had been largely deductive and idealistic. Claims about "what should be" were logically derived from axiomatic premises about the nature of political institutions, and these claims were used to judge political conditions with little regard to the actual circumstances. But now "political theory is inductive" and a matter of observation, classification, and generalization based on "what is." Political theories are "studies of political structure and function, conceived in the same scientific spirit as that of a zoologist examining the fauna of a particular region." Gettell suggested that political theory as a field of study could be divided into three distinct but related elements. The "history of political theory" was concerned with the origin and development of the state including both the ideals that attended successive stages and the ideas on which institutions were actually based. The second element, "analytical or descriptive" political theory, was not to be understood as sharply distinguished from the historical dimension but rather just the latest stage and the basis for political reform in the present. It consisted of the "philosophical concepts and principles concerning the notion of the state, its essential attributes, and the meaning and justification of authority." Finally, there was "applied political theory" which was concerned with the "immediate present and the future" and consisted of "principles and ideals concerning the proper purpose and function of the state" and obtained from observing the state "in motion" and in its relationship to the individual and to other states. It was involved in practical matters of reform and progress and included the whole spectrum of political thought from anarchism to socialism.[64]

In 1915, an APSA report on political science instruction in higher education listed "political theories (history of political thought)" as one of twenty subjects surveyed, and it recommended that curricula include courses in "political theories and history of political literature." It noted a tendency in the discipline away from institutional analysis in favor of studies of "government in operation" and more factual and practical matters. Some were worried about a decline in the study of theory, since it was not as "popular" as it had been. It had the lowest enrollments of all subjects and was taught only in 11 of 150 institutions surveyed. Political theory tended to be confined to graduate schools and small study groups.[65] For the next few years, political theory as a specific subject and object of reflection was increasingly neglected as the concerns of political scientists focused more sharply on practical issues in domestic and international politics. "Political Theory" as a literature category even disappeared from the *APSR*—and then reappeared in conjunction with "miscellaneous."

One of the principal causes of this recession was the advent of World War I and the ostensible rejection of the German philosophy of the state on which so much of political theory had been based as well as of the style of thought associated with this philosophy. In England, pluralist theory was already hostile to the theory of the state. Sir Ernest Barker not only condemned German philosophy and the "worship of power" in the work of writers such as Nietzsche and Treitschke but criticized Austin's theory of sovereignty as never having fit English "polyarchism."[66] The state was nothing but organized individuals. In the United States, Dunning held on to the view that German idealism, from Kant to Hegel, had a profound and salutary effect on the "form and method of political philosophy" and had produced a "refined psychological analysis" whereby the "classification of political ideas assumed great scientific precision." Yet "like all other idealists, the German philosophers in fact achieved little more than to clothe certain institutions and aspirations of contemporary politics with the sanctifying garb of mystic form and nomenclature." While idealism initially sought to defend the individual, Hegel's glorification of the state, in its "Bacchic frenzy," threatened the very ethic of individualism.[67]

John Dewey attacked German idealism and its evolutionary philosophy of history in favor of a critical and "experimental philosophy" which, he believed, undercut the kind of nationalism which led to the war. As early as 1894 Dewey, drawing upon Leon Duguit, had attacked Austin's theory of sovereignty and argued that the state and sovereignty must be understood as the sum of complex activities. Although Dewey maintained that politics was the "controlling factor in the formation of philosophical ideas," such ideas also "served to articulate and consolidate" politics. And this was the case in Germany where "an apriori and an absolutist philosophy has gone into bankruptcy."[68]

The state was hardly rejected as the subject of political science by individuals such as Willoughby, who had done so much to make it coincidental with the domain of political science, but the association with German philosophy precipitated a reevaluation. Willoughby argued there had been a conspiracy between political authority and German professors of political philosophy in propagating Prussian ideals in the form of the myth of the state and a philosophy of history celebrating the evolution of the Teutonic people. He argued that these "principles are related to one another and are logical deductions from the general political philosophy which has been dominant in Prussia." Like Dewey, he contrasted this with the "political ideals" of America which included legal equality, the people as the ultimate source of authority, and a written constitution. The German philosophy, as represented by Kant, Fichte, and Hegel, pretended that there was an overall "meaning to human history" which passed through an evolutionary process of conflict, claimed the superiority of the Teutonic people, and advanced the idea of a mystical divine state. And there was a unity between the professors, such as Treitschke, who advanced this political philosophy and the nationalistic state.[69]

Franklin Giddings, the Spencerian founder of academic sociology who had been much involved with the discipline of political science as a member of the Columbia school, stated the case most dramatically.

The thoughts of sober-minded men have turned anew to theories of political life because a Teutonic philosophy of authority has incited, has directed, and sought to justify the most diabolical collective conduct that the human race, in all its career since the Heidelberg jaw was clothed in flesh, has infamously committed. This theory has seized upon a creation of the demoniac imagination and called it The State, spelled with a large "T" and a capital "S."

Even Giddings, however, did not reject the state, which he maintained was the "noblest expression of human purpose," but only the idea of sovereignty advanced by "metaphysical theorizing" and the idea, of the "Treitschkes and Kaisers," that the state was "absolute" rather than "finite and relative."[70]

The theme of the "discredited state" was also pursued by Laski. He argued against both the idea of the omnipotent state as the source of law and the notions of philosophical absolutism with which it was allied. But, at the same time, he systematically turned to pluralism not only as an account of social reality but as a theory of democratic society. His early work represented a constant attack on idealism, on the monistic theory of the state, on the idea of state sovereignty, and on the Austinian inspired emphasis on formal legal aspects of the state as the subject of social science. Most of this work, largely in the form of collected essays, was published while he was at Harvard (1916–20), and much of his philosophical inspiration, and justification, came from his reading of Dewey and William James.[71] Laski left Harvard and returned to England, after negative student and administrative reaction to his public discussion of the Boston police strike. The university had offered its services to the city, and Lowell, now president, admonished Laski that it was not the place of a professor to speak out on political issues.[72] What he precipitated, and left behind, was a debate which had a profound impact on both political science's vision of political reality and its conception of liberalism.

After the war, political theory did not again receive focused attention until Merriam set out to revolutionize, and further Americanize, political science. The idea that the key to the transformation of the discipline resided in political theory would be a persistent notion. Merriam was also reacting to both the hopes and failures of those who had tried to make social science meaningful to the practical world. The reaction against the German philosophy of the state was also, if more subtly, a rejection of related assumptions about the relationship between the academy and politics. Although most of the voices of progressive social science did not directly join the conversation about political theory, the context is crucial for understanding Merriam's conception of political theory and his view of the relationship between social science and politics.

4

Politics and Political Theory

Least of all can there be anarchy in social science, or chaos in the theory of political order.

Charles Merriam

Woodrow Wilson is surely an instructive case: charter member of the AEA, eminent political scientist at Hopkins and Princeton, president of the APSA, governor of New Jersey, and president of the United States. Merriam pondered why a person of such obvious political talents had for so long remained in political obscurity, that is, an academician. Wilson never contemplated collapsing the roles of scholar and political actor, but rather was dedicated, until he finally left the university, to finding a way in which political science could be instrumental in practical affairs. For Wilson, the machinery of government, as it stood, was incapable of dealing with the complexities of advanced industrial society. His famous critique of congressional dominance and inefficiency and plea for more responsible government based on the parliamentary model assumed that both government and citizens must become more rational.[1] The social scientist, like the statesman, was to play a crucial role. Wilson wanted to avoid socialism and European statism and yet achieve a national state that, through a science of public administration, could direct increasingly random social and economic forces while remaining responsible to democratic majorities. The world had changed since the founding, and new paths of democratic and institutional development were necessary.[2]

On several occasions Wilson attempted to specify the role that political scientists could play. As a student of Ely, he found a lesson in the career of his teacher and rejected advocacy. He initially saw the political scientist as a "literary politician" who would be a mediator between the statesman and citizen,[3] but eventually he came to see the scholar and practitioner as distinct but complementary. In his presidential address to the APSA, Wilson noted that he did "not like the term political science" which seemed to suggest that human relations could be reduced to a science when, in his view, inquiry was ultimately a matter of "sympathy" and "spiritual comprehension"—knowing people not as "congeries of interests, but as human souls." Thus he preferred the term "Politics" which, for him, implied a certain unity between inquiry and its object as well as a bond between what he called "the statesmanship of thought" and the "statesmanship of action" which had not "hitherto often been partners."[4] But the issue was hardly a conceptual one.

The role of political science, he claimed, was not to provide practical expertise but knowledge. The goal was to achieve an "accurate and detailed observation of these processes by which the lessons of experience are brought into the field of consciousness, transmuted into active purposes, put under the scrutiny of discussion, sifted, and at last given determinate form in law." The volatile world of politics with its overwhelming mass of facts could be intellectually subdued by the political scientist who "out of his full store of truth, discovered by patient inquiry, dispassionate exposition, fearless analysis, and frank inference" would "enrich the thinking and clarify the vision of the statesman of action" who did not have time for reflective study. Each, in a sense, must think like the other but perform their distinctive roles. Wilson maintained that the facts were prior to the law and were "precedent to all remedies," and the task of political science was to study those facts and provide the knowledge required for leadership.[5] Yet exactly how articulation was to be achieved seemed as elusive for Wilson as it was for others of his generation.[6]

For individuals such as Beard and Arthur Bentley, there was still a faith that social science could produce facts that revealed political reality and raised the consciousness of a democratic majority and responsible elites. They had a singular commitment to social science as a method and tool that could pierce ideology, understand human behavior, and educate the public. Bentley was never successful in establishing an academic career, and, consequently, he never faced as directly as some the problem of reconciling politics and professional social science. His concern with the philosophical basis of scientific inquiry was linked to the Progressive ideology, but he held fast to the idea that science must precede reform. He had applied to Hopkins to study with Ely, and although Ely had left for Wisconsin by the time he arrived, the atmosphere remained hostile to social Darwinism and classical economics. Following his undergraduate studies, he spent a year (1893–94) in Berlin and Freiburg where he became deeply involved with the literature of the *Methodenstreit* and theorists such as Dilthey and Simmel. By the time he had begun his graduate work at Hopkins in 1894, his concern with the foundations of science had already begun to overshadow, and diverge from, his dedication to social reform.

During 1895–96, he held an academic post in sociology at the University of Chicago where he encountered Dewey and pragmatism—an experience which contributed significantly to undermining his belief in the psychological basis of social science and set him toward seeking a more fundamental ground of social science and human action. But he had no further academic success. In 1896, he took a job as a newspaper reporter, and both his substantive and methodological work remained largely outside mainstream political science. Bentley's realist antiformalist notion of a social science that would cut to the essentials of human action and the process of social activity was probably the most epistemologically radical vision in the history of American social science. Published in 1908, *The Process of Government*, however, had little general impact on the direction of political science, and when his ideas about "groups" took hold in the work of political scientists of the 1950s, the substance and concerns were in many respects far removed from those of Bentley himself.

His opus went beyond nearly all predecessors in its search for an objective observable social reality that was free from subjective overlays. And his unpublished *Makers, Users and Masters* (1920) indicated that his notion of the social implications of such a science was very different from that of many of the other reformist social scientists of the period. In Bentley's view, an enlightened middle class, supplied with the "facts," would rise up against the political and economic ills for radical ends but not with radical means. Although he claimed that industrial capitalism was out of control and that American society was dominated by concentrations of economic power, he argued that a proletariat revolution could be avoided by raising the consciousness of a democratic majority who, through regular political channels, would regain popular control.[7] While Bentley could not afford to stay in the academy, many could not afford to leave. Beard, however, could afford it, both intellectually and financially.

After graduating from DePauw (1898), Beard worked at Hull House in Chicago for a year before spending four years at Oxford. Here he was one of the founders of Rusking Hall which was devoted to the education of the working class. He entered graduate school at Columbia determined to promote the interests of industrial workers. He worked with Burgess and did his doctorate on the institution of the justice of the peace (1904). Although he initially accepted much of Burgess's perspective on history, their ideological differences became considerable, and he was drawn to individuals such as Seligman and Goodnow. Although Beard was initially appointed to the history department at Columbia, Burgess chose him for a chair in politics and government in 1907. He was, at this point, supportive of education in political science and optimistic about its future.[8] He was strongly influenced by Bentley's book and pursued a progressivist agenda as an activist on issues such as suffrage and municipal reform. His political views as well as his vision of social science increasingly brought his work into tension with Burgess who had not allowed Goodnow to succeed him as Ruggles Professor. Differences at Columbia had been growing for some time, and Beard's book on the constitution (1913) was a decisive statement of the substance and method of a position which caused both public and academic concern.[9]

Beard's work was widely denounced as socialist or Marxist, but it was less his limited acquaintance with such literature that inspired him than the more immediate and continuing contact with Seligman who was one of the generation that studied in Germany and was influenced by both Marx and the historical economists. The Jewish exception in the Protestant world of progressive historical economics, Seligman, although clearly critical of the operation of capitalism and an advocate of social change, had attempted to formulate a non-Marxist economic interpretation of history and distance himself from Ely during the latter's more radical moments.[10] Seligman was deeply inspired by the idea of an ethical social science, but he saw hope in capitalist abundance and attempted to build a bridge to classical economics. But whatever the exact source of Beard's method, the motivation was alienating him from the establishment at Columbia.

Nicolas Murray Butler, a protégé of Burgess, had been appointed president of the university in 1902. In 1890 while still a dean, he had recruited J. McKeen Cattell who became an eminent psychologist but also an abrasive and outspoken critic of autocratic university governance. Butler and the trustees attempted to force him into retirement, but there was considerable faculty resistance (including individuals such as Dewey and Seligman). In June of 1917, after many years as a pacifist and supporter of Germany, Butler decided that there was no room at Columbia for dissent from war policies adopted by the president and Congress and that he, with the full support of the trustees, would consider such actions treason and sedition. Cattell's son, a student at Columbia, was among a group who had circulated a petition protesting the draft. The courts brought action against them, and Cattell both appeared on their behalf and sent a letter to several congressmen urging resistance to conscription. The letter was published in the *New York Press,* and Cattell was dismissed by the trustees at Butler's request.

Although Beard had not been a vocal supporter of Cattell, he himself had been twice summoned before Butler and the trustees to explain comments defending dissent. He resigned charging the trustees with reactionary attitudes that betrayed the idea and mission of the university and demeaning the role of the professor. The *New York Times* headlined Beard's resignation as "Columbia's Deliverance." He continued his efforts on behalf of civil liberties and, along with Robinson who also left Columbia, was one of the founders of the New School for Social Research in 1919. But he eventually withdrew from academic life for a long period.

Beard's voice was much louder in the profession than that of Bentley, but it reflected the same progressive faith in social science as showing the way to a nonsocialist antiauthoritarian answer to the evils of capitalism and corrupt politics through the revival of democratic citizenship. Like so many of his contemporaries, he rejected speculation in favor of factual realism and believed that objective science and history would motivate a potentially rational and democratic public. Critical research in universities, training civil servants, and educating citizens were to be the tasks of professional social science and the basis for the partnership of science and democracy.[11] Merriam's goals were similar, but his strategy for the articulation of academic and public discourse was different.

After a somewhat dormant period, as far as attempts to identify what kind of thing political theory was and its place in the discipline, Merriam set out to give it a distinct meaning. In doing so, he in some ways departed from his own work, which up to World War I had largely involved the traditional attempt to recount the ideas of past thinkers. There is, however, probably no more prevalent and persistent, but misleading, conventional wisdom about the history of political science than the assumption that Merriam's work represented a fundamental break in either the theory or the practice of the discipline.[12] To hold Merriam's post-1920 work up against the arguments of some of the most influential members of the Columbia school seems to evoke a sense of contrast, but exactly how to specify the transformation is a great deal more difficult. To characterize it as a transition from historicism to scientism or from formalism to realism is inadequate. It was, after all, Burgess's goal to apply the methods of natural science to the study and transformation of politics.

When Merriam summed up his ideas in his manifesto of 1925, *New Aspects of Politics,* he was explicit about not asking "our older friends to go," and he never took issue with his principal teachers—Burgess and Dunning.[13] If Merriam did not put as much emphasis on the state as an object of inquiry, he nevertheless perpetuated the idea of the state, now conceived as government, as a means of political salvation. And the nineteenth-century vision of political science as a vehicle of civic education found its most enthusiastic extension in Merriam's work. Although it may be reasonable to suspect that Merriam in part had Burgess in mind when he spoke of the "intoxicating effect of the undiluted Hegelian philosophy upon the American mind," he noted in his study of the modern history of the theory of sovereignty, his doctoral dissertation, that with respect to political theory "the results of the American development finally took scientific form at the hands of J. W. Burgess," and he consistently emphasized his debt to Dunning, his "teacher and guide in the study of political theories."[14]

Despite all his talk about a new kind of political science, the intellectual bond with Burgess and Dunning remained. Political institutions and behavior were, as for his teachers, essentially a matter of ideas which were to be explained contextually, and ideas, in turn, were understood as the transforming forces in society. Writing at the high point of his advocacy of scientific method, Merriam said of Dunning that "no one in the last generation has done more . . . to advance the study of formal political theory, and to prepare the way for the increasingly intensive study of the human mind."[15] Merriam was probably in effect saying something about himself as well as Dunning when he distinguished the latter from Laski on the basis that "one type of man prefers a degree of isolation from current world events and another is interested in mingling with the stream."[16] But despite differences in the attitude toward political action, there was a short intellectual distance from German historical idealism, Comte, and Spencer, as adapted to American social science by individuals such as Dunning, to Merriam's vision of the psychological bases of politics. And it was an equally short distance from Burgess's notion of political theory as a source of both social scientific and practical order to Merriam's constant conjunction of the problems of cognitive and practical control of political phenomena. The problem that Merriam inherited was how to at once remain in the academy and yet enter the "stream" of political life.

The institutionalization of political theory after 1900 was not simply a matter of academic professionalization but part of a conscious search for social scientific legitimacy and authority. Theory was presented as the special province of those who *know* as opposed to those who *do* and as the key to both worlds. Historically it was viewed as the source of political change and urged as the vehicle of social transformation. It was not an accident that the focus on theory increased as the distance between politics and social science grew wider. Political science, as a professional discipline, had from the beginning engaged the question of how to achieve political purchase from an academic fulcrum. The search for political theory was part of the search for the authority of knowledge vis-à-vis the authority of politics. Merriam's basic goals continued to be those of the Progressive Era. Political science would aid in creating democratic citizens and in providing the basis of rational public policy. But Merriam's vision was of a science that would explain human behavior and contribute to the tractability of that behavior by intervening in public policy at the level of governmental and social elites.

Merriam's project must be viewed in the context of the war and such events of the early part of this century as the "Red Scare." This period was not one in which academicians felt secure in seeking social change through direct political advocacy.[17] And the war inspired both his concern about the need for democratic social control and his conception of the instrumentalities to effect it. Merriam also worked diligently, through the Social Science Research Council (created as an extension of the National Research Council which had been organized to facilitate national preparedness) and private foundations such as the Laura Spelman Rockefeller Memorial. The goal was to find nonpartisan sources of research funding and to propagate the idea of state action, particularly through the executive branch with the aid of social science expertise.

As Dunning's student, Merriam had identified himself from the first as a political theorist. Although economics had been his initial choice, "political theory emerged triumphant."[18] Merriam noted "the poverty of English literature on the history of political theory in general," and while he was most indebted to Dunning, "under whose direction all of the writer's work in the field of political theory has been conducted," he acknowledged his debt to Burgess "whose doctrine of sovereignty first stimulated interest in the present study."[19] This history of sovereignty, which ended with the American theorists Burgess, Wilson, and Willoughby, was viewed by Merriam as a "development." During Merriam's early years at Chicago, Dunning remained his close advisor and confidant. Merriam had read the proofs for Dunning's second volume, and the latter acknowledged that he had "rendered inestimable service by his sound critical judgment and his accurate scholarship." It was at Chicago, however, that he stepped away from "pure" scholarship to "political involvement" which he viewed as the mandate of his graduate education.[20] He had begun his dissertation in Berlin, and Gierke, his codirector, had been the Chair of the Imperial Code Commission. Another teacher, Hugo Preuss, would be the principal drafter of the Weimar Constitution. The practical disposition was very much reinforced by the intellectual climate at Chicago. Contact with Dewey,

Thorstein Veblen, E. J. James, Albion Small, and others turned him toward political practice.

Merriam published *A History of American Political Theories* in 1903 shortly after arriving at Chicago. In form, it was, like the dissertation, a Dunning-type exercise, but it also embodied his optimism about the compatibility of democracy and a national state devoted to social control. Dunning warned him that reviewers might jump on him as a "socialist."[21] Merriam noted that the "development" of American political theories had received little attention from historians, because, unlike the Germans, Americans had characteristically little interest in "systematic politics" and philosophy. But, he argued, there was in fact "no dearth of political theory from the days of the Puritans to present times"—it simply was buried in political life. "Like all other political theory, American political ideas are of little importance aside from the great historical movements of which they are an organic part." On the whole, however, he concluded that although to say that there was "no American political theory" would be an exaggeration, there had been "no remarkable development of political philosophy" or "contributions to systematic politics." Americans, he suggested, as had his teachers before him, tended more toward "action than reflection." Yet he did see some hope in the last half of the nineteenth century with the emergence of "a group of political theorists" who in method were "more systematic and scientific" and in doctrine represented a "pronounced reaction from the individualistic philosophy" of earlier periods.[22]

Such individuals as Lieber, Woolsey, Burgess, Lowell, Wilson, and Willoughby had developed, in their historical-comparative method, "a more scientific way of approaching the questions of politics," and sociologists and economists had taken a new interest in social forces and social control. The ideas of natural rights and the social contract had been rejected, and the state was seen as a positive force in general welfare and as a source of liberty. Merriam believed that many of these ideas were, in general, ahead of popular thought, but he claimed that with respect to the "function of government," the public "has gone beyond political scientists, and is ready for assumption of extensive powers by the political authorities."[23] Knowledge and power were ready for one another.

Although Merriam upheld the sovereign supremacy of the Union, he, like Beard after him, but unlike his teachers, saw the *Federalist* as a reactionary tract that was suspicious of popular government and turned away from the principles of the revolution. He praised Jefferson (over Adams) and the triumph of Jacksonian democracy. Although some believed that, with such trends as those toward the concentration of wealth and imperialism, there was, in the present, a movement away from democracy, he said that this was "not proven." He was optimistic that the "drift" was in the direction of social equality which would "call out a greater extension of democratic activity" expressed through "governmental control and regulation." With respect to national expansion, he remained close to Burgess and suggested that "democracy does not demand that barbarians be admitted with equal political rights with peoples long trained in the art of self-government, nor, on the other hand, does it require that democratic states leave the work of political civilization to countries where constitutional liberty is unknown, or to states possessing a less degree of constitutional liberty than their own."[24]

Although he was, in his words, "well on the way toward a five-foot shelf of erudition in political science," Merriam's deep involvement in Chicago politics, during the next decade and a half, dominated his career despite some limited academic publication.[25] But his frustrations with often petty aspects of everyday political life, his failure to become mayor, and the experience of the war all contributed to his sense of the need for a practical catalyzing role for political science and political theory—for a new way to bridge scholarship and political action. From his earliest years in Iowa, Merriam had been involved in practical politics, and it might not be too fanciful to suggest that after the period as a political scientist *in* politics, he concluded that meaningful political change could only be effected by the impact of political science *on* politics.

In 1920, Merriam published a book dealing with recent American political thought. Although this was in many respects a continuation of his 1903 volume, it was his first comprehensive statement of where he stood both politically and as a social scientist. The emphasis was on the social turmoil engendered by capitalism, urbanism, and other forces during the last part of the nineteenth century and their implications for democratic ideas and institutions. But he also again devoted considerable attention to what he took to be the development of the "systematic study of politics" which included Darwinism, the Webbs, and various German thinkers including Marx (whose "philosophy deeply influenced political activity and speculation throughout America"). He stressed that it was in the United States that there had been the greatest emphasis on the "scientific study of politics."[26] Here, once more, he counted the appearance of the professional social science associations and the work of Lieber, Woolsey, Burgess, Wilson, Bryce, and Willoughby which was continued through the efforts of individuals such as Goodnow and Beard. Through a concern with such topics as public administration and municipal government, political science and political theory were moving away from abstract speculation, rationalism, formalism, and natural rights and toward a concrete pragmatic consideration of the activities of the state and a concern with political reform.

Merriam argued that the sociological tradition from Comte and Spencer through Lester Frank Ward and later professional sociologists such as Giddings and Small had contributed to furthering systematic inquiry. But he also emphasized the role of those thinkers who were "not systematic" but who had raised their voices against political and economic abuse—Carl Shurz, William Curtis, E. C. Godkin, and Horace Greeley. For Merriam, as for Dunning, political theory was *in* politics as well as *about* politics. And the task was to bring the two dimensions together. Herbert Croly's *The Promise of American Life* represented the Progressive hope for increased social and political democracy through state leadership, and Walter Lippmann's *Preface to Politics* protested formalism and legalism while pushing experimental pragmatism. Thinkers such as Dewey and Beard, activists such as Jane Addams, and economists such as Ely, Veblen, and Commons all counted in this story of the progress of American thought.

Merriam optimistically summed up the period as one in which there was a "gradual tendency toward the concentration of political and economic institutions" with a decline of laissez-faire policies in favor of a broader purpose and centralization of the state.[27] He suggested that three principal "philosophies of action and interpretation" had succeeded one another: conservatism and natural law, liberal or progressive theory advocating popular control, and a collectivist theory of industrial democracy. The "latent ideal" all along, however, had been to "translate the hope and faith of democracy into more effective form under the new social and economic conditions."[28] Like Dewey (e.g., *The Public and its Problems,* 1911), Merriam was disenchanted with localism as a basis of democracy, but he rejected socialism in favor of democratically legitimate but authoritative political control of the economic system.

In his famous 1921 analysis of the condition of political science, Merriam announced that while he had initially intended to survey the development of the field over the past four decades (a task that he had already accomplished in the 1920 work), he decided instead to speak to the "present state" of political science and to the more pressing problem of the "reconstruction of the methods of political study and the attainment of larger results in the theoretical and practical fields." This, he argued, required a fundamental change in the "theory of politics" which had now "come in contact with forces which in time must modify its procedure in a very material way" and which "constitute a challenge to all systems of thought." What he was referring to was, first, what he claimed to be "the comparatively recent doctrine that political ideas and systems . . . are the by-product of environment" and, second, the methodological advances which made it possible to measure these determinative "facts and forces" within the field of politics.[29] Merriam's notion of social scientific explanation was largely a synchronic version of the historical approach coupled to the application of new research techniques. His observation of the manipulation of public opinion during the war only further confirmed his belief that ideas were the essence of politics and that psychology was the way to study and control it.

Dunning, he argued, had demonstrated how in the past "political theory had been conscripted in the service of class and race and group," and Merriam now wanted to demonstrate how, through the advance and redirection of political theory in political science, "political prudence might be more effectively organized" on a national and international level.[30] What theory would do in political science was basically serve as an intellectual instrument for dealing systematically with the vast amount of information that was being produced. The facts did not speak for themselves in either an explanatory or a prescriptive sense. He believed that it was in part simply the complexity of modernity that led to the overwhelming amount of facts, but it was also the increased ability to gather them. This in turn meant for Merriam the need for a strong interdisciplinary emphasis.

Other disciplines of what he called "kindred stock," such as psychology and sociology, were "producing masses of material facts, of interpretations and insights, correlations and conclusions" which were relevant to politics and which required ordering. Political theory, as Burgess and, particularly, Willoughby had already argued, was to serve as a "medium for the collection and classification of political material," and the availability of such instruments as "statistical observation" made it possible to "definitely and measurably advance the comprehensiveness and accuracy of our observation of political phenomena." The goal was the "cross fertilization of politics with science." Could it be, Merriam asked, that we can know and control physical nature and yet not "interpret and explain and measurably control . . . the forces of human nature?" He argued that "the processes of social and political control may be found to be much more susceptible to human adaption and reorganization than they are now." But before this practical goal could be achieved, there was a "necessity for better organization of our own professional research," and political theory was to be the answer to this problem.[31]

Merriam was hardly a philosopher of science, but he adopted, without much reflection, an instrumentalist interpretation of scientific theory that would ever after retain its hold on mainstream political science and which would be reinforced by its later exposure to logical positivism. There were complementary cognitive and practical dimensions to instrumentalism. Theory was understood as an intellectual construct for ordering and manipulating facts that were epistemologically primitive and accessible to immediate experience. Such a notion of theory had been advanced by Ernst Mach at the turn of the century, but Merriam was probably more directly influenced by the American pragmatist tradition and the work of Dewey in which the cognitive claim was closely related to the practical image of science. Merriam referred to the influential work of Karl Pearson who had developed this image of theory, but who had also urged the application of scientific method, statistics, and psychology to all aspects of life. His discussion of Pearson was superficial, but Pearson's *Grammar of Science* (1892, and republished in 1911) emphasized the idea that science began and ended with facts and that science was, in the end, description with a social purpose.

Since there was considerable suspicion of theory as a speculative enterprise that was ideologically dangerous and in some way inimical to empirical science, there was a distinct problem of reconciling the belief that theory was scientifically important and necessary with other assumptions about social scientific inquiry. Instrumentalism provided a basic, if not always consistent, answer to this problem. Theory was an important but subservient element in scientific explanation that functioned as a tool for better understanding and organizing observed facts, but it was something that must be defined in terms of such facts. The sense of being overwhelmed by facts and information was common, and theory was consistently understood as a means of producing intellectual order. But the instrumentalist perspective extended even further.

This position coincided with the Progressive vision and the emphasis on factual realism as well as with its image of the functions of social science and government. In science, theory ordered facts and made them manageable, and, within politics, governmental institutions and agencies of control ordered individuals and the elements of society. There was a definite and, in Merriam's case explicit, parallel between the theoretical organization of political nature and the political organization of human and social nature. As in the case of Woodrow Wilson, there was the notion that the social scientist and the statesman play parallel and complementary roles in their respective intellectual and practical ordering of political nature by creating meaning and unity out of disparate elements of reality. But for Merriam, most important was the idea that social science and political theory were institutional instruments for joining and mediating these functions. Social science itself, that is, theory as opposed to practice, was understood as an instrument for the explanation, prediction, and control of politics.

Merriam was not only impressed with methods in other disciplines, but with the idea of social control so dominant in contemporary sociology and the possibilities that seemed to be inherent in the study of psychology. In the same meeting of the APSA at which Merriam delivered his critique of political science, Henry Elmer Barnes gave a paper surveying the "contributions of sociology to modern political theory." He had earlier published an article on the "representative" contributions of Sumner and Ward to "political theory," and this theme of sociology and political theory was expanded into a book. Barnes found the emphases of Bentley to be similar to those of the sociologists Giddings and Small. For too long political science had been under the spell of the "abstract metaphysical and legislative approach and concepts of Hegelian dialectic, the Austinian analytical jurisprudence and the German *Staatsrechtslehre.*" The new trends had put "the lawyers of the metaphysical and 'mechanical' schools to rout" with an "infusion of Darwinian and Neo-Darwinian biological and functional and behavioristic psychology." He saw the new trends represented in the pluralist and realist approach of such individuals as Roscoe Pound, Duguit, Graham Wallas, Bentley, Laski, Hugo Krabbe, Lippmann, and Beard. Most new developments in political theory, he argued, had taken place under the influence of sociology, and, in fact, this had been the case from Aristotle to Madison and only more recently interrupted "by the influence of lawyers upon political theory and practice."[32]

Barnes, like Merriam, used "political theory" to refer to both an element in social science and ideas in society, but in both cases he stressed the importance of the relationship between ideas and their social context. This position inhibited any incipient tension between history and political science. Barnes had attacked certain historians but not the enterprise of history. He claimed that "little sympathy or interest can be expected from the 'eminent' and 'respectable' historians as a group" for the intellectual direction in which he was moving, which stressed the evolution of science and the "progressive establishment of human control over nature and the increasingly perfect adaption of nature to human use." But the "new history," represented by a "renegade and outlaw" such as Robinson, had "transcended archaic and illogical conventions and dared to view history psychologically as a record of human achievement."[33]

The notion of the identity of science and history, then, was by no means obsolescent. The practice of history was still perceived as an empirical antidote to philosophical excess and a way of understanding both the past and present. As one author put it, the "historical method" offers an "approach to the problem of social order" which serves "to clear the atmosphere of speculation and permits events to speak for themselves. In brief, we have in history the foundation of science and a scientific view of life."[34] The relationship between ideas and context had always been assumed to be one of mutual causation, and Barnes emphasized "the correlation between successive advances in social and political theory and the changes in the social and political environment." Political theory was defined as part of a study of political action that would give guidance to the statesman in managing the conflict between various social interests and guiding the "evolution of the political community" and the "development and functioning of all the organs of social control" including the state.[35]

The question of whether political theory was to be understood as something in politics or something in political science or both would never be entirely settled, but it was becoming clear that it was political science that would in all cases decide the criteria of existence and location. The statement of one political scientist at this time did not appear odd, but it would have been singular two decades earlier. In a discussion of methods in the study of politics, he noted that with regard to public law and political philosophy, neither actually "*is* political, at least not nowadays," since "political theory comes into politics only in the determination or explanation of political activity."[36] It was increasingly becoming an autonomous self-ascribed entity in political science. In a 1923 essay on "the nature of political thought," Gettell (now at the University of California) offered little that was distinctly new, but he attempted to synthesize the views about political theory that had developed by the end of the first quarter of the century.

Gettell emphasized the functional and practical characteristics of political theories. He stressed the tenuous character of abstract ethical theories that could not be proven and that would be "untenable" if carried to their "logical conclusion." Political theories served best to give "precision and definiteness to the meaning of political terms" in political science, and they contributed to "clarity and honesty of thought" by examining the "actual meaning" behind the use of many political terms. He also made the common point that political theory was valuable for interpreting history and explaining contemporary politics, since it made it possible to understand the beliefs and ideals of which political action was an expression. Finally, like Willoughby, he allowed that political thought was in some measure an end in itself and represented "a high intellectual achievement apart from any practical application of its principles."[37]

In 1922, the APSA Committee on Political Research, under

Merriam's leadership, had examined what it took to be the "recent history of political thinking" which it equated with the "development of methods of inquiry in recent years in the field of political science and of the related social sciences." In its 1923 progress report, it concluded that the "a priori speculation" that had characterized the past two centuries was on the "decline" as were historical and comparative studies of law and institutions. What was on the rise was the "observation and description of actual processes of government," and what made this possible was the use of methods from all the various fields of social science.[38] Merriam suggested that political inquiry had evolved through four principal stages. While natural law and the a priori deductive method had informed political inquiry through the mid-1800s, the historical and comparative approach had dominated until the turn of the century. The present tendency was toward quantified observational surveys, and the future was pointing in the direction of the "psychological treatment of politics" characteristic of the work of individuals such as Wallas and Lippmann and intercourse with other fields such as statistics, history, sociology, anthropology, geography, and biology.[39]

While Merriam argued that it was necessary to make political science more scientific, he also claimed that "the political scientist must be something of a utopian in his prophetic view and something of a statesman in his practical methods." Scientific method was not in itself sufficient, even though it was necessary for the development of political control. If we were not to "drift at the mercy of the wind and waves," it was necessary to organize "public intelligence" through "technical knowledge of human nature" in order to prepare for the "next great stage in the advancement of the human race."[40] The final report of the committee was published in 1924, and Merriam's discussion of psychology and politics appeared as a separate article. He stressed the significance of psychology both because it focused on the springs of human behavior and because it held promise for the "development of scientific method in the observation, measurement and comparison of political relations."[41] Some were concerned about the implications of this perspective for the autonomy of politics and political studies, but, as one political scientist of the period had put it, "if political science is not psychology, what is it?"[42] Nevertheless, this attempt to find an identity for political science in methodology would be strongly contested.

Merriam, however, was far from totally sanguine about the current situation. There was a lack of sufficient data and analysis, there was too much bias in the interpretation of data, measurement was inadequate, the problem of striking a balance between political conformity on the one hand and criticism and social change had not been solved, and gen-

eral causal explanation was underdeveloped. Merriam actively participated in three national conferences (1923, 1924, 1925—in Madison,
New York, and Chicago) on the science of politics that were designed to
provide a coherent vision of political inquiry. The emphasis enunciated
by the principal organizer, Arnold Bennett Hall of the University of
Wisconsin, was on the development of scientific methods for the purpose of social control. Rather than undertake a "frontal attack" on the
problem of developing a "scientific method," the executive committee
decided to conduct roundtables on a variety of subjects.[43] Merriam led
the roundtables on psychology and politics.

In the first conference report, Hall claimed that "the great need of
the hour is the development of a scientific technique and methodology
for political science" that would aid in guiding legislation and administration on such matters as civil service reform and finance by supplying
knowledge to those in government who do not have the time for such
research. The burden, he suggested, was "primarily on the teacher and
scholar." There must be a "fact-finding technique that will produce an
adequate basis for sound generalization" and put political research on a
"scientific, objective basis."[44] The emphasis in political science had
been on historical and descriptive research without adequate attention
to "analytical and statistical" studies that would allow the facts to be
gathered and conclusions drawn. Without such methods "political science cannot make any substantial contribution to the success of our political democracy." Hall argued that the "perfection of social science is
indispensable to the very preservation of this same civilization" which
created modern science. What was required was a "system of social
control which will guide humanity by its intelligence rather than by passion, by which the true course of social progress may be more prophet-
ically discerned; in short, which causes mankind to become the creator
rather than the helpless creature of destiny is essential if civilization is to
survive the caprice of ignorance and passion."[45]

In the report of the second conference, Hall lamented the danger
that natural science would continue to outstrip social science. He posed
the question of whether this was something "inherent" in these endeavors or whether it was principally a "methodological" problem. But
he indicated his certainty that "new political theories" and the work of
the "political pioneer" were neglected because of the "unscientific character" of the conclusions.[46] While Merriam saw a reasonable division
and complementarity between "political prudence" and "political science," Hall argued that the former could not be the basis of the latter. It
was necessary to "extend and perfect" scientific technique so "that more
and more of the field now preempted by political prudence will be occu-

pied by a science of politics" and that, "if we can only find the method," more issues of "political theory" can be reduced to objective treatment in terms of material facts. He attempted to demonstrate at some length how natural science in its early years was also undeveloped and to suggest that statistics and psychology must become an integral part of political science if parity was to be achieved. If reason was to dominate over passion and mankind was to be the "conscious arbiter of its own destiny," the "power-controlling sciences" must "equal the efficiency of the power-creating disciplines."[47] Hall argued that "most writing that appears under the name of political theory might better be called political literature." It was rationalization, propaganda, dogma, speculation, and the like which based its persuasiveness on "literary form." What Hall had in mind was largely progressivist writings. "Certainly it is not theory in any scientific sense, for a true theory is a generalization that accurately explains the facts of political behavior."[48]

In 1924, Merriam and Barnes edited a volume of essays by Dunning's students dealing with contemporary political theory. Merriam devoted a long encyclopedic piece to the topic of "Recent Tendencies in Political Thought" which recapitulated and extended the themes discussed in his APSA progress report. He seemed somewhat overwhelmed by the proliferation of ideas in both society and social science, but he wanted to determine the "outstanding social forces" and the kinds of "systems of political rationalization" and other "intellectual equipment" that were being employed in the competition between the "most conspicuous groups." And what, he asked, were the "ways of arriving at political truth" and what "progress" was there in the "discussion of what are commonly regarded as the fundamentals of political theory?"[49]

He suggested that the basic forces were the "development of industrialism and urbanism, the new contacts with diverse races and nationalities, and the rise of feminism" and that the principal groups were the working class, capitalists, the middle class, and racial and religious factions. There was, however, a "lack of coordination between religion, science, and philosophy" which had produced a "great break in civilization" and "a tragic gap in the mores of the day," and "political theory itself was embarrassed by the lack of agreement upon many of the fundamentals of human conduct." He counted the "advancement of science" in recent years as a landmark but lamented that this had not been adequately reflected "in the domain of social phenomena" where political philosophy and the name of science still remained tools of interest and power. Although there had been a decline in older philosophical perspectives, such as the neo-Hegelian, neither pragmatism nor psychology had significantly influenced political thought. A variety of approaches to political inquiry had developed, but methodological progress in political science had been slow even though developments in the fields of anthropology, ethnology, and archaeology were of "great significance" for the "methods of political theory."[50]

Merriam claimed, however, that although progress had been slow and although there was a bewildering array of ideas, it was possible to discern "actual progress in political speculation" on matters such as democracy and to ascertain that an "objective scientific attitude" was emerging, and "standards of impartial intelligence were entering the domain of political theory." Although it was premature to suggest that Comte's vision was being realized, scientific disciplines were beginning to converge on the understanding and control of human behavior and "political nature" and cut into "the language of traditional authority, of custom, or group propaganda" which was "still the official language of the time." Although overall progress was not overridingly clear in all sectors, "the signs of dawn" were apparent as the "human mind advanced during this period toward the understanding and control of political forces and the political process."[51]

As Merriam consolidated his claims about the scientific study of politics, he also made clear the purpose of that science. He argued that through "minute thorough patient intensive studies of the detail of political phenomena [political scientists] will bridge the gap between art and science and bring us to more precise methods of political and social control than mankind has hitherto possessed."[52] The aim was to produce social cohesion and consensus through scientific education and scientific government. Merriam was concerned with irrational political behavior and the manipulation of the public for unscrupulous purposes. His notion of science was one that would cut through ideology and achieve scientifically credible political and social reform. "Politics as the art of the traditional advances to politics as the science of constructive intelligent social control."[53] *New Aspects of Politics* was basically a compilation of his earlier essays and addresses. It was rhetorical and exhortative, and there was very little sustained analysis of political theory. In fact, in Merriam's work, despite the influence of his claims about theory, there never was any such analysis. Political theory meant ideas about politics, and in Merriam's view these ideas had become too often possessions of special interests, classes, and other forms of prejudice. Political theory in political science was to be in part method, but it was also a purification of political thinking that would transcend particularities and thus contribute to unifying the political society. Merriam argued that "jungle politics and laboratory science are incompatible," and the "modern movement" in the study of politics is both "democratic and scientific."[54]

Merriam indicated no conflict between what had become the traditional study of political theory and his vision of "a science of political behavior" with a "real political purpose."[55] In his presidential address to the APSA in 1926, he once again paid homage to his predecessors and stated that "political theory had been embellished" by individuals such as Willoughby and Dunning. He did, however, argue that the greatest progress had been made in the area of political theory as "method" and that within this area the "most striking tendency" had been "toward actual observation of political processes and toward closer analysis of their meaning." He saw certain dangerous signs in society such as the tendency toward "political fundamentalism" evidenced in the Scopes trial, but it was precisely such tendencies that he believed political science and political theory, correctly conceived and applied, could ameliorate. Merriam's vision was that of a "new politics" that would be achieved through a science that would include "the mechanisms of education and eugenics."[56]

Whether science so conceived served, or could serve, a real, or proper, political purpose, however, was for the first time to be a matter of significant contention. And while Merriam still clung to the instrumentality of the state, the concept of the state and the idea of democracy associated with it, and the identity of political theory and political science, were confronting a serious challenge from the emerging theory of pluralism. Meanwhile, however, disciplinary practice during the 1920s was marked by the further institutionalization of the history of political theory as a field and a subject matter. In addition to an increasing number of specialized studies of the thought of particular individuals, periods, and countries, there were a number of books devoted to general treatments of the history of political theory. Although the authors were not always American, the genre was distinctly American.[57] As Eric Voegelin later noted, and many came to forget or, for various reasons, deny, the history of political theory had been "almost an American monopoly from its beginnings."[58] The story was one of the progress of Western consciousness, of the manner in which political action and institutions were the manifestation of political ideas, and it was seldom other than a vindication of liberal ideas and institutions with an emphasis on the past as providing lessons for the present.

A. R. Lord emphasized, without argument, what had become a dogma—"the theory of politics is the peculiar product of Western thought," and "only in Western civilization has the social consciousness of men attained that superior grade of political interest at which it demands a theory of the State and its relation to the individual citizens who compose it." His "historical and philosophical" inquiry also took the position that "institutions are what they are in virtue of the ideas they embody: the history of institutions is a history of ideas," and thus "history and the criticism of political ideas are complementary." The purpose was to examine the "atmosphere in which modern Politics grew up."[59] C. E. Vaughan, noting that "political theory goes hand in hand with history," saw his particular study of modern political thought as focusing on a series of perennial issues, such as the relationship between the individual and the state, and as a segment of a tradition that began in ancient Greece with Plato.[60]

Gettell, arguing that there was "no satisfactory single-volume history of political theory," offered one of the first comprehensive accounts after Dunning. Although Dunning's work was "a splendid monument to his scholarship, and must serve as the basis for the work of any later writer," it omitted theories that emerged during the last half-century as well as literature pertaining to the United States and international relations. Also, Gettell claimed, it "shows little realization of the connection between economics and political theory" and was more "a survey of political literature than a history of the development of political thought in relation to its historical, institutional, and intellectual background."[61] Political theory, he claimed, arose as a result of the "natural" development of the state—at first unconscious but then reflective. The theory of the state was the "subjective" complement to the "objective phase" of the state. For Gettell, the "theory of politics" was the "peculiar product of Western thought," and there was not "a single controversy of our day without a pedigree" that could be uncovered by such historical studies.[62]

He claimed that it was evident that there was "a close relation between the political thought of any given period and the actual political condition then existing." Since "political theories are the direct result of objective political conditions," they tend, no matter how speculative, to be addressed to concrete situations and emerge as forms of either legitimation or criticism. The conclusion that "political thought is essentially relative in its nature," that it could lay no claim to "ultimate" or "absolute" truth, and that it was the result of "judgments or emotional intuitions" that could not be "proved" did not diminish Gettell's belief that, as in the case of "actual political organization, a continuous growth may be traced" and that "progress toward democracy, individualism, liberty, and internal justice owes much to the doctrines of a long line of able thinkers."[63]

Ludwig Gumplowicz made a German entry into the genre by presenting a survey reaching from Hammurabi to Lester Ward and beyond, and later Gaetano Mosca offered a rendition. Robert H. Murray, noting his debt to Laski, identified the history of political theory with the history of political science and asked if there was "a single controversy of our day without a pedigree stretching into distant ages?" In a compendium of "original works" dedicated to Dunning, his former student Francis Coker offered a vehicle for introducing students to "political theories" and providing "helpful illustrations for such general histories of political philosophy as those of Dunning, Pollock, Janet, Willoughby, and Bluntschli."[64]

F. J. C. Hearnshaw moved further in the direction of attributing synoptic meaning to the history of political thought. "So far as we know . . . political philosophy in its pure and systematic form had its rise in Ancient Greece"—and it ended with the conflict between individualism and socialism.[65] In a second edition of this volume, nine years later, he noted that an "immense amount of work has been done on the history of political ideas"—which required an entire chapter to catalog. Hearnshaw also edited several collections of essays on various periods in the history of political ideas. In a volume on medieval thinkers, Barker, adumbrating a later conventional distinction, took pains to distinguish between "political thought" and "political theory" and suggested that while this period had a great deal of the former, it had little of the latter. Political thought referred to the general body of ideas, "the immanent philosophy of a whole age, which determines its action and shapes its life," while political theory was "the speculation of particular thinkers, which may be remote from the actual facts of the time" and more self-conscious and explicit.[66]

The history of political theory, however, carried different meanings for different people. Few would disagree with the contention that "there has been very little, if any, political thinking really independent of quite rapidly changing circumstances."[67] And going back to the "*political* theory" of Plato and Aristotle was a search "for solutions of modern social and political problems." But while for Hearnshaw the history of political theory documented the rise of socialism and the danger of descent into the "abyss," another author read it as support for the idea of a collectivist interventionist state and a critique of "the modern plutocratic gospel."[68] Whatever the message, the "presentist" character of these histories was evident.

One idiosyncratic text was important less in its influence, or ultimate intelligibility to readers of this period, than in the extent to which it was an intimation of things to come. It was written by a Hungarian scholar, Gesa Englemann, and translated and introduced by two Hungarian émigrés, Karl Geiser and Oscar Jászi, who together largely constituted the political science department at Oberlin College. It was offered in response to the "revival of interest in political philosophy in American colleges and universities." The author, it was claimed, employed "an entirely new method" involving "artistic intuition" whereby "he saw in his imagination these leading spirits . . . reincarnated at a phantom round-table, presenting their views to our own generation." The purpose was to "bring the best of political thought of two thousand years to the problems of the present," and this was relevant because there were "constant tendencies in human nature, and in the aspirations of our soul" which allow us to extract general knowledge from the past. Jászi believed that there was a critical need to aid students in "discriminating between good and bad political thinking in our own day."[69]

The work of Hegel and Marx, Jászi argued, had produced "an entirely relativistic attitude" which had become a "driving force in present-day America where the materialism, relativism, and subjectivism of pre-war Europe are in a manifest ascendancy." He believed that this crisis of thought was evident in work such as that of Lippmann which, by its suggestion that political theory was only a rationalization of elite power, was an example of "relativistic subjective political thinking" and, at least by implication, a "refutation of all claims, on the part of moral and political science, to give direction and purpose" to human affairs. The notion that human nature was malleable and that there were no permanent ideals was a product of the "scientific attitude" that was expressed by the Russian Bolsheviks and was now promoted "by the pragmatist and pluralist." This perspective had engendered a "dismal political science" which has jettisoned our "moral background" and the ideas of the classics who knew more than modern "boosters of relativity."[70]

In Hungary, in 1900, Jászi had founded and led the "radical" Society for Social Sciences—an association patterned after the Fabians and devoted to social and political reform and, later, along with Georg Lukács, was associated with the Free School for the Social Sciences which was dedicated to educating the working class and utilizing positivist social science as a critical instrument of political liberalization. While socialist in outlook, they rejected revolutionary Marxism in favor of parliamentary politics, education, and state planning. The path that had brought Jászi from this position to his analysis of the condition of modern political thought in the United States is a subject that belongs to a later chapter, but it was one example of the transfiguration of political ideas that would take place as intellectual and political exiles from Europe came to America. Jászi became closely involved with Merriam during the decade after his emigration in 1923. He looked to Merriam for aid in publication as well as financial support, while Merriam employed him in his comparative civic education project.[71] Despite this long association, there is little indication that their intellectual horizons genuinely intersected. The issues involved in Jászi's arguments, however, bore a conceptual, even if not historical, relationship to what emerged as the principal debate in political science during the 1920s.

5

In Search of Identity

. . . too many theories, not enough theory.
Charles A. Beard

From the beginnings of the discipline, if not the nation, political diversity had been construed as a political pathology. While the *Federalist* had sought an institutional remedy, most nineteenth-century theorists, as well as the progressivists, had looked for an answer in the idea of the state. The circumstances of the late nineteenth and early twentieth century did little to ameliorate this concern which cut across ideological lines. For Wilson, the problem was fragmentation in both government and society, and Macy, as well as many others, continued to see political science, through government, as an answer to the problem of controlling proliferating and conflicting interests.[1] In the work of both political scientists and sociologists, the focus on interest groups, as political reality, increased. Although Bentley's work was neither well understood nor immediately very influential, his emphasis was neither unrepresentative nor unnoticed. And Beard's account of the founding challenged the idea of collective unity that had sustained the traditional theory of the state. Pluralism, as an account of social reality, was by 1920 gaining strength and, at least implicitly, displacing the concept of the state.

Pluralism, however, was hardly congenial to individuals such as Merriam who pursued a vision of national democratic consolidation and social control. As one eminent political scientist asked, How could conflicts between groups be resolved without the supreme will of the state?[2] What was emerging in the 1920s was an image of an irrational pluralistic society, propelled by self-interest and acting through the vagaries of public opinion, in which there was no definable public. This was exemplified in the work of Wallas, Lippmann, Lowell, and Frank Kent. Merriam himself found that American society was fractured by parties and that individuals did not participate.[3]

It fell to Harold Laski, and to some extent Mary Parker Follett, to redeem pluralism as a normative thesis.[4] Although Laski was primarily concerned with what he perceived as the lack of pluralism in England

and referred to the United States as something of a model, it was principally in response to Laski's claims, and to the ideas of those whom he implicated in his arguments, that the debate about the state was generated and one of the most important transformations in the history of American political science was effected.[5] By the mid-1920s, the concept of pluralism and the idiom of pluralistic theory had become common currency, while a decade earlier the concepts had been absent from the literature. Pluralism was viewed as a "critical political theory" directed against the "conservative political theory" of the state.[6] By the 1930s, it had begun to be equated with the theory of liberal democracy. The controversy about state and pluralism, however, was also, in the end, one about the identity of political theory and political science.

Ellen Deborah Ellis was the first to identify the controversy and give an account of it. She noted Laski's dependence on a long list of thinkers which included Gierke, Maitland, Figgis, Duguit, and Barker as well as on ideas of guild socialism and syndicalism, but she emphasized that what emerged from all this was an increasingly distinct theory of "pluralism" which could be juxtaposed to "monism"—the "long accepted state theory of political science" which represented the state as the distinct, unitary, and absolute political association and sovereign organ of society and as something standing behind government and as the creator of liberty and rights.[7] Ellis noted, accurately, that the pluralist challenge to these assumptions sprang less from a factual disagreement than from the normative belief that the state should be limited. She suggested that pluralist theory leavened some of the more dubious elements of traditional statism, such as the excessive emphasis on authority exemplified in German philosophy, and that it called "attention to the present bewildering development of groups within the body politic, and to the fact that these groups are persistently demanding greater recognition in the governmental system." The difficulty, however, was that pluralism tended to destroy the distinction between state and government. It offered no solution to the problem of competing interests and tended to "lay the way open to a very disorganized and casual political organization" which would be a threat to both order and liberty and which disguised the inescapable fact that, in the end, any real and true state must be a "unitary state" in which there is "one supreme loyalty and political sovereign."[8]

Sabine's sympathies were clearly on the side of pluralism, and he claimed that "the traditional notion of the state is out of accord with present day political conditions." But he tried to mediate somewhat the debate between "monism" and "pluralism" regarding state sovereignty and suggested that these were less competing theories than different points of view—one looking to legal structure and the other at process or development.[9] Sabine, now at Missouri, also participated in the translation and introduction of Krabbe's work on *The Modern Theory of the State*. He still associated political theory with the philosophy of the state, but he applauded Krabbe's theory as offering a new conception of sovereignty as embodied in law and free from organic images of authority. He also took the opportunity to say something about the nature of political theory.

A theorist, Sabine argued, must feel a "scientific reverence" for the facts or "what is" but yet can never escape the "ideal dimension" and the question of what "ought to be." Political theory involved "not only the generalization of facts but also the valuation of tendencies." He embraced the characteristic view that political theory was entwined with the development of political institutions, and although one might at times go back to the Greeks for inspiration, it should always be done in the context of seeking "an intelligence which in the midst of change can look before and after and so make itself the master of its fate." Although political theory might lapse into "special pleading," it was, at its best, continually reflective about both ideals and actual tendencies and "at once negatively critical and constructive." Both the citizen and the statesman needed "the cobwebs of obsolete theory cleared from his mind" so as to achieve a "clearer vision of political and social realities" and the "*whither*" as well as the "*whence*" of institutions. He claimed that "at the bottom political phenomena belong to the realm of mind," and political theory is the "product of the need to clarify the mental vision."[10]

Coker (Yale) worried about an emphasis on pluralism and interest groups and about theorists such as Sabine who, he believed, tended to concur with Gierke, Figgis, Laski, Krabbe, and Duguit in disparaging the idea of the state and the role of state authority in preserving liberal values.[11] But it was William Yandell Elliott, an assistant professor at the University of California, who began systematically to attack those whom he believed were undermining the idea of state sovereignty. He believed that the pluralist position was tied to scientism, realism, pragmatism, interdisciplinary enthusiasm, and other "varied currents of contemporary political theory which seems to have set against the conception of unitary sovereignty as the basis of the structure of the state."[12] These views, he claimed, were out of place "in so closely knit a unity as is formed in the modern state." For Elliott, pluralism was closely allied to syndicalism and such dangerous doctrines as those of Sorel. Laski was his principal target at the time, but Elliott saw him as following Barker's attack on the idea of the state and as a "disciple" of William James and an advocate of Dewey's experimentalism.[13]

In a review of the Dunning festschrift, Elliott suggested that the book was a "fitting memorial to a great political theorist and historian." But although the contributors had turned their attention to some of the issues connected with the contemporary revolt against the state (which Dunning had found "unintelligible"), he judged the general "tone too largely sociological." While acknowledging Merriam as "the dean of American theorists," he questioned his use of the term "political theory." While general issues of "the methodology of research" should not be excluded, political theory properly understood was "chiefly concerned with a political evaluation of the descriptive material" produced by the social sciences. He was also "astounded" at Merriam's suggestion that pragmatism had exercised little impact. This was contradicted by the very content of the volume with all the references to Laski and other pluralists and socialists who were "pragmatic in the extreme."[14]

This was the beginning of the first distinct jurisdictional dispute about the concept of political theory, but by the middle part of the decade, the main currents of the debate about political science and political theory had swung away from Merriam. He seldom criticized specific individuals, and there was little direct criticism of his work. His ideas had produced minimal impact on the normal practice of the discipline, but some strong reactions against the themes with which he was associated had appeared by the mid-1920s. William Ernest Hocking, for example, a Harvard philosopher, struck out against the trends in political theory that involved pluralism (and anarchy), pragmatism, and relativism. He argued that there was too much emphasis on psychological explanation, which only provides part of the truth about human nature, and that ethics and metaphysics, which take into account conscience and reason must be part of the theory of politics.[15] The changing image of the state, however, was apparent in a work such as that of R. M. MacIver who, while seeking something of a middle way in the controversy, succeeded in undermining many of the assumptions that were crucial to earlier state theory. This somewhat ambivalent formulation was still not at all congenial to Elliott, since it gave the state no ultimate authority over social groups.[16]

Ellis suggested that after attempting to extricate itself from "a supernatural or metaphysical theory" and from the field of law and a formal juristic analysis of the state, political science was now besieged by disciplines such as sociology, economics, and ethics. Political science was at a "crossroads" where it was necessary to ask whether it was any longer possible to "attempt to reestablish it as a distinctive discipline?" The pluralists may have attempted to reach the "realities" behind the idea of the state, but, she argued, they had also tended to eliminate any distinctive political reality or meaning of sovereignty. In her view, even Willoughby did not adequately articulate what she called "the political."[17] While Sabine continued to argue that juristic formalism was too simple an approach to deal with modern political developments, Willoughby, despite his criticisms of Burgess and German philosophy, still clung to the more traditional view of the state and argued that the pluralist position and the critique of sovereignty threatened the domain of political science and political theory. But he also attacked the critics on the same grounds that he had attacked Burgess, that is, for failing to distinguish between fact and value or political science and politics.[18]

Beard, on the other hand, while at this point still a strong supporter of science, clung to his vision of a muckraking "realism" that exposed the real economic interests that stood in the way of rational policy. Early on he had come to the conclusion that, while once people of affairs had directed the discourse of public life, "after the Civil War politics fell into the hands of professors, who proceeded to systematize it and sterilize it."[19] "Natural science made its great forward advance when it climbed down out of the realm of rhetoric into the humble kingdom of organic and inorganic things."[20] He agreed with Merriam that lawyers and historians were an "incubus" that kept political science behind the times, but in his 1927 presidential address to the APSA, he presented a stinging indictment of the discipline and profession and stressed the extent to which "creative thought" and "constructive imagination" were suppressed.

The universities, he claimed, were "essentially conservative" and run by administrators attached to business interests. There was too great a teaching burden and a lack of research money which together bound faculty to writing textbooks. In political science, the emphasis on measurement and too much detailed "induction" rather than "deduction" and imagination created excessive specialization and the "peril of narrowing the vision while accumulating information." Where, he asked, had such a "microscopic" approach brought Germany? In Beard's view, creative speculation and significant critical analysis ended with the detachment of political science from politics and a professionalization that curtailed free inquiry through a preoccupation with the attitudes of trustees and a concern with salaries, promotion, and pensions.[21] Elliott's critique of trends in political science sprang from a distinctly different philosophical and ideological position, but there was a certain affinity.

It is something of an irony that Elliott, the leading critic of scientism and pluralism during this period, was an American who did his undergraduate work at Vanderbilt and his doctorate at Oxford (1923) under

A. D. Lindsay, while G. E. G. Catlin, who emerged as the most articulate defender of these persuasions, was an Oxford undergraduate who took his doctorate at Cornell (1924). In the same volume of the *APSR* in which Beard's address was published, Catlin declared that "politics is concerned with a field of human behavior characterized by the recurrences of specific behavior patterns" and which can be defined psychologically and measured by various quantitative and statistical means.[22] Floyd Allport, one of the strongest supporters of psychological analysis, stressed the same theme and insisted that there was "no break between the natural and social sciences."[23] He claimed that political behavior was a type of social behavior and explicable in terms of stimulus-response psychology.

Despite all the talk about science, much of it was little more than rhetorical overture. William B. Munro, who succeeded Beard as president of the APSA, argued that Bagehot's analogy between physics and politics should be revised and taken even more seriously. He claimed that political science was still encased in the "abstract formalism" of classical political thought and, at best, reflected the "atomic theory" of "abstract individual man" that characterized the eighteenth century. Munro recommended looking at the "sub-atomic" possibilities and the "invisible and hitherto much neglected forces by which the individual citizen is fundamentally activated and controlled." He did not make very clear what all this entailed, but he claimed that "it is to the natural sciences that we may most profitably turn . . . for suggestions as to the reconstruction of our postulates and methods."[24]

Only Catlin, now on the faculty at Cornell, attempted to give philosophical substance to claims about scientific method and an extended analysis of the issues involved—an analysis that would not be rivaled in sophistication for a quarter of a century. He applauded the pluralist position and its attack on the "absolute state" and natural rights theory as well as its embrace of factual realism, but he complained that it was still an "ethical philosophy," which treated politics from a "liberal" perspective, rather than a "dispassionate study of actual human behavior." Catlin left no doubt that the purpose of social science was social control (e.g., the need for a "social Wasserman test" as part of a "profession of social medicine") just as the purpose of natural science was control over nature, and he clung to the inherent complementarity of science and democracy. He argued, however, that it was first necessary, as in the relationship between biology and medicine, to find some "basal principles of political method" and establish "a behaviorist science of politics" that would allow sound diagnosis of political problems and administrative and legislative treatment.[25]

History, he concluded, "is not and never can be a science," but "it provides the data of the social sciences" which must be subjected to measurement and quantification and analyzed according to the deductive method. The historian may have critical impact, but "social therapy is not his affair." The latter is the responsibility of political science, but at present, he argued, political science is only "a barren name." It was necessary to "go back to Aristotle" and imitate his approach by creating a comprehensive science with a distinct method based on empirical observation and generalization.[26]

Catlin specifically adopted Pearson's instrumentalist notion of theory as, epistemologically, an a priori mental construction independent of facts but nevertheless generated a posteriori from particular facts—"a logical structure superimposed upon the observation of a highly frequent occurrence." His model among the social sciences was economics, and he wished to construct an abstract fiction called "political man" (the power seeker) and the "political situation" (competing wills) that would lend itself to a hypothetical, predictive, deterministic and causal, experimental science that derived data from history, form from economics, and substance from psychology.[27] Except for the work of Laski, Catlin was largely dismissive of trends in political theory. He castigated Hegelianism, Comtean positivism and its philosophy of history, *Staatslehre* and its residue, and the inadequate scientific basis of Progressive tracts such as Walter Lippmann's *Preface to Politics* (1911): "Hitherto the unguarded field of political theory has been a veritable Valley of Hinnom wherein men have been permitted to cast without challenge the rubbish of uncritical speculation and the burning oil of enthusiasm, to fling the bodies of opponents and to sacrifice to strange idols."[28]

It was now time for political science to carve out its domain among the social sciences, develop a theoretical structure to define and explore it, and put science in the service of democracy. In a more methodological vein, Stuart Rice's influential book on *Quantitative Methods in Politics* was published in 1928. He studied under Giddings, and he viewed politics as part of group life in general and within the province of sociology, but, against some sociologists such as Small, he stressed the distinction between science and moral philosophy and argued for the unity of scientific method. As with Catlin, there was more systematic concern with the nature of scientific inquiry. He relied on Pearson but also on literature emerging in the philosophy of science such as P. W. Bridgman's *Logic of Modern Physics* (1927).

In Gettell's account of American political thought, the last chapter dealt with issues of liberalism and new influences springing from the use of scientific methods. He largely followed Merriam's story of the evolution of the discipline, but his general position reflected the now familiar line that American government neither possessed nor needed much in the way of "abstract philosophical speculation" or a "comprehensive philosophy of politics." Like the English and Romans, from whom many of our ideas and institutions had sprung, our political life was shaped by "practical considerations" rather than "a priori deductions of political doctrine," "impractical ideals," and even "logical consistency." Although he rejected the notion that political thought was basically a rationalization of interest and reiterated his notions about the reciprocal relationship between thought and action, he argued that, in America, "political theory has usually been able to adjust itself to changing conditions" and that "political speculation" has, from the beginning, been immanent in principles underlying political practice.[29]

Elliott was now an assistant professor at Harvard where, along with Carl Friedrich (the "eagles," as they were called), he would dominate the study of political theory for many years, direct over a hundred dissertations, and become "the primary mentor of Henry Kissinger."[30] At this point, he brought together his strictures against "the pragmatic revolt in politics." Elliott set out to rescue the concept of the state, but he was also seeking to rescue political science and liberalism.

For Elliott, pragmatism was not only a specific philosophy but a global world-historical mode of theory and practice which, while led by James and Dewey in contemporary academia, was also characteristic of Hobbes, Marxism, and fascism. Most specifically, he claimed that it was the philosophy of Mussolini who, as a "political pragmatist," had attributed his ideas to James as well as Machiavelli, Nietzsche, and Sorel. Pragmatism, for Elliott, was the intellectual basis of a modern "revolt against rationalism" and against the theory and practice of "the constituted and democratic state."[31] This was not just a revolt against the idea of the state but a move against the very idea of politics. Elliott argued that pragmatism had captured the main stream of political science which was "behavioristic in terms of psychology and positivist in terms of philosophy."[32] Its skeptical anti-intellectual attitudes could also be detected in natural science and the philosophical instrumentalism of Poincaré, Eddington, and Pearson, as well as in theories of relativity and probability. Dewey, in his view, was a positivist in the tradition of Comte, Durkheim, and Pareto. And Laski and Duguit were part of the same intellectual tradition.

Elliott argued that pragmatism was "skeptical of absolutes" and provided no norm of action or basis for the evaluation of action. What was needed was a restoration of the "normative side to political theory" and engagement of "ethical principles" appropriate to statesmanship and to man as a purposive creature. Pragmatism might be suitable for natural science, but when appropriated by social philosophy, he argued, it ultimately "results in an apology for the Fascist ideal of a 'disciplined' national organism" and in a fundamental break with liberalism. Elliott called for a return to the idea of the "organic character of group life"— or what he labeled as a "co-organic theory" which he contrasted with the recent theory of pluralism and which involved the idea of constitutional government under laws reflecting a shared moral purpose and ideal. It was necessary to recognize the "value of moral personality in the individual, and the necessity of a social structure that will protect it." This notion of a "co-organic community" might ultimately be a "mythos," he suggested, but it was one worthy of embrace.[33] He believed that Coolidge's handling of the Boston police strike was an example of the co-organic state in action.

Elliott claimed that although the ideal had been partially achieved in the United States, the problems of economic monopolies, urbanization, class conflict, overpopulation, and war threatened to escape the control of constitutional morality and the discipline of law. Pluralism and the problem of the autonomy and power of "voluntary associations" was the great problem facing modern political theory. Individualism and pluralism, carried to an extreme, opened up the door, in both theory and practice, to fascism by passing political power to subpolitical groups. In some ways, this same concern about the lack of a "great community" in the United States was not very different from that of those such as Dewey whom Elliott attacked, even though the underlying philosophical premises were different.[34] Like Lieber and Burgess, Elliott stressed the idea that while the government possessed limited sovereignty, "not the federal state created by the Constitution." The "government is the creature of the political community," and the "constitutional state . . . is the political community."[35]

It was not, however, simply the state as a unity behind diversity that Elliott wished to salvage. It was as much political theory and political science as their subject matter. In his view, there was "not a single contemporary political theorist in America who is to be counted among those of the first order." There were simply "too few political theorists and too many technicians, engineers, scientists or artists." He suggested that "most of our professors of politics would disdain the term *theorists:* they prefer to be called political 'scientists.'" For Elliott, a political theorist was someone who sought to understand facts but brought to bear principles and normative concerns. Thus the "political theorist" was both a "political scientist" and a "political philosopher" and paralleled, in the world of ideas, the fusion of ends and means that characterized the statesman.[36]

How, exactly, Elliott came to see pluralism, scientism, and pragmatism as identical was less than clear, and although he may have worried more about the professional identity of political science and political theory than those he criticized, his basic concerns were not that different—especially with respect to the anxiety about growing distance between academic and public discourse. Despite the intellectual distance between them, Catlin presented a long and surprisingly temperate, if somewhat wry, review of Elliott's polemic. He claimed that it was "indubitably the book of the year in political theory" and an important exposition of the "new liberalism"—which would actually be welcomed by those wishing a defense of the old liberalism with its emphasis on idealism and statism. Catlin suggested that Elliott stood to Laski like T. H. Green to Mill—a characterization that fitted Elliott's image of himself.[37] Merriam's student Harold Lasswell, while obviously in disagreement, also reviewed the book cautiously and suggested that because it broadened the perspectives of students of government, it should be "welcomed with enthusiasm."[38]

Catlin did, however, take serious issue with the notion that Mussolini could be best understood as a pragmatist, since he appeared closer to a Platonist. He argued that it was in fact the kind of philosophy espoused by Elliott that threatened individual rights through its view that the "state is the good, the beautiful, and the true." Nationalism, Catlin claimed, was "one of the most dangerous social poisons of our age" and a danger to the rule of law and constitutional morality and that in this respect Elliott was "on the side of Mussolini." For Catlin, internationalism and respect for local rights offered a better hope. Although he agreed with Elliott that the "facts" do not yield norms, he maintained that knowledge of facts explains norms and illuminates what is possible for human purpose. Maybe, he suggested, their differences rested "upon an irresolvable diversity of aesthetic judgment on values."[39]

By the end of the decade, various general treatments of science and scientific method had begun to appear, and these were reflected in attempts to develop some systematic sense of what social scientific research was all about. The concern was to give substance to the belief that the social sciences were progressing from "philosophical and analogical study toward scientific research and real social theory" and that they were "on the eve of a new development of assured scientific proportions yet to be determined and perfected." The basic problem, which made the situation "unsatisfactory," was the proliferation and plurality of approaches and techniques and the lack of an "agreement concerning definition, scope, and method" which could provide a text in "the fundamentals of social research" and grounds of "appraisal."[40]

Beard, however, remained disaffected with both the university and political science. He continued his critique of scientific enthusiasm by distinguishing "scientism" from "realism" and focusing on the problem of the relationship between the university and politics. The dream of making politics into a science was, he claimed, largely the product of "rationalizing great passions into word patterns." While science required "disinterested reason" and a stable subject matter, investigators inevitably had prejudiced minds and political reality was in constant flux. He believed that "we should be slow to assume that the . . . method of natural science is equally appropriate to human affairs" and must conclude that "no science of politics is possible; or if possible, desirable." Herbert Hoover's engineers were, he claimed, a case in point.[41]

Political theory, political philosophy, and political science could not, he argued, be validly distinguished, and what we should aim for was simply the application of increased intelligence to the "social organism," a broad reflective imaginative intelligence nourished by the "Socratic method," which is most attuned to the discursive character of political reality and grounded in experience but yet remote from immediate interests. He saw little alternative to the university as the training ground for such political thinkers, but although in principle it provided "the most favorable climate for creative work in America," it was in a sorry state. At least it needed "more humor."

There are in the university too many charming friends who must not be offended; too many temporal negotiations that call for discreet management; too many lectures to be delivered; too many promotions requiring emphasis on the amenities of life rather than on the thinking process; too many alumni eager to apply in 1928 what they learned in 1888; too much routine, not enough peace; too much calm, not enough passion; above all too many sacred traditions that must be conserved.[42]

He did suggest that the rise of the new "realism" had brought "gains for truth and justice," that there had been advances in administrative science, and that events had undermined the "Manchester economics" and allowed for more "constructive" economic thought. "But on the whole our political thinking has not kept up with our factual evolution." Creativity was dulled by burdensome teaching loads and other demands, and the "passionate faith in 'doing something'" led only to "heaving up piles of printed matter" of little ultimate significance. And the discipline's attempt to emulate natural science had "not added a single concept of any importance to the science of human government."[43] Although he continued to stress the difference between natural and social science and the role of the latter as "ethical sciences," his general account of the social sciences, and even empiricism, a few years later was considerably more optimistic—suggesting that without them "modern civilization would sink into barbarism." Yet in the case of political science, he still found scientism and the cult of objectivity a profession of faith characteristic of those who, unlike the classic authors from Aristotle to Madison, were "academic by profession and more or less remote from politics as practiced."[44]

Edward S. Corwin was explicitly cynical and wary regarding the trend toward scientism both with respect to its faith in method and its substantive research product. He noted that certain political scientists, from a desire to gain credibility for their field, "have registered a vow to convert political science from a 'normative' or 'telic' science . . . into a science which will hereafter be printed in lower case instead of in upper case, and will, moreover . . . be able to predict the future just as astronomy, physics and chemistry are able to do." He saw this as basically a response to the belief in the possibilities of behavioristic psychology, but, like Elliott, he was concerned with the way in which research along these lines was undermining the "democratic dogma" by suggesting that citizens were indifferent and irrational.[45]

Although Sabine did not believe that pragmatism (which he associated with Dewey, Veblen, and others and such ideas as empiricism, evolutionism, and instrumentalism) was ultimately a sound "philosophical" position, he wished to distinguish it from "recent forms of mechanistic behaviorism." Although its hope for social "control" was probably "utopian," it was also "honorable." He suggested that it "may force us to get down to actualities" and that it offered the "best available method at the present time for inducing a strict realism in political theory." With its emphasis on purpose and problems, questioning of tradition, rejection of abstractions and juristic formalism, stress on imagination as the center of thought, belief in an ad hoc test of truth, commitment to interdisciplinary studies, and its emphasis on keeping political theory in touch with "real situations," it promised the best path forward in the next "dozen years."[46] Willoughby continued to defend the idea of political theory as a speculative pursuit of ideals (but not utopias) with practical significance.[47]

While Catlin wished to distance himself from the literature concerned with the theory and history of the state, he pointedly attempted to project the image that the contemporary search for a science of politics was the perpetuation of a tradition that began with Plato and had always been concerned with more than seeking "ideals."[48] Catlin attempted to identify "political theory" in "professional political science" as something distinct from "political thought," "ethics," the "opinions of literary men," and "the approach to politics from the angle of political philosophy and of the humanities." He argued that the proper approach involved psychology, sociology, and statistics and that it required, following the lead of Bentham, Mill, and Dewey, searching for "substantial uniformity" in the behavior of the "human atom." This in turn required the development of hypotheses and laws that would simplify and generalize human behavior in "political systems" or that aspect of the life of the community that involves the activity and control of wills.[49] He left no doubt that, as in the case of Aristotle, "the end in view is practice and not mere knowledge" and that the "positive science of politics" was "one of the most hopeful elements for the more intelligent and . . . purposive ordering of society."[50] But the ability to "form a grounded judgment on the practical strength or weakness of institutions and conventions" (such as Mill's analysis of women's rights) must be predicated on the creation of a systematic body of knowledge, like mathematical axioms, from which could be deduced predictive laws.[51]

Beginning in 1923, the Social Science Research Council (SSRC) had conceived a project that involved "an inductive approach to the study of methods in the social sciences" which largely paralleled the efforts of the meetings in which Merriam had actively participated. By 1926, the notion had evolved of creating a "casebook" that would constitute a "synthesized integration of the methods so far developed." Stuart Rice began the planning in 1927, and Lasswell became a coinvestigator. The attempt at a general centralized survey, broken down into various categories such as "logic" and "technique," ultimately foundered, but the committees of the various disciplines (which included Merriam and Lasswell in the case of political science) were asked to compile the contributions that they "regarded as of outstanding significance."[52]

The product was less than unequivocal. Rice noted that the very notion of method was "cloaked in ambiguity," and that while some saw it as the essence of science, others believed emphasis on the concept was a sign of "decadence." He concluded that at best "method must be regarded as a term of variable meanings" and that they would proceed to use the term in whatever way seemed useful—which in the end they concluded referred to the "concepts and assumptions underlying scientific activity" that established the units and boundaries of inquiry in a field.[53] The argument was that these basic concepts were of particular importance in social science, since the "facts of human history," which constituted the "raw material" of social science, were, compared with those of natural science, so amorphous. Since "experience notoriously changes in accordance with the ideational system to which it is related," causal analysis requires conceptual stability. If the facts "are to have any coherent meaning, they must be selected in accordance with some guiding point of view, some preconception" that determines methods in the more narrow sense of techniques and that constitutes "*instruments* as well as *frameworks* of investigation."[54] Although what was called for was largely what the next generation of political scientists, following the lead of Merriam and Lasswell, would understand as theory, the contributors had limited confidence in either their scheme or the validity of the final project.

The tentative character of the undertaking was symbolized by the inclusion of invited comments by Elliott who addressed the issue of the very possibility of a science of politics. It was not clear exactly whom Elliott was speaking for when he declared that "political *theorists* as a group" deny the possibility of a "political *science*," but he at least wished to distinguish himself from "political scientists proper" and their "positivistic confreres" who believed that the discipline could emulate the experimental sciences. He suggested that Munro's notion of following the lead of physics and Catlin's attempt to abstract a general concept of political man captured the spirit of the day but actually indicated the limits in social science of "universalized abstraction" and deterministic prediction.[55] The complexity and autonomy of human activity, he argued, rendered some of the goals of the casebook dubious. Elliott, however, had no difficulty with the idea of political science as "an objective description of observable and describable external characteristics of human behavior" or with the assumption that it was possible to discover such things as "an observable and measurable regularity of recurrence in the behavior of certain interest groups" which social scientists might "dispassionately observe and compare." He did not believe that it was impossible or undesirable to develop classificatory schemes and even formulate "rough laws." But this factual investigation, he claimed, must be supplemented by "political philosophy" or the formulation and critique of ethical principles and values which together might be called "political theory."[56]

The differences between the proponents of the casebook and Elliott were, in the end, as Catlin himself noted, relatively narrow. He was more inclined, for example, to think of "rough laws" as incomplete formulations rather than reflecting inherent limits on the explanation of political behavior, but he was quite willing to concede that "a study of values is indubitably quite as valuable as a study of social forces and controls."[57] It would be a mistake to extrapolate too directly from the tensions between individuals such as Elliott and Catlin during this period to later controversies about political theory and the science of politics. Although these tensions contributed to the framework of later discussion, the content would be fundamentally transformed by the infusion of European ideas—both those defining the logic of science and those attacking scientism. The future of the conversation was adumbrated in Karl Mannheim's lengthy review of Rice.

Mannheim, at this point at the University of Frankfurt, charged that the volume yielded "too much to the fascination of natural science" and that it indicated a "mistrust of 'philosophy' or 'metaphysics.'" He argued that the work suffered from American social science's "excessive fear of theories, from a methodological asceticism which prevents it from putting forth general theories," as well as from a "curious lack of ambition to excel in the quality of theoretical insight." But on the whole he approached the discussion from the standpoint of issues in German sociology. When he claimed that this work represented the manner in which "American studies start from questions nowise connected with those problems which arouse our passion in everyday political and social struggle," he simply failed to grasp the context in which the pursuit of science was generated in the United States.[58]

By the early 1930s, the issue of the nature of political theory began to recede from discussions regarding the direction of the discipline. During the next few years, the concept would tend more to stagnate than evolve. Even as a literature classification, the criteria of inclusion, apart from something having to do with ideational matters both cognitive and ideological, was ambiguous. The equation of theory and "mentalisms," already sedimented in the study of the history of political theory, gained support with the emphasis of Merriam and others on psychology during the 1920s, but long before and after, dissertations in political theory were listed in the *APSR* under "Political Theory and Psychology." There were facts, events, circumstances, institutions, and behavior, and then there were concepts, ideas, ideologies, and various other mental predicates that were both the reflection and cause of the objective half of the world.

It was not until 1930 that political theory was designated as a section in the annual meetings of the APSA, but there was no distinct identity to the subfield or even a pointed concern with such an identity. It was largely defined, substantively, by issues involving trends in legal and political thought and various matters relating to the concept of democracy in the American state. In a report of the APSA Committee on Policy, there was no mention of political theory as a division of either research or curriculum.[59] And within a short time, political theory even disappeared from the annual program as increasing pressures of domestic and international affairs continued to draw attention away from issues about scope and method in political science.

What political scientists were concerned about was the nature of democracy, the rise of antidemocratic movements in Europe, international relations and diplomacy, representation and parties, Southern politics, constitutional guarantees, the "government of backward peoples," the New Deal, social planning, and the economic order in general.[60] Yet issues of substance and method were not totally disjoined. One of the most remarkable documents in the history of American social science was the "Ogburn Report."[61] In 1929, Herbert Hoover had appointed a committee of social scientists to conduct an extensive survey of social trends in the United States for the purpose of dealing constructively with pressing issues of public policy. William F. Ogburn, the fervent exponent of quantitative methods from the department of sociology at Chicago, was the director of research, and the committee worked closely with the SSRC. Merriam was vice-chairman as well as author of the section on "Government and Society" in this massive and comprehensive volume.

Although the emphasis was on matters related to "instability" and "social stresses," the concern was with broad issues of social change. Such immediate and specific problems as the Depression and international relations were purposely excluded from extended treatment, but they were very much in the background. The goal was to present a "scientific" analysis free from "bias" and "ideology," but the spirit that informed the project was that which Merriam had supported so strongly: social scientific intelligence linked to constructive governmental action. Modernity, it was acknowledged, had brought social disruption on many fronts, but it had also produced both science and the governmental forms and ideas that promised a solution. Although "democracy as a way of life" was becoming pervasive, the "corruption and inefficiency" of government and the need for a better system of social control was just as evident.[62] As in his earlier work, Merriam argued that "the trend of American government cannot be understood . . . without reference to the movement of American political theories and attitudes"—which involved both "ideologies" and the more "systematic" work of political scientists, publicists, and philosophers. He suggested that Dewey was "the foremost philosopher of democracy," and that even "Mr. Dooley and Will Rodgers are not without deep meaning."[63] Yet in the end, despite challenges to their most basic ideas and institutions such as capitalism and democracy, Americans had "remained relatively docile as far as revolutionary movements on the one side and political philosophy on the other." They continued to be "non-theoretical," "intolerant," and "non-experimental." This, however, Merriam claimed, was an attitude that they could no longer afford.[64]

There would continue to be (sometimes eccentric) speculations about how to develop a scientific study of politics,[65] but with respect to the trends initiated by Merriam, it was principally Lasswell who undertook their perpetuation. In many respects, the "chief," as Merriam was called, was more an impresario than a substantive academic performer. While chair of the department in the late 1920s, he continued to teach the history of political theory in a manner that "looked like notes from Dunning." He was, as his own students acknowledged, "not a great theoretician," but he stimulated others with his eclectic vision and dominated the department.[66] His energies were increasingly directed toward his work with various foundations, including the SSRC, and government agencies such as Roosevelt's National Planning Board. Although many students from the Chicago school (such as Gabriel Almond, V. O. Key, Quincy Wright, Harold Gosnell, and David Truman) would have much to do with shaping the direction of political science during the next generation, Lasswell was the most productive and influential protégé among this innovative group who were all devoted to Merriam's project of seeking a general framework for encompassing political phenomena.

During this period, Lasswell had little to say specifically about political theory, but the commitment to the idea of the reformation of society by understanding human psychology and behavior was not only sustained but radicalized in his notion of a therapeutic policy science. It is important to note the intellectual continuity, from Dunning to Lasswell, represented in the emphasis on a contextualist approach to social science. Even more than Merriam, Lasswell was concerned with effecting social change, but both understanding and manipulation involved ideas in context.[67] Part of Merriam's military service in World War I had been as a propagandist for the Committee on Public Information (the forerunner of the USIA), and the study of the uses and misuses of propaganda and the manipulation of public opinion would be a persistent part of the Chicago agenda. It was, however, for at least the next decade, the special province of Lasswell.

When Lasswell finished his undergraduate studies (1922) at Chicago, where he had worked closely with members of the empiricist/reformist sociology department, he began graduate work under Merriam. During the 1920s, he traveled abroad both while preparing his dissertation and later on an SSRC grant in Berlin where he studied psychoanalysis and Marx and was exposed to the work of a wide range of European social theorists such as Weber, Mannheim, Michels, and Pareto. Before finishing his graduate work, he coauthored a study of the attitudes of the working class which stressed the need for knowledge about the "influence of environmental factors upon human opinions, motives, and action," before diagnosing and treating "disease" in the "social body" for the purpose of substituting "wise co-operation for wasteful conflict."[68]

That Lasswell had been influenced by Dewey, and by the general direction of the social sciences at Chicago, was apparent from an early age. However, his image of a rational society and the place of intellectuals in creating it was reinforced during his travels in Europe.[69] While visiting England, he wrote to his mentor about the differences in the position of academics in the two countries and about the "absence of the authority of intellectuals in America." In England "academicians have a sense of power. They actually feel that they have a hand on the wheel of the state," while "our serious students of social problems moon in their cubby holes over plans of world reformation which include long eras of time or plans of world comprehension which require an infinity in which all lines meet in fruitful union with reality." They find themselves "relatively impotent, and driven to vagaries in consequence."[70] The dilemma of the politically motivated academician in America would continue to haunt Merriam and Lasswell. Lasswell represented the fourth, but still not the last, generation of American political scientists to be enthralled with what they took to be the union of theory and practice in Europe and to mourn its absence in the United States. Although the war had occasioned an overt turn against German philosophy and toward the Americanization of political science, continuity with the nineteenth-century vision of the integration of public and academic discourse was by no means broken.

Lasswell's 1926 dissertation, on *Propaganda Technique in the World War*,[71] emphasized the dangers, and possibilities, of elite manipulation of masses and was closely related to Merriam's subsequent extensive series on the comparative study of civic training and political socialization. In a review of Lippmann's *Phantom Public* (1925), Lasswell seemed to accept the limitations of the people as a source of substantive decisions, but, doubting that the public would bow out except for providing procedural checks on government as Lippmann had urged, he stressed the need for the leadership of the "intelligentsia and academics."[72] Lasswell put less emphasis on civic education than on the development of scientific hypotheses that would expose the psychological reality behind politics and political ideology and make society manageable. His early work might even be construed as devoted more to the elimination of politics than its management, but the idea of politics as pathological was hardly without precedent. In Lasswell's work, however, the idea of democracy found expression principally in terms of elite scientific social planning and mass manipulation.

Given his therapeutic concerns, it may not be surprising that Lasswell made the leap to Freud from more familiar forms of psychology such as that represented by Watsonian behaviorism, the work of Wallas on *Human Nature in Politics*, W. I. Thomas's studies of social personality, and the interactionism of George Herbert Mead. But it is also not surprising that it was the neo-Freudian emphasis on social rather than biological determinism that ultimately held his attention.[73] *Psychopathology and Politics* was indeed a radical, but in retrospect, consistent move in the conversation of political science.[74] Much of politics was presented as symbolic manifestations of illness rooted in the individual psyche. Solutions to political conflict and the attainment of social harmony, Lasswell argued, were not likely to be achieved through normal democratic processes but through a social scientific program of "preventive politics" based on psychological analysis.

Like Merriam before him, Lasswell argued that scientific political analysis required not just the collection of data and the application of scientific techniques and tools but "the invention of abstract conceptions" that would order data in a meaningful way.[75] This notion of theory as a conceptual instrument to be judged by its cognitive utility would be developed by Lasswell in his later work. How, exactly, he related this to his reliance on Freud, and Marx, is not clear, but more and more he came to view such formulations as part of a family of constructs for guiding an exploration of reality and predicting, and controlling, trends.[76]

Lasswell's ideas took some bizarre turns—such as suggesting that judges give up "logical thinking" for "free-phantasy," but the principal direction of his thought was toward the view that political order in the modern, and at least Western, world required the leadership of a technically oriented middle class and an elite in control of symbols and devoted, where possible, to peaceful means rather than coercion.[77] This project became part of Merriam's attempt to develop a comprehensive study of power in the face of the emerging crisis of world politics. In 1932, Lasswell, on his way to Moscow, visited Merriam in Berlin. Merriam was beginning an extended essay on power where he had commenced his dissertation on sovereignty—but now "in the midst of a furious struggle for the possession of the substance of political power (the Reichstag election of 1932)."[78] "In the mornings he wrote," finishing his essay in six weeks, while in the afternoons he and others became "observers and students of Hitler, Bruening, Reds and Whites from Russia, of all manner of folk who came streaming through the town and stopped for a glass of lemonade."[79]

For Merriam, realistically understanding power and its role "in the process of social control" and mastering the phenomena under modern conditions might "mean light or darkness for individuals and civilization." The need was to "fuse intelligence with faith" and move from "blind adaption to creative evolution." This meant largely the "New Deal" and the rejection of anarchism, laissez-faire, Marxism, and all other doctrines that did not allow for a proper role of government in achieving social progress. But it also meant in all respects, as for Lieber and Burgess, a belief in the efficacy of reason in governing human affairs.[80] For Merriam and Lasswell, there was a basic commitment to the notion that such realism in social science implied ethical principles.

Merriam challenged his colleague, the philosopher and sometime politician T. V. Smith, to explicate "a realistic ethics" that would be comparable to what Machiavelli did for politics. Smith, like Lasswell, believed that it was possible to use organized "intelligence for social direction" and that capitalism could take a lesson from the "Communistic experiment." Democracy, he suggested, was simply "politics no longer innocent of philosophy."[81] Smith took up his task through a critique of an ethic of conscience. Such an ethic was, he argued, a danger to civilization. Such doctrines, theological and otherwise, were merely rationalizations for interest. At best, claims of conscience provided self-identity, but individualism did not automatically lead to "a dependable social order" or one based on something other than coercion. Smith argued that reference to conscience inevitably ended in the pursuit of dominance rather than the renunciation of power as the goal of life. Liberalism meant above all a rejection of absolutes.[82]

Lasswell's *World Politics and Personal Insecurity* was the most important work in what, in effect, was the trilogy that emerged from the Chicago school's study of power.[83] Here he defined political analysis as "the study of changes in the shape and composition of the value pattern of society," which meant in effect "the study of *who gets what, when, and how.*"[84] Elites inevitably dominate the masses through the manipulation of symbols, and this meant possibilities for good as well as evil. "It is indubitable that the world could be unified if enough people were impressed by this (or any other) elite. The hope of professors of social science, if not the world, lies in the competitive strength of an elite based on vocabulary, footnotes, questionnaires, and conditioned responses, against an elite based on vocabulary, poison gas, property, and family prestige."[85]

Lasswell believed that academicians who seek the truth were "bound to have some control," and he pursued his idea of a "politics of prevention" which was the "special province of political psychiatrists" who would control the masses, maybe through some "myth," and succeed in "mastering the sources and mitigating the consequences of human insecurity in an unstable world."[86] He likened the extensive study of power in which he and Merriam were engaged to the "political-totalistic" studies of Marx and Engels. The concern in this period was more with global than domestic politics, and Lasswell believed that by an "intensive personality study" and "by concentrating on the unconscious aspects of human action, the possibility of controlling mass security by manipulating significant symbols" was at hand. War and revolution, he argued, were the product of the discharge of collective insecurities, and leaders manipulated this force.[87]

Lasswell also continued his search for political realism on the domestic scene. The truth of politics was that there was always an elite which tended to get the most of what there was to get, and the remainder of society constituted the masses. He suggested that this interpretation of politics "underlies the working attitude of practicing politicians" and that therefore the study of politics was essentially a study of "influence and the influential." Although he began to press the distinction between "political science" and "political philosophy," on the basis that the former "states conditions" and the latter "justifies preferences," and although he saw his work as declaring no preferences and "restricted to political analysis," this was, in large measure, because the preferences, and the ends of science, were, as much as for Merriam, largely given.[88] Lasswell noted that his findings in *Politics: Who Gets What, When, How* largely coincided with the views expressed in the last chapter of the book published in the same year by his friend and colleague T. V. Smith. That chapter was titled "Americanism" which Smith defined as "liberalism" in both the broad and narrow sense of the term.[89] No one went further than Smith in explicitly equating democracy with individualism and equality, and in equating, and arguing for, the symbiotic relationship between democracy with the spirit and method of scientific inquiry and its application to the study of human behavior.[90]

Lasswell's work leaves little doubt that his pursuit of science was instrumental. It was in the service of a distinct set of values. It is ironic that his separation of political science and political philosophy prepared the way for a generation who increasingly repressed the search for the *connection* that informed his *distinction*. For Lasswell, as for most of those who had preceded him, the hope of authority and efficacy for political science rested on its ability to establish itself as a genuine science.

6

The Crisis of Liberalism

. . . any political philosophy of the present time, no more than those of the past, can step out of the relationships in which it stands to the problems, the valuations, the habits, or even the prejudices of its own time.

George Sabine

During the 1930s, the history of political theory continued to crystallize and evolve as a distinct literary form. The idea of the "great tradition," stretching from Plato to the present, fully emerged as the past of both modern politics and political science. Although there were no pointed criticisms of the study of the history of political theory, there was, by the early 1930s, some sensitivity to a, not very widely articulated, concern that too much emphasis on the "development of ideas" had isolated it from the "realities of human life." With the recent focus on science, it did not "hold the preeminent position that it formerly held," and some considered "political philosophy" to be "vague, ethereal, and unrelated to the workaday world."[1] A typical response was to stress the characteristic notion that political theory was rooted in the institutions and activities of politics and contributed to shaping "future practice." Studies of the history of political theory demonstrated "the relativity of ideas to environment and circumstance" and thus made us "analytical and critical of those political ideas that are today considered as absolute and immutable divine revelations."[2]

C. H. McIlwain's influential text on the *Growth of Political Thought in the West* did much to solidify the notion that what was being studied was an actual historical tradition that had intrinsic meaning. McIlwain dominated the study of political theory, and to a large extent the whole department, at Harvard during the 1920s, before Elliott and Friedrich gained prominence. Like his predecessors, he noted the close connection between ideas and institutions and even omitted Machiavelli from his lectures because he stood outside the main historical current of his time.[3] McIlwain stressed the extent to which what was being studied was an organic whole—a "stream" whose "first faint trickle" could be discerned in ancient Greece and which constituted thereafter an "evolutionary process" that revealed the *"growth"* and *"development* of our ideas about the state and about government" and the appearance of values and practices such as "legislative sovereignty." He had little sense, however, that the historian had much to offer in the way of practical judgment.[4]

When Coker undertook a survey of "recent political thought," it was a very different picture than that produced by Merriam and Barnes a decade earlier. He noted, but omitted discussion of, developments in psychology and "political behaviorism" as well as quantitative methods in favor of analyses of Marxism, socialism, and anarchism. Political theory was defined functionally as "dominant political ideas" about the state both in "theoretical writings and active social movements." Although, as a distinct form, it had begun with the Greeks, "some sort of political theory has existed even among the most primitive peoples." The purpose of his study was to seek the roots of "our political reasoning."[5]

By the early 1930s, the assumption of relativism was closely tied both to the study of the history of political theory and to the concept of liberalism. An early version of the emotivist theory of ethics had been articulated in Edward Westermarck's popular book. He argued "that the moral consciousness is ultimately based on emotions, that the moral judgment lacks objective validity, that moral values are not absolute but relative to the emotions they express."[6] The continued emphasis on the relativity of political ideas was, however, consistently complemented, and compensated for, by the assumption that, overall, history exemplified development and progress. By mid-decade, writing and teaching the history of political theory was to a great extent a matter of understanding and legitimating American liberalism and distinguishing it from alien ideologies and regimes. Doctrinal and political developments in Europe required a self-conscious position. Americans had become too unreflective about their institutions and values which were now being challenged by communism and fascism.[7] But the literature was also a vehicle for pursuing remnants of the debate about scientism, statism, and pluralism.

T. I. Cook, dissatisfied with the available textbooks and the influence of pragmatism and individuals such as Laski, emphasized the need to deal with the normative dimension of social studies and with "problems of ends and values." He insisted that "political theory is indeed part of politics; and political activity cannot be understood, and in sophisticated societies, at least, could not be carried on, without it." And "to study the history of political ideas is to study our own ideas and see how we came to hold them."[8] On the other hand, Edward Lewis's history of

American political thought presented a critique of state theory from Burgess to Ford and defended the pluralist position.[9] The paradigmatic work of the period, however, was Sabine's *A History of Political Theory.*

First published in 1937, this was the most important treatise since that of Dunning, and its subsequent significance was unparalleled. As David Easton noted in 1953, "it exercised deeper influence over the study of political theory in the United States . . . than any other single work."[10] In its successive editions and printings, it became the basis of most undergraduate, and graduate, programs in political theory for an entire generation as well as the model for scholarship and other textbooks. The title, significantly, referred to "theory" and not "theories," "philosophies," "thought," "thinking," or some more generic notion. Political theory was becoming a more reified concept, and Sabine, now teaching government (since 1931) at Cornell, attributed a certain identity and autonomy to political theory that went beyond many earlier works. He did not make any sharp break with the earlier literature, but a large part of his contribution was to synthesize secondary material and to give an authoritative structure to the history of political theory.

Sabine claimed that "modern political ideals" had begun with the Greeks and that there had been an organic continuity in the evolution of political thought—culminating in contemporary liberal democracy. His concern was with ideas and texts and not the theory and practice of the state, but, like previous writers, he stressed "that theories of politics are themselves part of politics. In other words, they do not refer to an external reality but are produced as a normal part of the social *milieu* in which politics itself has its being." They are reflections on ends and means, and as such are an aspect of political activity which "evolves along with" institutions. These ideas might to some degree control circumstances, but the important point was that they reflected those circumstances. Sabine presented the history of political theory as a dimension of the evolution of political history. "Thus conceived the theory of politics no more reaches an end than politics itself, and its history has no final chapter."[11]

Sabine hardly glorified political theory. He emphasized that "taken as a whole a political theory can hardly be said to be true." It could be analyzed into "judgments of fact" and "estimates of probability" which potentially could be "objectively right or wrong," and certain assessments of its internal logic were possible. But "invariably, however, it includes valuations and predilections, personal and collective, which distort" fact and logic, and "the most that criticism can do is to keep these three factors as much as possible distinct." Although the historian "ought to avoid the egoism that makes every generation fancy it is the heir of all the ages," there can be "no profession of impartiality beyond fidelity to sources . . . or beyond that avowal of conscious preferences which should be expected of every honest man." Sabine noted that his "philosophical preferences" were based on "Hume's criticism of natural law" and on the assumption that "it is impossible by any logical operation to excogitate the truth of any allegation of fact, and neither logic nor fact implies a value." It was, he argued, the failure to observe these distinctions that called into question transcendental doctrines such as natural law, Hegelianism, and Marxism. Values, Sabine argued, were "always the reaction of human preference to some state of social and physical fact," and he suggested that "the idea of economic causation was probably the most fertile suggestion added to the social studies in the nineteenth century."[12]

His point of view in writing the history of political theory was one of "social relativism." Political theory was always "a part of philosophy and science," an application of the "relevant intellectual and critical apparatus which is at the moment available," as well as a "reflection" on the problems of the "historical and institutional situation." It was thus necessary for the historian to make judgments about the significance and representativeness of the material encountered and to balance "political theory in action" and "political theory in books." Although Sabine did not stress any holistic intrinsic meaning or import for the present, he did believe that there was a principle of the survival of the fittest at work in politics and the history of political thought and that the theory and practice of liberal democracy represented the highest stage of human development—and one that was logically and epistemologically grounded. The totalitarian movements of the twentieth century were presented as aberrations. Communism and national socialism bore the "authentic mark of fanaticism." He claimed that "for anyone bred in the rational tradition of Western philosophy and modern science it is impossible to take seriously this claim to a higher form of knowledge," since it "violates the procedures" in terms of which "scientific knowledge is possible."[13]

This was, as a reviewer noted, "a text-book with a difference" and the "strongest statement yet" of the thesis that theories were relative to political circumstances. It was the work of "an empirical positivist" who rejected natural law.[14] By the end of the 1930s, the dominant image that informed the study of the history of political theory was that of the unity of liberal democracy, relativism, science, and historical progress. In his presidential address to the APSA, Arthur Holcombe, one of the principal members of the Harvard department, indicated the close alliance between political science, liberalism, and the history of political theory. He argued that "when the play of human will is examined on the grand scale of universal history, a regular march will be discovered in its movements"—but not of the kind claimed by Hegel and Marx. The direction was toward the rise of the middle class and "democratic-republican" ideals. And "the proper basis for such a political philosophy is a political interpretation of history."[15]

Writing the history of political theory had never been viewed as an antiquarian endeavor, and increasingly the "practical objective" became one of explaining the "crisis" of twentieth-century politics and justifying liberal democracy. "Truths," it was suggested, are "clothed in fading garments," and "in order to remain true, they require to be restated." The search was for "unity" and something not unlike "a philosophy of history" that would "portray the interweaving and continuous operation of the main decisive European political ideas" that "govern our present conduct."[16] Through the next decade, the history of political theory was understood as reflection at the "crossroads"—a way of making an informed choice between democracy and fascism as ways of dealing with modern problems—and sorting out the train of thought from Hobbes to Hitler.[17] Even Catlin took up the history of political philosophy in an attempt to confront the dogmas of communism and fascism.

His "story of the political philosophers," like that of those before him, revealed "a rational Grand Tradition of Culture and also (quite distinct) the beginnings of a Science of Politics." He argued that it was possible to "mount upon the bastion of three thousand years a searchlight that may project a ray for a few decades toward the horizon of the human future." Catlin, like Sabine, affirmed the contextual and relative character of political theory, but he stressed even more the extent to which meaning could be found in this "story," the degree to which modern problems were rooted in this tradition, and the way in which writing this history constituted a "philosophy of political history" that addressed current issues.[18] For Elliott, as well, the issue was that of understanding the "contemporary struggle between totalitarianism and constitutionalism" and the need to make clear the evolution and righteousness of "constitutional democracy" which has "flourished only in the soul of Western culture."[19] The vision of history that gave rise to this genre had its roots in German philosophy, but it had undergone a half-century of Americanization. By this point, however, the paradigm, around which individuals as diverse as Elliott and Catlin could unite, was not without incipient challenges from a new wave of European thought, but its identity was now fully formed.

First of all, political theory as a whole, as well as the study of the history of political theory, was seldom understood as out of phase with the basic goals and values of mainstream political science, and the history of political theory remained to some extent a history of the science of politics. Second, the history of political theory was essentially, either implicitly or explicitly, a justification of liberal democracy and an account of its progress in the world. Third, it was assumed that the path of democracy, and Western civilization in general, was congruent with, and symbiotically related to, the progress of science in general. Historical progress, science, and democracy were part of a general syndrome. Fourth, American political scientists and political theorists tended to equate the spirit of liberalism with moral relativism. This was despite, but maybe because of, their attachment to the underlying "givens" necessary to sustain pragmatism. The faith in liberal democracy and its historical progress, the belief in scientific knowledge, and other such anchors of certainty allowed them to be consciously and explicitly committed to the idea of relativism as the logic of both democracy and science. They were opposed to absolutism and transcendentalism in both epistemology and politics. Finally, there remained in American political science a persistent suspicion of, if not aversion to, politics and the suggestion that it represented something fundamental in the human condition. It was not simply that politics was often corrupt and in other ways inadequate but that it was inherently pathological and hardly the realm of basic human fulfillment—even if government was conceived as an instrument of such fulfillment.

The debate about political theory that would emerge in the 1940s was not, however, simply the result of a sudden confrontation between such indigenous values and the perspective of the émigrés. Although it would be a great mistake simply to extrapolate the character of the forthcoming controversy from earlier arguments between individuals such as Elliott and Catlin, the basic assumptions of the field were not without challenges, and these challenges provided, in part, a context for the new conversation about political theory. During the late 1930s and early 1940s, there was a fundamental disagreement about the foundations and character of liberal democracy and attending issues of pragmatism, science, progress, and relativism which reflected both domestic and international political concerns.[20]

It is ironic that it was at the University of Chicago that the critique of liberalism and social science was most distinctly articulated. President Robert Maynard Hutchins and allies such as Mortimer Adler were making the ambience less than congenial for the ideas that had traditionally informed social science and philosophy at that institution. Lasswell, for example, left for Yale Law School in 1938 when not promoted to full professor. When T. V. Smith and Leonard D. White edited *Chicago: An Experiment in Social Research* (1929), it was more than the purported summary of five years of interdisciplinary research on regional urban life. It was a celebration of the Chicagoan, and maybe American, idea of a social science—both in terms of method and social purpose. The term "Chicago school" derived from W. I. Thomas's ecological movement, that is, contextual explanation, which dominated so many aspects of research in the social sciences. White's loving description of the physical and intellectual structure of the new Social Science Building (erected in 1929) was a testimony to the faith in science as an answer to human problems. But if Chicago produced the archetype of the social science idea, it was soon to generate its opposite.

Nineteen twenty-nine was also the year that Hutchins arrived at Chicago, and one of his first duties was to dedicate the new temple of social science. Although in his earlier post (ironically, at Yale Law School), he had embraced legal realism, he turned, by the mid-1930s, toward a neoclassical Aristotelian/Thomist natural law philosophy and against the basic premises of the university's social science establishment and the philosophical heritage of Dewey. In 1930, he brought Adler and his emphasis on the "great books" from Columbia to the law school and recruited such individuals as John U. Nef and Stringfellow Barr who joined the attack on scientism and the related version of liberalism. In his manifesto, *The Higher Learning in America,* Hutchins argued that metaphysics must do for the modern university what theology had done in the Middle Ages—provide an ordering principle and an "intelligible basis for the study of man in his relations with other men." At present, however, "Karl Marx is the new God. Dialectical materialism is the new theology." Both the social and natural sciences, he claimed, rather than combating this doctrine, had degenerated into the "indiscriminate accumulation of data" and an emphasis on instrumental mastery of nature and society that had led to "vocationalism, empiricism, and disorder; and its moral consequences are an immoral morality." In political science, "power becomes the word," and the professional schools like public administration make no contribution to the university "except to intensify its disorder."[21]

Hutchins was intent on rejecting pragmatism in favor of more transcendental foundations of democracy. Adler's emphasis on classical education was accompanied by an attack on positivism, relativism, and pragmatism in the professoriate—suggesting even that there might be more to fear from this internal covert nihilism than from the acts of Hitler. Dewey's actual arguments could hardly sustain these characterizations of his philosophy, but he represented the identity of science and democracy and claimed that "the crisis in democracy demands the substitution of the intelligence that is exemplified in scientific procedure for the kind of intelligence that is now accepted."[22] He remained unequivocal in his belief that there was a connection between philosophical and political absolutism on the one hand and between critical nonfoundational rationalism and democracy on the other.

The two sides at Chicago aired their positions in a symposium on Hutchins's book. The Aristotelian philosopher Richard McKeon heralded Hutchins as a "prophet," while others warned of the dangers in this pursuit of "metaphysical unity" and the attempt to impose Cardinal Newman's "idea of the university."[23] The same year that Hutchins's book appeared, T. V. Smith, by then a member of the Illinois legislature, championed not only the liberal, pluralist, relativist, pragmatist view of democracy but the kind of joining of theory and practice that Hutchins attacked.[24] Dedicated to his "fellow-politicians—at once the hope and despair of the American people," he pondered the increasing "eclipse" of liberalism under the shadow of communism and fascism but stressed the need for central democratic control in the wake of the depression.

It would be difficult to say what constituted the core of democratic theory in political science, but many of the popular "dogmas" of democracy, both with respect to how it operated and how it should operate, had been called into question by realism. It was not simply that some of the assumptions were factually incorrect but that there was the beginning of the suggestion that they might be injurious if deployed in practice.[25] Beginning in the 1930s, with the work of individuals such as Pendelton Herring, political scientists had sought "empirical" bases for redefining democratic theory and emphasized that democracy was grounded less in a set of substantive values than in certain institutional processes.[26] What was emerging was a theory of liberal democracy in which order, consensus, and public interest were understood as a product of conflicts and compromises between group interests. There was, after all, a functional whole behind the diversity of the parts. This was increasingly presented explicitly as an alternative to totalitarianism.

Sometimes realist claims and counterclaims were distinctly linked to practical political platforms. Thurman Arnold's attack on ideals was in service of the New Deal, while Lippmann, shifting from his earlier views, turned against pragmatism in favor of natural law and criticized current notions of collectivism as a prelude to totalitarianism.[27] Similarly, the theologian Reinhold Niebuhr turned away from an earlier social scientific optimism and toward a different kind of realism which called into question the idea of progress and the hope for radical social amelioration.[28] The sense of domestic and international political crisis was becoming the focus of a call for transcendental grounds for democracy and human judgment in general.

One of the principal vehicles for the defense of pragmatism, liberalism, and social science at the University of Chicago had been the *International Journal of Ethics*. By the end of the decade, the issue of whether liberalism, as a philosophy and as a mode of public policy, was sound or bankrupt was informing discussion. The underlying concern was often the totalitarian challenge to liberal democracy and the domestic revision of liberalism represented by Roosevelt. Philosophers Charner Perry and Smith as well as Merriam and Lasswell were frequent contributors. There was a great deal of emphasis on the issue of whether the "liberal" view that values were subjective and experimental was preferable to some form of moral objectivism. Perry defended the former position and attacked natural law. He identified "political theory" specifically as the study of norms and of the art of their construction and reconstruction by elites devoted to social control. He pointedly argued that the belief in the subjective character of value judgments led to useful moral principles that aided in settling disputes, while objectivism only created an atmosphere of contention and doubt.[29] Benjamin Wright had noted in his study of American political theory that, although ideas of natural law often lurked in the background, they basically represented attempts to "solve the unsolvable" and were a way of dealing with issues that were not "capable of objective proof."[30]

One response to the growing concern that liberalism lacked a philosophical core that could withstand the challenge of antagonistic ideologies was to shore up or revise liberal philosophy, but others began to question the core of the new liberal vision. Elliott's colleague at Harvard, the sociologist Pitirim A. Sorokin, published the first volume of a massive work which attributed the decline of the West to nineteenth-century positivism.[31] And conservative members of the first wave of émigré authors, such as Aurel Kolnai and Hermann Rauschning, looked for an underlying intellectual explanation for the rise of totalitarianism. Kolnai had argued that communism was a result of mental illness and that Marxism was a social psychosis deriving from bisexuality. He now claimed that the Nazi movement was not some accident of personality and circumstance but rather a logical entailment of certain trends in German philosophy which could not be countered by utilitarian liberalism. What was required, he argued, was a vision of democracy based on Christian humanism.[32] Rauschning argued that Hitler's "nihilism" sprung from a will to power that was ultimately the consequence of forces unleashed by Enlightenment values.[33]

Americans such as Dewey had been convinced that there was something about the characteristic bent of German philosophy that predisposed it toward authoritarian politics, and this view was reinforced by a new and growing literature that attempted to explain the Nazi movement in terms of German idealism, romanticism, and the ideas of Nietzsche.[34] They were, however, quite unprepared for the view that liberalism and scientism were not only not antidotes but implicated in the problem. The intellectual crisis revolving around the issues of liberalism, relativism, science, and progress was also distinctly manifest in the short-lived *Journal of Social Philosophy* which began publication in 1936.

Initially, the journal was explicitly conceived as a counter to the emphasis on quantitative social science and the promotion of the narrow vision of scientism represented by individuals such as Ogburn. The goal was to introduce more historical and philosophical reflection into social science. It became, however, an outlet for a wide range of opinion from both social scientists and practitioners (e.g., Franklin Roosevelt and Charles Evans Hughes). Many of the contributions reflected a Deweyan perspective and represented the values of the New Deal, but issues of European politics and the condition of Western liberalism were principal topics. In the first issue of the journal, the historian Carl Becker argued for relativism as a basis for criticizing establishment values and claimed that both liberal democracy and communism were only slightly different secular ideologies of progress which had been preceded by Christianity. These were "useful social myths," but destined to be supplanted by "factual knowledge." For Becker, however, there seemed to be little doubt that the "Truth" of liberalism was somehow coincident with "matter-of-fact."[35]

Jászi now found a context for his claims. He argued that the relativism inherent in scientism had undermined conceptions of "right and wrong" and led to a theoretical and practical "breakdown of liberal democracy" which culminated in the "fatal collapse" represented by World War I and its aftermath.[36] For some, what was required, then, was a return to metaphysics.[37] Others, however, believed that it was precisely such metaphysical attachments that characterized modern antidemocratic movements. It was suggested that fascism and communism represented a return to "dogmatism and medievalism," while democracy rested on "a relativistic attitude toward all regulative ideas" and was the "practical expression of the philosophic doctrine of the relativism of political ideas."[38]

Some political and social scientists, like Carl Friedrich, reflecting judgments about the New Deal, warned that it was necessary either to get control of the economic and social system or give way to some less congenial form of government.[39] It was not uncommon to argue that in the face of Soviet and Nazi use of science, "scientific . . . control becomes crucial" in "designing a democracy."[40] Others, such as the constitutional scholar Alpheus T. Mason, allowed that while laissez-faire capitalism had created problems that threatened liberal values, it was important to avoid opting, like "some countries," for despotic rule as a solution. Although Roosevelt had not gone this far, it was necessary, after centuries of fighting various forms of political oppression, not to allow liberalism to be transfigured by "specious" forms of collectivism.[41]

Francis G. Wilson (of the University of Washington), who would be a prominent participant in the conversations about political theory during the next decade, was (by his own account) a "conservative" who saw the function of political theory as one of explaining and directing politics. He believed that National Socialism was "understandable" given modern conditions and that, although hardly liberal, would probably moderate. In his view, the modern "crisis in the economic, political, and social foundations of society" required the injection of "authority." He did not condemn pragmatism, which represented the basic spirit of the electorate, but he argued that during the "pragmatic age," liberalism and democracy had been "asleep."[42] Democracy would need to become more self-conscious and "militant" if it was to survive and avoid the fate of Weimar.[43]

By the end of the decade, one commentator summed up the amorphous condition of liberalism: "One who calls himself a liberal is nowadays diversely called by others traitor, coward, parlor-pink, eclectic, jelly-fish, a selfish or muddy thinker who wants both to have his cake and to eat it, rationalist, skeptic, conservative and radical. . . . But there is unanimity of opinion on one thing, namely, that liberalism is essentially negative, paralytic and disintegrative. Its boasted open-mindedness is nothing more than axiological anemia." He nevertheless defended liberalism and argued that this indictment was overdrawn but warned that liberalism could not afford to allow its principles to provide a forum for illiberalism.[44] Although there was little to indicate that academic political theory was finding its way into politics, political issues were distinctly reflected in the conversation of political theory.

The problem of relativism surfaced in a number of areas such as that of cultural anthropology and the work of such individuals as Ruth Benedict, but more relevant to the issues in political science was the controversy that emerged over the nature of historical knowledge. This reached its peak in the famous Bulletin 54 of the SSRC and the renewed focus on work of Charles Beard.[45] Becker's presentist or relativist theory of writing history may have been inspired by European authors such as Benedetto Croce, but it was in many respects continuous with the positions of Robinson, Barnes, and Beard in which history had been overtly advanced as an instrument of liberal reform.[46] Beard did not want to reduce history to rhetoric and, like Becker, held on to the idea of realism and the autonomy of facts, but he continued to push the relativity of interpretation—in part because of a commitment to the social uses of history and in part because of an epistemological dilemma.

The problem of objectivity had two sides to it. Although positivistic or scientific history, whether he took it to be the Rankean type or some American version, seemed to both eschew social relevance and pursue a goal not applicable in the human sciences, history could not be significant if it was unable to make some such reasonable claim to truth. The relevance of history depended on the authority of knowledge. For Beard, the search for objective history remained "a noble dream," since ultimately writing history involved "an act of faith" that was influenced by the perspective of the author and preconceptions that governed such matters as the selection of data, the issues discussed, and the form of interpretation.[47] His ambivalent conclusion was for a "limited relativity, not a chaos." It was necessary to be "emancipated from the illusion of the absolute truth of history," but it was equally important that there be a "scrupulous and critical use of sources and facts and, so far, a degree of scientific exactness." But the main message was still that history was a form of social thought and that "historians have a public responsibility" and that the practice of history provides "guides to ground public policy."[48] His concerns about scientific history, and his use of relativism to attack this position, were primarily a continuation of his critique of scientism in social science and a reflection of his belief that the development of a social philosophy required abandoning the idea of value-freedom. Maurice Mandelbaum had attacked Beard's and Becker's relativism, as well as the arguments of Croce, Dilthey, and Mannheim. He believed that European critics of relativism had failed to sustain the possibility of objective history, and he took it upon himself to mount a defense of recounting the past as it actually was.[49] Beard argued that Mandelbaum had gotten the "relativist" position quite wrong when he characterized it as the view that historical truth is relative and that a historical work is merely a reflection of the present. The point was rather that it was impossible to achieve verisimilitude and that historical writing was always a partial account in the context of a configuration of present concerns and circumstances.[50]

By the end of the decade, there was little in the way of renewed articulation or defense of scientism. One political scientist noted that while a "well-conceived scientific treatment" of politics was needed, this meant systematic analysis and not, as Merriam had well demonstrated, the neglect of ideas as the basis of human behavior. He rejected attempts at universality and oversimplification that failed to recognize the pragmatic point of view of Dewey and the "relativistic approach which is the distinguishing feature of the more recent interpretation of scientific method."[51] Merriam, speaking for the embattled social sciences at Chicago, specifically linked political theory to public administration and made a plea for setting aside debates about whether social science was really a science and for getting on with the application of practical intelligence to human affairs.[52] The émigré literature had yet to make its way into the conversation in any clear manner, but one of the first major works to appear was Leo Strauss's book on Hobbes which had been published in England before Strauss arrived in the United States. Reviews of the work indicated little grasp of the argument, and Friedrich's reaction is instructive.

Friedrich was one of the first émigrés to enter the field of political science. Although originally a student of medicine, he turned to the study of politics at Heidelberg under Alfred Weber and came to the United States in 1922. He began teaching at Harvard in 1926 and eventually succeeded McIlwain as the dominant person in the history of political theory. He accepted the widespread view at Harvard that "social science cannot benefit from applying the methods of natural science."[53] His emphasis on constitutionalism supported the view that democracy was grounded less in power residing in democratic majorities, or even consensual agreement on fundamental values, than in constitutional methods and pluralism. Friedrich argued that, in fact, pluralism in both ideas and politics was what in large part distinguished democracy from totalitarianism and from the whole line of political thought, from Aristotle to Hegel, that contributed to the "deification of the state."[54] Although Friedrich was, in various ways, instrumental in providing a bridge between European and American ideas, he was not particularly attuned to that dimension of the coming wave of European thought, and the intellectual world of Weimar Germany from which it emanated, that would reshape the contours of the discourse of political theory. Originally much taken with the ideas of Carl Schmitt, some of which he passed on to Elliott, he had believed when Hindenburg and Hitler came to power that Germany would "remain a constitutional democratic state," but he came to admit that the Nazis had made him "look like a fool."[55]

Friedrich recognized that Strauss's claim that Hobbes was the author of both contemporary liberalism and socialism involved a general critique of the "modern mind," which he agreed much needed a "purge," and represented a renewal of the "search for fundamentals." But he found it difficult to identify the exact character of Strauss's "own viewpoint." Here was an author who in some respects seemed to praise Hobbes, yet it was doubtful that he either agreed with him or was a "mere commentator." Friedrich concluded that there were "many indications that the author is a historical relativist."[56] There could be few stronger indications of the intellectual distance between the two traditions that were converging in American social science. Two political science journals began publication in 1939. One was the *Journal of Politics*, and the other was the *Review of Politics*. They, and their lead articles, adumbrated the divergent paths of political theory.

Although there had been little specific attention to the issue of the nature of political theory during the 1930s, the underlying premises regarding its character, function, and place in political science were sufficiently destabilized to suggest to Sabine the need to address the question "What is political theory?" His essay codified many of the assumptions that had evolved during the past century in the context of American political science. Political theory was, first of all, Sabine argued, a descriptively distinct mode of philosophy, devoted to the study of civic society, that had a distinct historical career and which, despite its various forms and contents, began in classical Greece and remained "a unit throughout its history."[57] It was never, he emphasized, a merely scholarly or "antiquarian" endeavor, and it arose, as an intellectual response to a "specific situation," in the "interstices of social and political crisis" such as that which obtained in fourth-century Greece and seventeenth-century England. To understand a political theory was to view it "as a part of or an incident in politics itself" but also to apprehend the wider social context of which politics is a part. Yet its situated character did not limit its applicability, since there was an important sense in which the basic political issues were perennial and universal. It pointed toward the future as well as the past and remained alive to the degree that it could "weave itself into the developing tradition of the subject."[58]

For Sabine, it was practical interest that gave rise to and defined political theory, and even conservative thought entailed "policy" or judgments of both probability and right. Thus, analytically, a political theory could be divided, following the description of thought advanced by pragmatists such as Dewey and Mead, into claims of fact, cause, and value. But while, in his view, the pragmatists understood these elements as logically connected, Sabine argued, in a manner that he believed ultimately involved "a destructive criticism of pragmatism," that they were "quite distinct." Although he stressed that political theories were intended to have, and had had, profound "psychological" or persuasive effects, Sabine strongly resisted the notion that the meaning of theories was reducible to their emotional impact. The existence of a theory and its effect on belief was a fact along with other facts, but he insisted that "their causal influence as existing facts is simply irrelevant both to their truth or falsity" as factual claims and to an assessment of their "logical consistency"—and that logic and truth were equally distinct. Theories characteristically, and even necessarily, consisted of both factual (and causal) and valuational claims, but, apart from the relatively narrow matter of logical consistency, there was no way to judge the validity of a theory as a whole. There was no way to bridge or equate claims of fact and value—of "is" and "ought to be." But in the rational criticism of a political theory, the first step was to discriminate these elements and apply tests appropriate to each.[59]

Sabine rejected the idea that theories could be made scientific by a deletion of evaluative references or that theorists should refrain from valuation. Intellectual honesty, as well as logic, however, required not passing off values as facts even though in practice the two often became confused. The problem was with certain philosophies, such as those of Hegel and Marx, that, like the natural law theorists that preceded them, claimed a logical synthesis, now through historical dialectic. This propensity toward conflation was also, in a "milder" manner, present "in the pragmatism of Professor Dewey and Professor Mead."[60] Sabine ended his essay with a set of questions about the possibility of general standards of judgment, but his intimation was that while "truth" was inevitably a relative concept, logic and the criterion of "coherence" offered something in the way of a universal critical standard.

For those seeking the authority of knowledge in an age marked by conflicting values and crumbling foundations, Sabine's account of political theory offered little. Sabine also attempted to articulate what was meant by liberalism and to assess its "historical position." Although he found it difficult to formulate a definition in terms of either philosophy or institutions, he claimed that, despite all the attributes that might be attached to it—from civil liberties to notions of limited government—and despite the substantial transformations that separated newer from older forms, the essence of this "attitude"—from Bacon to Dewey—was a moral commitment to and a "belief in the supreme social value of intelligence" as the basis of ordering human affairs. This was manifest both in the pluralism that allowed and propagated free discussion and in the attempt to apply knowledge to the rational direction of political life.[61]

The *Review of Politics* was founded by the émigré Catholic publicist

Waldemar Gurian and Fathers Frank O'Malley and Leo Ward. The express goal was "to revive the Aristotelian conception of politics" and to bring to bear "Christian wisdom" and "the Christian world-view" on modern problems and, with respect to "social and political philosophy," to take a "well-defined concrete political and social line" on temporal issues.[62] Gurian took the position that nazism was part of a more general crisis in European society growing out of the decline of liberalism.[63] Gurian came from a Russian Jewish family but was brought up as a Catholic in Germany. He was a student of Max Scheler as well as Schmitt's most dedicated disciple. He was greatly influenced by Schmitt's critique of liberalism and did not break with his teacher until just prior to the Nazi purge in 1932. He fled to Switzerland in 1934 and came to the United States in 1937 where he became a political scientist at Notre Dame.

Nef, of the Committee on Social Thought at Chicago, was closely tied to the *Review,* and it became a basic outlet for the ideas of the émigrés and particularly, during the next decade, for those in political theory such as Strauss, Voegelin, and Hannah Arendt whose major works would not appear for a number of years. Arendt, for example, published several articles that would eventually become part of her *Origins of Totalitarianism* (1951). The first issue led off with Jacques Maritain arguing that the modern "crisis of civilization," manifest in totalitarianism of both the Left and Right, was a consequence of the derailment of humanism by both rationalist and irrationalist tendencies. What was required, he suggested, was nothing less than the "liquidation" of the last four centuries of modern thought and the creation of an "integral humanism" which would provide a new basis for the democratic ideal and overcome the "general paganization of our civilization" by reconciling the natural and supernatural dimensions of human existence.[64]

The intellectual developments during the next decade were crucial for political theory as well as the discipline as a whole. The "behavioral revolution" of the 1950s, identified in terms of its self-ascribed attempt to appropriate and apply the methodology of the natural sciences and redefine political theory accordingly, did not come on the scene as suddenly as is often assumed. The conversation out of which it most immediately sprang took form in the previous decade in the context of a debate about liberalism, relativism, science, and history.

By the early 1940s, there was a distinct increase in literature dealing with political theory. This revitalization was in part a response to the war which prompted reflection on various issues concerning political values and their foundation as well as a renewed concern with making political science scientific. To some extent the focus on theory was a consequence of the sociological fact that those political scientists with practical skills and concerns were more deeply involved in the war effort and had left the academic field to the theorists. A list of political scientists' wartime activities published in 1946 indicated that few political theorists were engaged in nonacademic pursuits. But much more significant was the beginning of the impact of the émigré scholars on the field and on issue definition—even if they were only minimally visible in the major published literature.

Although the behavioral movement was revolutionary in that it was an attempt, and ultimately a successful one, to break away from certain forms of institutional, historical, and legalistic research that tended to dominate much of the practice of political science, it was in many respects a distinctly conservative revolution. First of all, it would be difficult to find any major tenet of behavioralism that had not been articulated by individuals such as Merriam and Catlin. Even its research practices were rooted in work that was well advanced in the 1920s and 1930s. At least in qualitative and conceptual terms, the continuities were more striking than the innovations. Second, it was conservative in the broader sense that it embodied and rearticulated the basic liberal values of political science and political theory. Although most of those instrumental in defining the behavioral movement understood themselves, more narrowly and immediately, as involved in realizing the promise of a scientific study of politics, their arguments emerged in a context in which a fundamental challenge to the liberal science of politics was taking shape. The behavioral revolution was not consciously perceived as a preemptive strike, but its self-understanding, and external image, as basically a revolt against an obsolescent indigenous idea of political theory and political science is misleading. It was in large part a revolt against an alien philosophical incursion and a response to a hostile intellectual ambience that by the mid-1940s was presenting an increasingly articulate challenge to the traditional image of political science and, particularly, to the idea of political theory as exemplified in the work of individuals ranging from Sabine to members of the Chicago school.

This challenge was, indeed, in part the persistence of voices from the past that to some degree provided an access for émigré thought. Elliott, reflecting on his critique of pragmatism, concluded that his assessment had been correct and, given the course of modern events, historically sustained.[65] Adler and Nef argued that such movements as fascism and other political pathologies were rooted in cultural distortions, and, unfortunately, culture sprang from universities controlled by relativists and positivists who, in their opposition to values such as those advanced by Hutchins, constituted a threat to democracy. While Hitler's nihilism was open and could be confronted directly, the threat to democracy from within was more subtle and in some ways more insidious and could be combated only by a conscious return to absolute principles such as those advanced by Plato and Aristotle and by a rejection of pragmatism, relativism, utilitarianism, and allied ideas.[66] Often the claim was that democracy should be grounded in religion which offered the only answer to "atheist communism" and "Nazi radicalism." And any attempt to ground morality in a theory of ethical relativity was impossible.[67]

This position gained an increasingly broad base of support in the American academy, and the proponents of ideas associated with the Chicago school, Dewey, and much of mainstream American social science, now found themselves more on the defensive than in an intellectual vanguard. Dewey, who had borne the brunt of much of the criticism and become the symbol of pragmatism, relativism, and the like, pointedly rejected any idea of natural law and responded to Hutchins's attack on relativism and liberal professors and Hutchins's theory of education as an "attempt to form human character in terms of such an ideal."[68] Dewey rejected the return to the Greeks and the Middle Ages as a misguided and reactionary attempt to seek standards from societies in which there was little social democracy and little grasp of scientific principles. He argued that the path forward required accepting "the scientific way, not merely of technology, but of life in order to achieve the promise of modern democratic ideals."[69]

For Merriam religion had constituted a singular threat to democracy and scientific progress, and although the war required a justification of liberal principles, he and his intellectual progeny were unrepentant in their attachment to the convergence of science, democracy, pragmatism, relativism, and social progress. Lasswell held on to the idea of a "science of democracy" that was dedicated to "removing the physical and technical barriers to perfection." Smith once again struck out against the "politics of conscience," and while admitting that "compromise" had its limits, as in the case of dealing with Nazis, he insisted that it, along with pluralism and tolerance, was not only the essence of politics but the basis of morality and democratic progress.[70] Broader philosophical defenses for this position were forthcoming from such philosophers as Sidney Hook who argued for a methodological justification of democracy. It was to be understood as a scientific hypothesis which could be applied and tested like any form of empirical analysis. It did not require metaphysical support but only an attachment to the values associated with scientific procedure. Philosophical absolutism was in fact, he argued, antidemocratic just as closure to inquiry was unscientific.[71]

This position also gained support from certain émigré philosophers such as Philipp Frank (Harvard) who claimed that the kind of thinking characteristic of science sustained democracy. Frank pointedly argued that, in search of a "scapegoat" on which to blame the crisis marked by totalitarianism, certain people had focused on an "attitude" that had "been called by different names: empiricism, positivism, negativism, pragmatism, relativism, operationalism, instrumentalism, scientism, rationalism, anti-rationalism, etc." But he claimed that, quite to the contrary, the scientific attitude and "this 'relativism' has been for centuries the only effective weapon in the struggle against any brand of totalitarianism" and represented "the only method compatible with the progress of human knowledge" and "democracy."[72]

Although Sabine never exactly embraced pragmatism as philosophy, it was because he continued to believe that it shared with ethical naturalism the tendency to conflate facts and values. Their logical separation, however, did not entail that social studies could eliminate its evaluative dimension. He argued that the arguments of Beard and others that social science involved values had become "overworked," but "the fact remains that political theory has always contained a large amount of valuation" which was ultimately a matter of "choice" rather than "objective" determination. This did not mean, however, that social science could not be objective. What was required was keeping the two realms analytically distinct and avowing one's values in order to ensure "clarity."[73] Sabine would remain adamant that the search for the meaning of democracy could not return to the "pre-conceived ideas" and metaphysics of earlier years. Science and philosophy had undercut transcendent reason, which had been replaced by psychology, and values were reactions to given states of affairs.[74]

It was in this intellectual context that a distinct conversation about political theory began to emerge, and by the early 1940s, the émigré scholars had joined, and begun to transform, that conversation as they converged in the attack on scientism, liberalism, and relativism. In 1958, Crick argued that one of the failures of the American science of politics, which he attributed largely to the growth of scientism and professionalism joined to a stifling form of unreflective conservative liberalism, was that it spoke neither "to problems nor to public" and had become "profoundly at odds with almost all that is best in American political experience and expression." He found hope, however, in the post–World War II period, in the "infusion of émigré and refugee scholars" such as Friedrich, Hans Morgenthau, Arendt, Gurian, Franz

Neumann, Sigmund Neumann, Strauss, Voegelin, and such American partisans as John Hallowell. Their ideas, he maintained, had "helped to widen perspectives" and rescue political science and political theory from its "nativism."[75] Crick failed to say much about either what these broadened perspectives involved or what these individuals had effected and affected in the previous two decades. But he had largely inverted the historical relationships. By the end of the 1950s, the issue at hand was actually less a matter of the anticipation of transformation than an understanding of it. By this point the émigré scholars had become a fundamental part of the story of American political science and the evolution of the concept and practice of political theory. Their work was less a reaction to the behavioral movement than its catalyst. But to understand this work, it is necessary to penetrate the world from which they fled but in which their ideas had taken form.

7

The Idea of Theoretical Intervention:
The Weimar Conversation

Is it conceivable then, that the sphere of human activity on the mastery of which our fate rests is so unyielding that scientific research cannot force it to give up its secrets?

Karl Mannheim

What pervaded the intellectual world of Weimar was a sense of crisis manifest in culture, philosophy, and politics. Although this image of crisis would be projected retrospectively on the advent of nazism, the basic concerns were articulated long before. The problem at the center of the Weimar conversation was the relationship between theory and practice or, more specifically, the academy and politics. The crisis was ultimately a crisis of *Wissenschaft*. The republic that had evolved from the revolution of 1918–19 and lasted until Hitler's ascendancy in June of 1933 was one in which intellectuals flourished but one which they also deserted—or, as some suggested, deserted them. Liberalism, pluralism, egalitarianism, mass politics, political parties, and materialistic middle-class culture were rejected by many on both the Left and Right.[1] Although there were many supporters of the republic, the intellectuals, for the most part, "tempted by distance," were a "stunning exception."[2]

This alienation was in some cases forced on them because of their status as Jews or Eastern Europeans, but the estrangement of *Geist* and *Macht* was more deeply rooted. The integration of these two realms at the high point of the mandarins had not, for the most part, entailed direct political participation, and now the unity that had allowed more priestly participation was shattered. Although the work of such individuals as Lukács, or the members of the *Institut für Sozialforschung* at Frankfurt, may have centered on dilemmas in Marxist theory, such specific foci were in large part either displaced or particular manifestations of the more concrete but general structural problem of the relationship between the authority of knowledge and political authority and, more specifically, the university and politics.

Max Weber's addresses on politics and science as vocations were sym-

146

bolic of, and touchstones for, the engagement of this issue. Although Weber's arguments have been construed in a variety of ways and although the essays are hardly one-dimensional in either intention or content, there has seldom been sufficient attention to the fact that they were the culmination of a dialogue about academic and public discourse in which he had been engaged for a quarter of a century. The continuing problem which sustained his attention was that of recasting the role of the scholar vis-à-vis politics—a problem that was generated both by his personal crises and by the structure of the world in which he resided. Weber's relationship, both theoretical and practical, to the politics of his time is a complicated matter, but never more so than in the period when these lectures were delivered.[3] After years of ambivalence about commitments to both political life and academia, he was intensely involved with both.

In 1918, he both accepted a chair in political economy at Vienna and joined the German Democratic Party. And it was in this context that he accepted the invitation from the Union of Free Students at Munich and presented the two lectures. The lecture on science was delivered late that year and the lecture on politics in January 1919, eighteen months before his death. He campaigned for the Democratic Party in the 1919 elections and even accepted a nomination for the Reichstag. The year that he delivered the lecture on science, he stated that he "was born for the pen and the speaker's rostrum; not for the university," but he declared by mid-year in 1919 that he was "finished with politics" and accepted a chair at Munich.[4] It is easy to suggest that his bifurcation of the vocations of science and politics was the culmination of his own inability to find an accommodation between them, but the dilemma was much more than a personal issue.

Science as a vocation, Weber claimed, required passion, commitment, and an "inward calling." This was particularly true in the specialized, and often impecunious and mediocre, world of the contemporary university which was "chained to the course of progress" and obsolescence and which reflected the same rationalized "disenchantment" that was characteristic of modernity in general.[5] "Science today is a 'vocation' organized in special disciplines in the service of self-clarification and knowledge of interrelated facts. It is not the gift of grace of seers and prophets dispensing sacred values and revelations, nor does it partake of the contemplation of sages and philosophers about the meaning of the universe."[6] Politics was "out of place in the lecture room"—for both students and faculty. Science gave no answer to questions about "what we shall do and how we shall live." Thus "to take a practical political stand is one thing, and to analyze political structures and party positions is another," and it would be an "outrage" to conflate the languages appropriate to these spheres. Weber argued that "the prophet and the demagogue do not belong on the academic platform." Even though students might "crave a leader and not a teacher," it was, he claimed, the duty of teachers to exercise self-restraint and refrain from exploiting their position by proselytizing.[7]

A teacher could properly play a critical role by, for example, exposing students to facts that were "inconvenient" for their ideological position, contributing to the knowledge employed in the technological control of objects and activities, and providing methods for thinking about choices and their consequences and achieving clarity and self-consciousness about one's ideas and actions. But "whenever the man of science introduces his personal value judgment, a full understanding of the facts *ceases*," and science was meaningless with respect to arbitrating between the basic and incommensurable "value spheres of the world." Science offered means but not ends, and ends were ultimately matters of decision and not cognition.[8]

Although Weber was contemptuous of certain aspects of American higher education where students bought knowledge as if it were a commodity, "just as the greengrocer sells my mother cabbage," the atmosphere was such that "no young American would think of having the teacher sell him a *Weltanschauung* or a code of conduct." For Weber, it was not simply a matter of the propriety of the position but also the fact that "the qualities that make a man an excellent scholar and academic teacher are not the qualities that make him a leader to give directions in practical life or, more specifically, in politics."[9] Yet even if the qualities of a leader were present in a teacher, the obligation was to exercise them in the appropriate realm and not in the classroom with its captive audience. If the modern age lacked a charismatic saviour, it was vain to believe that a substitute could be found by having "thousands of professors, as privileged hirelings of the state, attempt as petty prophets in their lecture-rooms to take over his role."[10]

Although Weber's model of the scientific attitude may have represented more a regimen that he wished on his ideological opponents than a norm to which he himself adhered, it evoked a sharp distinction between academic and political life. It was, however, a distinction which reflected what was happening in Weimar, and it represented what he believed was essential for a reconstruction of the relationship between the two spheres. What he was claiming, most simply, was that in a world that was becoming academically and politically pluralistic, the idea of an authoritative monolithic academic voice coincidental with political authority was obsolescent and that, paradoxically, the reconstitution of the relationship between academic and public discourse presupposed their separation. This was an idea that was deeply embedded in the American experience, and it was in no small way part of the subsequent appeal of Weber's work to social scientists in the United States. The assumption that the call for value-freedom sprang from a passion for political disengagement has been a constant source of error in understanding the history of social science. Only if science was distinct from politics, with separate standards of validity, could it speak with authority to politics and constitute a critical voice.

Weber characterized the politician, or the political actor, ideally, as an individual who also embraced a vocation and passionately took a stand in the practical world and assumed personal responsibility for it. The calling of politics required, however, a tolerance of complexity and a refusal to succumb to a chiliastic "ethic of ultimate ends." He contrasted this attitude not only with that of the "prophetic politician" but with both the "sterile excitation" of many intellectuals, who lacked a sense of both proportion and responsibility, and with the "vanity" of those academicians for whom it had often become an "occupational disease."[11] For Weber, both science and politics were fraught with an internal, and humbling, paradox. In each case, one must make commitments to ideas that were destined to be rejected. Thus it was only the vocation itself that could sustain fealty.

Neither in general nor in his own life was Weber successful in articulating exactly the character of the rapproachment between theory and practice that he sought. He did, nevertheless, understand that it was in itself a practical problem. For many of his peers, however, the practical problem had been transformed into a philosophical one. The problem of the authority of knowledge had become an epistemological issue. Weber entered public life speaking for his generation and dedicated to linking scholarship and politics, and it would be a mistake to read any of his major statements as a renunciation of that commitment. The generation he represented reacted not only against the politics of the past but against the manner in which academicians had valorized that politics, and nearly every statement Weber made about the separation of science and politics was directed against a specific atavistic configuration of politics and academia and presented in the service of a clarification of what he considered to be the emerging situation. There was a purposive ambiguity in Weber's image of science. It at once represented *Wissenschaft* or philosophy but also science in the narrower sense of the natural sciences and emerging specialized social scientific disciplines. He was fusing what had been traditionally distinct, and this was in part the cause of the negative reaction to his presentation.

The higher educational establishment had been dominated by the Prussian Ministry of Education and by its director, Friedrich Althoff who gave Weber his first academic appointment (Berlin, 1892). Although Althoff retired in 1907, his policies continued to govern the system. The cultural sciences were viewed as adjuncts of the state, and emerging social science had little chance of legitimation except in terms of its public policy utility. Weber began his intellectual life as a student of *Staatswissenschaft* under individuals such as Treitschke and Mommsen, and he was a member of the *Verein*. He never argued for a social science that was not fundamentally a *political* science or without political consequences. But he did argue consistently for a science that was not an instrument of the state and one that gained its authority from its academic and scientific status. The establishment within the *Verein* was supported by Althoff, and it, in turn, often gave intellectual legitimacy to the state's paternalistic welfare legislation.

The sciences of sociology and political economy championed by such individuals as Weber were not only theoretically innovative and concerned with such matters as a more materialist account of history but involved efforts to reform both politics and the university. The latter had largely excluded Jews, socialists, Eastern Europeans, and various cognitive dissidents who, after the turn of the century, were represented in Weber's circle and who belonged to the generation that created the German Sociological Association as a counter to the *Verein*. These individuals, centered in non-Prussian institutions, usually held unsalaried and irregular positions *(Privatdozenten* and *Extraordinarien)* and were often associated with a movement for educational reform, constitutional change, radical politics, and scientific innovation. In addition to Weber's salon (which included his brother, economist/sociologist Alfred, George Simmel, Ferdinand Tönnies, Werner Sombart, Emil Lederer, and Ernst Troeltsch), there were socialists and radicals such as Gustav Radbruch, Eduard Bernstein, Lukács, Ernst Bloch, Preuss, and Roberto Michels.

Weber spent much of his life *between* science and politics, rarely solidly situated in either. In his inaugural address, after accepting a chair in political economy at Freiburg (1895), Weber posed the question of whether his generation could make a contribution that equaled that of the nation-builders of the past. His answer was that progress toward internal unification would come through a political and economic science that explored social reality but at the same time provided a vehicle of political education for citizens. This would require, however, some resolution of the dilemma of the relationship between academic intellectuals and politics, and he began his attack on the *Kathedersozialisten* and the Gustav Schmoller school.

Although the professoriate of Weber's era still had considerable public influence and although there was an expectation of leadership, the decline of academic authority, the traditional aversion to party or interest politics, and increasing pluralization in both the university and politics raised severe questions about the articulation of public and academic life. The persistence of the, sometimes extravagant, mandarin style among individuals such as Treitschke only exacerbated the situation. A reconstitution of academic authority was necessary, but at the same time, however, Weber was concerned about a less than realistic and responsible politics that could be influenced unduly by certain elements of academic discourse. In this period, when there was an imminent clash between the older vision of *Bildungbürgertum* and the ideas associated with such groups as the Stefan George circle and the Ethical Culture movement, Weber in many ways sided with the older school. The newer persuasions were too utopian for Weber and symbolized for him the absolutist ethic of pure intention. This was as problematical as the establishment position of the *Verein*.

In 1898, shortly before the illnesses that would take him away from the profession of teaching for two decades, Weber could have been a National Liberal candidate but chose to remain at Heidelberg, where he had taken a chair in 1896, and commit himself to the vocation of science. In the critical methodological essays written shortly after the turn of the century, he attempted to accomplish several things, but often the least noted theme of these essays was his emphasis on freeing social scientific inquiry from the entanglements of philosophical epistemology, such as those that characterized the *Methodenstreit*. He insisted that such metatheoretical claims were ex post facto judgments about scientific practice rather than the foundation of that practice.[12] The authority of social science required independence from the traditional domination of philosophy. But the autonomy of science with respect to the language and practice of philosophy must be complemented by independence from politics.

The famous essay on "objectivity," was published when he assumed joint editorship of the *Archiv für Sozialwissenschaft und Sozialpolitik* in 1904, and it was written shortly after he resigned his formal faculty position and in the midst of the conflict with Schmoller and the *Verein*.[13] Weber stressed the many ways in which value judgments impinged upon, or were otherwise involved in, empirical inquiry. Furthermore, the enterprise of science both arose from a practical concern and had wide implications for value choices. Yet there was still inadequate recognition that science and political valuation were distinct enterprises. There was a fundamental logical distinction between the kind of claims that largely defined each sphere, that is, existential knowledge of what "is" and normative claims about what "should be."

Weber's concern at this point was less to keep science out of politics than to keep politics out of science. His celebrated and maligned distinction between fact and value served, first of all, to establish the autonomy of science and, second, to make possible, through their distinction, an analysis of the issues involved in their relation. Even though he insisted on the categorical distinction, his formulation of the ways in which science, through explanation, information, and reflection, could, potentially, circumscribe the terms of practical judgment left, in principle, a narrow realm for unrestrained decision and commitment. Where once in Germany the spheres were neither in fact nor consciousness distinct, they now were, and even though the membranes might be permeable, the question of the existential relationship between political practice and the practice of knowledge could not be avoided.

During this period, Weber began a series of attacks on the lack of academic freedom in Germany. He focused on the case of Michels's exclusion, and he attempted to obtain chairs for Simmel and Sombart who were Jews. Here he claimed that "alleged academic freedom is obviously bound up with the espousal of certain views which are politically acceptable in court circles and in salons, and furthermore with the manifestation of a certain minimum of conformity with ecclesiastical opinion or, at least, a facsimile thereof. The *freedom of science' exists in Germany within the limits of political and ecclesiastical acceptability.* Outside these limits, there is none."[14] His confrontation with the Althoff system and the manner in which it restricted and demeaned the university teacher and scholar, as opposed, for example, to his understanding of American universities, continued for several years.

The generational differences within the *Verein* became increasingly prominent in the years prior to World War I, and Weber led the opposition. His arguments for academic freedom implied both the freedom of academics from political authority and the freedom to hold less than orthodox positions. The thrust of his work was in the direction of taking the image of scientific objectivity away from the conservatives in both their political and academic roles. He organized the German Sociological Association in 1909, but he had difficulty maintaining the practice of separating science and political rhetoric within the organization. He withdrew from its leadership in 1912. Weber succeeded in having inserted into the charter of the association the clause that sociology "rejects the pursuit of any practical goals, whether ethical, religious, political, aesthetic, etc.," but it would be a mistake to take his intention as one of neutralizing the impact of science on social practices or as merely a strategy to limit the influence of his opponents.

His essay on "ethical-neutrality" in social science (1917) had been prepared (originally in 1913) as a memorandum for discussion at the *Verein* during the height of the *Werturteilsstreit*. He bracketed the issue of the logical distinction between fact and value claims and, instead, focused on what he insisted was the separate issue of the freedom of scientific disciplines from value judgments. This, he argued, was a matter that neither logic nor science could answer. *"It is itself entirely a question of practical judgment and cannot therefore be definitively resolved."*[15] Weber argued that simply renouncing the passionate delivery of value claims was not enough—those florid lecturers such as Treitschke were at least recognizable for what they were. It was one's duty to make clear which statements were statements of practical evaluation and which were scientific claims, but more important was the need to eliminate the former in the first place. According to Weber the university was not an arena for moral training and character formation but rather a sphere governed by intellectual integrity and specialized knowledge. His goal, however, was not to neutralize the authority of the academy with respect to practical matters, but to make that authority once again credible.

In an age in which there was a unified social ethic, the position of such individuals as Schmoller had its place, but given the ethical and political pluralism of the contemporary world, it was anomalous. Weber, by this time, had come to the basic position that was reflected in the essays on the vocations of science and politics.

Of all types of prophecy, this "personally" tinged type of professional prophecy is the most repugnant. There is no precedent for a situation in which a large number of officially appointed prophets do their preaching or make their professions of faith, not as other prophets do, on the streets, or in the churches or other public places—or if they do it privately, then in personally chosen sectarian conventicles—but rather regard themselves as best qualified to enunciate their evaluations on ultimate questions in the name of science and in the carefully protected quiet of governmentally privileged lecture halls in which they cannot be controlled, or checked, by discussion, or subjected to contradiction.[16]

Weber noted that some faculty even tried to keep classroom discussion confidential in order to maintain their cult of personality. He argued that the professor who wished to pursue practical affairs possessed other avenues. This was not a matter of rejecting the value of academic freedom, because the political use of the classroom by individuals such as Schmoller was not complemented by tolerance for other persuasions such as Marxism and laissez-faire economics. The university was at best little more than a training center for civil servants or at worst a "theological seminary." Since there was not freedom for many political positions, all should be excluded.

Weber's point was less the epistemological claim that value judgments as such lacked definitive criteria and were matters of will, decision, and faith, or the defense of a liberal ethic of tolerance, than an insistence that *there was no philosophical, or academic, solution to practical judgment.* Although it may be true that Weber embraced some version of the neo-Kantian or Nietzschean idea that there was no transcendental ground for values, the more immediate concern was that in the contemporary situation, there were so many contending points of view that there was not even a conventional ground. The problem was more cultural than epistemological. This same position was reflected in Radbruch's "relativistic" theory of law which stressed that the legal system could not identify itself with one political ethic and therefore must be decisionist or place responsibility in the hands of political actors.[17]

Although Weber's addresses on the vocations were presented to a group of democratic and socialist students caught up in utopian hopes for revolutionary change through intellectual avenues, he was speaking both directly and indirectly to some of the leading intellectuals of Weimar. Weber's argument was that in this world marked by the inexorable rationalization of life and by a struggle between conflicting values that seemed to promise only "a polar night of icy darkness and hardness," the young could at least embrace a vision of responsible prudential politics that avoided chiliastic commitments *or* pursue the path of scientific reason that spurned illusion and was committed to realism in understanding the world.[18] His basic assumption was that these realms would be complementary.

Although much of Weber's work had limited influence during the Weimar years, the lectures on the vocations occasioned an immediate response.[19] With the fall of the Wilhelmine Reich, the authority of the university receded dramatically, and it became a place of nostalgia and resentment. Although it was predominately conservative as an institution, those on the Left were also unhappy with the decline of intellectual authority. It is not surprising that many of the individuals, such as Max Horkheimer, who were students or peers of Weber during this period, registered "disappointment."[20] They expected a more pointed statement from the most prominent social scientific intellectual. Weber's position seemed to hold out little hope for those who were committed to the idea of theoretical intervention, and this included both those academics who had characteristically enjoyed participation in public authority as well as those intellectuals who sought it.

In the same year that Weber delivered his lecture on science, the first volume of Oswald Spengler's *Decline of the West* was published. Although it reflected much of the same pessimism and sense of cultural crisis that permeated intellectual life in the postwar period, it was initially scorned by the academic establishment. It became, however, a best-seller during the 1920s and gained intellectual credibility. Maybe no other work illustrates as well the fine line between vastly different political positions with respect to the sense of crisis and the critique of Weimar parliamentary democracy. Spengler, himself an archconservative and eventually close to National Socialism, articulated widely shared views about the dangers of liberalism and its intellectual counterpart. The skepticism and attacks on rationalism that had haunted German philosophy in the century from F. H. Jacobi to Nietzsche once more resonated.

One response was that of Husserl. In his influential essay on "philosophy as rigorous science" (1911), he had attacked both naturalism (positivism) and historicism as leading to an extreme skepticism. He also rejected traditional metaphysics but aimed at transforming philosophy, as phenomenology, into a science of the a priori consciousness that could recapture universal standards of validity.[21] By the mid-1930s, this sense of malaise had been extended into a broader historical and philosophical analysis of "the crisis of European science" which, he believed, was reflected both in the political situation and in the path that phenomenology had taken, for example, in the *Existenz* philosophy of his student, Martin Heidegger. Modern antirationalism and irrationalism, and historicity, could only be overcome by a transcendental reconstitution of the "natural" pretheoretical attitude.[22]

This was the abyss that Weber seemed to have left unbridged. Many saw Weber's arguments as only an accentuation of the crisis of *Wissenschaft*—and, consequently, the crisis of politics. And both seemed to be grounded in a crisis of neo-Kantian philosophy which failed to underwrite science and to give it any authority to speak to politics. It was in this context that the positions of many of the young intellectuals who emigrated to the United States were formed. For many of the émigrés who became so influential in redefining political theory in the United States, the core of the Western crisis was ultimately a crisis of relativism, and Weber's work, emphasizing the inability of science to answer fundamental moral questions, became a prominent symbol of that crisis and of the failure to respond to intimations of nihilism. The crisis of relativism was in fact a crisis of the intellectuals and their relationship to politics, and Weber's image of science did little, in their view, to solve the problem. Two of the first and most influential books of the émigré generation—Strauss's *Natural Right and History* (1953) and Voegelin's *The New Science of Politics* (1952)—began with responses to Weber and with the problem that they believed he bequeathed to contemporary political theory. Although the significance was dimly grasped in the United States, this was an explicit projection of the Weimar conversation.

The neo-Kantian philosopher, Heinrich Rickert, whose work had influenced Weber considerably, noted that Weber had resisted the contemporary idea of a philosophical "super-science" and that his essays expressed less some scientific asceticism and value relativism than the "anguish" of the relationship between the *"vita contemplativa"* and the *"vita activa."*[23] Weber's critics often understood him in the same way. The classical philologist, Ernst Robert Curtius, interpreted the essay on science as a response to the young intellectuals who dreamed of reaching philosophical absolutes and returning the university to a position of social leadership. Curtius argued that Weber had mistakenly assumed that modern science was the archetype of knowledge. There was, as Plato had demonstrated, philosophical knowledge which transcended the "anarchy of values" that marked the modern world, and this was the property of the university.[24]

One of the first, and most important, responses to Weber was that of Erich von Kahler who was among the émigrés.[25] Kahler, like Curtius, was much influenced by the Stefan George circle but also in close contact with those around Weber who attacked what he believed was Weber's truncated view of science—or what he considered to be the now "old" positivist naturalistic and specialized view of science. He called, following George, for a "new science" that would not "submit to the utterly bleak project" outlined by Weber and that *would* search for the "meaning of life" and work for a "renewal" based on "spiritualization."[26] Kahler's "new science" was, of course, actually a return to the older vision of *Wissenschaft* as a comprehensive philosophical project with public significance. Kahler emphatically insisted that "the connection between political liberal-democratic relativism and scientific-conceptual relativism could not be closer."[27]

Those around Weber who defended his position, such as Arthur Salz who, like Kahler, carried the debate to the United States, were quite explicit about the underlying issue: the authority of intellectuals. Salz maintained that Weber was against the pretensions of both Marxists and those such as Kahler who sought in aesthetics "some highly questionable natural law." Science had application to practical life, but honesty required accepting the fact that academic and political life were different spheres that could not be bridged by philosophy.[28] Ernst Troeltsch, the philosopher of religion who was a friend of Weber's and best known for his *Der Historismus und seine Probleme* (1922) also criticized Kahler along similar lines but offered a different solution.

Troeltsch noted that Kahler's position was part of an emerging intellectual syndrome that was a reaction against the specialized sciences as well as neo-Kantianism and that wanted to once again connect science to practical life by seeking universal foundations and an image of unity modeled on Greek philosophy. This idea of an aesthetic organic community, sprung from individuals such as George, was, he claimed, an unrealistic response to modernity. This movement and call for a "new science" was a romantic reaction to "democratic and socialist enlightenment" and simply confused science, philosophy, and practical life. Troeltsch, however, argued that what was needed was not a new science but a "living leader" who would extricate society from the "directionless cacophony of today's fanatasists."[29]

The pervasive influence of the George *Kreis* was evident in these discussions.[30] There was a rejection of liberalism, socialism, democracy, and modernity in general while embracing an aristocratic position based on classical images of heroism and religious mysticism. This strain of prophetic neoromanticism touched many around Weber including his brother, Sombart, Salz, Simmel, and Ernst Kantorowicz. And there were affinities with Georg Lukács's Tolstoian mysticism and antimodernism. Weber was himself in close touch with George in the years just prior to the war, and he was interested in the idea of cultural renewal. Although there was considerable crossover between the two circles and although Weber was reticent in criticizing George, the cultic character of this group of antimodernist poets and social critics and its rejection of modern science were in many respects uncongenial. Many perceived a parallel between political disorder and philosophical relativism, and there was a belief that the former was rooted in the latter. But what was understood as having a philosophical cause was also conceived as having a philosophical solution. Simply seeking some reconstitution of, or substitute for, rationalism, however, spoke only obliquely to the existential situation of multiple ideologies and the dilemma of the university.

This was indicated in Max Scheler's turn from philosophy to the sociology of knowledge and his emphasis on the mediating role of the university.[31] Scheler also responded to Weber and defended him against Kahler's notion that science could create a *Weltanschauung*. The Marxists and the romanticists were, he claimed, both wrong. Science and ideology were different spheres. Yet he joined the critics in noting that Weber did not allow for a third element—philosophy as an *"essential mode of human cognition"* which could not, any more than theology, be displaced by the scientific study of worldviews.[32] What Weber's work signified, according to Scheler, was the limitations of positivism and democracy. Morality and philosophy were transcientific—and even science was grounded in a preconstituted *Weltanschauung*. Weber's neo-Kantian nominalism failed, he claimed, to see that philosophy, as conceived by Husserl, could mediate between the spheres that Weber had separated and "drive history forward" through "elites." Scheler, like Mannheim later, sought a basis of objective valuation in immanent social perspectives that manifest an element of a potential synthesis. And, again like Mannheim, he attempted to extend this to a more general social analysis that took account of the Weimar situation and its political pluralism and provided for the university as a mediating vehicle.[33]

Mannheim ultimately came to take his bearings from Weber in the course of his intellectual and political journey through Weimar. *Ideology and Utopia* was published a decade after Weber's essays, and it set the agenda for subsequent discussions that took place during the last days of the republic.[34] Like much of the Weimar intellectual Left, he came from, and was in part materially supported by, an assimilated Jewish middle-class family even though challenging the bourgeois culture which they had accepted. His earliest involvement, beginning in 1910, was with the circle around Jászi and Lukács in his native Hungary, and Mannheim attempted to reconcile his early commitments with Lukács's changing vision.

The son of a wealthy Jewish capitalist assimilated to German culture, Lukács followed a long road from middle-class Protestantism to radical Marxism. In his father's house, he was introduced to many prominent European intellectuals, including Weber, and his family encouraged his academic pursuits. Shortly after the turn of the century, he studied in Germany with Simmel and Dilthey and became acquainted with the work of Marx. Failing in his *Habilitation* at Budapest, partly because of prevailing anti-Semitism, he broke with Jászi and went to Heidelberg in 1912 where he became part of Weber's circle as well as involved with the ideas of George. Although Lukács's eschatological socialism eventually placed him in a very different position from Weber, there was intellectual overlap and mutual respect.

Lukács returned to Budapest in 1915 where Mannheim came under his influence. By this point Lukács's position was an antiliberal antipositivist one dedicated to radical renewal through cultural critique and a general rejection of party politics. Mannheim, after attending the University of Budapest, went to study in Germany with individuals such as Simmel (where he stayed until the war), and he became a leading member of the Lukács group. Intellectually and politically, Mannheim, however, remained torn between Jászi and Lukács. In the revolution of 1918–19, Jászi became a minister in the Karolyi government, while Lukács played a similar role (in education and culture) in the succeeding Soviet Republic under Bela Kun. When this regime was overthrown in 1919, Mannheim became a refugee in Germany.

Implicit in Weber's separation of science and politics was the widely shared assumption that the latter, maybe irredeemably, was a realm infused with irrationality. Although Weber attributed value to politics, many of the philosophical Left in Weimar were as antipolitical, with respect to actual party politics, as the establishment. They envisioned something in the way of a return to an organic cultural order informed by an academic elite. They still advanced the notion of philosophy as a master science and viewed the specialized sciences, with their flirtations with the natural sciences, as both inferior and dangerous. Mannheim held on to the Enlightenment idea of immanent reason in politics and the susceptibility of politics to rational reordering. While Weber, despite his struggle with the tensions between politics and science, had moved rather freely between the spheres, Mannheim, the doubly alienated émigré scholar, focused more pointedly on the mechanisms of mediation.

Although initially at Freiburg, Mannheim became a *Privatdozent* at Heidelberg in 1926 where his *Habilitationsschaft* was *Conservatism*. He was not naturalized, however, until some time later. His association with Marxism was more a problem than his status as an Eastern Jew, but he received the patronage of Alfred Weber (as long as he submerged his Marxism and reformist concerns) and the economist Emil Lederer on the basis that he was not "political." Mannheim was at this point much taken with Lukács's *History and Class Consciousness* (1923) even though he did not accept Lukács's partisanship—and, indeed, could not, given his tenuous academic situation.

Lukács's solution, to both the problems of Marxist philosophy and the contemporary issue of theory and practice rooted in the relativist dilemma, was to argue for a privileged historical moment and for revolutionary action. He claimed that the proletariat occupied a unique epistemological position from which the totality of human relations was theoretically transparent. It was the first subject in history that was capable, in part because of its alienated position, of achieving an objective social consciousness. But it also had a practical interest in transforming society, and thus theory and practice were joined in a singular manner. However, there remained the theoretical and practical problem of how the proletariat was to escape imprisonment in the reifications of bourgeois society. For Lukács, this was the task of the Communist party which would represent a catalyzing form of proletariat consciousness.

In his 1924 essay on "Historicism," Mannheim had already enunciated the main theme of *Ideology and Utopia*—the idea that out of the modern reality of intellectual and political pluralism could be derived a dynamic and synthetic notion of truth that would replace traditional foundational epistemology. Yet it would avoid the dilemma of relativism and provide a basis of resolving conflicting interests and ideologies. *Conservatism* continued the development of this line of thought and provided a historical foundation. The work was itself strategic in that it suggested a reconciliation between contending ideologies by arguing that the ideas of both the Left and Right involving such matters as the rejection of natural science, liberalism, and capitalism had a common genealogy rooted in post-Enlightenment conservative romantic historical thought. In this work, he also first announced his theory of "socially unattached intellectuals" who had become apologists for various interests but who were also somewhat homogeneous and in a position to undertake critical reflection and work toward mediation.

The problem Mannheim set for himself, or which was bequeathed to him, was how to claim authority for knowledge while rejecting some sort of ontological turn. By 1929, he had achieved academic security, and *Ideology and Utopia,* his answer to this problem, became the focus of an intense debate. The controversy had been initiated by his 1928 paper "Competition as a Cultural Phenomenon" in which he had stressed the manner in which political "knowledge" was socially rooted. There was no ambiguity about the fact that the argument reflected, and was directed at, the Weimar context—political and intellectual pluralism and the crisis of philosophy. And it was hardly a matter of speculation to suggest that the work was dialectically related to the arguments of Weber and Lukács.

Mannheim's starting point was the failure of traditional epistemology, and particularly its attempt to ground knowledge outside of convention and in a subject that was independent of history. He argued that it was necessary to start by accepting the "rootedness of knowledge in the social texture" and the "amalgamation of political and scientific thought."[35] From the Enlightenment to Marx, the growing sense of the social grounds of knowledge had led to a situation where the "unmasking" of ideologies had become everybody's game. The task now was to move to a more "non-evaluative" and "total" conception of ideology that would form the basis of a sociology of knowledge. The problem was how to move from this descriptive-explanatory posture back to an "evaluative" position. Like Weber, Mannheim stressed the loss of a unitary world—of both politics and science—and focused on the danger of science being absorbed in politics. Such an "alliance" destroyed science and obscured the fact that "political discussion possesses a character that is fundamentally different from academic discussion."[36]

The specter that Mannheim confronted, the source of both intellectual anxiety and the anxiety of intellectuals, was "relativism." This he took to be the product of the recognition—which he urged as a critical force and a basis of self-clarification—that all thinking is bound up with the concrete position of the thinker. For Mannheim, relativism was a problem only from the standpoint of the old epistemology in both its positivist and antipositivist versions regarding the foundations of knowledge. He argued that it was necessary to "emancipate" ourselves from this absolutist syndrome and adopt a "transitory" or dynamic epistemology which reflected changes in the substantive meaning of truth that emerged in the practices of life.[37] The guiding concept would be "relationism," the "non-evaluative insight" that within a particular period or historically situated "framework of thought" there was a basic interdependence of the elements of meaning. The real issue was the basis of particular judgments within that framework. The question, then, became which "social standpoint" promised "the best chance for reaching an optimum of truth" about that historical situation and provided an opportunity to become "masters of the situation."[38]

Mannheim believed that the very "crisis" of modernity promised opportunity, that from the pseudoproblem of relativism could come the truth of relationism and a kind of reflectiveness that was "comprehensive" and separated "the true from the untrue," that allowed evaluative claims, and that eliminated "false-consciousness." For Mannheim, there could be a pragmatic test of the most ethically valid attitude. It was one that called for more than merely compromise and adjustment but with which action could comply, that is, it escaped "ideological and utopian distortions."[39]

The second major section of the original edition of Mannheim's work was "The Prospects of a Science of Politics: The Relationship between Social Theory and Political Practice." For Mannheim, the problem of theory and practice was negligible in the aspects of life that had been routinized and encompassed by administrative structures. Politics, however, was a different matter. It was the residue of the "irrational" and the field of "emotion" where things were in constant flux and where observers were encased by proliferating partisan positions.

These even entailed different logics and different ideas of the relationship between theory and practice and heretofore had prevented the emergence of a science of politics—either a science of understanding or a science of control. "Is there a science of this becoming, a science of creative activity?"[40]

Mannheim's answer was, yes, right at the point at which such a science seemed most unlikely because of the contending images of science in party schools. A "turning point" was discernible that made "politics as a science for the first time possible," a "science of the whole" based on "political sociology" that involved "the possibility of an integration of many mutually complementary points of view into a comprehensive whole."[41] Such a science would discern the manner in which the elements of thought in a certain historical matrix were emerging in a sort of dynamic synthesis and how there might be a dimension of truth that is valid for all parties and objectively accorded with the historical situation. This was an attempt to find a compromise between Weber's image of irreconcilable partisan positions and Lukács's notion of totality. But who was in a position to practice this science? The "relatively classless stratum" of "socially unattached intelligentsia."[42]

This concept was not really an extrapolation of Mannheim's own situation, since his image of the intelligentsia was conceived as more closely tied to parties. It was a science directed toward practice, but it was also a science independent of practice. The kind of knowledge they would possess was the kind that would be produced in "universities" and "other institutions of higher learning" where the pursuit of this "advanced form of political science" would be conducted.[43] Thus for Mannheim there was a vision of a three-tiered arrangement whereby socially homogeneous but politically heterogeneous intellectuals, possessed of a university-based science of politics but bound to particular interests, would facilitate decisions in politics that mediated between conflicting parties and represented a kind of microcosm of the society. The argument was for the mediation, not the fusion, of theory and practice. There was still the persistent problem of politics intruding into science, and "the fact that sciences are cultivated in academic surroundings constitutes a danger in that the attitudes adequate to the understanding of an actual sector of human experience are suppressed in the contemplative atmosphere which prevails in academic institutions."[44] But in an age in which social relations were no longer a mystery and were in some measure predictable, it was possible to break away from "fatalism" through a science of politics that prepared the "road for political action."[45]

Mannheim's arguments, although in many respects sympathetically received, at least in terms of the significance of the issues raised, were, like those of Weber, ultimately congenial to only a few.[46] Much of the extensive response appeared in the theoretical journal of the Social Democrats, *Die Gesellschaft*, and focused on the implications for Marxism, that is, whether Mannheim rescued or distorted Marx. These arguments often failed to grasp precisely what he was saying—particularly with respect to the relationship between intellectuals and the science of politics. Hans Speier, for example, who had been Mannheim's first doctoral student and an active Social Democrat, believed that Mannheim's position was ultimately too "apolitical." The general concern evoked, however, was much broader. For most, on both the Left and Right, it was not sufficiently rationalistic and succumbed to a kind of relativism that could not really establish the authority of knowledge.

In response to Mannheim's essay on competition, Alfred Weber admitted that much knowledge was "relational" but insisted that there was a "sphere of thinking" and "a body of knowledge which is universally imposed on all humanity" as well as a shared "method" for obtaining it. Similarly, Sombart maintained that there was "a cultural science of universal validity" and that "values remain absolute and objective."[47] Although Curtius applauded Mannheim's emphasis in *Ideology and Utopia* on the problem and the role of the intelligentsia, he attacked his "imperialism of the specialized sciences" and his depreciation of the idea of philosophy as "queen of the sciences," as well as his surrender to "a variant of European nihilism" and "a recurring form of skepticism."[48] He later (in *The German Mind in Danger*, 1932) warned against Mannheim's ideas as a threat characteristic of Jewish thought which depreciated the state in favor of society.

Those who would be associated with the Frankfurt *Institut,* such as Horkheimer, Paul Tillich, and Herbert Marcuse, focused on Marxist issues, but they also stressed that, although truth might arise historically, it transcended history. Horkheimer maintained that the social rootedness of ideas "in no way affects the validity of science," and Marcuse argued that history pointed beyond itself and that "truth once discovered, *transcends* the sphere of ideology from which it emerged."[49] Arendt viewed the book in broader but similar terms. She asked why "it can so disturb philosophy" and suggested that its purpose was to reveal "the precariousness of modern spirituality." She believed that if Mannheim were correct, the existential ontological project of her teachers, Heidegger and Jaspers, would be rendered otiose, and she interpreted the book (without any concrete evidence) as "polemically directed" toward their work and their attempt to speak about freedom, authenticity, and the like as universal structures of the human condi-

tion. With the emphasis on the "ontic" and "essent," ontology and consciousness would be exposed as ideology and denied their "absolute
claims" about reality and, consequently, their authority in specific situations. What was implied was a "radical relativization and historiciza-
tion" which she could not accept. There was a realm of "existence"
beyond historical particulars about which "philosophy is perfectly capable of speaking" and which cannot be reduced to sociological analysis.[50]

Mannheim replied to the critics by insisting that sociology was required by the pluralistic conditions of the age. Much of the criticism, he
claimed, was grounded in the old prejudice against the specialized sciences, but he argued that sociology had both philosophical and political
implications without replacing either. Far from nihilistic, it reflected a
faith in the possibility of overcoming the crises of both theory and practice as well as that of the relationship between them. What it rejected, he
claimed, was the old metaphysics, while it was much more in tune with
new work in ontology such as that of Heidegger.[51]

Many of those who were involved in the debate about Mannheim's
work were among the émigrés to the United States—where the conversation and its tributaries continued. These included Arendt and her
first husband, Günther Anders, Horkheimer, Hans Jonas, Lederer,
Adolph Löwe, Marcuse, Franz Neumann, Otto Neurath, Alexander
von Schelting, Speier, Tillich, and Karl Wittfogel. After 1933 and the
emigration, however, the concern about the relativistic implications of
Mannheim's work was accentuated by intellectuals on both the Left and
Right who were increasingly sensitive to the issue of relativism. If taken
to its logical conclusions, they argued, his argument was self-defeating
and involved a vicious circle whereby the sociology of knowledge and
the judgments of the free-floating intellectuals were themselves historically limited.[52] This kind of argument, however, failed to grasp what
Mannheim was saying which was, first of all, that the traditional epistemological quest for extrascientific transcendental standards of validity was meaningless—and thus there was little point in seeking answers
to questions posed from this point of view. Second, and most important,
the real issue was the practical one of the relationship between science
and politics for which, as Weber had demonstrated, there was no philosophical or scientific solution. It was this concern about the authority of
knowledge that became the focus by the late 1930s.

Jászi and Lukács, although now intellectually and ideologically estranged, both turned against Mannheim as fostering relativism and
abetting irrationalism. Speier, in a long review of the 1936 English edition of *Ideology and Utopia*, broke sharply with his former teacher.
Speier, now influenced by Strauss at the New School, claimed, in this

reassessment of the book, that Mannheim created a situation in which "philosophy becomes impossible" and in which one could not rationally choose between Kant and a "party-boss" or between a "moral philosopher" and an "engineer." His arguments depreciating the possibility of transcendent truth, Speier, argued, reflected the "self-hatred of the intellectuals" and amounted to "obliterating the differences between philosophy and rhetoric."[53] By 1935, and his exile to England, Mannheim had himself lost hope in political solutions, and liberal politics, and turned toward an elimination of politics and the substitution of rational planning and pragmatic social engineering in the pursuit of democratic values.[54] This position, however, was just as distasteful both to individuals such as Horkheimer and Theodor Adorno and to Jászi. Jászi condemned Mannheim's *Man and Society in an Age of Reconstruction* as "not less totalitarian than the Bolsheviks or the Fascists" and as "making freedom a thoroughly vague and relativistic concept."[55]

Despite ideological differences, many during this period were drawn in various ways to the arguments of another thinker: Carl Schmitt. Schmitt, who lived until 1985, was a legal scholar and government adviser who eventually affiliated himself with National Socialism and did much to validate Hitler's regime.[56] His association with the Nazis would tend to suppress a recognition of his influence, but even as late as 1933, many were drawn into the orbit of his thought. These included Michels, Mannheim, and Walter Benjamin as well as a wide range of thinkers who eventually emigrated to the United States: Friedrich, Gurian, Strauss, Arendt, Marcuse, Horkheimer, Speier, Hans Morgenthau, Neumann, and Kirchheimer.

Schmitt was one of those who attended Weber's lectures, and he moved within his intellectual ambience and accepted much of his image of the modern age. There was, however, by no means unanimity among those who were disenchanted with modernity—Weber, for example, despite his historical pessimism, debated Spengler, and Schmitt hardly shared Weber's sympathy and hopes for parliamentary government. One thing that made Schmitt so attractive to so many was his persistent and articulate critiques of bourgeois liberalism, faith in science, and historical progress. In speaking to the crisis of politics and the crisis of political reflection, Schmitt endorsed Weber's image of the autonomy of science, but he went even further than Weber in seeking the autonomy of politics. What Schmitt believed must be preserved was the very idea of what he called, maybe without precedent, *"the political."* In a world in which politics as a distinct form of life was viewed as disintegrating, Schmitt invented the idea of the political much as Aristotle had invented the idea of the *polis.*

Like so many of the critics of the Weimar republic, Schmitt had a deep antipathy for parties and interest politics, which he saw as a threat to the state and social homogeneity. He sought to recapture a more essential sense of what was political, but unlike many in the academic elite, he did not stand aloof from political issues and from concrete political analysis. Even though he was primarily a professor of public law, much of his work was more closely tied to the emerging specialized social sciences than to traditional legalism. He had a continuing association with the liberal *Deutsche Hochschule für Politik* which opened in 1920 and emphasized the empirical study of politics. This school, with which individuals such as Neumann and Scheler were affiliated and which Americans such as Beard visited, probably came closer than any other institution in Germany to developing a notion of a science of politics as a distinct field in a world where jurisprudence and philosophy were the accepted modes of political analysis.[57]

Through much of his early life, Schmitt was a strong Catholic and worried about the impact of relativistic materialistic liberalism and socialist attacks on religion. Although he originally sought answers in normative neo-Kantian images of law, he turned increasingly toward an emphasis on the state and sovereignty during the postwar crises of the republic. For a number of years he was closely associated with the Catholic Center Party which, along with socialist and democratic forces, supported the Weimar Constitution and which he saw as more than just another vehicle of political interest. There can be little doubt that Schmitt was a consistent defender of the constitution, and he was allied with Preuss as well as being a supporter of Friedrich Ebert, a socialist and the first president. It is equally clear, however, that his focus was on the extraordinary measures, as opposed to regular laws, that were required to sustain the regime—on emergency powers and executive authority. He could hardly be construed as sympathetic to the basic principles of the constitution or with the conditions of the Versailles Treaty. Liberalism and pluralism were always an anathema, and he wished to replicate in some way the conditions of the traditional authoritative state. But at the same time he accepted the legitimacy of Weimar as the only practical hedge against the extremism that he saw as precipitating the revolution of 1918–19 and which continued on both the Left and Right.

His rise to prominence came while at the University of Bonn. In a series of early works including *Political Romanticism* (1919), *The Dictator* (1921), *Political Theology* (1922), and *The Crisis of Parliamentary Democracy* (1923), Schmitt challenged the culture, values, and institutions of liberalism and began to advance his idea of sovereign political leadership that would take temporary measures to preserve a constitution and represent the people as a whole. His concrete concern at this point was to ward off the claims of both communists and reactionary monarchists but also to seek political answers divorced from ideas of abstract right and the identification of the state with law and legal norms such as those advanced by liberal neo-Kantian jurists such as Hans Kelsen.

Bodin and Hobbes had recognized that sovereignty must be defined in terms of "who decides on the exception" which meant that it stood outside and above the normal order as does a miracle in the religious sphere. It was in times of political crisis and breaks in the routine that the nature and locus of sovereignty and state authority, or lack thereof, became most clear. Liberal theory fostered, at best, an image that corresponded to normal or basically nonpolitical times and failed to capture the essence of politics. What was most immediately at issue in Schmitt's analysis was Article 48 in the Weimar Constitution—to which he wished to attribute a more decisive executive authority (than did the formal legalists) in bringing about or restoring a true sense of the constitution.[58]

Schmitt argued that legal positivists and normativists, who believed that the state was identical with the constitution, and pluralists such as Gierke and Krabbe, who suggested that sovereignty was an atavistic residue of absolutism, had negated the very idea of the political. The loss of epistemological and ontological authority in philosophy was paralleled by a loss of any transcendent ground of political authority. It was necessary, Schmitt argued, to hark back to Catholic thinkers such as Maistre, Bonald, and Donoso Cortes who recognized the need for decision. Although these conservatives were sometimes viewed as romantic conservatives and reactionaries, the real romantics were the liberals and their idea of politics as "everlasting conversation."[59] Liberalism made democratic legitimacy impossible by its heterogeneous conception of the people and its fractioning of authority. Even Marx and Engels saw the need for decision and for dictatorship that expressed a general will. Schmitt's indictment of modernity was striking less in its particularity than in the manner in which it represented sentiments reflected by a number of theorists who would eventually come to reject any association with him.

Today nothing is more modern than the onslaught against the political. American financiers, industrial technicians, Marxist socialists, and anarchic-syndicalist revolutionaries unite in demanding that the biased rule of politics over unbiased economic management be done away with. There must no longer be political problems, only organizational-technical and economic-sociological tasks. The kind of economic-technological thinking that prevails today is no longer capable of perceiving a political idea. The modern state seems to have actually become what Max Weber envisioned: a huge industrial plant. Political ideas are generally recognized only when groups can be identified that have a plausible economic interest in turning them to their advantage. Whereas, on the one hand, the political vanishes into the economic or technical-organizational, on the other hand, the political dissolves into the everlasting discussion of cultural and philosophical-historical commonplaces. . . . The core of the political idea, the exacting moral decision, is evaded in both.[60]

Schmitt supported the presidency of Hindenburg, and the years from 1926 through 1928 constituted a period of relative stability. In this sense, his arguments were recommendations for preservation through system mechanisms. By the mid-1920s, however, he had largely turned away from his Catholic affiliations and pursued a "realist" mode of political analysis which he associated with Hobbes and Machiavelli. He gave a seminar at Bonn in political philosophy in 1925–26, and it was here that he developed his essay on "the concept of the political," the first version of which was presented to a largely socialist audience at the *Hochschule* in 1927 and published in the *Archiv* the same year. Schmitt argued that "the concept of the state presupposes the concept of the political" but that this becomes obscured through the pluralistic interpenetration of state and society and the attempt of liberalism to reduce the state to society. The former was defined, he insisted, by the relationship between "friend and enemy," just as morality was defined by the relationship between good and evil, and this applied to both domestic and international politics.[61] The task was to establish the "objective nature and autonomy of the political," and this required, among other things, not confusing economic and political categories and not conflating such concepts as enemies and competitors.[62]

His concern was in part about the political extremes that were developing, and his fear was that liberalism might allow parties to emerge that would negate the very basis of the constitutional order that permitted them. But in more general terms, what the theory of pluralism (from Gierke to Laski) did, based as it was on "liberal individualism," was to deny the sovereignty of the state by reducing it to other associations. It in effect, he claimed, denied the existence of the political. And the pluralist practice of party politics weakened the state and inhibited its ability to perform the functions of maintaining external security and internal order. One of Schmitt's claims that would resonate in the work of individuals such as Strauss and Morgenthau was the historical irreducibility of the state and its grounding in human nature, a point, he suggested, that was recognized by Machiavelli, Hobbes, and Hegel. All "genuine" political theories are based on the recognition of the problematical, "evil," self-seeking dimension of human being. He also argued that there could be no "world state," since the very concept of the state presupposes otherness. Despite the claims of natural law and individualistic liberalism, the "state and politics cannot be exterminated."[63]

In 1928, Schmitt accepted the Hugo Preuss chair at the Berlin School of Business Administration. This was the point at which Weimar fell into extreme economic and political problems, and Schmitt, noting the endemic weakness of parliament, began to urge the idea of the president as a neutral and flexible defender of the constitution. To favor a strong executive that could stand above party politics was not at the time in any clear way connected with the rise of the Nazi party, and it was defended by people such as Friedrich at Harvard. It was this argument, however, that drew him inexorably into the position of government adviser after 1930. In *Legality and Legitimacy* (1932) he stressed the necessity for parties to recognize the legitimacy of the constitution, but the work, which stressed the difference between formal legality and political legitimacy, was also read by many as a theoretical justification for presidential absolutism. This book and his defense of the presidency in the case of *Prussia vs the Reich* (involving Chancellor Papen's appointment of a Reich commissar over Prussia) tended to brand him as an apologist for the Right and began to lose him the support of some of those, such as Gurian and Kirchheimer, who had been most attached to his ideas.

Heller, for example, worried about Schmitt's increasingly amoral position and the threat of dictatorship, became his principal adversary in the battle over von Papen's seizure of the Social Democratic Prussian government in 1932.[64] But many of Heller's arguments were similar to those of Schmitt. Neither individual could accept the normative law theories of Kelsen which seemed to obscure political realities. For Heller, this analysis masked the interest of the bourgeoisie and lent strength to what he saw as the social anarchy of capitalism and the pluralism that destroyed the possibility of democratic homogeneity (*Politische Democratie und Soziale Homogenität*, 1928). Heller, like Neumann, sought a solution within the Weimar framework, but he believed that liberalism was as dangerous as the traditional theories of the state (*Die Krisis der Staatslehre*, 1926). Those involved in the *Hochschule* such as Ernst Frankel, Neumann's law partner, continued to support Schmitt as late as 1932. With Hitler's ascendancy as chancellor, however, things changed. Although Schmitt may have initially believed that Hitler would be contained by Hindenburg, Schmitt began to collaborate with the Nazis and provide the basis for legalizing the regime that was purging so many of his colleagues. Even though he did not embrace the Nazi ideology in any direct sense, ambition and concern for self-preservation moved him to become a theorist for the Third Reich. But, like Heidegger, who believed that he could be the philosopher of the new order and who personally urged Schmitt to join him in underwriting it, he found that the Nazi regime ultimately neither needed nor wanted philosophy and legal theory.[65]

What drew many on the Left to Schmitt's ideas, just as Schmitt was drawn to Marx and Lenin, was the imagery of the resolute sovereign and the idea of an exceptional moment of truth, the critique of materialism, and the view that liberal institutions were inherently illegitimate and did not constitute true democracy.[66] This alliance between the Left and Right in political theory would become a persistent feature of the discourse. It was not just the claim that totalitarianism in this particular case emerged from liberalism but that the former was philosophically inherent in the latter. Although Schmitt's notion of decision as a way to close the gap between theory and practice was not exactly the strategy of activist Social Democratic legal theorists such as Neumann and Kirchheimer, who took part in Schmitt's seminar in Berlin (1930–31), there was a common belief, following Mannheim, that the republic could in some way be reconstituted to make it a more genuine state.

These individuals took seriously Schmitt's claims about the failure of parliament, but they believed that party conflict could be overcome by Socialist politics and legal strategies that would facilitate synthesis along the lines envisioned by Mannheim.[67] Similarly Rudolf Hilferding, the Marxist Social Democratic theorist and editor of *Die Gesellschaft*, believed that the bourgeois state and parliament could be transformed into a vehicle of the proletariat. The relative autonomy of the state could, and should, be utilized, and thus he came to defend the republic and the idea of the state and "the political" as a basis of social change.[68] Kirchheimer found in his teacher Schmitt not only a method for applying legal analysis to politics but, more substantively, a way of criticizing both liberal and socialist (Bolshevik) practice yet vindicating socialist theory.

In a series of essays published in *Die Gesellschaft*, he developed a theory of democracy that, combining Marx and Schmitt, postulated a homogeneous society. For Kirchheimer, liberal democracy was not, any more than dictatorial Russian communism, a true state. His most famous essay, "Weimar—and What Then? An Analysis of a Constitution," was published in 1930. Beginning with a quotation from Rosa Luxemburg about the limitations of legislative reform that did not issue from a revolution, Kirchheimer argued that Weimar was a compromised republic which did not carry forward the principles of 1918. Formal or political democracy was not real or social democracy. Countries such as the United States, he argued, tended to think of themselves as democratic because of a wide franchise, but this only concealed a "bour-geois dictatorship" rather than providing for the dictatorship of the proletariat and a new social order.[69] Majority rule was only meaningful when it virtually represented the will of a homogeneous community. Kirchheimer, following Schmitt, argued that Weimar was a constitution that "did not come to a decision"—that is, one that did not ratify the ascendancy of a social class. It represented the "serious lack of political decision-making capacity which marks the agony of our contemporary life"—it "stood for nothing and permitted everything."[70]

No work more represented the sense of crisis permeating the Weimar conversation than Jaspers's *Die geistige Situation der Zeit* (1931), but it also symbolized the distance between intellectual images and po-litical particularities. Jaspers noted that when the book was written he "had scarcely any knowledge of National Socialism" and was "shocked" by its success in the elections of 1930. Although the image of crisis would later be projected on Hitler's regime, it was in fact the pluralistic liberal culture and politics of Weimar that gave rise to it. There is no doubt that Jaspers was much taken with Weber's work, but the sim-ilarities with Schmitt cannot be ignored.[71]

For Jaspers, the problem of the modern age was an epochal crisis de-riving from human uprootedness and social disintegration, decline of authority, destruction of the natural world, the loss of faith in transcen-dence, relativism, historicism, positivism, irresoluteness, nihilism, the domination of technology and technique, rationalization, mechaniza-tion, bureaucracy, Marxism, sociology, and psychoanalysis. These were all productive of and consequent to the emergence of mass society and mass rule and a leveling of human existence marked by conformity in social and intellectual life. In this world, the individual and the human essence disappeared. Even "the races of man interbreed."[72] He claimed that Spengler and Walter Rathenau *(Zur Kritik der Zeit)* provided the "two most outstanding mirrors of our time."[73]

Although the basic solution required reaching back to the question of "human existence," the most immediate answer for Jaspers was for individuals to transcend the everyday "life-order" through the "State as expressive of the will towards the whole" and find a new home in a world in which they had become homeless. The power "politically in-corporated in the State," and in the necessary variety of states, was the medium through which individual "human beings can attain to a unity of will" and, with decisive leadership, achieve "safeguards against the mass-order"—"in a self-hood which enters into ties with others."[74] "To be able to think politically denotes the attainment of so high a level in the human scale that we can scarcely expect everyone to reach such a level," but it is the state upon which "all human life depends."[75] Ulti-mately, the salvation of the individual was to be found in education and the "life of the mind" and the pursuit of "Existence-philosophy." This required, however, a transcendence of the specialized sciences. Both here and in politics the search was for "heroic action" and "nobility." True science was "an aristocratic affair" destroyed by "mass-life at the universities." A different style was represented in the ideas of Kierkegaard and Nietzsche, as well as in the actions of resolute political leaders and those individuals who rose above themselves and confronted "Nothing-ness" while "safeguarding the fatherland" in the "Great War."[76]

Many of Jaspers's ideas resonated in the work of his friend and stu-dent Arendt, as well as in that of other émigrés such as Speier, but similar images characterized the arguments of Heidegger who was the most pervasively influential philosopher of the period. He and Jaspers had become friends by 1920, and despite philosophical differences, both sought a revolution in philosophy and a turn away from neo-Kantianism. Unlike Jaspers, however, Heidegger fell in with National Socialism as Rector of the University of Freiburg and joined the Nazi party in 1933—the same year he wrote to Schmitt inviting him to partic-ipate in intellectually underwriting the Third Reich—after Schmitt had sent him a copy of the "Concept of the Political."[77] By 1934, Heidegger and Schmitt were central figures at the reconstituted *Hochschule* (now under the Ministry of Propaganda) and influential in integrating its programs with the new regime. And the connection between the two individuals was more than practical. The affinities with respect to deci-sionism and a search for a fundamental ontology were apparent. The extensive controversy over the extent and implications of Heidegger's Nazi affiliation should not obscure the *fact* of his involvement.[78] He was much taken with the ideas of Spengler and Ernst Jünger, and although it is difficult to sort out the contentious issues that turn on the rela-tionship between his philosophy and his practical actions, what drew him to the Nazis was less any intrinsic relationship between his ideas and National Socialism than the search of the philosopher for social authority—or, in the case of Germany, the reconstitution of that au-thority and the reintegration of philosophy and the state.

Few of the émigrés may have been strictly Heideggerians in the man-ner exemplified by H.-G. Gadamer who remained in Germany. It has been noted that Gadamer's account of his own intellectual development appears to treat the years between 1933 and his accession to Jaspers's chair at Heidelberg, in 1949, as largely an irritating intrusion into his academic career. What the account may reflect is that while he refrained from political involvement, he made compromises to maintain his career.[79] It is too facile to assume that Gadamer's quietism, any more than Heidegger's collaboration, was the consequence of their rejection of traditional rationalism, but, as in the case of so many thinkers of this period, there was a kind of surrogate politics being played out in their philosophical arguments and in the interplay of concepts such as nihilism and resoluteness.

Although Heidegger's politics would lead many to depreciate their intellectual debt to him, his influence extended not only to those, such as Arendt, Marcuse, and Karl Löwith who studied directly and closely with him for several years and who, as with those who worked with Schmitt, found the break over nazism and the Jewish issue an agonizing one, but others such as Strauss who came to intellectual maturity in an intellectual atmosphere in which Heidegger's fame was unsurpassed. The dominant themes included: the critique of modernity (and the domination of technology and the growth of mass society), the attack on neo-Kantian doctrines, the reading of images of historical decline into liberal society—particularly in the United States, the fusing of history and philosophy and the project of deconstructing the Western tradition, the cult of antiquity and the return to Greek philosophy and the transcendental emphasis on heroic action and "the political" as exemplified in the polis, the hermeneutical emphasis on texts and language, the return to ontology, the celebration of the vocation of philosophy as standing above the specialized natural and social sciences, the antipathy toward pluralist politics and the support of the state, and the practical mission of *Wissenschaft* in joining the university and the people.[80]

One of the last outposts of the Weimar conversation was the group that came together at Frankfurt just prior to emigration.[81] Mannheim had been appointed to a chair at the university in 1930, and Tillich, the Christian socialist, had joined the philosophy department. Here Horkheimer, with the sponsorship of curator and classical philosopher Kurt Reizler, had assumed the directorship of the *Institut* which included Adorno, Friedrich Pollock, Leo Lowenthal, and Karl Wittfogel. In this circle, the main concern was, strangely, still not the imminent political catastrophe but the more abstract issue of cultural crisis and the crisis of rationality and the question of whether answers were to be found in a return to the Greeks, religion, Marxism, or sociology. Reizler, who had been the aide to wartime chancellor Bethmann Hollweg and had supported the idea of a new *Reich* over Europe, had pessimistically anticipated the "age à l'americaine" that he believed would be the cultural future.[82] Mannheim, stripped of his academic position, would soon be in England and the others, in the United States. Benjamin, hard at work on his own neo-Marxist critique of modernity and story of history as decay, moved to Paris where he remained until the city fell to the Nazis.[83] Failing in an attempt to cross the border into Spain, he died of an overdose of morphine. The character of the Weimar conversation as it entered the United States was in part determined by such accidents of history.

8

Coming to America

Who is Leo Strauss?
Charles Merriam

When Strauss received what he referred to as his "call" to the University of Chicago in 1948, he had been at the New School for Social Research for a decade. He had already begun to enlist the personal following and effect the change in the discourse of political theory that would distinguish him as the most influential émigré in the field. Morgenthau, who was already at Chicago, eased the path, and Hutchins, meeting Strauss after a summer lecture, in the absence of chairman Leonard White, offered him an appointment as full professor with the highest salary in the department.[1] Merriam was then emeritus but teaching the history of political theory.

For several years prior to emigration, after receiving his doctorate in philosophy at Hamburg (under Ernst Cassirer) in 1921 and pursuing subsequent studies pivoting around Hermann Cohen, Franz Rosenzweig, Husserl, and Heidegger, Strauss had worked at the Academy of Jewish Research in Berlin where he focused on a critique of Spinoza and on law and reason in medieval Jewish philosophy.[2] He had actively entered the Weimar conversation during his last year in Germany (1932), in the form of a reply, in the *Archiv,* to Schmitt's "Concept of the Political." Strauss accepted much of what Schmitt had to say about modernity and the irreducibility of the political. He suggested, however, that the critique of liberalism did not go far enough and that it failed to recognize that Hobbes was actually "a founder of liberalism" and the originator of the notion that the political was not natural.[3] Strauss presented early portions of his book on Hobbes to Schmitt who supported Strauss's application for the Rockefeller fellowship that sustained him in France and England during 1932–34. In this work, Strauss pursued the theme that Hobbes had turned away from classical political philosophy and its conception of the political as well as its concern with justice and paved the way for modern liberal society by reducing politics to an arrangement for protecting the pursuit of egoistic self-

175

interest. It may be true that the "time was ripe" for Strauss and that he came at the "right moment," when an interest in history and values was growing, but his exact position was as dimly understood in England, by such patrons as Barker, as it was during his early years in the United States. It is surely one of the ironies in the annals of the émigrés that Strauss, hardly typical of the individuals recruited by the New School for Social Research, came in 1938 on the basis of Laski's strong recommendation and subsidized by fees donated from the latter's American lecture tour.[4]

The story of the emigration is complex.[5] Heinrich Brüning, for example, the right-wing Weimar chancellor who preceded Hitler and fell victim to his own policy of rule by presidential decree, reappeared as an anomalous visitor in the Department of Government at Harvard. Although the issue of the relationship between public and academic discourse was part of the émigrés' former world, the advent of totalitarianism only accentuated their concern. While few had been active in mainstream politics, there were many political persuasions with which they were at least intellectually involved—such as Zionism and Marxism. Although some found aspects of American politics, such as the New Deal, to which they could in some way relate, Lowenthal spoke for many when he lamented that "what makes me so sad is that there aren't any real political movements with which I can identify."[6] But while many had been politically marginalized in Germany, it was, in the end, political action that, quite unexpectedly and in a manner which many could never quite comprehend or bring themselves to confront, turned on them.

The story of John Herz, who eventually came to teach political science at Howard University and the City University of New York, was in many ways typical. As a young man, he was deeply steeped in German cultural life at the gymnasium, and, as a university student, moved freely from one center to another, following Husserl, Jaspers, Nicolai Hartmann, and others while pursuing a varied humanistic curriculum with an academic career in mind. As for many, however, the study of law was ultimately a fail-safe—particularly for a Jew, and he became Kelsen's first doctoral student at Cologne. Since he felt totally assimilated and never really considered himself a member of a minority, the "purification" which purged both his father and himself from the court system came as a shock. Biding his time for two years as an assistant to a lawyer, who assured him that the Nazis would not last, he finally joined Kelsen in Geneva and studied international relations until he came to the United States in 1938 (as an assistant at the Institute for Advanced Studies at Princeton).[7]

While Herz's passage to the United States was by no means without difficulty and anxiety, it was hardly the stuff of high drama, and he was fortunate in his personal contacts and in keeping his family together. Henry Ehrmann's experience was distinctly different. He was a Social Democratic judge until dismissed in 1933 and arrested by the Gestapo and confined to a concentration camp. He managed to bribe his way out and escaped to France where he spent six years as a journalist before hiking over the Pyrenees a few weeks before the German invasion. He finally reached the United States via Portugal and, after working as a military specialist and on prison reform, began a teaching career in comparative politics that took him from the New School to Columbia, Berkeley, and eventually Dartmouth.[8]

Many refused to believe that someone such as Hitler could appear, let alone last, in Germany or to believe that the culture was inherently anti-Semitic. Lowenthal, like Neumann, clung to the belief that Hitler was an anomaly and that Germany was the least anti-Semitic country in Europe. Speier, like many enthusiastic Social Democrats, believed, at best, that the proletariat would rise up in a general strike and that, at worst, Hitler would drop the Jewish issue once he had gained political ascendance. When they did confront the matter, many spent much of their life seeking some philosophical, world-historical, or unitary sociological explanation. Arendt, years later, commenting on Eichmann, would speak of the "banality of evil," but few, including herself, treated totalitarianism as anything less than the culmination of modernity.[9]

Although it is impossible to understand adequately the émigré perspective, either individually or collectively, without examining the imprint of Weimar, many of these individuals were quite young (often in their early thirties) when they reached the United States. Maybe without exception, their most noted and defining work and influence was in this country. Their ideas were fundamentally shaped by their image of political life in the United States and by the ideational and institutional academic context. Whatever functional continuity there may have been with their vocational lives in Europe, it was only in the United States that they became political theorists. In a 1964 television interview, Arendt said, "I am not a philosopher. My profession—if it can be called that—is political theory. I have bid philosophy my final farewell."[10] It was not simply a matter of words but of their professional identity and its relationship to politics. The difficulty, however, was that this identity carried with it no clear image of the relationship.

Although many did not for some time, if ever, gain a very clear grasp of the past and present of American political culture, this did not necessarily inhibit them from creative insights, any more than it had

Toqueville or Lieber before them. And this image of the visitor was appealing as a rationalization of their intellectual and sociological status. Arendt, for example, stressed that "outsiders and spectators gain a sharper and deeper insight into the actual meaning of what happens . . . than would be possible for the actual actors. . . . It is quite possible to understand and reflect about politics without being a so-called political animal." And she wrote to Jaspers that she was "more than ever of the opinion that a decent human existence is possible today only on the fringes of society."[11] Even though in many ways they valued American democracy, both in the university and society at large, many continued to share much of the spirit of the German professoriate, and this included the general disdain for everyday politics and politicians. Lowenthal's claim that "politics" and the "revolution" abandoned them, rather than vice versa, was not an atypical response to the perception that theory often seemed only vaguely related to actual practice.[12]

The negative attitudes toward Weimar and the attending image of politics was projected on the United States. The lack of structure and authority, the tendencies toward mass politics, and the materialism, pluralism, acquisitiveness, and egalitarianism of bourgeois society were not generally congenial. Weimar represented the threshold of totalitarianism and became the symbol of what was wrong with modernity, and that symbol often informed their conception of liberal democracy in America. Much like John Heartfield's artistic image of German history as a natural metamorphosis from the larva of Ebert to the chrysalis of Hindenburg to the moth of Hitler, they saw historical decline rather than natural progress in political ontogeny.[13] Although Arendt would resist any facile identification of liberalism with totalitarianism, she noted that "liberalism, the only ideology that ever tried to articulate and interpret the genuinely sound elements of free societies, has demonstrated its inability to resist totalitarianism so often that its failure may already be counted among the historical facts of our century."[14]

While many political theorists in the United States may have been critical of political processes and institutions, their perspective was reform—which, in the end, implied a validation of the values of liberal society. The basic problem was one of means and not ends—or, at most, it was a matter of realizing those ends. For many of the émigrés, on the other hand, there was, although in varying degrees, often an inherent antipathy toward both liberal politics and the very idea of liberalism. It was in part this attitude that had already distanced many from what was happening in existential politics in Germany. It was, for the most part, the liberals such as Kelsen and Brecht who, among the émigrés, had actually confronted the Nazis. What many of the émigrés, and particularly those most influential in reorienting the conversation in political theory, brought to America, then, was a critique which struck directly at the informing values and assumptions of American political science and political theory. America, with its emphasis on technology and science, represented the embodiment of historical fallenness.

Liberal society was an island of safety from totalitarianism and maybe the best practical hope in the contemporary world, but, seen through the lens of Weimar, it seemed, if not inherently flawed, at best tenuous and in need of some root and branch reconstruction. The emphasis was on: the genetic limitations of liberalism; the idea that liberalism in some manner, either through institutional decline or inherent defect, spawned totalitarianism; an image of science as a threat to humanism and the dangers of scientism and scientific specialization in social inquiry; historical pessimism and the demand for a deconstructive approach to the history of thought; and the search for transcendental grounds of political and moral judgment which would combat the philosophical relativism that was understood as the intellectual counterpart of the practice of liberal politics.

The New School for Social Research, founded in 1918, was in part the project of such intellectuals as Herbert Croly associated with the *New Republic,* and it became a home for a number of academic dissidents such as Beard and Thorstein Veblen. The school was reorganized in 1923 under Alvin Johnson who, in 1927, was also appointed by the SSRC as associate editor of the *Encyclopaedia of the Social Sciences (ESS).* Johnson was a graduate of the School of Political Science at Columbia and was generally influenced by individuals such as Dewey. When many of the Jewish and socialist contributors to the *ESS,* whom he had enlisted in Europe, were expelled from their university positions, he created the University in Exile which eventually became the Graduate Faculty of the New School in 1935—under a governing committee which included Dewey, Felix Frankfurter, Hutchins, and Oliver Wendell Holmes.

Johnson came from a populist Nebraska background, and although he enlisted in the Spanish-American War, his propensities were pacifist. The story of his career indicates how the atmosphere at Columbia, where he came to study economics in 1898 and which was dominated by Burgess's imperialism, Giddings's anti-Semitism, Dunning's aloofness, and the like, could have spawned the generation of Beard and Merriam. Part of the answer was, of course, the liberal historical economics of Seligman and other such voices, but even the fact of their presence testified to the degree to which Burgess had been committed to academic freedom. After teaching at Bryn Mawr and Columbia and

working with Beard on the *PSQ*, Johnson was urged by President Butler to remain (and at the same time warned by Butler that as a radical he
would not be hired back to a conservative institution). He left in 1906,
however, for a series of jobs at Texas, Chicago, and Stanford before finally returning to New York to join Croly at the *New Republic*. Croly
eventually saw the New School as too academic, but for Johnson it represented the possibility of an institution that could be "honestly free"
and dedicated to the "education of the educated" in order to free them
from "dominant opinion," through the work of a "true galaxy of liberal
professors."[15]

The main idea behind the *ESS* was not only to help integrate and
strengthen social science but to give it "a voice on practical issues." It
was, in effect, a continuation of the Columbia vision. Johnson and
Seligman, the editor and his mentor, made frequent trips abroad seeking contributors and, while noting the continual disintegration after
World War I, became well acquainted with European academics and impressed with those who drew their inspiration from Weber—"the most
creative thinker of our time."[16] Johnson began the process of facilitat-
ing the emigration with the aid of Lederer, the socialist professor of
economics at the University of Heidelberg. Lederer, an Austrian, who
held degrees in jurisprudence and political studies from Vienna and
Munich respectively and who had been coeditor (with Sombart) of the
Archiv, had been instrumental in coordinating the work on the *ESS*.
Convinced that Hitler would gain control, he emigrated in 1932 and
became the first dean of the Graduate Faculty.

The journal *Social Research* began publication at the New School in
1934. Johnson noted that it was a product of "spontaneous growth"
which served as an outlet for the great body of thought that was being
created by the refugee scholars. He suggested that what was "striving
for expression in the collective mind of continental scholars" was a "new
kind of thinking." The "methods employed are obviously continental,"
and the journal was the sign of a "coming intellectual movement."[17] Although some of the themes that would characterize this "movement"
were apparent from the beginning,[18] the work of the individuals who
would be most influential in the revolution in political theory was not
yet prominent. Johnson received generous and crucial financial support from the industrialist Hiram Halle, and during the next decade,
there were 178 appointments. One of Johnson's goals was to bring this
group of intellectuals to bear on American academia—and on American public life—and he attempted to find people who had practical as
well as scholarly experience. His image of the European university was
once more one in which "philosophy extending to state and society" lay
at the center, and it was this that he wished to bring to America.[19]

Some universities, such as Columbia under the leadership of Dewey, also created organizations to help, at least temporarily, refugee scholars. The Emergency Committee in Aid of Displaced German (later, Foreign) Scholars was created in 1933, but the efforts were largely confined to well-established middle-aged individuals. The Rockefeller Foundation had, for a number of years, supported a program that brought European scholars to the United States for study, and it also participated in the rescue mission. However, the foundation's efforts were somewhat inhibited, because it was worried about Jewish quotas in American universities and about the saturation of academia with Jewish scholars. Also the purpose of the program had not been to Germanize scholarship in the United States but to Americanize the German university and support empirical work which it conceived as related to the American style of social research—and democracy.

Although a few American social scientists who were contemporaries of the younger émigrés had studied in Europe, notably Talcott Parsons (Heidelberg), who had worked with Lederer and had Alfred Weber and Jaspers on his doctoral committee, *most of those who would dominate political science during the next three decades were the first generation innocent of a European education just as those who came to oppose mainstream political science were either émigrés or heavily influenced by their ideas.*[20] What the emigrants brought to the United States was a new literature and a new set of ideas associated with such thinkers as Weber and Mannheim, and, given the issues of the day, political science and political theory were among the areas most immediately affected. While many were, at best, ambivalent about American liberalism and empiricism, some accommodated quite easily to the American intellectual and political context. Others found it profoundly disquieting. Often, however, the problems were as much matters of personal style and sociocultural accommodation as issues involving ideology and philosophy.

Many, as Jews (or, like Hans Speier, spouses of Jews), socialists, and dislocated intellectuals, had been less than entirely at home in their own land and had already embarked on a version of what many of those who remained in Germany called the "inner emigration." Coming to America was a further psychological and sociological rupture. In an extended and poignant reflection, Adorno spoke for more than himself when he noted that "every intellectual in emigration is, without exception, mutilated" and "lives in an environment that must remain incomprehensible to him"—where "his language has been expropriated, and the historical dimension that nourished his knowledge, sapped."[21] Speier, one of the early group to come to the New School in 1933, wrote a somewhat abstract essay some years later dealing with the "Social Condition of the Intellectual Exile" from Seneca to the present. He was not very specific about himself and his peers, but the reference could hardly go unnoticed when he spoke of the dilemma faced by so many between "empty fatigue and moribund preoccupation with cemeteries" or the "hectic activities untouched by any awareness that their context has changed."[22] Speier had managed to integrate with relative ease, but even so it meant changes in professional identity. As for so many who went to work for the United States government during the war, and organizations such as the Rand Corporation in the context of the 1950s, it involved suppressing earlier socialist affiliations and criticisms of liberalism and capitalism.[23]

There was a great deal of ambivalence about the United States. It was one of the allied nations that many believed could have prevented the rise of Hitler if the peace settlement had been more just. On the one hand, it provided shelter and acceptance that was less available in, for example, France where there was considerable hostility to those on the Left, but, on the other hand, anti-Semitism was often quite visible. Emigration meant for many, at least initially, a loss of status, and it involved for most a struggle to speak, write, and think in a new language. As Arendt noted, they did not "like to be called 'refugees,'" with all the loss of autonomy that the term implied, since they had "committed no acts and most of us never dreamt of having any radical political opinion."[24]

Despite all the elements of culture shock, many found positions to which they could never have aspired in Germany. As Morgenthau noted, "I would never have been able to establish myself as a scholar were it not for the opportunity offered me by the United States."[25] In the end, however, there was a distinct sense in which the émigrés felt that "going to America was itself an admission of defeat," and "being an exile is not a matter of needing a passport; it is a state of mind." Some assiduously sought assimilation while others, such as Arendt, "made a fetish of the exile condition" and distanced themselves from bourgeois life. America was also a bewildering place. Not only was the society so pluralistic that it was difficult to identify or categorize, but even individuals embraced a variety of, seemingly incompatible, beliefs and values that puzzled those who had lived in a more ideologically and culturally vertically integrated world. There was great nostalgia for many of the more minor aspects of European culture, but there was also a great deal of concern about the lack of structure, the failure to valorize elites, the "general permissiveness," and pure tolerance which all seemed to signal danger—even for the survival of liberalism itself. Arendt was disturbed by the "country's fundamental anti-intellectualism" and puzzled by the paradoxical "coexistence of political freedom and social oppression."[26]

For scholars such as the sociologist Paul Lazarsfeld, who had such a profound impact on political science and the application of survey research, assimilation was in many respects relatively easy. He came to the United States from Austria under Rockefeller auspices in 1933 but elected to stay after the German occupation. With his interests in empirical research, he had found himself uneasy in a European atmosphere "dominated by philosophical and speculative minds." He understood himself as a "positivist" who "became a connecting cog" to American social science.[27] Maybe largely because of uneasiness about anti-Semitism in the United States, Lazarsfeld was socially not quite as comfortable as he was methodologically. Politically, however, he was a socialist activist, and the New Deal was appealing.

The Austrians, as a group, assimilated easily. Some, such as Erich Hula (at the New School) and Voegelin, had previously spent time in the United States as Rockefeller Fellows and could already identify themselves as political scientists. But there was a general intellectual orientation that facilitated integration in the case of such individuals as Lazarsfeld, Kelsen, Hula, Felix Kaufmann, and Alfred Schütz. Although not a political scientist, Joseph Schumpeter's 1941 work on *Capitalism, Socialism, and Democracy,* which suggested that democracy involved less any particular set of substantive values or ends than a kind of political method, not only reinforced the image emerging in political science during the late 1930s but became an explicit rationale for mainstream political science's account of democracy in the 1950s. Schumpeter, whose fellow students at Vienna included Lederer and Hilferding, came to Harvard in 1932. Among other scholars from Vienna, such as Friedrich von Hayek, Ludwig von Mises, and Karl Popper, the orientation tended to be liberal, antinationalist, anti-natural-law, individualist, and empiricist. With respect to political science, the key figure emerging from the heritage of the Viennese enlightenment was Kelsen.[28]

A Jew, born in Prague, he wrote his dissertation at Vienna on Dante's *De Monarchia* and became an influential and popular professor of state and administrative law as well as a prominent figure in the postmonarchal Austrian state, where he played a major role in drafting the 1920 constitution. His legal positivism, substantively, stressed the identity of law and the state and struck out against natural law, abstract notions of justice, and the traditional *Staatslehre.* As a method, it emphasized the separation of a scientific analytical description of systems of legal facts and norms from values and ideology. He was a committed liberal democrat but steadfastly clung to the view that democracy was intellectually best supported by relativism rather than value absolutism.[29]

By the late 1920s, both Kelsen and the constitutional state were un-

der attack, and in 1930, fearing a fascist takeover, he took a position at
Cologne—only to be proscribed in 1933 while lecturing in Holland.
Practicing his commitment to the separation of fact and value, he had
actively participated in recruiting Schmitt, at a higher salary than his
own, respecting the latter's ability even though he did not care for him
personally, intellectually, or politically. The generosity was not recipro-
cated, and Kelsen moved to the Rockefeller-supported Institute of International Relations in Geneva. Hula, Kelsen's assistant from Vienna,
stayed on to work for Schmitt, while living in Kelsen's house, until the
political situation became too tense. Schmitt was friendly but jested that
"we don't need any Austrians now." After stays in Switzerland, France,
and England, Hula accepted, in 1938, an invitation from Johnson, extended four years earlier on the recommendation of Kelsen. Kelsen
continued his work for seven years in Geneva before coming to Harvard, where he spent two years, before settling on a permanent post at
Berkeley in 1942.

The career of Karl Deutsch was another case of successful integration. A German Jew who had attended the German University of
Prague, where his studies were interrupted by conflict with pro-Nazi
groups, he spent a period in England studying optics and mathematics
before taking a degree in law (at the Czech National University) and, in
the same year (1938), emigrating to the United States where he served
in the military. He did his graduate work in political science at Harvard
where he received a doctorate in 1951 and, teaching at MIT, Yale, and
Harvard, became one of the leaders in postwar American political science and the use of quantitative approaches.

For others, however, the transition was more difficult. Maybe the
paradigm case was Adorno who entered the United States in 1938 after
a period at Oxford. Although associated with the transplanted Institute
for Social Research at Columbia, he initially came with an invitation to
become musical director of the Rockefeller-sponsored Princeton Radio
Research Project which was headed by Lazarsfeld and devoted to the
study of the effects of radio on American society. Although he was interested in studying trends toward conformism and mass society, his Marxist orientation and emphasis on the critique of culture were not easily
adapted to a project largely underwritten by and shaped by the mass
media industry. Although it might be an exaggeration to claim that
"Adorno's disdain for American culture bordered on the pathological,"
neither American society nor social science were ultimately compatible
with his disposition.[30] It is something of an irony that both he and the
Nazis came to conclude that American jazz was decadent. His estrange-

ment was probably rooted less in his philosophical and political perspective than in his elitist intellectual attitude, but, whatever the basis, he represented the extreme in émigré alienation.

He was perplexed by what he perceived in American social science as the "demand to 'measure culture,'" since "the direction prescribed for my development" had hitherto been one in which it was "my fitting and objectively preferred assignment to *interpret* phenomena—not ascertain, sift, and classify facts and make them available as information."[31] Although he may have eventually developed some appreciation for "empiricism," he believed that "the full scope of experience is fettered by empirical rules excluding anything that is inherent in the concept of direct life experience."[32] These perceptions, however, cut both ways. Robert Merton, referring to Lowenthal, noted that "the German style of social philosophical thinking is not compatible with American methodology."[33] Adorno admitted, somewhat grudgingly, to being impressed by the manner in which democracy was a way of life in the United States, particularly in the university, and he believed that there was in England and the United States a strong indigenous power of resistance to illiberal forces. Yet he was quick to emphasize that he did "not mean to say that America is entirely immune from the danger of an upset in the direction of totalitarian domination. Such a danger is inherent in the trend of modern society per se," of which the United States was in many respects the exemplification.[34]

The émigrés, then, were hardly intellectually monolithic, yet there was a striking uniformity across a broad spectrum of the émigré experience and perspective that was in sharp conflict with the values of American social science. Few were able to break fully with perceptions of scholarship and politics formed in Germany. The personal, political, and intellectual tensions that divided individuals in Europe were perpetuated in exile and exacerbated the divide that separated them from Americans. Some could not immediately, or ever, secure academic posts, and those that did often could not find exact vocational parallels in the structure of American academia. There is the often related story of how Morgenthau, interviewed by a woman in an agency for helping the flood of displaced scholars, was urged to take a job as an elevator operator.[35] For most who had established themselves academically, the opportunities were not quite so restricted. Lowenthal, for example, originally a professor of comparative literature specializing in the Elizabethan period, redefined himself as a sociologist. Political theory, and even political science, was not a familiar vocational category. Except possibly for some of those associated with the *Hochschule* such as Franz

Neumann and Sigmund Neumann, the idea of political science as it had evolved in the United States was strange to those for whom political studies still meant primarily *Staatswissenschaften* and *Staatsrechtlehre*.

Had the republic survived, Franz Neumann would probably have been a politically prominent figure. Upon his expulsion in 1933, he went to England and studied with Laski before coming to the United States, with the help of the Emergency Committee, in 1936 and, on the basis of Laski's recommendation, joining the Frankfurt group at Columbia. The political climate of the New Deal was congenial, and he served with the OSS and the State Department during the war before returning to Columbia where he was an important academic figure in the 1940s. Shortly before his death in an automobile accident in 1954, he reflected on the plight of the émigré in America. He noted that "the German exile, bred in the veneration of theory and history, and contempt for empiricism and pragmatism, entered a diametrically opposed intellectual climate: optimistic, empirically oriented, a-historical, but also self-righteous." He believed that the exiles had brought to the United States a "note of skepticism" and a "theoretical framework" but that the general mood which they confronted was one in which the emphasis on the collection of empirical data threatened to destroy theory and create a disdain for history as well as subvert a critical attitude by a dependence on funding sources that rendered the scholar a social functionary.[36]

This image reflected his view of what had happened in Germany during the last quarter of the nineteenth century. There, he claimed, the university had given up authentic political science and had become basically the training ground of "functionaries" rather than "reformers." By the 1950s, he worried about a repetition of this syndrome in the United States. Neumann's image of the proper role of the scholar was that of the "critical conscience of society," but this role was in danger in the modern age. The basic problem of modernity was, he suggested, the reconciliation of freedom and coercion, and "this fundamental ambiguity of modern political theory is manifested in the ambiguous position of the intellectual."[37] His own personal ambiguity was reflected in this assessment. Although he claimed that "a conformist political theory is not theory" and saw political theory as an instrument in the struggle for social change, he never found it possible, despite his unhappiness with the Cold War and McCarthy period in the United States, to play either a critical or activist role in his new home.[38]

The explanations for what had happened in Germany were diverse, but intellectuals often found intellectual answers. Ehrmann, for example, argued that the republic was undermined, and totalitarianism

fostered, by the Spenglerian mood that dominated secondary education. For some of the émigrés such as Neumann and Brecht, who had
worked within the framework of Weimar, however, there was a tendency to look for more concrete causes of the failure of the republic.
Neumann began *Behemoth* while he was at the Institute. It advanced the
thesis that Nazi Germany was not a real state and legal system at all and
that National Socialism was simply a negative movement that could not
be related to Hegel or to relativism, positivism, or any coherent set of
ideas—it simply lacked any "rational political philosophy."[39] Weimar
fell because its pluralism was not based on an underlying community of
values. Out of group conflict came mutual neutralization and a vacuum
of power filled by the state bureaucracy and the executive, and an elite
politics based on decisionism that arose with the support of the masses
and was sustained by a monopolistic economy and racial imperialism.

Although the New School was hardly part of the mainstream of the
American academy, the émigrés responded to the new environment
and almost immediately began to influence it. Lectures and interdisciplinary seminars, on fascism as well as on the methodology of the
social sciences, drew an audience of New York academics—including
individuals such as Merriam's student Gabriel Almond who was teaching at Brooklyn College. Here began the process through which "American social theory emerged deprovincialized," but the transformation
was mutual.[40] The democratic socialists, such as Lederer and his former student Speier, led the critique of Weimar at the New School. For
many Americans, it was a paradoxical argument—that totalitarianism
was somehow the product of democratization. It was not simply, as the
émigré historian Hans Kohn would argue, that it was the result of the
eventual consequence of the historical failure of liberalism in Germany,[41] but rather that there was something internally problematic
about liberal society and its pluralistic and egalitarian character which
made the fate of Weimar a warning to the West.[42]

Speier, the youngest of Johnson's recruits, picked up on Lederer's
earlier concern about the middle class's loss of status and alienation
from the republic and its susceptibility to nazism. He pushed the idea
that totalitarianism grew out of social disintegration and the emergence
of mass society which was a perversion of democracy.[43] Some, such as
Hans Staudinger, who had been an administrative and elected official
in the republic and had succeeded Lederer as dean of the New School,
put less emphasis on the sociology of the Nazi success and more on its
ideological effectiveness. But the more general vision that emerged was
one of totalitarianism resulting from liberal decay.

The general seminar at the New School in the early years focused on the issue of fascism and the differences between Weimar and the United States. The emphasis tended to be on the deficiencies of the institutions of the former, and many believed that totalitarianism was the result of excessive majoritarianism as well as of inequities in the parliamentary system. It was caused by the breakdown of social structures resulting in growing atomism and mass politics and a kind of perversion of liberal democratic politics in which leadership and structure broke down. In 1941, the Study Group on Germany was formed, consisting of Hula, economist Eduard Heimann, philosophers Horace Kallen (who along with Beard and Robinson had been one of the early permanent faculty), Strauss, Kaufmann, Riezler, and sociologists Karl Mayer and Albert Salomon. The emphasis continued to be on the crisis of European liberalism and the triumph of illiberalism in Germany both in the late 1800s and early 1900s. Some such as Kaufmann were reluctant to see nazism as the heritage of German philosophy while Kallen, much like Dewey, emphasized the contrast with the Anglo-American liberal model.

Brecht was a political actor who participated in the final days of Weimar before being driven into geographical and vocational exile. He was a Prussian and Lutheran who had attended the University of Berlin and subsequently trained for the law and accepted a judgeship at Lübeck. In 1910, he began work with the Department of Justice in Berlin where he remained in various capacities until he joined the staff of the Chancellery in 1918 and later the Ministry of the Interior in 1921. In these posts, he saw, and participated in, the major events of the postwar period from the birth of Weimar to the rise of the antidemocratic forces. He was dismissed from federal office in 1926 whereupon he became a Prussian delegate to the Reichsrat. When Hitler was appointed Chancellor in 1933, his first official appearance was, as tradition demanded, before that body.

Following Hitler's speech, Brecht, as the delegate from Prussia, was expected to respond. He in effect challenged Hitler by lecturing him on the need to work within the structure of the constitution. This was the last free speech in the Reichsrat. Brecht was attacked by the National Socialist press, and, along with the Prussian ministers, he was "retired" from official duties. Eventually publicly charged by Goebbels with embezzlement and put under surveillance and temporary arrest, he met discreetly with Speier who passed to him an invitation from Johnson to come to the New School. "Thus, on November 9, 1933, in my fiftieth year, we left Germany on a boat called 'Germany.' We scattered flowers on the North Sea, a symbol that we would return."[44]

Brecht did return from time to time during the 1930s. He was ambivalent about leaving Germany initially and reluctant to make a final break. He was worried about participating in the public discussions about nazism at the New School, "since he alone of the group had not broken with Germany" and it would be financially difficult and "unsafe" for him to participate as well as "personally painful besides to hear the government of one's country attacked." Johnson was impatient about his indecision and stressed that the school was created as a "protest against German policy" and "maintained solely as such a protest," and thus his equivocal position would undermine the project. And Brecht finally concluded that, even as an Aryan, he could no longer "function" in Germany.[45] His last prewar visit, in 1939, was to aid his sister and her Jewish husband, but before he could reach them, they committed suicide. Although Brecht and his wife continued, during all their American years, to live simply in New York hotel rooms, bereft of their former belongings, he, at least by his own understanding, integrated easily into American culture.

He found himself in the New School—and the profession of political science—"exalted by a community of fate and by shared, constructive work." He had left politics as well as Germany and now, "half-German, half-American," committed himself, with Weberian sentiment, "body and soul, to science, and the proper discharge of this commitment commanded the undivided man. This was incompatible with an active political life."[46] Brecht noted that while many of his "academic colleagues were more or less frustrated practicians," he, "the practician, longed for theory" and threw himself into the world of academic scholarship (which he referred to as "science") and the study of political theory and the history of political ideas.[47]

There was a great contrast between Brecht and the members of the Frankfurt school. Although critical theory, or the work of those individuals associated with the Institute for Social Research, would not be fully visible in the conversation of political theory for many years, it was nevertheless part of the ambience that surrounded the transformations of the 1940s and 1950s. Like many of the émigrés, critical theorists contributed to an interpretation of American liberalism and pragmatism cast in their image of Weimar European positivism. There are few greater ironies of this period than the fact that this group of German philosophical Marxists, partially subsidized by an Argentinean grain merchant and sustained by stock market investments, left the University of Frankfurt and found a home at Columbia under the sponsorship of President Butler. They self-consciously "built there an island of German radical intellectuals" who were "upper class Jews."[48] The invitation had been arranged through the offices of individuals such as the sociologist Robert Lynd, but the group was careful to keep its intellectual character obscure to its host.

One of the most distinguishing characteristics of the Institute was that while the notion of critical theory called, in principle, for political engagement, the commitment was always more to theory than to politics. They were men ultimately "undivided" but intellectually unreconciled to their choice of pure "science." Although Horkheimer, the intellectual and organizational leader of the group, claimed that they were bound together in the "belief that formulating the negative in the epoch of transition was more meaningful than academic careers,"[49] such careers in fact dominated—and when they did not, it was because they, unlike most of those at the New School, could financially afford to do otherwise.

They were opponents of Weimar who viewed it as part of a transition to socialism and who had not accurately perceived the extent of the Nazi threat. Even in Germany, they had remained aloof from practical politics, and in the United States their philosophical claims, for the most part, rarely either reflected or responded to the particularities and peculiarities of political life. They continued in America to live in a bourgeois style while pursuing an unrelenting attack on bourgeois society—or at least a philosophical image of it. Lowenthal, bridling at the common suggestion that they should have been closer to the oppressed, argued that, after all, Marx's aim was to abolish the proletariat. "Luxury is not an evil," since "enjoyment leads to a higher degree of differentiation" and theoretical reflection.[50]

When the *Institut* was shut down in 1933, it moved, after a year in Geneva (with Horkheimer and Marcuse) to Columbia where it continued to publish its journal *(Zeitschrift für Sozialforschung)* in German and otherwise conceal the intellectual position while maintaining the European orientation. Although the journal was discontinued in 1942 (due largely to bad investments), it was published in English *(Studies in Philosophy and Social Science)* the previous two years as the group took a more permanent stand in the United States. They proclaimed, at this point, a "desire to devote our work—even in its external form—to American social life," since "America, especially the United States is the only continent in which the continuation of scientific life is possible. Within the framework of this country's democratic institutions, culture still enjoys freedom."[51] Except for Adorno, the others (including Horkheimer, Marcuse, Lowenthal, Pollock, and Kirchheimer) took steps toward naturalization, and during the war many went into government service where some, such as Marcuse and Neumann, remained until the 1950s. This interlude was surely one of the most ironic chapters in an ironic story: "a cadre of the most outstanding Marxist scholars of the European emigration forged a tactical alliance with the executive wing of the U.S. government."[52] Here, as Herz, another recruit to the intelligence service, put it, the "Hegelian *Weltgeist* found its temporary abode."[53]

Lowenthal went to work for the Domestic Media Department of the Office of War Information and, later, the Bureau of Overseas Intelligence. Neumann, Marcuse, and Kirchheimer were among a large number of prominent émigré academics (including historians Felix Gilbert and Hajo Holborn) who (with the aid of the American Council of Learned Societies, the SSRC, and the Library of Congress) were recruited to the Central European Section of the Research and Analysis branch of the OSS (later the CIA). Although they had some sense of efficacy (Marcuse, for example, drafted the order that formally abolished the Nazi party) and although they attempted to apply their theories about totalitarianism, the government failed to utilize their knowledge very fully, and most were disappointed with the results of their efforts. The experience probably, in many cases, heightened their moralism and concern with practice, but most eventually drifted back into the isolation of the university.

Although the formal headquarters of the Institute remained in New York, Horkheimer (partly for reasons of health) and Adorno moved to Pacific Palisades in California in the early 1940s where, with the support of the American Jewish Committee, they began their critique of American mass culture. The approach was still informed by the idea that totalitarianism was ultimately the working out of the inherent logic of liberalism and the ideas of the Enlightenment. In their view, Dewey and American pragmatists were positivists, and although positivism was not the cause of fascism, its surrender to the "facts" was destined to confirm any existing order and disable critical thought.[54] The series on *Studies in Prejudice* included the five-year project headed by Adorno which culminated in the famous study of the *Authoritarian Personality* (1950). Although Marcuse remained in the United States (first with the State Department and then at Brandeis, 1954–65), Horkheimer and Adorno returned to Frankfurt in 1949. Lowenthal became research director of the Voice of America (1949–53) before joining the sociology department at the University of California, Berkeley, in 1955. Neumann and Kirchheimer returned to Columbia.

The story of Schütz and his work, which also eventually found its way into the story of political theory in the United States, was distinctly different. Despite predilections to the contrary, Schütz did not have a mainstream academic career—in part because his opportunities, as a

Jew, were limited in Austria. He worked in the world of finance, which he disliked, and scholarship remained his avocation. He studied with individuals in the liberal positivist Austrian school such as Kelsen and von Mises, but his work was ultimately grounded in the social action theory of Weber and the philosophy of Husserl. Schütz came to the United States in 1939 after the Nazi occupation of Austria, but although affiliated with the New School, he worked on Wall Street while pursuing social philosophy. He found a great deal of intellectual overlap between his social theory and the American pragmatic tradition and social interactionist theory, which in turn found inspiration in his work.[55]

Schütz's phenomenological approach to social science, which focused on the understanding of subjective meaning on the part of social actors, conflicted with the dominant form of empiricism in American social science, but it was also resisted by the Frankfurt school. Horkheimer, Marcuse, and Adorno had come down hard on Mannheim and what they took to be his pragmatism and his universalization of false consciousness. His relativism smacked too much of the kind of decisionism that they associated with individuals such as Schmitt. In a somewhat similar way, which would be reflected in the work of such "critical theorists" as Jürgen Habermas, a generation later, they were unhappy with Schütz's *Lebensphilosophen*. They believed that it not only provided little in the way of purchase for a critique of society but even tended to suggest an acceptance of appearance as reality. Although they were critical of the implications and limitations of positivism, both as an attitude toward social phenomena and a mode of inquiry, they did not want to reduce social inquiry merely to understanding—to the exclusion of structural explanation and normative/critical claims based on transcendental grounds.

The positivist image of science that many of the émigré theorists struck out against in American social science was, ironically, less one generated in this country than one that they brought with them. And although the American and European images of science would begin to merge by the 1950s, as the logical positivist account of science gained hegemony both as an object of approbation and disapprobation, positivism was itself part of the migration of ideas. Although there was some increased awareness of the literature in the philosophy of science during the early 1930s, and works such as those of Poincaré and Duhem, this material was seldom in any way systematically encountered by American social scientists.

The philosophy of science was not an institutionalized form of scholarship before the mid-1930s, and it was not fully developed until the school of logical positivism emigrated to the United States. The 1934 entry (by Guido de Ruggiero) on "positivism" in the *ESS* defined it in terms of a general tradition of philosophical scientism extending from Bacon through Comte to such later philosophers and scientists as Mach. It was suggested that "in a broad sense Dewey might be considered a positivist in that he champions a scientific view of reality and extols that active experimentalism which has in modern times profoundly modified the attitude of the mind toward physical nature," but little attempt was made to link positivism to the American academy. Logical positivism was briefly discussed as a recent trend and as involving the study of "pure mental structures" and the rejection of essentialist metaphysics, but it was passed off as "generally sterile in social and political application."[56]

Moritz Schlick, the leader of the Vienna Circle, had visited the United States (Berkeley and Stanford) at the turn of the decade, and Herbert Feigl, who defined himself as the "first propagandist" of logical empiricism in America, came on a permanent basis (University of Iowa) at the same time.[57] Although he was one of the inventors of the term "logical positivism," he strenuously worked to change the label to "logical empiricism." By the late 1930s, however, the Vienna group, which had disbanded after Hitler's invasion of Austria, along with its Berlin contingent, had, with some exceptions (such as Popper and Wittgenstein in England) reestablished itself in the United States. Carnap, maybe the central figure in the movement, came to Chicago in 1935 and was followed by Hans Reichenbach (UCLA), Gustav Bergmann (Iowa), Carl Hempel (Chicago), Kurt Gödel (Princeton), Frank (Harvard), and others. A. J. Ayer's *Language, Truth, and Logic,* which did much to make positivism accessible to social science, was not published until 1936. Seldom, before the 1950s, were the doctrines of logical positivism distinctly reflected in the theory and practice of political science. Although the logical positivists, for the most part, had only a vague knowledge of the work of American philosophers (such as Dewey, William James, Charles S. Pierce, and Bridgman) and although Americans were not well acquainted with the most immediate intellectual forebears of positivism, such as Wittgenstein, there were some obvious potential affinities. These included an empiricist epistemology, an instrumentalist account of scientific theory, and a commitment to the unity of scientific method.

Charles W. Morris at the University of Chicago, the pragmatist and follower of Dewey, was, along with W. V. O. Quine (Harvard), Carnap's sponsor after visiting him in Prague. Morris viewed logical positivism and pragmatism as complementary aspects of a movement toward the ideal of a unified science based on "scientific empiricism."[58] The American and European philosophers (including Dewey, Carnap, Hempel, Feigl, Morris, Nagel, and Bertrand Russell) all joined together in the unified science movement toward the end of the 1930s and, under the leadership of Neurath, created an *Encyclopedia of Unified Science* for the purpose of propagating "a universal scientific attitude."[59] Carnap found "considerable interest" among Americans in the "scientific method of philosophy," and for a number of years he participated in an influential interdisciplinary colloquium at Chicago dealing with scientific methodology.[60]

In America, as opposed to Europe, the influence of metaphysics and German idealism seemed to be at a low ebb, and Carnap perceived the atmosphere as "very congenial" to the kind of project that he pursued. On the other hand, unlike Europe where he had been more closely associated with the natural sciences, he found himself in a philosophy department where "historicism" and traditionalism were indeed strong forces. He was "depressed to see that certain philosophical views which seemed to me long superseded by the development of critical thought and in some cases completely devoid of any cognitive content" were still current. He was particularly struck by Adler's attempt to refute, on metaphysical grounds, the theory of human evolution. He noted that sometimes he had the "weird feeling" that he "was sitting among a group of medieval learned men with long beards and solemn robes"—a feeling that was heightened by the Gothic architecture at Chicago.[61]

The leading figure in the philosophy of science on the American scene had been Morris R. Cohen. He was one of Charles Morris's teachers, and probably as much as any work of the period, his discussion of "Method, Scientific" in the *ESS* was a primary source for claims about science advanced by social scientists—particularly at Chicago. Cohen and Ernest Nagel (a student of both Dewey and Cohen) also wrote *An Introduction to Logic and Scientific Method* (1934) which became an even more popular authority. Although Dewey's name was prominent in discussions of science, he had little to say about the logic of science—emphasizing more its goals, attitudes such as experimentation and control, and instrumental social role. Cohen's work assumed, and implied, that scientific activity was grounded in a set of procedures and principles that could be in some manner codified and applied.

Cohen argued that the "essence" of science, and scientific "imagination," was not to be found "in the content of its specific conclusions but rather in the method whereby its findings are made and constantly corrected." Method "denotes any procedure which applies some rational order or systematic pattern to diverse objects" and ranged from logic to laboratory techniques. In the end, the sciences were at one in their logic which involved, contrary to Bacon's view, basically deduction from former knowledge and testing of propositions against facts. Ultimately, it was the method of science which "minimizes the shock and uncertainty of life, so that man can frame policies of action and of moral judgment fit for wider outlook than those of immediate physical stimulus or organic response."[62] Cohen made no reference to the literature of logical empiricism. He did not embrace the idea that social science could acquire nomological knowledge characteristic of the natural sciences, but he did believe that it could employ scientific method which would both aid in the control of human circumstances and enhance social freedom. As a defender of scientific values, he was in conflict with some of the humanists at Chicago during this period, such as Adler, but although he got along with Carnap, there were some distinct points of divergence from the positivists whom he perceived as ambivalent about theories and as too closely allied with cruder images of empiricism which he believed depreciated theories, speculation, and the role of reason in science.[63]

One of the important vehicles for joining the work of European positivism with the American tradition, and at the same time for providing formulae for discussing the character of scientific inquiry in a manner that bridged the worlds of philosophy and social science, was Kaufmann's analysis of methodology. He had published *Methodenlehre der Sozialwissenschaften* in Vienna in 1936, and in 1944, now under the influence of Dewey, produced a comparable work that advanced an image of science as an activity defined by "rules of procedure" and as a combination of "systematic observations and their interpretation in terms of theoretical principles."[64]

The University of Chicago was a crucial nexus for American political science and the émigré perspective—with respect to both the defense and critique of scientism. The tradition of Merriam and Lasswell was perpetuated by Easton, beginning in the late 1940s, but the university eventually became the host of such individuals as Strauss, Arendt, and the Thomist disciple of Maritain, Yves Simon. Nef noted that Simon was recruited (1948) because he shared the group's "belief in the reality of truth, in the realm of being, and in man's capacity, by research in philosophy, to edge a little closer to it."[65]

One of the pivotal figures in the development of the new perspective at Chicago was Morgenthau. Like many of the émigrés, Morgenthau came from an affluent German-Jewish family and faced the dilemma of assimilation. Although originally a philosophy student at Frankfurt, he studied law and history at Munich where he was introduced to Weber's ideas about political realism and the tension between theory and practice. The failure of liberalism in Weimar transfixed Morgenthau, and he found little in the way of answers in the brand of Marxism associated with the *Institut für Sozialforschung*. He received his doctorate at Frankfurt in international law in 1929 and worked as a legal assistant to the Social Democrat Hugo Sinzheimer where he became close to Neumann and Frankel. He taught at Geneva from 1932 until 1935 and officially emigrated in 1935 when, along with Heller and others, he went to the University of Madrid.

He arrived in the United States in 1937 and taught at Brooklyn College and the University of Kansas for several years. He was admitted to the bar in 1943. He began, that same year, to teach political science at the University of Chicago, and he was affiliated with the State Department's Policy Planning Staff until the early 1950s. Although he did not fit easily into the intellectual climate created by Merriam, Lasswell, and White, he was supported by Hutchins and soon became a prominent theorist of international relations. What tied him most closely to the dominant émigré perspective was his attack on both the premises of liberalism and the assumptions about the possibility of a science of politics.[66]

The life and work of Arendt has been extensively examined.[67] She arrived in the United States in 1941 (at age 35) after escaping from internment in France. She had been a student of philosophy who had studied with Husserl and Heidegger. Her relationship with the latter evoked considerable passion, both intellectual and otherwise. Heidegger remained a decisive influence, despite continuing personal and intellectual tensions and reconciliations over the years, but she did her dissertation (in 1928 at Heidelberg on St. Augustine's concept of love) with Jaspers. Much of the next two decades was spent working with the Jewish community and dealing with Jewish political issues which included work on her biography of Rahel Varnhagen.[68] After the Nazis came to power, she aided German communists in Berlin but eventually went into exile in Paris in 1933 and commenced eighteen years of statelessness. During the 1930s, she associated with Jewish intellectuals such as Benjamin and became involved with the Zionist movement. During her early years in the United States, she was research director of the Conference on Jewish Relations, an editor for Shocken Books, and executive director for Jewish Cultural Reconstruction.

Despite what, at a certain level of abstraction, became a somewhat common assessment of liberalism, positivism, relativism, the crisis of the West, and its historical roots, there was considerable tension between some of the leading émigré scholars. Viewed from the American perspective, individuals such as Arendt, Strauss, and Voegelin appeared very similar, but they were, by their own assessment, in many ways intellectually distant from one another—if not something of rivals.[69] The Marxist orientation separated the Frankfurt group, but there was also personal estrangement. For example, Adorno had blocked the academic career of Arendt's first husband, and he had been less than helpful with respect to the escape of Benjamin. She believed that Adorno had tried to ingratiate himself with the Nazis and spoke of him as "one of the most repulsive human beings I know." When Jaspers asked her for information about Strauss, she noted that he was "highly respected" but a "convinced orthodox atheist. Very odd. A truly gifted intellect. I don't like him." While still in Germany, Arendt had at one point rebuffed Strauss's romantic overtures and later chided him, a Jew, for his conservative political leanings.[70]

While it would take Arendt some time to assimilate (intellectually, personally, and professionally) in the United States, the situation was different for Voegelin who was the first of the major figures to engage directly in the conversation of political theory. By the early 1940s, Voegelin had become an active participant in the world of professional political science.[71] Although born in Germany (1901), he spent much of his early life in Austria. He studied law at the University of Vienna under Kelsen and worked with von Mises. He finished his doctorate in 1922, within the framework of the positivist orientation along with individuals such as Schütz and Kaufmann, but he was also introduced to philosophy and was much influenced by Weber. After studying Greek history in Berlin and visiting Oxford where he worked with classicist Gilbert Murray, he received a Rockefeller Fellowship in 1924 and lived in the United States until 1927, visiting institutions such as Columbia, Harvard, and Wisconsin.

This period in the United States represented the beginning of a great intellectual change. He became well acquainted with American philosophy and social science and took courses with Dewey and Giddings. He was influenced by the ideas of Whitehead and Santayana and began to immerse himself in the philosophy of history and the work of Spengler and Toynbee. Upon his return to Austria, after some time in France and at Heidelberg, working with Alfred Weber and immersing himself in the ideas of the George circle, he published a book on the "American mind."[72] He became a lecturer at Vienna in 1929 and witnessed the rise of Nazi influence and anti-Semitism in the university. During the early 1930s, he published two books on the idea of "race" which traced the history of the idea and critically examined the scientific pretensions of racial theories.[73] While implicitly critical of Nazi ideology and its attitude toward Jews, the works more explicitly criticized both liberal and Marxist ideas including the faith in progress and the methods of natural science. By the mid-1930s, he had broken entirely with Kelsen. This was precipitated by his book on the "authoritarian state."[74]

Here he analyzed the Austrian government created in 1933, as well as the prior evolution of the constitution, with an emphasis on the concepts of "total" and "authoritarian" states in modern times. He also undertook a criticism of Kelsen's neo-Kantian theory of values and legal positivism on the basis that it neglected the communal bases of politics, and he suggested that the Austrian regime might be a bulwark against radicalism of both Left and Right. Voegelin began to study neo-Thomism during the next few years, but he was dismissed from the university in 1938, the same year that he published a book on "political religions" which argued that the roots of modern ideologies were to be found in Averrorist doctrines and a subsequent deformation of Western thought.[75]

He was so incensed that the "rotten swine who called themselves democrats—meaning the Western democracies," allowed the *Anschluss* that he "contemplated for a moment joining the National Socialists" whom he also hated, but he decided to emigrate.[76] Eluding the Gestapo, Voegelin escaped to Switzerland. Schumpeter, Elliott, and Holcombe facilitated his entry into the United States by sponsoring him for an instructorship at Harvard. He taught at Bennington for a year (1938–39) but found the leftist orientation "was no more to my taste than the National Socialist environment that I had just left."[77] He moved, first, to the University of Alabama where he began to teach the history of political theory and then, in 1942, to Louisiana State University where he remained for most of his academic life.

While at Harvard, he began to conceive an extensive study of the history of political ideas, and many of his early publications in the United States during the 1940s reflected this project and situated him squarely in the field of political theory. Although drawn to certain aspects of American life, such as the attachment to "commonsense," which he believed connected American thought to the classics and the exposure to which he believed help "immunize" him against ideas such as those of Heidegger, he was contemptuous of American subservience to foreign intellectual fads and of the "populist" attitudes that brought "functional illiterates into academic positions."[78]

It was precisely the alien critical theological perspective of individuals such as Voegelin that would precipitate the new conversation about political theory that marked the next decade. The split at the University of Chicago that began in the late 1930s continued to develop, but it was only a microcosm, even if a catalyst, of the polarization that would begin to overtake political theory, and the discipline of political science, by the early 1950s.

9

Political Science and Political Theory

Our contemporary world is losing its confidence in the inevitability of Progress.
Robert S. Lynd

When Lynd noted that "Nazi power politics has stripped the social sciences in Germany of their intellectual freedom," he probably had in mind his new colleagues at the Institute at Columbia.[1] His critique of barren empiricism and timid social theorizing and his plea for an engaged social science may have resonated with the émigrés at some level, but his vision of social science was not ultimately congenial to the European scholars. Lynd argued that the "crisis" of American culture and world politics required reuniting "the scholars and the technicians," political philosophers and public administrators, and remembering that it was "the *interested* desire to know in order to do something about problems that had predominantly motivated social science" from Adam Smith to Harold Lasswell. Social science was now suffering, he believed, from excessive specialization which led to "the centripetal tendency to shrink away from the marginal area where insistent reality grinds against the central body of theory." In political science, there was a "traditional body of inherited theory, and a growing body of empiricism somewhat disregardful of theory," and both managed to neglect basic questions about the character of modern democracy.[2]

At the 1940 meeting of the APSA, Benjamin Wright (Harvard) was approached by an army general who requested that he help enlist a group of political theorists to write a field manual for soldiers in order to explain the character of liberal democracy and to counter the writings of Hitler and Marx.[3] By this point, however, it would have been difficult to find a clear consensus among political theorists on this issue. Strauss reached back to suggest that while Dewey's *German Politics and Philosophy* had properly warned against the practical dangers of absolutist philosophy, the "experimental method" was equally problematical and obscured the need for moral absolutism. And he condemned traditional studies in the history of political theory, such as that of Vaughn, for embracing the assumption of "continuous progress."[4]

199

The early writings of certain individuals such as Arendt, Strauss, and Voegelin would not be incorporated into major and highly visible works until the early 1950s, but the literature produced by the émigrés was, as a whole, already creating a distinctive intellectual ambience—even if its exact character was not easily defined by contemporaries. The concerns at this point were seldom pointedly with American politics, but with the philosophical and political dimensions of totalitarianism and the history of political thought. This work, however, at first often inadvertently, struck at the intellectual core of American political science.

Marcuse published *Reason and Revolution* in 1941 (dedicated to Horkheimer and the Institute). Although he praised America as having a rational spirit and "as the only land of the future," his critique of positivism as abetting the rise of totalitarianism, and his resurrection of Hegel as an exemplification of critical rationalism and the belief in the state as a vehicle of individual realization, ran counter to American perceptions.[5] Benjamin Lippincott, an associate professor at Minnesota who had taken his degree at the London School of Economics, noted only that the author "frequently stands for absolutes." Sabine, however, took strong exception to the idea that "the characteristic philosophical expression of an authoritarian social philosophy is positivism."[6] Some of the émigrés would soon be entering more directly into the discourse of political theory. The exact manner in which this conversation took shape in the 1940s was somewhat accidental, but it precipitated a profound transformation in political theory.

Early in the decade, Lippincott argued that, in practice, the discipline of political science remained much as it had been at the turn of the century. The greatest deficiency was theoretical. What passed as political theory had been devoted to recounting past ideas, and even among those committed to science, there was, except for a few individuals such as Willoughby, an "aversion" and "hostility" to theory. The dominant notion of scientific method defined empiricism as collecting facts and viewed "theories or ideas about the facts [as] not only unnecessary but positively dangerous." This rejection of theory, he claimed, was not only detrimental but in an important sense an illusion, since, as Cohen had demonstrated, theories were always implicit in the selection and interpretation of facts, and their denial only served to conceal bias.[7] Lippincott's criticism foreshadowed claims that would be common a decade later, but it was not the immediate catalyst for the controversy about theory.

In 1943, William Foote Whyte, a social anthropologist, published an article in the *APSR* which presented a "challenge" to political scientists.[8] Whyte's argument largely reflected the views of the Chicago school and was related to the current controversy about social science at the university, but there was no indication that he had any clear notion of the nerve endings that would be agitated by his comments. He suggested that the war had occasioned a concern about the fate of democracy that had led some political scientists to "write political philosophy and ethics" and neglect the study of "plain politics." He argued that "a scientific study of politics requires the discovery of certain uniformities or laws" and that political scientists should direct their attention to "the description and analysis of political behavior" which in turn required that they "establish themselves as participant observers in the field of practical politics." Whyte thought it was a sad fact that, from Machiavelli to Riordan *(Plunkitt of Tammany Hall),* most important contributions to knowledge about politics had been "made by men outside of academic life."[9]

The most immediate and pointed response to Whyte was by John Hallowell, but Hallowell identified Whyte with an intellectual position that was still unfamiliar to most Americans, including Whyte—positivism. Even though Hallowell noted Cohen's reservations about positivism, his image was largely derived from the *ESS.* This outlook, with its attempt to separate "ethics and politics," threatened, he insisted, to distort social inquiry and undermine "all belief in transcendental truth and value" and open the way to intellectual and political "nihilism." Hallowell suggested that Whyte's views represented the "increasingly positivistic" trends in political science that were evident in the claims of individuals such as Rice and Catlin as well as much of mainstream political science since the turn of the century.[10] Hallowell, however, was less concerned with Whyte's particular claims than with finding a vehicle for voicing an objection to what he believed was the general growth of scientism and modern liberalism.

Although Hallowell's work would, by the middle of the next decade, be overshadowed by similar and related claims in the work of such individuals as Strauss and Voegelin, his critique was in many ways novel and, at this point, certainly more influential in shaping the dialogue. Hallowell had recently published an article and a book on the "decline of liberalism" in which he attributed the rise of nazism to the acceptance of positivism among German academics and jurists.[11] And now he interpreted American political science as a tributary of this tradition. This was far from the first challenge to scientism in American political theory, but it was distinctly different. The ideas that science was a threat to liberal democracy, that democracy should rest on religious values, and that the development of political thought was not essentially a story of progress were, in general, quite anomalous, but at this point not isolated, notions.[12]

Hallowell took his undergraduate degree at Harvard, but despite what night be construed as the similarity between his arguments and those of Elliott, the context of his concern was considerably different. After his graduation in 1935, Hallowell took his master's degree at Duke where he was aided by Taylor Cole, who had observed first-hand the rise of nazism in Germany during the early 1930s, in gaining a fellowship to Heidelberg.[13] The experience was, indeed, a transforming one as he witnessed the growth of Hitler's hold on the country and particularly on the university. He studied with Jaspers and noted the pressure to which he was subjected both as an academician and, socially, because of his Jewish wife. Faculty members greeted each other with the Nazi salute, and half the faculty appeared in uniform at the first convocation. Those who were less than enthusiastic about National Socialism were drummed out of the classroom by students. The husband and wife managing his rooming house sent their children out of the room before discussing politics, his letters home were intercepted, and he was called in by the Gestapo for questioning.

When Hallowell returned to the United States, he found few people who understood, or were interested in, the situation he had encountered. He was offered an assistantship at Princeton in 1938, and two crucial events transpired as he attempted to grapple emotionally and intellectually with the sense of urgency precipitated by his experiences in Germany. First, although he had rejected religion after being raised in an unconventional sect, he underwent a conversion and became a dedicated Episcopalian who sought to link theology and political theory. This direction was in part the consequence of attending lectures by Reinhold Niebuhr who attacked modern liberal thought and argued for a Christian foundation of politics.[14] But, second, Hallowell began to work with Gerhart Niemeyer, an émigré and student of Heller who had followed the latter to Madrid. While vacationing in Germany in 1936, Niemeyer found himself unable to return to Spain because of the civil war. In view of the situation in Germany, he came to the United States via France and accepted a position at Princeton where he taught until 1944.[15] Through Niemeyer, whose focus was law, Hallowell began to absorb the Weimar critique of modernity and liberal society, and he also found inspiration in the work of Kolnai and Rauschnung as well as in Lewis Mumford's attack on pragmatic liberalism.[16]

Hallowell's concern was with the issue of how nazism could have gained a foothold in a liberal world. The answer that he gave was the one that would come to characterize the émigré literature—positivism and relativism, but his dissertation, and subsequent book, was the first expansive exposition of this argument to appear in the United States. After teaching briefly at UCLA and working for the Office of War Information, Hallowell, with the aid of Cole, who was then with the OSS, secured a position at Duke where he remained for his entire academic career—directing over forty dissertations.

Why was it, Hallowell asked, that liberal political institutions had collapsed like a "house of cards" in Germany? His answer was that their "original spirit" had undergone a "heretofore unsuspected stage of inner degeneracy." It was no longer "deeply rooted in the spiritual consciousness of the people," and this was why professors, judges, lawyers, and civil servants gave way before National Socialism. Hallowell argued that the cause was actually less Hitler than liberals themselves and an "inner flaw" in their ideology that made it vulnerable; liberalism was not "murdered," it "committed suicide." And if this defect was not recognized and confronted, liberalism would continue to fall in the West before communism and other totalitarian movements. For Hallowell, the intellectual dimension of this defect was to be found in ideas such as the legal positivism of Kelsen—which Radbruch, for example, had finally repudiated in favor of natural law. And the intellectual dimension was the key to understanding the fate of political institutions which were "the structural expressions of conceptual schemes" and required "a consistent ideational foundation" in order "to enjoy a vigorous and live existence."[17] What was necessary was a reconstruction of liberal ideology, and this, in turn, required a critical analysis and recovery of its historical roots.

Hallowell claimed that liberalism had devolved from its original "integral" form to its present "degenerate" condition. In its original formulation, at the point of the Renaissance and Reformation, liberalism was based on an individualistic ethic and on the absolute value of the "human personality" which in turn was predicated on "eternal values" of natural law. These ideas had, however, been undermined by romanticism and neo-Kantian and neo-Hegelian forms of positivism, subjectivism, and historicism in the nineteenth century as well as by trends toward "collectivism" in political thought. This was not simply a problem in political theory but in modernity in general—cubism in art, Schoenberg and Stravinsky in music, Barth in religion. The consequence of all this, Hallowell claimed, was a trend toward intellectual nihilism which culminated, politically, in anarchy and tyranny. Liberalism, internally weakened by its inability to defend transcendentally its own substantive values and convictions, collapsed, and nazism developed as a practical "corollary." And "the spiritual crisis out of which totalitarianism emerged is a crisis, peculiar not to Germany, but to Western civilization."[18] The reconstruction of liberalism could be effected, Hallowell argued, only by a religious and philosophical grounding in modern theology as characterized by the work of such individuals as Niebuhr, Tillich, and Berdyaev.

Voegelin reviewed this work sympathetically—suggesting only that Hallowell might have sought the roots of the decline of liberalism further back than the nineteenth century. Where the tradition of political philosophy went wrong would be the principal concern of historians of political theory by the 1960s. Voegelin was working on his general (but later temporarily abandoned) history of political ideas which attributed the decline of the West, which culminated in Marxism, to the secularization of Christian images of history during the Enlightenment.[19] Similar critiques of liberalism would be enunciated by émigrés, of various ideological and philosophical persuasions, by the end of the decade. Niebuhr, in 1944, argued for a reconstitution of democracy on religious grounds and on the basis of higher law. He claimed that liberalism, too optimistic and morally sentimental, had failed to see the capacity for evil in human nature and that secular theories of democracy had failed.[20]

Hallowell was not the only one to join these issues. J. Roland Pennock also claimed that democracy could not be taken for granted and that its defense required finding "some standard of right which is universally applicable." He believed, however, in the more typical American manner, that such a standard could be derived from an understanding of human nature through "rational empirical methods." He pointedly rejected Hallowell's analysis and any turn to "pure faith."[21] When Hayek's attack on collectivism and social planning as the "road to serfdom," with the attending critique of relativism, historicism, and scientism, was published, T. V. Smith, reflecting the general mood of perplexity and anger among many American social scientists in the face of these criticisms, called Hayek's attitude "hysterical." He suggested that it was "almost the inevitable result of a book written by any European who had fled bondage in one land . . . and carries his fears with him into the land which he does not intimately know."[22] It was, however, not only the philosophical grounding of social science and liberalism and the entailed approach to public policy that was at issue but the image of political reality.

By this point, liberalism in political science largely meant pluralism, and pluralism was both a descriptive and normative thesis. During the 1930s, as Americans searched for a concrete image of liberal democracy, pluralism and the "group-theory of politics," modulated by ideas of government intervention, had increasingly provided a paradigm.[23] For the émigrés, however, pluralism was cast in the image of Weimar and perceived as the political counterpart of defective liberal doctrines and as the precursor of mass society. Kirchheimer warned against the dismissal of the idea of the state and about "group interests superseding the . . . sovereign community." He claimed that the pluralist image of an "arbiter" free of consensus only concealed the locus of real power and produced ad hoc justifications for government intervention.[24] Hallowell attacked the theory of pluralism characteristic of the empirical work of Herring and the theory of compromise advanced by T. V. Smith. The idea that conflict and compromise were the heart of democracy was, he argued, the consequence of positivism, pluralism, and relativism and reflected the denial of objective values. Democracy required a grounding in substantive truth or else it would lapse into "nihilism."[25]

The political theory research committee of the APSA had been inactive for a number of years, but in November 1943, the committee was reconstituted, under the chairmanship of Wilson (now at Illinois). The other members included Ernest S. Griffith (director of the congressional Legislative Reference Service), Wright, and Voegelin. A symposium attempted to sort out the issues facing the field and to move toward a redefinition of political theory. Wilson, a Catholic, had suggested that thus far in American politics conservatism had been a failure, but now the time had come for "an ethical restoration in politics" based on tradition, Christian values, and morality.[26] Although this view did not determine the exact agenda of the committee, the image of political theory that emerged diverged sharply in many respects from past constructions.

In summarizing the committee's discussion, Wilson stated that there was an explicit recognition that political theory was in part a philosophical consideration of political science—which analyzed the "metaphysical principles embedded in the work of those who study primarily political institutions and processes." There was also a reaffirmation of the long-standing belief that one of the main functions of political theory was to "define the concepts of political science" and provide "usable definitions of political terms." But the group also set out to articulate the substantive problems in political theory.[27]

Wilson noted that there was a "deep cleavage among political theorists in the area of primary ideas" on an "ultimate issue." The exact nature of this issue and cleavage was, however, something that the participants had some difficulty in specifying. One issue involved a conflict between those who took metaphysics seriously, as did "the great political thinkers" of the past, and those who believed that metaphysics was "little more than the name given to logical thought." Was scientific "detachment" and the search for "value-free discussions" a mark of "progress" or "ineptitude?" Another issue was the clash between those who embraced a "theological approach," and believed that there was more to the study of politics than "clinical observation," and those who pursued the "method of the positivists," and accepted the "empirical" or "now traditional 'positivistic,' scientific, or liberal technique of social study." Some claimed that a theological perspective was necessary to understand the past as well as contemporary society, but there was also a question of what constituted such an approach and the manner in which it was challenged by "traditional approaches of idealistic and rationalist liberalism."[28] All agreed that it was important to "formulate and criticize values," and most believed that to some degree it was possible to formulate "valid social and political principles." There was much the same kind of discussion about knowledge of the "recurrence of political behavior." There was a willingness to compromise at some point and acknowledge that both "utopia" and the "facts" should be stressed.[29]

Some, Wilson noted, believed that the fundamental issue was reflected in the differences between the thought of the Middle Ages and the nineteenth century, while others perceived the basic problem in terms of natural law versus majority rule. One division was between those who argued that America needed a consciousness of history and that an examination of our philosophy of history was in order and those who wanted to concentrate on pragmatic social choice and the "ends-means relationship." But all agreed that there should be an emphasis on the history of values in American political society, that there was a need for greater availability of the "texts of the great thinkers," that "the political tradition of the West must be subjected to close scrutiny," and that "we should study the ancients because they are really modern" and "timeless." The classic texts were perennial either because they were part of our political tradition or because they discerned an "essential nature of moral man or the moral universe (or even Satanic man and the Satanic phase of the universe)."[30]

In his individual statement, Wright announced his conviction that

the greatest need in this country today is a statement of objectives in terms of ideas and ideals. We lack any clear conception of what we are fighting for, what goals we should seek to attain, even in this country, after the war. . . . We have been too inclined to hide timidly behind the excuse of objectivity. Interpretations of the history of political thought and analyses of current winds of doctrine can alike make great contributions to the future course of American democracy.[31]

Griffith, however, took a distinctly different position. He argued that "research in political theory hitherto has been largely synonymous with searches for the origin, growth, and decline in ideas, principles, and doctrines," while what is required if there was to be "precision" in the field was more attention to "the basic concepts that underlie all theory," to the definition of these concepts, and to the development of better "conceptual *systems*." Such research, he cautioned, should not be understood as a search for *"correct"* concepts, since theorists have too long looked for absolute principles and failed to recognize that they are subjective and historically relative and reflect various institutional arrangements. He suggested that there are "timeless" concepts, but they were not to be found in the ephemeral world of politics and the state. The "constants" must come from other fields such as psychology, sociology, history, geography, and anthropology. Like Merriam and Lasswell, he saw political science as "derivative."[32]

Voegelin offered a research scheme that would be reflected in his *New Science of Politics* (1952). He argued that the general history of political ideas had been represented with distinction by such individuals as Dunning, McIlwain, and Sabine and that problems in this area were of particular importance to American scholars who had done the most to develop this field. But it was necessary to rethink the field in light of both the vast new historical knowledge now available and the general philosophy of history. Dunning, he argued, had taken the first step by focusing on "political theory" as a category rather than on the broader concept of political science or the narrower concept of political ideas, but his work was weak on the Middle Ages and somewhat distorted by his emphasis on "progress." Sabine had taken the further step of making political theory distinctly subordinate to the structure of political history, but it now remained to recognize the work of individuals such as Toynbee who pursued this task in a much more philosophical manner.[33]

In reviewing Brecht's analysis of the decline of the German republic, Hallowell was concerned that Brecht did not sufficiently stress the degree to which that decline was "a direct consequence of the liberal's lack of conviction in his own philosophy."[34] Hallowell's attack on liberalism became increasingly strident, and his argument was hardly congenial to the traditional values of American political science and to individuals such as Merriam.[35] Merriam had been appointed to a chair at Chicago in 1944 and was lecturing on the history of political theory. His reaction to claims such as those of Rauschning about the decadence of Western civilization and the decline into nihilism was largely one of bewilderment. Here, Merriam noted, was a former Prussian soldier and Junker and erstwhile Nazi leader who had turned against the party and fled to Southern California and decried faith in science and human progress through liberal democracy while awaiting his naturalization papers.[36]

One theme that had originated in the 1930s, and persisted through the 1940s, was the claim that it was necessary to construct a democratic theory, or ideology, that, as Herman Finer put it, would "accomplish for Democracy what Marxism had done for Soviet Communism."[37] Almond, who had taken his degree at Chicago under Merriam and would be one of the principal actors in the behavioral movement, spoke out strongly for the ethical involvement of political scientists and against Whyte's suggestion that values should be the province of the philosopher. The problem was less the critics' emphasis on values than the fact that political science could not countenance the disjunction between science and democracy and the idea that liberalism was the exemplification of social and intellectual decline.

The symposium on "Politics and Ethics" in which Almond participated was an attempt to explore further the issues that had been raised by Whyte, but it was clear that for the most part the individuals were still talking past one another.[38] Almond strongly defended the "ethical purpose" of political science on the grounds that the goal of social science was better "public policy" and the production of the kind of "emotional clarity" and "knowledge" that would further "rational judgment and action" in choices between "good and evil." Almond argued that the social scientist stood in the worlds of both science and action, embracing "warm advocacy and cool objectivity," and although science could not create values, he believed, following Weber, that it could make judgments about possibilities and consequences.[39] Lewis Dexter (Bryn Mawr) articulated a somewhat similar position. He was more than willing to admit the relevance of values and accept the many ways in which values entered into empirical research. His immediate concern, however, was to separate value claims from reports and predictions and to develop a theoretical science based on "valid generalization about political behavior, regardless of immediate crises," which could then be applied to practical problems.[40]

Whyte reiterated his original position and labeled as "ridiculous" Hallowell's claim that an "amoral description of dirty politics" encouraged the propagation of such politics. In his view, "the academic moralist can enjoy only the pleasure of self-expression." Like Almond and Dexter, he agreed that the ultimate test of social science was its "practical value," but he argued that the separation of fact and value made the greatest contribution to democracy. Whyte stated that he did not recognize the target of Hallowell's criticism—that he had never even met anyone who represented the position described. He insisted that he was not interested in "positivism" and the "philosophy of science" and that Hallowell had gone off on a "tangent" and created a "straw man." Hallowell, however, delivered a yet more passionate statement about the role of social science. He argued that what was needed was not yet more research techniques but "convictions based on principles," since "a social science not committed to the search for freedom and justice has already signed its own death warrant." It was "not only our right, but our responsibility, to unmask sophistry, and to guide men along the paths most likely to yield happiness and freedom."[41]

In 1946, Morgenthau published *Scientific Man and Power Politics* in which he claimed that there was a fundamental "inability of our society to understand, and to cope with, the political problems which the age poses." This failing was attributed to a "general decay in the political thinking of the Western world" that could be traced through the works of Hobbes, Bentham, Mill, Marx, Spencer, Dewey, Beard, and Mannheim. It was manifest in a faith in science and rationalist philosophy as well as in various forms of liberalism allied with a rising middle class. Liberalism, with its notions of "reason, of progress, and of peace," simply failed to recognize that fascism was not an aberration and a temporary form of repression but something rooted both historically in the "bankrupt age that preceded it" and in human nature. Now that the war was over, the world had another chance but only if it overcame liberalism with its attachment to the rule of law, science, the repudiation of politics, and social planning which together left democracy weak in the face of its enemies.[42] The turn away from liberalism found further expression in the successive editions of his popular textbook, *Politics Among Nations* (1948). This study in political "realism" and "power" was distinctly different, in both theory and motivation, from what, terminologically, might have seemed to have had an affinity with the work of individuals such as Merriam and Lasswell.

Not all of the émigrés accounted for the problems of modernity in terms so alien to American intellectual propensities. Ernst Cassirer, for example, unlike his student Strauss, defended the Enlightenment and the ability of its concept of reason to counter the "myth of the state" and its contemporary totalitarian manifestations.[43] But although the differences, both ideological and philosophical, between many of the émigré scholars would be much more apparent in the succeeding years, the criticisms of science and liberalism that were advanced were strikingly similar. Morgenthau, for example, was far removed from those associated with the Frankfurt school, and Horkheimer was hardly sympathetic to neo-Thomism and much of the philosophy that inspired individuals such as Hallowell, but to American political scientists, the messages sounded remarkably similar.

Horkheimer had, at best, a dim grasp of American politics and American political thought when he transposed his criticisms of Weimar into a critique of American culture. His book, which reflected the then un-translated collaboration with Adorno on the *Dialectic of Enlightenment* (1944), was the product of a series of public lectures at Columbia, and it was indeed a pessimistic work responding to and reinforcing what he claimed was a "universal feeling of fear and disillusionment." Horkheimer undertook a critique of the "concept of rationality" on which, he claimed, modern liberal democratic industrial society was based. His purpose was to demonstrate that this idea of reason was self-destructive and that its implementation was "accompanied by a process of dehumanization."[44]

The idea of reason that he attacked was what he called instrumental or "subjective reason" as opposed to the "objective reason" that had characterized classical philosophy and German idealism and which had aimed at transcendental truths as a basis of critical judgment. The growth of instrumental reason, and its urge to dominate nature—beginning with Locke and the Enlightenment and culminating in modern liberalism and the work of individuals such as James, Pierce, Dewey, Veblen, and Beard—was really a process of the destruction of ratio-nality. Its lack of principle had allowed it to "tilt over into fascism" and accommodate itself to its "opposites." In the contemporary age, it was exemplified in positivism (which he essentially identified with pragma-tism) which underwrote relativism and recognized only the authority of science.[45] Horkheimer found all of this at work in American culture and political history from the founding period to the conformity of con-temporary mass society and its pluralist image of democracy.

Although Weber and Mannheim had understood the rationalizing tendencies of modern society, their ideas of reason had provided noth-ing to combat the domination of technique. He suggested that National Socialism was a product of modern reason and the "revolt against na-ture." It played upon repressed "natural drives" and gained the sup-port of the alienated masses who were the "victims of instrumentalized reason." Horkheimer interpreted America as a culture in which the metaphysical depreciation of nature was in some ways less pronounced than in Europe, but, in practical terms, the "tendency to real domina-tion of nature is equally strong" and manifest in the attraction to Dar-winism and pragmatism.[46] What all this produced was a mass culture in which everything, including classical music, had been turned into a rei-fied commodity devoid of objective value and meaning. Liberalism led to a loss of real individualism as much as in totalitarianism and to the creation of cultural "conformity through the leveling principle of com-merce and exchange." In this situation, workers took on the ideology of business leaders and real "political theory" disappeared and was replaced by "empirical research" which offered no barrier against the encroachment of "nihilism."[47] Although not directly attacking liberalism, Lowenthal's study of racial prejudice in America suggested that it was only a "surface manifestation of deeper social and psychological currents" discerned by Horkheimer and Adorno.[48]

Few during this period struggled as sincerely as Brecht to work their way through the issues that had surfaced in the conversation of political theory and to reach some accommodation between the American and émigré perspectives, and no one focused more pointedly on the problem of relativism. During this period, he published several articles dealing with relativism, absolutism, and science.[49] Brecht shared the concern about relativism so characteristic of many of the émigrés. In a review of Maritain's book, he had noted that "totalitarianism has greatly profited from the value-emptiness which has been the result of positivism and relativism in the social sciences."[50] But he did not accept the characteristic solution. In reviewing Voegelin's *New Science of Politics*, he noted that it was a "leading expression" of the fact that "the mid-century revolt against positivism, scientific method, and relativism in political science is making headway." There was, indeed, as Brecht was clearly aware, a revolt against the values of mainstream political science before the behavioral "revolution" reaffirmed those values. But Brecht argued that although such work pointed toward the danger of believing in "automatic progress" and indicated the "significance for political research of the yearnings and needs of the human soul," it made the mistake, like Maritain, of believing that metaphysics could be transformed into a science and of "indulging in the fashionable spirit of decrying relativism."[51]

Like many others, Brecht was concerned about the influence of legal positivism on German judges and lawyers who applied laws that were morally reprehensible, but he believed that it was incorrect to seek scientific cum philosophical grounds for moral principles and natural law. Moral judgment was, as Weber had maintained, a matter of human volition but not therefore lacking validity. For Brecht, the dilemma was that scientific value-relativism, that is, the inability of science to ground moral judgments, as expounded by Weber, Kelsen, Radbruch, and Lasswell, had once seemed a liberating philosophy, but in the face of nazism, it became a paralyzing one. As a consequence, many intellectuals "turned from being political scientists to becoming ethical philosophers or theologians (if not simply bad logicians) and *they called this science*." Since, he believed, there was no scientific knowledge of values, his solution was to teach "the *limits* of science" and urge other ways to bridge the "is" and "ought." He was an intensely religious Lutheran, particularly in his later years, and he rejected the attempt to "bracket God" and ultimately sought to ground political theory in faith and religious values.[52]

Brecht explained the rise of relativism in Germany as part of a critical philosophy advanced by liberals and socialists living under an authoritarian regime. They wished to demonstrate that ethics was, or should be, a matter of individual choice. He concluded that relativism was characteristic of democratic societies and that Americans never found it to be a problem. They were comfortable with the idea that basic values could not be proven and that the "is" and "ought" could be separated, because there was an underlying consensus and unconscious dogmatism with respect to liberal values. They were never forced to confront the issue of making fundamental choices or justifying the beliefs to which they were attached, while the rise of nazism forced intellectuals in Germany to face the dilemma.[53] But he nevertheless believed that political theory must face the issue of justifying democracy. "I do not accuse political practice; I accuse political theory."[54]

In 1947, Brecht reported on a roundtable dealing with relativism and political theory which included Coker, Pennock, Lippincott, Wright, Voegelin, Hallowell, Almond, and Wilson. Some individuals such as Morgenthau entered the discussion from the floor. Kelsen was invited, although unable to attend, but sent a message indicating that despite the growing unpopularity of relativism, he remained a critic of "absolutism." Kelsen's legal positivism continued to be a prime target of those who wished to ground political theory in natural law, but Kelsen was adamant in claiming that philosophical absolutism led to political absolutism, while democracy was pluralist and analogous to, and supported by, philosophical value-relativism and the separation of science from politics.[55]

Brecht saw the issue as deriving from the contention that "modern science and modern scientific methods, with all their splendor of achievement, have led to an ethical vacuum, a religious vacuum, and a philosophical vacuum." Social science found itself in a position where it could not distinguish between right and wrong, good and evil, or justice and injustice. None of the social sciences were as affected by this problem as political science which was forced to deal directly with the phenomena of communism, fascism, and nazism which had "settled down in the area abandoned by science." Brecht argued that "no political theorist can honestly avoid the issue"—the issue posed by "scientific relativism." Brecht wished to focus on the "higher forms" of relativism such as that represented by Weber which admitted that there was priority among values but no intersubjective demonstration.[56]

All participants agreed that more study of values was necessary. Wilson, Pennock, Almond, Morgenthau, and Hallowell joined in the claim that "at least some *approximation* to proof often seems possible regarding the validity of value judgments," and Almond stated that the "greatest challenge of political theory today is the task of participating in the search for a valid natural law theory." Hallowell made his case for Christianity, despite its basis in faith, as a rational ground of values. When asked how he would deal with a Muslim, he replied, "Convert him." Lippincott, while noting that he was a believer, did not see any basis for proof. Wright sided with Coker and pointedly warned against "claims to absolute knowledge." While he did not believe that political science had gained much from its more "scientific" pursuits, he argued that "even the worst aberrations of our quantitative brethren are preferable to the mystical lucubration of their antagonists on the opposite wing." Relativism and pragmatism offered a more reasonable position. Voegelin joined the discussion by suggesting that the whole definition of the issue had been rendered obsolescent by the advances in philosophical anthropology which had reconstituted a more classical notion of science and placed us "far beyond relativism."

Lippincott again criticized the emphasis in political theory on the history of ideas and argued that it failed to "discharge the main purpose of theory, which is to ascertain the chief facts, concepts, and principles that do, may, or ought to arise as a result of governance."[57] With respect to the relationship between scholarship and teaching and between theory and practice, most agreed that one's values should be made explicit and that political science should be made relevant to political practice. Almond pushed for value-neutrality in the presentation of research despite one's value position, while Hallowell argued for being a "partisan in favor of all that is good for humanity" and suggested that it was the notion of objectivity as neutrality and the "abdication of such responsibility on the part of the academic profession in Germany that drove so many university students into the hands of the Nazis."[58]

There was an increasing polarization of the field. Voegelin had found his stride attacking modernity and charging that science, from Newton onward, had brought relativism into the world and created a tradition of "spiritual eunuchs." He argued that "as a consequence of the interlocking of science and social power, the political tentacles of scientistic civilization reach into every nook and corner of an industrialized society, and with increasing effectiveness they stretch over the whole globe."[59] For someone such as Coker who had been a critic of scientism and pluralism, and for Wright, who along with Elliott, Friedrich, and McIlwain, was a principal in the highly traditional program of political theory at Harvard, such arguments presented a dilemma. Faced with the new challenges emanating from the émigrés, where Marxism and natural law all sounded much alike, he found himself choosing the side of empirical political science which was not simply a choice about a profession and discipline but a choice for liberalism.

While conventional histories of political theory had been, and continued to be, in effect, histories of the development and progress of liberalism, the challenge was now sufficiently focused that a more specific recovery of the liberal tradition seemed necessary. Frederick Watkins (at McGill) noted that while "most people are aware that liberalism is in the throes of a major crisis," the "full significance" was not yet adequately understood. His study was an attempt to "recapture" the meaning of liberalism and make it "whole." He set out to demonstrate that liberalism was not just a "policy" or even *a* tradition but "the modern embodiment of all the characteristic traditions of Western politics. If liberalism fails to survive, it will mean the end of the Western political tradition." In his view, the choice was a stark one—between liberalism and totalitarianism, and the meaning of liberal democracy was pluralism.[60]

The defense of scientism that would culminate in the behavioral movement was in part a response to the new criticism, but there was also an independent if complementary worry that political science had not achieved its traditional goals. While much of the conversation in political theory was absorbed with issues generated by the attack on political science, political scientists were also concerned, by the postwar period, that the discipline had not agreed on a definite set of scientific principles and methods that would allow it to fulfill its aspirations. This was the theme of William Anderson's survey of political science in 1949.

What the discipline required, he argued, was an "established body of tested propositions concerning the political nature and activities of man that are applicable throughout the world and presumably at all times." Anderson was no enemy of the study of the history of political theory and concerns about values, but he, much like Willoughby, argued that it was necessary to distinguish between politics and science and pursue the latter.[61] The way to do this was to study individual "human political behavior," or the political atom, and produce knowledge in the "field of scientific method" that would be useful in developing postulates and propositions. Such claims had been at the core of political theory for over fifty years, but it was now increasingly difficult to find political theorists committed to that calling.[62]

The call to science would be increasingly accompanied by an attack on the existing practice of political theory which was often described as excessively historical, teleological, utopian, antiscientific, moralistic, and generally obscurantist. This was an image that would be difficult to ascribe to the literature published before 1940, but it can be more easily associated with the trends in the field after that date. By 1950, Hallowell had brought together his arguments in a comprehensive work on modern political thought. This book embodied, summarized, and reflected the claims that had emerged during the past decade, and it was in many respects prototypical of, and initiated, a new genre of literature in the history of political theory. It also presented a new substantive image of that history which would begin to dominate the field by the end of the next decade and which would be paradigmatically represented in the work of Voegelin, Strauss, Arendt, and Wolin.

Although Hallowell's work was about "modern political thought," a large portion was devoted to a general interpretation of the development of political ideas from ancient times up through the emergence of what he designated as "integral liberalism" which he claimed was an outgrowth of the ideas of such individuals as Grotius and Locke.[63] The image projected was one of a seamless web of evolution that moved from the classical world through the emergence of modern science, the Renaissance, and Hobbes to the rise of liberalism. However, *the story of modern political thought was now a story of decline* which was offered as an explanation of contemporary political problems and "the crisis of our times" exemplified in socialism, Marxism, Soviet Communism, fascism, and the theory and practice of totalitarianism in general. But the most basic problem was the decadence of contemporary liberalism and its inability to defend and maintain itself.

In Hallowell's saga, the main villain, positivism, was the direct outgrowth of the Enlightenment, utilitarianism, and German idealism. His notion of positivism was still the very general one of an "attempt to transfer to the study of social and human phenomena the methods and concepts of the natural sciences" as exemplified in the work of Comte, Mill, Spencer, and Ward.[64] Positivism, with its attendant separation of fact and value, and relativism, with its rejection of transcendental grounds, undermined liberalism and both allowed and abetted the rise of antiliberal political movements. For Hallowell, the answer to the modern crisis was once again Christianity and the reconstitution of liberalism on the basis of religious values. The book received a less than enthusiastic reception in the political science community. Watkins claimed that it "must be read with great caution," and he questioned the "propriety of asking students, outside a confessional school, to accept Christian orthodoxy as an unquestioned standard of judgment."[65]

In 1950, Lippincott attempted, as he had a decade earlier, to make sense out of what constituted political theory in the United States and to provide a critical analysis of the field. Although his discussion did not gain the attention attracted by some of the statements that would be made in the next few years, it is remarkable in that it included most of the points that would be understood as central to the behavioral manifesto. The basic themes of what would become the behavioral movement had been formulated well in advance of the 1950s, but they were distinguished less by their novelty than by the extent to which they were a reaffirmation of the traditional values of political science.

Lippincott suggested that political theory was at least potentially, or correctly understood, the "most scientific branch" of political science. It was, however, an area in which political scientists had "produced little," if theory were defined, as he believed it should be, "as the systematic analysis of political relations" in descriptive, explanatory, evaluative, and prescriptive terms. It should, he argued, be concerned with "general" claims about the "actions and behavior of men" and with particular facts and institutions only as objects for testing its principles. Only Willoughby, MacIver, Dewey, Merriam, and Lippmann qualified as making a "serious attempt." It seemed to him that the aversion to theory remained as it had a decade earlier. Up to this point, Lippincott argued, "the greatest effort has been devoted to writing the history of political ideas" and "defining and classifying terms and principles of politics." Although there had been impressive work in the history of political theory and although history could in some ways contribute to science, history and the description and classification of political principles had not "advanced science in any marked degree," and it had not done much to promote understanding of the great political issues and events of the age.[66]

Many of the shortcomings of political theory could, Lippincott believed, be attributed to the "inadequacy of empiricism," or the crude inductivist misunderstanding of empiricism that eschewed both evaluation and generalization and held that only "'facts' are real, and that values are subjective and not susceptible of scientific treatment." He maintained, on the contrary, that universals were as real as facts, that scientific method does not assume that facts speak for themselves, and that evaluation is necessarily built into the subjective organization of data on the part of the observer. Lippincott's prescription was for political theory finally to take stock of itself, develop some definite agreement about what it was and what it can do, identify its proper place in political science, specify the basic problems it should engage, give up old-fashioned nontheoretical empiricism, adopt a "more creative type of scientific method" that would resemble that of the "great physicists," become more interdisciplinary, and, finally, confront the main political problems of the day such as the threat of communism to the foundations of democracy, the nature of political power, and the issue of state intervention.[67]

This was a remarkable statement, and it signaled the agenda of the next decade. Merriam's analysis of the discipline in the same volume was a striking contrast in that it reflected an older paradigm and suggested none of the tensions implicit in Lippincott's discussion. The growing sense that political science in the postwar period must be more than a science of American politics and that liberalism was more than an American mission would be one factor in moving the discipline further in the direction of articulating a vision of a universal political science. Yet that vision was as much a defense of liberal values as it was a claim for the authority of science.

Behavioralism effected significant changes in the research programs of the discipline, but philosophically it represented the resumption of the project that had been formulated and pursued at Chicago. Such a resumption, however, required, at this point, more than a token justification and more than merely overcoming the inertia of some of the characteristic historical, institutional, and legalistic analysis in the field. First, the very idea of a science of politics was under attack, and political theory, which had been so closely allied to that idea, was being transformed. Second, the liberal image of politics which had been inseparable from this science was also being called into question. For all those involved, proponents as well as opponents, the behavioral movement was understood as revolutionary, but although it led to the constitution of a new disciplinary order, it was initially, like the American political revolution, fought as much to redeem the past as to realize the future, to institutionalize an ideal that was in danger of slipping away. The question is not so much one of who fired the first shot in the behavioral revolution, though the answer would seem to be that it came from the antibehavioral ranks. By the end of the 1940s, however, the battle lines were forming. The basic reason that the genre of the history of political theory became the target of much of behavioral criticism was that it was the repository of much of the literature that challenged the values of the discipline.

Despite its continuities with the past, behavioralism was not merely a rerun of ideas from the 1920s and 1930s. The behavioral movement would have a much greater impact on the actual practice of the discipline. Although in retrospect the claims of Merriam and Lasswell appear prominent and the influence of Chicago was significant, more traditional forms of inquiry continued to dominate the field as a whole well into the 1940s and beyond. By the early 1950s, the belief that the practice of political science had not lived up to its promise and that it lagged behind other dimensions of the scientific enterprise was enunciated with new vigor. Although some, such as those associated with the Chicago school, would still link the need for a "profound understanding of political behavior" to practical issues and the advance of democracy,[68] few would explicitly hold fast to the old alliance.

Lasswell would be the most consistent advocate of political science as a practical science with an end in action and would steadfastly hang on to this idea until the image of political science as a policy science once again became an essential part of the identity of the discipline in the 1970s. But in the early 1950s, he was, at best, ambivalent, and this ambivalence probably reflected the dominant underlying sentiment. The latent ethos was still social control, and the "dangers" implicit in this idea would be fastened upon by many of the postwar critics of behavioralism who viewed it as antihumanistic. But increasingly the discourse of political science centered on developing pure science despite the normative emphasis in comparative politics in which a science of politics was tied to the modernization and Westernization of "developing" countries. There have been many general contextual explanations for the behavioral emphasis, and numerous factors can, and have been, noted.

There was the growing sense of danger in the Cold War era, and during the McCarthy period, of becoming involved with normative issues—dangers to both individuals and the credibility of disciplines.[69] This was also a period when educational and research emphasis was on pure science, and political scientists were testifying to the scientificness of political science to gain research support. Political science adopted the term "behavioral" to represent its affiliation with the wider movement in the behavioral sciences. In 1949, a group of scientists at the University of Chicago, interested in developing a general theory of human behavior, chose the label "behavioral sciences," both because of its "neutral character" which facilitated the interdisciplinary approach it reflected and because, repeating the nineteenth-century concern, people (and especially those who voted research funds in Congress) "might confound social science with socialism."[70]

The impetus of the pressures and incentives of increased professionalism was significant, and the return of political scientists from involvement in various dimensions of the civilian and military war effort carried with it as much disillusionment with the world of practice as enthusiasm, as well as a sense, often, that scientists and practitioners belonged to different cultures. There was a belief that with the end of the war the normative issues had been settled and that government had more than enough expertise to govern. Finally, there was the oft-noted liberal complacency of the postwar period and the assumption that democratic values had been assured and that politics required more description and explanation than reformation—that the process of description and explanation was at once a kind of validation that did not require a distinct normative claim. Yet despite all the elements in this putative inducive and conducive ambience, there were some persistent and powerful internal dynamics that moved the field in the same direction.

There was still the pervasive, and now maybe explicitly Weberian, belief that unless political science could establish itself as a real and legitimate science, it would never play the policy role that had fallen, and was still falling, to fields such as economics, that practical authority required scientific detachment. The retreat to scientific purity was in part a function of the long-standing idea that political contamination entailed a loss of credibility as well as of objectivity. But more immediate was the emerging need, in the conversation of political theory, to defend the very idea of science and to give meaning to the concept of scientific theory. The core meaning of behavioralism would be the commitment to emulating natural science, but this had always been the commitment of political science. Political scientists were still suffering from an envy for the certainty that seemed characteristic of "real" science. But what was required was a new definition and defense of this traditional goal.

Discussions about science focused in a much more specific way than ever before on the concept of theory and on the place of theory in science. The controversy over the meaning of theory would contribute to fracturing the discipline, and in the course of that controversy political theorists on all sides would be increasingly drawn into critical and defensive philosophical arguments. Many behavioralists, as well as antibehavioralists, would view the behavioral revolution as basically a theoretical revolution, and there are several reasons for agreeing with that assessment.

First of all, there was an unprecedented metatheoretical consciousness about not only scientific theory and the nature of scientific explanation but about all dimensions of the concept of theory. Second, much of the energy of political scientists went into calling for, creating, and applying the research strategies and conceptual constructs that they equated with theory. Theory was understood as the key to scientific progress and as a distinct element of scientific explanation. Third, to the extent that one might take "theory" as the counterpart of practice, the behavioral revolution was marked by the already-noted emphasis on the development of a theoretical, as opposed to an applied, science with the emphasis, at least ostensibly, on scientific rather than political issues. Finally, the behavioral revolution was theoretical in that many of the individuals most responsible for effecting and sustaining that revolution were, in fact, political theorists. They were primarily trained and wrote dissertations in that area. Even setting aside those whose work had been prominent before the 1950s, such as Lasswell, the list is impressive. It includes, at least, Robert Dahl, Deutsch, Easton, Almond, Heinz Eulau, Alfred and Sebastian de Grazia, Morton Kaplan, Herbert McCloskey, Ithiel de Sola Pool, James Prothro, Austin Ranney, Albert Somit, and John Wahlke.

The debate within the discipline would often be understood as a conflict between political *scientists* and political *theorists*, but this was more a matter of field and literature designation than a question of education or concern about theory. Certainly few of the behavioralists understood themselves as antitheoretical, and probably very few initially understood their concern with scientific political theory as a rejection of their earlier education any more than political scientists and political theorists of the 1930s saw any incompatibility between a commitment to science and a concern with the history of political thought. To some extent, what was involved was a lag between the graduate educational establishment and the literature of political theory. The theorists educated in the 1930s and 1940s were for the most part not exposed to the new arguments that appeared in political theory, and they felt a good deal more at home with the traditional goals of the field than with the new wave of antiliberal and antiscientific thought. They eventually felt constrained to make a choice between scientist and theorist as a primary identity. The imminent debate between scientific and traditional political theory, however, would be far from simply one about method and political inquiry or even about an emphasis on values as opposed to facts. It was, in the end, a debate about liberalism and its fate. Lynd, at the beginning of the decade, had worried about what had happened to the idea of progress. By the end of the decade, Karl Löwith had declared that the idea was an "illusion" originating in a secularized theology of history and that society was "at the end of the modern rope."[71]

10

The Behavioral Reformation

The ultimate aim of scientific generalizations about politics is to increase the determinancy of important political judgments.

Harold Lasswell

The political scientist must live within the political world without being of it.

Hans Morgenthau

Beginning in the early 1950s, the call for scientific theory was characteristically accompanied by an attack on current practices in the discipline and particularly on political theory. The tensions that had developed in the field of political theory became institutionally manifest, but the political scientists who pursued a "revolution" were often less than specific about, or fully aware of, what they were revolting against. When, in 1961, Robert Dahl labeled his account of "the behavioral approach" in political science "an epitaph for a monument to a successful protest," he found that it was easier to say what the approach was *not* than what it was—not the approach of "the speculative philosopher, the historian, the legalist, or the moralist." But he designated neither a single piece of literature nor a concrete genre against which "the deviant and unpopular views" of these "revolutionary sectarians" were directed. Although it was difficult to conduct a revolution without someone to revolt against, the problem was less the absence of an enemy than one of identifying it and determining its location.

In the end, Dahl suggested that behavioralism might best be described less as an approach at all than a "mood" or "outlook" engendered by "a strong sense of dissatisfaction with the achievements of conventional political science, particularly through historical, philosophical, and the descriptive-institutional approaches," and, in turn, a "sympathy toward 'scientific' modes of investigation and analysis" and a concern with what "'is' as opposed to what 'ought to be.'" But who represented "conventional" political science was not mentioned, and Dahl did not address the content of the commitment to explain politics "by means of the methods, theories, and criteria of proof that are acceptable according to the canons, conventions, and assumptions of modern empirical science." His historical sketch of this "protest movement" suggested that most of the history of the field was the story of the fermentation of this rebellion.[1]

Apart from emphasizing various attributes such as a concern with quantitative methods and a focus on aggregate human behavior, political scientists in general had considerable difficulty describing the core meaning of behavioralism.[2] Herring, who became president of the SSRC in 1948, had urged the creation of a Committee on Political Behavior which focused on furthering the systematic study of the "behavior of individuals in political situations" for the purpose of "formulating and testing hypotheses, concerning uniformities." The "orientation or point of view," in David Truman's words, summarizing a seminar at the University of Chicago, was one that incorporated the goal of *"stating all the phenomena of government in terms of the observed and observable behavior of men"* in a rigorous, empirical, and theoretically informed manner. All this may have indicated a different distribution of research emphasis, but it was hardly revolutionary.[3] Truman later argued that the "advance in our discipline lies in the acceptance of generalizations as its primary objective and of empirically testable theory as its principal method," but he also noted that this had been a basic theme since the early years of the discipline.[4]

By 1950, the notes section of the *APSR* substituted "Political Theory, Research and Methodology" for the category "Political Theory," and a section on "Methodology and Research in Social Science" was added to the Political Theory bibliography. The direction of political theory as a subfield of political science was clear. But the intellectual distinctiveness of behavioralism was not to be found in a revolutionary break with mainstream political science. Its conception of political reality, its ideology, its commitment to the idea of science, its persistent practical concerns, its theoretical goals, and even its research techniques belonged to the very essence of the field. What *was* new was the crisis and reconstitution of its scientific identity and its perception of a need to defend its most basic presuppositions.

An articulate concern about linking political science to political practice would, however, become increasingly attenuated during the 1960s, and this direction was apparent in Dahl's analysis. Although Dahl stressed the difference between science and values, the practical uses of political science were not discussed. He did not banish "political evaluation" from political science, and even spoke of the need to reintegrate this function, but he denied the "political philosopher" any special role and emphasized instead the manner in which "evaluation cannot be performed in a sterile medium free from contamination by brute facts." His own work indicated that "brute facts" were not easily divorced from values, but even in terms of Dahl's own career, the break with practical concerns indicated a shift in emphasis.

Dahl had come from a poor midwestern family with populist leanings and had early on embraced democratic socialism. Although he had initially intended to be a lawyer, he drifted into political science (receiving his Ph.D. from Yale in 1940) but without any design to be a teacher and scholar which he looked upon with "disdain, as a domain for people not concerned with the active world." Subsequent government and army service contributed to disabusing him of a belief that his vocation was other than academic, and he returned to Yale as an instructor, in 1946, where he remained for the rest of his career.[5] By the 1960s, Dahl, as well as most behavioral political scientists, had largely ceased to discuss the relationship between public and academic discourse. There are many reasons that might be adduced for this shift, but not the least of these was the fact that they understood the functioning of American politics as satisfactory. If politics was not in need of fundamental change, description and explanation were in effect a form of political action. But the issue still shaped discussions in the 1950s, and the early years of the behavioral movement continued to reflect concern with the public role of political science. Scientific authority remained the perceived key to practical efficacy, but science was no longer an uncontested value. The attempt to construct a more self-conscious scientific identity was to some extent the product of a concern about the inadequacy of progress in empirical research, but it was more fundamentally a function of the belief that there was a need to defend the traditional vision of social science against the emerging antiscientific philosophies.

In the early 1950s, political scientists began explicitly to embrace positivism as a vision of science and as a philosophical legitimation of the commitment to scientific inquiry. Carnap's presence at Chicago contributed significantly to the appropriation of philosophical discourse. In a symposium on "The Semantics of Social Science," Perry argued that natural science had made its great advances by going beyond the "anthropomorphic and teleological" language of common sense but that in social science there was still "no important contribution in the field resulting from the application of scientific method." This could be attributed, he argued, to the "teleological, normative, or even moralistic terms" of "political theory" which "belong to a subjective or fictitious universe of discourse quite inappropriate to a general science of society."[6] There was an extravagant dimension to the rhetoric on both sides of the debate. The actual research and publication in the field hardly matched the picture of "positivism" that was being painted by the critics, and the image urged, by someone such as Perry, of political theory was equally counterfactual. To claim, as Perry did, that political science was "mostly history and ethics" and that "the propositions of political theory have a character of 'unreality' and futility that bars out any serious interest in their discussion" was to speak generically about an unspecified body of literature.[7]

Lasswell, his student Herbert Simon (who studied with Carnap in the 1930s), and the sociologist George A. Lundberg joined in this discussion and pressed for making the language of political science more scientific. Unlike Merriam and most earlier political scientists, they were no longer strangers to the philosophy of science. The whole symposium reflected the logical positivist semantic model of science advanced by Carnap. Simon enunciated an account of scientific explanation to which behavioral political scientists would routinely subscribe within the next few years. Science was to be understood as a system of predictive cum explanatory generalizations from which could be deduced testable propositions about concrete observables. Science, it was argued, was methodologically a unity, and social scientific inquiry was logically symmetrical with the methods of natural science.

For Simon, it was essential that political science adopt what he considered to be the more advanced methods of the other social sciences, and *central to this task was a transformation and redefinition of political theory* that would entail "consistent distinctions between political theory (i.e., scientific statements about the phenomena of politics) and the history of political thought (i.e., statements about what people have said about political theory and political ethics)." Lundberg endorsed Simon's image of science and stressed the need to abandon the approach of the humanities and "adopt the orientation of modern natural science" which would involve, as a first step, finding out "what the methods of natural science are." While Lasswell advocated "more attention to the construction of theoretical models" that would guide research, he also warned against excessive concern with the question of what "science" means and neglecting the practical ends toward which social science was ultimately directed in a democratic society.[8] But the argument was that the values that informed the goals of social science had nothing to do with the objectivity of descriptions and explanations of political phenomena—and that the authority of policy science rested on that very objectivity. The idea of science as a means, however, was being increasingly displaced by the idea of science as an end.

Ambivalence on this point was expressed in Lasswell's 1950 collaboration with the philosopher Abraham Kaplan, who had been a student of Carnap, in developing a general "conceptual framework" for political inquiry. Kaplan's positivism was, like Lasswell's, a peculiar hybrid version that was mixed, although not altogether homogenized, with the American pragmatic and instrumentalist tradition. The manuscript of *Power and Society* had actually been completed in 1945 before Lasswell left Chicago for Yale and Kaplan went to UCLA. The work had been funded during the war by the Rockefeller Foundation as part of a project on mass communication designed to recruit and train people in propaganda techniques. After the war, the authors saw their endeavor of creating a value-free operational language of political inquiry as an exercise in scientific "political theory" but as one nevertheless prompted by political issues such as the dangers created by "war, famine, and atomic destruction" as well as the developing confrontation between the "liberal-democratic and the Bolshevist" ideologies.

Although they stressed that they were concerned with practice, they also insisted that their purpose was neither "to provide a guide for political action" nor to develop "techniques of political practice." Yet they maintained that their goal, through the development of a systematic language for "inquiry into the political process" and the phenomenon of power, was "to bring the languages of political theory and of practical politics into closer harmony."[9] The premise that informed the project, and which made sense of these less than obviously compatible claims about scientific purity and practical purpose, was the persistent belief that the development of a science of politics comparable to natural science was the key to the practical authority of political science. Exactly how that articulation was to be achieved, however, remained nebulous.

They noted that "in recent decades a thoroughgoing empiricist philosophy of science has been elaborated in a number of approaches—logical positivism, operationalism, instrumentalism—concurring in an insistence on the importance of relating scientific ideas to materials ultimately accessible to direct observation." One purpose of the book was to legislate the meaning of "political theory" as part of empirical science and to reject explicitly what the authors believed was the tendency toward the identification of the term with both "metaphysical speculation" ("abstractions hopelessly removed from empirical observation and control") and the history of political thought from Plato to the *Federalist*. The latter had not, they claimed, been concerned with "political inquiry" and the formulation of "concepts and hypotheses of political science" but rather with what "ought to be" and with the justification of "political doctrines." Yet they again stressed that their scientific interest did "not exclude a political interest in its outcome and applications"— science and public policy were "intertranslatable" and "complementary" and "both manipulative and contemplative standpoints may be adopted."[10]

This tortured attempt to embrace simultaneously these standpoints was based on what the authors referred to as the *"principle of configurative analysis"* in which the "functions of the scientist overlap and interact with those of the policy maker." The policy sciences stood in "the grand tradition of political thought," but in that tradition, ethics and politics had been fused. Advances in social science, they claimed, required "giving full recognition to the existence of two distinct components in political theory—the empirical propositions of political science and the value judgments of political doctrine." They emphasized that they were not "unconcerned with political policy" and the "justification of democratic values" and "their derivation from some metaphysical and moral base" and that their "values are those of the citizen of a society that aspires toward freedom." But even though the end of science was to further the democratic ideal and achieve "human dignity and the realization of human capacities" by gaining control of political power, such goals were a matter of political doctrine which should not be confused with an empirical science devoted to constructing an analytical framework for developing hypotheses that would provide the basis for a "naturalistic" treatment of *"homocentric politics."*[11] Yet Lasswell, more than anyone else of the period, continued to emphasize the policy orientation of social science and the idea that political science was a science of democracy. In his 1956 presidential address to the APSA, he continued to call for scholars armed with science to lead society into the future and achieve a "reconciliation of mastery and freedom."[12]

The goal was to emulate theory in economics. This required, however, in Lasswell's view, a break with the tradition in the discipline that equated "political theory" with "political philosophy." The practitioners of the latter were actually "historians of past writings on the 'State,'" and "possessing a voluminous and dignified tradition they were so weighed down with the burden of genteel erudition that they had little intellectual energy with which to evolve original theory for the guidance of either science or policy."[13] Lasswell did not specify to whom he was referring, but if he really believed that the study of the history of political theory in American political science was fundamentally responsible for the theoretical deficiencies of the discipline, it would have implied a fundamental break with the views of his mentor, Merriam, which he never acknowledged. The real issue was not a conflict between history and science, but something much more specific.

The new intellectual regime taking shape at Chicago was evident in Morgenthau's review of Lasswell and Kaplan's book. Despite its emphasis on the concept of power, which Morgenthau stressed as the essence of politics, this work was, he claimed, a total failure. It made no contribution to political theory and was nothing less than a "monstrosity," an intellectually barren "theoretical pretense" that represented "a thorough misunderstanding of the nature of political theory and of its relationship to empirical research." He predicted that while their approaches, behavioralism and positivism, were gaining popularity, their position actually represented "an obsolescent point of view" and constituted "the most extreme, and therefore self-defeating, product of the fundamental errors" of the schools on which it was based. It would "contribute to their demise by virtue of its own absurdity." It was not simply the tragic misdirection of two brilliant minds, but a symbol of the "tragedy of political science."[14]

The project was a quite conscious attempt to create a scientific practice modeled on the logical positivist account of linguistic meaning and empiricism, but it was not alone in seeking to translate philosophical analyses of science into research procedures.[15] The economist J. J. Spengler endorsed the idea of a political science focusing on power. He claimed that it was time that "political science was transformed into a full-bodied social science even as economics was" and that it could do this by focusing on "'power' and power-oriented behavior just as economics has centered itself about scarcity and scarcity-oriented behavior." In a discussion of this summons, an earlier critic of scientism urged the development of a general unified science of theories and postulates similar to that "developed in natural science before, and first completed by, Newton." Some traditional advocates of empirical science such as Rice were, however, beginning to lose sight of the context of the argument. Wilson joined the discussion and argued that American social science had now come to share a common metaphysic regarding theory, knowledge, and social reality. This was based on scientism, empiricism, pragmatism, instrumentalism, positivism, relativism, and operationalism. He claimed that "the discussion of method has reached a crisis" and suggested that there were limits to the positivist idea of rationality which must be supplemented by ethical knowledge.[16]

By this point, Paul Appleby, attempting to anticipate the direction of political science during the next twenty-five years, argued that a much broader value-oriented vision was required than the one that was then developing. Oliver Garceau suggested that the great issue facing the discipline was whether the emerging emphasis on the scientific study of political behavior could be reconciled with democratic values and the "liberal democratic faith" in the human capacity to determine ends.[17] In 1951, the APSA undertook a comprehensive study of the teaching of political science in the United States. The widely discussed report stressed such practical goals of the field as citizenship education and preparation for public service, but it also expressed distinct concerns about the identity of the field. The report noted that although political theory was popular and although there was widespread belief that it should be "the heart of the subject," it was in fact not the "core" of the discipline and not sufficiently "systematic and conceptual." Further progress in the direction indicated by Lasswell and Kaplan was required.[18]

When viewed against the background of the preceding decade, Easton's provocative statement about the "decline of political theory" is more intelligible than when it is characterized as an unprecedented attack on traditional political theory. In some respects, the behavioral revolution was initially less a distinct and circumscribed historical phenomenon perceived as such by contemporaries and participants than a creation of commentaries and retrospective accounts such as that of Dahl. During the decades of the 1950s and 1960s, Easton played a singular role in defining behavioralism as a theoretical endeavor and as a distinct intellectual configuration.

Easton had come from a Canadian family of, at most, modest circumstances in which he was the first to attend college (University of Toronto). He had been involved in left-wing politics as an undergraduate during the depression years of the late 1930s and had chosen a career in political science, over law, in the belief that it was a calling better equipped for the pursuit of social change and for preparation as "a practical politician of some sort." He chose Chicago as a graduate school, but with the advent of the war, he remained in Canada and eventually took a master's degree at Toronto. He later reapplied to Chicago and Harvard and chose the latter for financial reasons. He was, however, from the beginning, intensely dissatisfied with the program—and with his dissertation director, Elliott. Part of the difficulty was the number of faculty absent while involved in the war effort, but in addition the curriculum was loosely organized and, in content, far from what Easton had expected. Although individuals such as Elliott and Friedrich frequently disparaged the Chicago school, Easton remained intrigued by its image of a simultaneous emphasis on empirical analysis and political action which contrasted sharply with the politically and intellectually conservative curriculum in political theory at Harvard. After completing his degree, Easton accepted, in 1947, a joint appointment at Chicago in the graduate division of social science (teaching Scope and Method of Social Science) and the department of political science. It was in this interdisciplinary atmosphere, with the emphasis on theory, methods, and empirical research, that he found his intellectual home and remained for thirty-five years, but he also stepped into a volatile situation.

By this point, the department had changed considerably despite the persistence of its external reputation. Individuals such as White still wished to link a "profound study of political behavior" to practical tasks and democratic values, but much of what Easton found stimulating was in extradepartmental forums dealing with issues such as values and systems analysis.[19] Merriam, though still a presence in the late 1940s, had retired, and Easton inherited his office (and a metal telephone baffle for ensuring the privacy of "political" conversations). Lasswell had left, and political theory had become largely the province of Strauss and Morgenthau. Jerome Kerwin (chairman of the Walgreen Foundation and lecture series), along with individuals such as Nef and Yves Simon (also of the Committee on Social Thought) stressed Catholic social theory and supported the views of Hutchins. While empirical analysis was still represented, the orientation was not particularly theoretical.

Easton eventually joined the department full-time before receiving tenure (1953), but there was, at best, tentative support for, and understanding of, his emerging position, which was a perpetuation of the spirit and substance, of the Merriam-Lasswell-Catlin tradition.[20] Easton's dissertation had been on "Concepts of the Elite in English Political Thought during the Nineteenth Century," and shortly after coming to Chicago, he had published articles on Bagehot and Lasswell. The impetus behind this work was the concern with the "threatened eclipse of liberalism," and the context was discussions such as those of Hallowell. But Easton's answer to the fragility of liberalism was considerably different from that which had been developing in the recent literature.

The problem of modern liberalism was, he claimed, its "unconscionable indifference to the material conditions of society," such as the "lack of equal economic opportunity," and its general "failure to put its theories to the test of social reality." Easton found some hope for revision in the ideas of late-nineteenth-century thinkers such as Bagehot, Mosca, and Pareto, who advocated "political positivism," or the "use of scientific method to discover social facts about the source of political power" and empirically test values in the context of actual social conditions. "Realism" also led to the recognition of the role of the elite in society and of the fact that social change required creative intellectual leadership. Although Bagehot tended to wrap his (conservative) liberal values in "a mist of science," he offered a "methodological hint vital for the very survival of liberal doctrines" such as equality and self-government and one that could convert "wishful thinking and utopianism to liberal realism." Easton concluded that the "liberal must turn to the laborious task of rigorous empirical study of society" and incorporate its findings "into the body of active liberal thought."[21] He pursued this theme further in his analysis of Lasswell's search for a link between science and democracy.

Easton began by noting that there was a contemporary "attack" by philosophers on scientism and on the very idea of a "science of man" as well as a general skepticism, even among social scientists, about its possibility. The basic issue, raised by individuals such as Strauss and Brecht, was whether social science could escape relativism and say something decisive about public policy. Easton saw Lasswell as passing through two basic intellectual phases—the first in which he eschewed political value judgments, while focusing on objective accounts of politics, and a second, beginning with World War II, in which he claimed that the social sciences must say "something about our ultimate social objectives" and, as policy sciences, come to a defense of democracy. Although Lasswell's work might seem to imply that social science could not break out of the Weberian impasse, Easton found subtle indications of another answer. Through scientific findings about human nature, there might be a "scientific validation of values."[22]

Lasswell, Easton claimed, was passionately committed to a science of and for democracy defined in terms of "majority rule" and the "dignity of man." The question was whether his "monist views on democracy" could be reconciled with his "permissive relativism." Easton argued that in the end there was coherency even if Lasswell had not articulated it. If certain human values and goals were scientifically and demonstrably rooted in universal basic impulses, then it might be argued that only certain institutional arrangements might satisfy these needs. For Easton, what this implied was the "need for the social scientist to return to an apparently discredited past in order to assert once again the possibilities of transcending the insecurities of relativism for the greater certainty of a science of values."[23]

What Lasswell's career indicated to Easton was the impossibility, and danger, of attempting to avoid political evaluation in the pursuit of a science of politics. The attempt to speak to the needs of a democratic community led Lasswell, almost unwittingly, to reformulate his claims about the "nature of politics." He had moved from a narrow theory of elitism and power in his early work, to a more general theory of decision making which opened new avenues for "the development of a systematic theory of political science," maybe the most important in the "history of political research," as well as a more accurate understanding of democracy. The lessons to be learned from Lasswell's work were the need to be aware of the value premises and conceptual principles governing political research and the need to seek the kinds of knowledge that are "immediately relevant" to democratic goals rather than simply searching for "pure truth."[24]

The actual context of the 1951 article was a symposium "on the relation of political theory to research" with other contributions by Alfred de Grazia, Donald Smithburg, and Samuel Eldersveld. The purpose of the discussion, de Grazia noted, was to determine how political theory might better "adjust" itself to the needs of research methodology and go beyond a concern with "utopian goodness."[25] Smithburg argued that there was too much emphasis on "ought" and insufficient on "is." He noted that the National Roster of Scientific and Specialized Personnel which had been created to list "useful talent" during World War II, had, "on the advice of the APSA, classified political theory as concerned with political ethics and the history of political ideas." His prescription for developing testable scientific hypotheses and making "a coherent logically consistent system out of the hodge-podge of sensory fact" was hardly a novel one, but he emphasized that the current obstacle was the political theorists' self-image as "historians or theologians."[26] Eldersveld argued that "we must predict, if we are to understand," but that the state of theory was such that it was still not possible to go beyond Merriam's 1925 statement about there being "signs of hope that genuine advance may be made in the not distant future toward the discovery of scientific relations in the domain of political phenomena."[27] De Grazia urged that the task of political theory was to lead this advance by creating "political theory of a high order" that would tell political scientists what they "ought to know" and make sense out of the facts that they collect.[28]

Political theory, then, was both the problem and the solution, but the attack on conventional political theory as historical, utopian, and theological remained vague in its reference. Easton's contribution was the most sophisticated and thorough analysis of political theory that had appeared in many years. It was primarily an extended argument about how historicism and relativism had led to the demise of creative value theory and applied causal theory as well as of their fruitful conjunction.

"Why is it," Easton asked, "that today in political theory we must turn to the past in order to find inspiration and genuine freshness?" The contemporary "poverty of political theory" and its failure to engage in its "natural and traditional role" and develop "revolutionary creative thinking" was, he argued, because it "lives parasitically on ideas a century old." The preoccupation with "historical interpretation" had also undermined "the task of building systematic theory about political behavior and the operation of political institutions" and had inhibited bringing the "two major orders of knowledge," facts and values, together in their proper relationship which had been so evident in the work of classic theorists such as John Locke. Easton claimed that political theory, properly understood, consisted of four types of analytically distinguishable propositions: values or preference, factual or descriptive, generalized causal theory about the relations between facts and between means to ends, and applied principles linking the former three.[29]

Although he noted some exceptions (Dewey, Barker, Croce, and Laski), he claimed that political theory had been dominated by a type of literature (Dunning, McIlwain, Sabine) that had "managed to crush the life out of value theory" by "retailing information about the meaning, internal consistency, and historical development of past values" and by concentrating, in various ways, on the relationship between values and their historical "milieu." Historicism, which reduced discussion of values to a kind of sociology of knowledge, and the "relativistic attitude toward values," which had characterized the tradition of thought from Hume to Weber, had, Easton claimed, led political theory far from the tradition that reached from its "birth as a discipline in ancient Greece" to Marx and that had arisen out of "political struggle" about "practical policy." Yet, he argued, moral relativism was neither logically nor historically the underlying cause of the decline of creative value theory. The decline, and even the emergence of relativism itself, was a function of the consensus and complacency that marked the late nineteenth and early twentieth centuries—a situation that had been profoundly changed by the "end of the first World War and the subsequent spread of totalitarianism" and by the recognition that theory was once again required for "guidance for our conduct in practical affairs." The historicist/relativist approach which sanctioned and urged the exclusion of values from empirical analysis was also, as Lynd had argued, detrimental to social research and, as Mannheim had demonstrated, impossible. "Research is inevitably immersed in an ethical perspective" that determines the selection of problems and facts as well as the interpretation of data. To neglect this obscured the fact that "social science lives in order to meet human needs," deflected research away from relevant issues, and perpetuated the "feeling today that social science lives in an isolated ivory tower."[30]

In urging the reconstitution of value theory, Easton adopted a distinctly minimalist position on the status of values—"the traditional social science assumption" that values were relative emotivist preferences and "responses fixed by our life-experiences" rather than "objective principles." If creative theory could be justified on this basis, acknowledging the very relativism that had contributed to its demise, it could certainly be defended on the basis of a stronger theory of values. Easton argued that the justification was pragmatic, that the age was one in which serious and sophisticated "political guidance" was necessary for both "the politician as well as the humble citizen." Although this task could conceivably be left to the "statesman," it was within the "competence" of "those social scientists who are most closely associated with analyzing the content of past value systems" and who are "in a strategic position for contributing to a reformulation of contemporary theory." Easton argued that the "task of the social scientist has been too sharply and artificially divorced from that of the politician." The well-rounded political theorist with knowledge of both contemporary "empirical relations" and "involved with human goals," who had grasped the "art" of value theory from the study of traditional political theory, rather than simply talking about that art, potentially possessed a discernment of which "neither the politician nor the citizen is normally as well-equipped." Creative value theory would make empirical research meaningful and relevant and "provide once again a bridge between the needs of society and the knowledge of the social sciences," and provide "the grounds of political action."[31]

Although the principal emphasis in the article was on the reconstitution of value theory, a second attribute, and cause, of the decline of political theory was "indifference to causal theory," or "systematic empirically-oriented theory about political behavior" which could "permit the construction of a meaningful applied science" that went beyond "the rank of exceptional common sense" provided by the journalist or statesman. Easton argued that political theory in political science had "never been guided by an image of itself as a truly theoretical organ" for the discipline. Even though the "creative political theorists of the past" had been concerned with empirical phenomena, they had failed to "develop genuine theoretical causal knowledge," and the advent of historicism had brought an end to the effort. The few contributions made in this direction were by individuals such as Lasswell, Simon, and Catlin who were not in the area of "traditional theory." The whole blame, however, could not be attributed to the subfield of political theory, since, compared to the other social sciences, the discipline as a whole had "a low level of theoretical development." Easton assumed that there were uniformities in political behavior to be discovered but that this required moving beyond "crude empiricism" and low-level generalization to general or "broad-gauge theory or the conceptual framework within which a whole discipline is cast" and which eventually and incrementally "might reach the stage of maturity of theory in physics."[32]

Easton was responding to a much greater substantive and methodological threat to the position he wished to defend than the dead hand of the discipline's past. The "historicism" that he attacked was, first of all, not explicated very well by his reference to Karl Popper's definition. It more closely reflected the position of Strauss with whom he discussed the content of his article and on whose image of the tradition of political philosophy he explicitly drew. Those chosen for criticism were in many ways surrogates for a mood and a literature that was at this point still not easily characterized and identified. Easton's analysis of the elements of political theory was, for example, virtually identical with that of Sabine, and his description of traditional American historians of political theory as retreating from value concerns and the support of empirical science to a kind of sterile historicism was a less than convincing characterization of either their motives or the content of their work.

Despite his attempt to deal with the issue of relativism, Easton had at this point not taken the full measure of his senior colleague, Strauss, and the latter had not discerned the direction of Easton's intellectual development. The impending split would be both academic and ideological. Strauss would soon be attacking Easton's scientism, and, as a defender of Joseph McCarthy and Richard Nixon, Strauss took umbrage at those like Easton who were strong critics. Although exchanges between the diverse elements of the Chicago faculty were limited, the department was becoming a microcosm of the intellectual division that would characterize the field of political science as a whole. The emerging battle between "ancients and moderns," between "philosophers" such as Strauss and "scientists" such as Lasswell, had been announced.[33] The fundamental issue, however, was less a matter of the choice between science and philosophy than one of the nature and status of liberalism. This was again evident in Coker's analysis of the situation.

He saw a danger to liberalism from some political scientists who, he believed, advocated separating morals and politics and presented a majoritarian account of democracy with no inviolable rights for individuals and minorities. The other, and maybe greater, danger to liberalism, however, was from those such as Niebuhr and Hallowell who were distrustful of human nature and individualism on principle and wanted to subsume political theory in moral and theological discussions. In response to the arguments of individuals such as Hallowell, Coker suggested that there was little basis for assuming that conditions in Germany and certain misguided notions about Hitler on the part of some people were a product of legal positivism, much less any part of liberalism.[34] But the debate in political theory was widening, and the idea of the danger of scientism was beginning to reach beyond the literature directly associated with the émigrés.

In a symposium on "Recent American Political Theory" in honor of Coker, his student at Yale, Dwight Waldo (now an assistant professor at Berkeley), singled out theories of democratic administration as constituting "a significant development in political thought." Waldo had written what would become the classic study of the political theory of American public administration, and, as in the book, he suggested certain dangers approaching "nihilism" in the tendency to separate politics and values from administration and efficiency and to call the latter a matter of evaluatively neutral science and fact. In a footnote, Waldo noted that Herbert Simon was among those who had made a great contribution to the study of administration but that this was most apparent when he was unencumbered by the methodology to which he was attached and which prevented him from seeing that there was no realm of factual judgments from which values were excluded.[35] In a sharp reply, Simon charged that Waldo's arguments were typical "of the writings of those who call themselves 'political theorists' and who are ever ready to raise the battle cry against positivism and empiricism." Furthermore, attacking Waldo's phrasing and terminology, he argued that there could be no

progress in political philosophy if we continue to think and write in the loose, literary, metaphysical style that he and most political theorists adopt. The standard of rigor that is tolerated in political theory would not receive a passing grade in the elementary course in logic. . . . If political philosophers wish to preserve democracy from what they regard as the termitic borings of positivism, I suggest as a first step they acquire a sufficient technical skill in modern logical analysis to attack the positivists on their own grounds.[36]

Although Waldo did not elaborate the point, his reply to Simon suggested an issue which had not yet surfaced in the literature. This was the incipient problem of the relationship between the philosophy of science and scientific practice—particularly in the social sciences. Waldo suggested that "Simon needs to examine whether the logical positivism of which he is enamored has become an obstacle in his pursuit of science to which he is dedicated. To me, at least, logical positivism, empiricism, and science are far from being the nearly or wholly congruent things which they are to Professor Simon."[37] This issue would not really be confronted by political science until the implications of Thomas Kuhn's analysis of *The Structure of Scientific Revolutions* made their impact on the critique of behavioralism in the late 1960s.

Easton's book on *The Political System* decisively shaped subsequent discussions about political theory as well as the practice of political science. It incorporated his discussion of Lasswell and the decline of political theory, but there was a distinct change in the distribution of emphasis. Although the concern with the reconstitution of value theory remained, most of the book was devoted to criticizing past empirical and theoretical work in political science and pursuing, as expressed in the prefatory quote from Beard, the worthy, even if ultimately impossible, goal of developing a general causal theory that would bring politics, and the future, under rational human control. Political science research had, he claimed, been characterized by "hyperfactualism," a failure to marry empiricism and theory. Although the focus on concepts such as "power" and the "state" had yielded some results, it had failed to provide a basis for formulating "a conceptual framework for the whole field." Easton here proposed what would become his influential definition of politics as "the authoritative allocation of values" and laid down the rudiments of his systems analysis which would be the focus of his extensive and detailed theoretical endeavors during the next decade.[38]

Although the book has been characteristically understood as the seminal theoretical tract of the behavioral movement, its immediate reception and interpretation was positive but ambiguous. Anderson, for example, perceived it as representing nostalgia for a "Golden Age" of political theory and as urging the creation of an autonomous group of theorists separate from political science. More perceptive was his belief, however inaccurate, that the book represented the growing pessimistic mood of the times and his puzzlement about how the historicism of Sabine and similar writers could have had the devastating effect on theory that Easton alleged.[39] What has been most neglected in Easton's book is his own account of the context in which he wrote it. There are few books in the field whose meaning has become so much a function of their interpretative history. Although Easton continued to cite Strauss's work, and noted once again that he had profited from his "friendly criticism and challenging scholarship," the intellectual chasm between the tradition to which Easton attached himself and the climate of political theory at Chicago was becoming apparent. As Catlin noted, "today there seems to be a 'Chicago School' of a markedly different temper."[40]

Arendt had published *The Origins of Totalitarianism* in 1951, and she stressed that this "crisis of the century" and "burden of our times" was not an aberration, but something deeply embedded in modernity and rooted in the collapse of the nation-state and the political order in the face of the rise of bourgeois and mass society. What made the phenomenon difficult to understand, however, was the pervasive positivist liberal bias of social science which obscured the role of the political dimension of life.[41] Yves Simon had published his *Community of the Free* (1947) and his Walgreen lectures (*Philosophy of Democratic Government*, 1951) which attacked the idea of progress and sought a theological basis of democracy. Voegelin's Walgreen lectures (1951) were published in 1952 as *The New Science of Politics*. This work was featured (certainly a unique moment for academic theory) in detail in *Time* magazine. Its thesis about the decline and decadence of Western thought was offered as an explanation for the mid-century issues of the Cold War, the Korean conflict, totalitarianism, and McCarthyism, as well as the general inability of American society to cope with the problems that it confronted.[42] Strauss's Walgreen lectures (1952) and a series of essays published during the early 1950s appeared as his most defining work, *Natural Right and History*, in 1953, following *On Tyranny* (1948) and the republication in the United States of his book on Hobbes. Journal articles in political theory were now increasingly and widely reflecting this literature. Although this work was not originally published in English, Lukács had undertaken (1952) to demonstrate that it was modern philosophy that had created "the path to Hitler." The "destruction of reason" grew out of German irrationalism, extending from Schelling to Heidegger, and relativistic ideas such as those associated with Mannheim, and the evolution had continued in pragmatism and positivism in America. Like Elliott, he concluded that Mussolini's basic ideas were attributable to William James.[43]

The philosophical and ideological issues that later would be recognized as dividing these authors were still not apparent to an American audience. Lukács's or Horkheimer's arguments, for example, were, in general terms, hardly distinguishable from those of Strauss and Voegelin. Strauss, however, pointedly distinguished his return to classical political theory from neo-Thomism, and he and Voegelin were at odds on a number of matters. Voegelin's review of Arendt was less than positive, even though she had cited his work on race, but there was basic agreement on issues such as the crisis of the West and the manner in which liberalism and positivism were implicated. He claimed that her book bore "the scars of the unsatisfactory state of theory" and the philosophy of history, bought into the "typically liberal, progressive, pragmatic attitude," and failed to discern the medieval intellectual roots of the problem and how much "liberals and totalitarians have in common." Arendt defended her approach to understanding history through subjecting facts and events to critical imagination, and she rejected "going back to religion and faith for political reasons." But although she stressed that "liberals are clearly not totalitarians," she emphasized "the fact that liberal or positivistic elements also lend themselves to totalitarian thinking." Although Voegelin's statements were the most extravagant, he was not alone in the sentiment that "the putrefaction of Western civilization, as it were, has released a cadaveric poison spreading its infection through the body of humanity" and created "a community of suffering under the earthwide expansion of western foulness."[44]

Voegelin had by this point given up his general history of ideas, based on the more traditional model, to pursue the project framed in his *New Science of Politics*.[45] After Hallowell's work, this was the first major attempt at a holistic account of the decline of political theory cast as an explanation of the decadence of modernity and liberalism. Wilson hailed Voegelin as "one of the most distinguished interpreters to America of the non-liberal stream of European thought" and as exposing the "presuppositions of liberalism" and leading political science "away from the obsolescence of positivist liberalism.[46] But few contemporary readers grasped the intellectual background. Voegelin emphasized the "derailment" of thought that began with Hobbes, the Reformation, and the Enlightenment, but the crucial point of origin was the Gnostic revolt against classical and Christian ideas that entered the modern age through the work of Joachim of Flora and led to the search for heaven on earth or an "immanentist eschatology" expressed in humanism, enlightenment, progressivism, liberalism, positivism, Marxism, and, eventually, totalitarianism. For Voegelin, communism was only the "radical expression" of liberalism. The modern crisis required a "restoration" and "retheoretization" of political science that would rescue it from the "degradation" effected by positivism, with its emphasis on method, facts, and the search for value-freedom, and turn it once again toward the search for transcendent principles that had characterized classical medieval Christian thought. Political theory, today, however, required, in the first instance, the historical recovery of forgotten truth.

Strauss, now Robert Maynard Hutchins Distinguished Service Professor, noted that the "unqualified relativism" that had taken over German philosophy a generation ago was now characteristic of Western thought in general and especially American social science and liberalism. It was not the first time, he suggested, that a victor had been defeated by the ideas of the vanquished. "Liberal relativism," historicism, and the triumph of natural science, with its emphasis on the separation of facts and values, led to a rejection of "natural right" and opened the door to nihilism and totalitarianism. To understand this crisis, a crisis of both ideas and politics, required the historical project of tracing its evolution in modern political theory—an evolution that was in fact a decline, since Machiavelli and Hobbes—and recovering the truth of classical political philosophy, as exemplified in the work of Plato and Aristotle.[47]

When read in this context, it is not surprising that Easton began his book with the claim that it was "increasingly difficult to appreciate why political theory should continue to be included as a central part of political science" and that it was essential to "win back for theory its proper and necessary place." In part, he attributed political science's shunning of the "scientific method" to a failure to understand the place of theory in empirical science and its relationship to facts, but the greater problem was a certain "mood of the age" that was "growing in political science." Apart from a reference to Michael Oakeshott as a supporter of "traditionalism" and to such things as the fears generated in the atomic age, Easton was not specific about the exact locus of this mood. But it was characterized by a "dissent against scientific method," a "growing disillusionment about the whole of scientific reasoning as a way of helping us understand social problems," and a turn "towards a greater dependence upon emotion or faith and upon tradition."[48]

Although Easton suggested that the mood was a general cultural phenomenon marked by "despair," which led people to put the "blame on scientific reason" and escape "its authority and use," it was also "ubiquitous" in "political philosophy" which had given up the idea that "progress is inevitable" and embraced the "humanistic feeling that scientific development, either social or physical, does not always lead to desirable moral results." What dominated was an attitude of "social pessimism" and a "disenchantment with the old utilitarian theories of man as an essentially reasonable creature," a turn toward "myth" and a "revival of an emotional attachment to high spiritual ideals," and a "movement back to theology." The search for social laws like those in natural science, represented by the work of individuals such as Lasswell, Catlin, and Simon, had been treated with hostility. Instead, "in political science criticism rather than approval of scientific method and its cognitive objects is almost imperceptibly becoming the criterion of judgment."[49]

Easton's suggestion that the cultural mood of the early 1950s was one of social pessimism and antiscientific sentiment was not easy to accept. Although others were reacting more pointedly to Strauss and defending the tradition of American social science, there can be little doubt that it was the work of Strauss and the other émigrés that determined the intellectual climate that Easton was describing.[50] It was principally neither Sabine nor, with the possible exception of Elliott, any of the figures who had dominated the field of political theory in American political science. Not only did the substance of Sabine's interpretation of the history of political theory, with its emphasis on liberalism and progress, differ from that of individuals such as Strauss and Voegelin, but he typified the relativism, pluralism, pragmatism, and historicism that they associated with the decline of political philosophy. And Sabine suspected that Strauss's interpretative approach to historical texts was little more than "an invitation to perverse ingenuity."[51] By the mid-1950s, the division in political theory that would structure the discourse for the next two decades was becoming evident. Strauss's position, for example, and its contrast with the philosophy of American political science, was now comprehensively visible.[52]

In a joint review of Easton and Voegelin, and their respective claims about the reconstitution of political science, Dahl suggested that the discipline was experiencing "serious intellectual tension" and that a new vocabulary might be necessary to deal with new "cleavages within the profession." The opposing types, however, were still not easy to label accurately despite what seemed to be their contradictory attitudes. This was partly, he suggested, because each side produced and attacked straw men, but also because the "political scientist" was in fact nearly always a theorist, while the "political theorist oddly enough often is not a theorist at all but a historian." What was required was more truth in labeling. Although Dahl was mildly critical of Easton's work and its metatheoretical emphasis, Voegelin's historical sketch of Gnosticism as the source of both liberalism and totalitarianism was, although accurately recounted, clearly something outside his intellectual experience.[53]

Hallowell's *The Moral Foundations of Democracy* was largely a reprise of his critique of scientism, relativism, liberalism, and pluralism and his plea for a theological defense of democracy, but Kerwin noted, in the foreword, that it represented a broad coalition of "the realists, the traditionalists, the Aristotelians, or the neo-scholastics" that supported the search for "rationally determined objective ends" and upheld the "ancient conviction that morals . . . lie at the very foundation of politics."[54] Those who gathered around Hallowell, such as his teacher Niemeyer and his student Father Canavan, would hold tight to the themes. Modern political thought was responsible for the political ills of democracy, and the "hallmark" of liberalism, the enemy of constitutional democracy, was nothing less than "permissive tolerance" and "pornography."[55]

Although the direction of his argument might have been discerned from his earlier work, Lippmann also picked up the theme of liberal democratic decay and explicitly threw his lot in with Strauss, Arendt, Voegelin, and Adler and accepted their vision of the "decline of the West" and their insistence on the need "to come back to the great tradition." The problem was mass society and the lack of leadership and resoluteness which produced the weakness in liberalism that allowed, and even encouraged, the rise of totalitarianism. Pluralism and the loss of a distinct public realm had led to the decline of a public consensus that could defend and sustain liberalism. The answer was a return to "natural law" and the academic propagation of a "public philosophy."[56]

An alternative thesis, however, was that the problem of liberalism in America was the tyranny of a less than conscious public philosophy. Daniel Boorstin was only one in a long tradition of commentators who had celebrated the "genius" of American politics as an immanent consensus on democratic values. Theory was embedded in practice.[57] Louis Hartz's (Harvard) neo-Toquevillean analysis suggested, however, that phenomena such as McCarthyism and messianic democratic chauvinism, characteristic of the Cold War, were rooted in this conservative "liberal absolutism." Despite the ostensible commitment to individualism and diversity, this irrational submerged faith in American exceptionalism produced unanimity and conformity. The lack of a feudal revolution meant that the United States evolved in the context of an unchallenged Lockean tradition of equality, freedom, and private property that limited real political alternatives, either Left or Right. This underlying consensus was what made pragmatism a viable philosophy, since the ends of politics were never in question.[58] Crick offered a similar assessment of the history of the American science of politics which, he argued, both reflected and reinforced the liberal consensus.

What liberalism and liberal democracy meant in political science was now, without any question, pluralism. Few would suggest that Dahl's descriptive study of New Haven politics, published the same year as his essay on the behavioral approach, was less than an implicit endorsement of pluralism as a normative theory of liberal democracy.[59] Truman's application of what he had taken to be Bentley's group theory of politics had provided an extensive account of both political reality and the essence of the process of representative government.[60] And Dahl had offered a more theoretical defense of "polyarchal democracy," which he suggested was actually an account of how the American system worked.[61]

Morgenthau's tortured analysis of the state of the discipline, and the relationship between theory and practice, in mid-decade was an indication of the difficulties in sorting out the issues. Although he complained about the abstract formalism and practical irrelevance of the dominant trends in political science, including traditional histories of political theory, he argued strenuously that it was nevertheless the practical attitude, which had long dominated American political science, that had rendered it hopelessly pluralistic and inhibited it from developing a theoretical core of general propositions. Although he did not mention Easton by name, he seemed to refer to Easton's work when he praised a contemporary effort to revive the "classics" by searching for a "theoretical framework" and developing "empirical theory" aimed at explaining "political reality." And he endorsed the idea that political science should, at the same time, be critical and "subversive" and seek normative truths and avoid the current tendency to "retreat into the trivial." Yet he did not attribute this concern to individuals such as Lasswell and to the behavioral movement. Distorted by positivism and relativism, there had been a separation of empirical research from political philosophy, and, he suggested, "perhaps no event has had a more disastrous effect upon the development of American political science than this dichotomy."[62]

The extent to which the behavioral identity was still in the process of formation was indicated by Harry Eckstein's report on a conference in which he labeled those seeking a more scientific study of politics "behaviorists." Nevertheless, the basic issues discussed in this unprecedentedly extensive gathering of academic political theorists were clear: the character of and relationship between political philosophy and political science, the status of the study of the history of political theory, and the role of contemporary political philosophy.

Eckstein noted that while there were extremists on both sides—those "behaviorists" who sought to transform political science into "a genuine scientific *discipline*" as opposed to the "anti-behaviorists" who believed that political theory should seek "something they called wisdom"—most accepted some "middle course" and argued against any strict "behaviorist-theorist" dichotomy. There was a general agreement that "political theory" should no longer be exclusively identified with political philosophy and that "the title 'political theory' has been unjustifiably appropriated by the historians of political theory." Political philosophy should be broadly construed to include such activities as "meta-theory," or "theory about theory." Most agreed that, for a variety of reasons, there was utility in the study of the "greats" and that political philosophy, in its various forms, and political science were mutually relevant.[63] But de-

spite the tendency among many to seek or accept some sort of reconciliation, at an abstract level, the very sense of a need for compromise
accentuated the fact of differentiation.

The tensions and hope for compromise were still evident in a volume
of related essays to which some of the participants in the conference
contributed. Waldo strongly voiced the idea that the basic role of political science was a practical one—citizenship training and preparation
for public service—and this required extensive and explicit attention to
values and ethical judgments which—he argued, against positivist and
similar claims to value-freedom—were, in any event, always embedded
in research and teaching. Hartz claimed that although much of the attack on "the traditional study of political theory" was "justified," he was
concerned about a retreat from political ethics, when faced with challenges to democracy like McCarthy, and from the obligation to be
"guardians of an ancient tradition of Western libertarian norms." The
contemporary emphasis on realism had also obscured the extent to
which theories were facts and to which politics was a function of "ideal
forces."[64] Frederick Watkins, Robert McCloskey, and Carl Friedrich offered similar arguments.

Watkins, noting that the historical or "traditional approach to political theory," and its relevance to political science, was being called into
question, claimed that there were grounds for reconciliation. Ideas
were both the moving forces in politics and the residue and reflection of
political history and thus a key to understanding the past as well as a
source of "observations and generalizations" about the "political behavior of contemporary men." McCloskey suggested that despite the less
than outstanding character of American political thought, American
institutions did reflect the "American political mind" and thus provided
a basis of understanding the past and present of American government. Consequently the "gap" between the political scientist and the
student of political ideas was not as great as it might seem. Friedrich
argued that political philosophy and political science were tightly
linked. The history of political ideas was not just a history of ideologies
and "highfalutin propaganda" but something that offered "nuggets of
insight," "approximations to the truth," and even "verifiable generalizations concerning established matters of fact."[65]

Norman Jacobson's essay was the first statement of some of the elements of what might be called the "Berkeley thesis" which would play a
significant role in the discussion about political theory in the 1960s.
Jacobson made his own plea for the "unity of political theory" in the face
of what he saw as the growing extremes of "moralism" and "scientism."
He acknowledged the "growing dissatisfaction with political theory"

and the sense that there was an "irreconcilable tension" between "scientific" and "traditional" approaches, but he believed that there was a great danger in "atomizing political theory" and that, on both sides of the debate, there was actually an underlying "hostility" toward politics and a neglect of the study of politics in its own right. Each pole, he suggested, had mounted abstract and dogmatic positions that in the end contributed to "professional political theory," that is, "producing political theorists in the universities," but which were quite removed from practical life and from the search for the kind of "political wisdom" that had been properly and traditionally the goal of political theory. Instead, they were motivated by a "passion for certitude" which implicitly denied both the "autonomy" of the political realm and the idea of political theory as "a unique enterprise." Jacobson noted that, despite all the rhetoric about science, he had "yet to read a proponent of scientific political theory who displays more than a primer stage acquaintance with the history and theory of a single field within the exact sciences or an appreciation of what the scientific spirit demands of its practitioners."[66]

The general claims by behavioralists about the nature of theory and scientific method were, as Eckstein's report suggested, and Jacobson stressed, distinctly vague. Despite increased borrowing from the philosophy of science, the explication of these concepts was not much more sophisticated than it had been in Merriam's era. The case for empirical theory required, many believed, coming to grips with these metatheoretical issues. "Methodology," it was argued, was more than a matter of research methods—it involved "reading in the fields of epistemology, logic, philosophy of science," and knowledge of other scientific practices and their history. Only on this basis could political science develop a "unique method" and theory be self-consciously constructed and validly understood as "the core of the discipline" rather than looking at the "great writings as the main repository of theoretic effort."[67]

It was no longer a simple matter to define the field of political theory. Thomas Jenkin (UCLA) was the first to attempt a general systematic and comprehensive survey of its functional and substantive characteristics. He suggested that its contemporary "complexity" was in part "responsible for a great schism in the ranks," but the reverse was probably closer to the truth of the situation.[68] Neither the contours of the academic practice of political theory nor the character of the "schism" emerged very clearly in Jenkin's analysis, but the idea that political theory was in a state of "decline" was now widespread. The issue was the criteria of declination. But despite the divergence in diagnoses, whether it was a withdrawal from moral judgment or insufficient attention to scientific method, there was a convergence of concern.

The underlying issue remained liberalism, but equally persistent was the problem of the articulation of academic and public discourse. Alfred Cobban, for example, noted that despite the new emphasis on value-freedom and relativism, the fundamental problem of contemporary political theory was not epistemological but rather its practical relationship to politics. While once embedded in political life, it had, under the influence of "history and science," become "disengaged from political facts" and "practice" and had "become instead an academic discipline." Political science had been "invented by university teachers, for avoiding that dangerous subject politics."[69] It was, however, the failure to distinguish between uses of "political theory" as referring to an academic field, a functionally defined entity or a linguistic form (such as prescription), and the canon of classic texts that created some confusion about its status. At this point, another kind of argument began to enter the conversation.

The British positivist school in analytical philosophy and representatives of the emotivist theory of ethics had questioned the cognitive status of normative, prescriptive, and evaluative claims.[70] While this kind of position was often congenial to behavioralists, reinforcing their image of the separation of fact and value and the objectivity of claims about the former, it created considerable anxiety in other camps. T. D. Weldon inspired much of the discussion by suggesting that the whole tradition of political philosophy had rested on a "mistake," the notion that normative claims could be validated, and that to enunciate a "political principle" was essentially to announce a decision and end rational discussion.[71] This kind of claim led Peter Laslett to announce that "the tradition has been broken" and that, since ethical claims lacked logic and meaning, "political philosophy is dead."[72] While this discussion lacked a good deal of coherency, with respect to exactly what was in danger, the threat to certain aspects of the enterprise of academic political theory seemed exceedingly real. At this time, there was little in the way of philosophical resources to counter the hegemonic authority of positivism in philosophy. Although the arguments that revolved around this set of claims had little immediate relevance for the issues that had developed in American political science, they served to further define those issues.

Not since the early years of the century had the identity of political theory been so pointedly discussed, and never had such a decisive split emerged. And there was a concomitant proliferation of the literature in all dimensions of the field. On the part of those who identified with behavioralism, the division often continued to be articulated in terms of a difference between those who wished to develop theory as the core of an empirical science of politics and those absorbed with the narrow antiquarian pursuit of studying the ideas of the past and the "great books." Value theory or "normative theory" was recognized as a third category along with the concern with making political science relevant to public policy.[73] For Catlin, the most fundamental issue, and problem, was still that of the relationship between "political theory" and "political action," but, like Lasswell, he argued that the basic distinction within the former was between "political science," and its search for general systematic explanatory theory which would provide "means," and "political philosophy," and its history which was concerned with "ends."[74] The real issue, however, was not the form and taxonomy of political theory.

Easton provided a fuller account of his systems theory, while also continuing to distinguish the "behavioral" approach from "traditional" political science. He suggested that the core differences revolved around the behavioral beliefs in the "possibility of predicting human behavior and the role of values." While behavioralism had come to accept the fact that values inform empirical research in a number of ways, it still represented "first and foremost the pursuit of pure or unapplied knowledge"—even if the ultimate concern was practical.[75] At this point, however, Strauss offered his own account of the "decline" of political thought, which was difficult to read as other than a response to Easton.

He too was careful to distinguish political philosophy from political science. Although, he claimed, they had once, in ancient Greece, been "identical," their modern separation was part of the problem and had led to a situation in which political philosophy was only a subject of historical treatises and a "matter for burial" rather than a vital enterprise concerned with the ends of human action. "Today, political philosophy is in a state of decay and perhaps of putrefaction, if it has not vanished altogether." What killed political philosophy was "Science and History, those two great powers of the modern world." Positivism, with its assumption that values were mere preferences, rejected political philosophy's search for the human good as unscientific and sought value-freedom. This, however, only drove values, such as the unreflective attachment to liberal democracy, underground and likewise submerged presuppositions about the scope and content of political reality, such as "group politics." While positivism in contemporary social science did not, itself, so much lead to "nihilism as conformism and philistinism," it transformed itself into "the serious antagonist of political philosophy: historicism" or a kind of radical relativism that rendered vain any search for true knowledge.[76]

Judith Shklar, at Harvard, a student of Friedrich, joined the voices of those proclaiming, but lamenting, the demise of political theory and offered her own version of the "spiritual antecedents" of the declination. For Shklar, the "entire tradition of political theory is at a standstill," and the sign of its "disappearance" was the absence of "radicalism," or an "urge to construct grand designs for the political future of mankind." She attributed this to the loss of utopian faith and the "decline of rational political optimism" after the Enlightenment, and this, in turn, she argued, was a product of the rise of "romantic and Christian fatalism" and "Christian social despair." The "absence of a satisfactory secular social philosophy" had left liberalism unsure and conservative, and "relativism, Marxism, the era of debunking have left no one in an intellectual condition to write about justice." Thus, she concluded, "the grand tradition of political theory that began with Plato is, then, in abeyance."[77] Sheldon Wolin entered the discussion for the first time in a long review of Shklar's book.

Wolin, while an undergraduate at Oberlin in the early 1940s, was introduced to political theory as a student of Jászi and held a position as his student assistant or "secretary." After serving in the Army Air Force, he returned to Oberlin before entering graduate school at Harvard (1946) where he worked most closely with Hartz, Elliott, and Wright. His master's essay on Dewey reflected the critical attitude toward pragmatism at Harvard, and his dissertation was on the history of British constitutional theory. After a year of postdoctoral study at Oxford, Wolin taught for four years at Oberlin before going to Berkeley in 1954 where, in his first year, he was given research leave under a Rockefeller grant. He remained in Berkeley during this period, however, and became acquainted with his visiting replacement, Arendt, who was working on *The Human Condition*.

Wolin placed Shklar's work in the same genre as Strauss's and Laslett's ruminations about the decline of political theory, but he suggested that her real concern was not the "grand tradition" but ideology and that her view of radicalism was too narrow, failing, for example, to include Dewey. He argued that her emphasis on Christianity and romanticism was misplaced, since this was not primarily political thought. Wolin had just completed his own book about what had happened to political theory, and, against Shklar's account, he presented an extended summary of his forthcoming argument about the pessimistic character of early liberal thought. Wolin suggested that the place to look for the functional equivalent of political theory was areas such as modern social science and the study of organizations. These were the alternatives to the tradition that had displaced political theory, and they had emerged from the eighteenth century in classical economics, the rise of society as an object, and the advent of modern business. Wolin argued that the task for the political theorist today was "not to administer artificial respiration, but to preserve the integrity of political theory" and to work against the trends in which "all sense of what is uniquely political is in danger of being lost or obscured. The task, therefore, is not to revive political theory but to rescue it."[78]

Dahl, however, was less than enthusiastic about any contemporary attempt to "do political theory in the grand style." In reviewing de Jouvenal's *On Sovereignty*, he took the opportunity to suggest that efforts of this kind were "obsolete" and that in the "English-speaking world, this type of political theory is dead," while elsewhere it was "imprisoned" or "moribund." Arendt's *The Human Condition* had been published in the same year as his review, but Dahl claimed that the real difficulty with "grand political theory" had all along been its lack of "scientific foundations" and its failure to take account of "truth conditions." Its demise, however, was in the West a consequence of the fact that the basic "political problems have been solved." Dahl's tone was not, on the whole, optimistic, but it may have been prophetic. In a world of liberal solidification, "the social sciences will move haltingly on, concerned with a meticulous observation of the trivial, and political theory will take up permanent residence with literary criticism."[79]

By the late 1950s, a participant in a symposium on the continuing issue of the relationship between political theory and political science noted that there was a "widespread conviction that political theory has entered upon a time of troubles." The representatives of opposing views were, however, beginning to sound like caricatures of their positions. David Smith took issue with those who advocated the development of "systematic, scientific theory" and argued that political theory was an "idiographic rather than nomothetic" endeavor and, in addition to the history of political theory, "largely a reflective literary discipline, more akin to moral philosophy." David Apter (Berkeley), on the other hand, claimed that the great amount of data now generated required training in the "canons and criteria of scientific work" and the advance of the "behavioral" approach as a successor to the "legal-historical" approach. It was necessary for political science to embrace "various theoretical approaches in the building of systematic theory" for organizing empirical data and to advance propositions "in the form of hypotheses with general rules for verification." Such "theory construction" required, however, "greater clarification of the epistemological foundation of science." A third participant, Arnold Rogow, held out the usual hope for the progress and complementarity of both points of view but asked, plaintively, in the context of the metatheoretical discussion attending this identity crisis, "Whatever Happened to the Great Issues?"[80]

The "theoretical" core that would be associated with behavioralism had begun to emerge by the late 1950s. These "approaches" to political research, or conceptual frameworks, included Easton's systems analysis, decision making, structural functionalism, communication, action, and power. One difficulty was that much of this material was interdisciplinary in origin and application and did little to establish the identity of political science. Although the "group approach" was sometimes advanced as a particular mode of analysis, it represented a more substantive and pervasive image of American political reality.[81]

When V. O. Key addressed himself to the condition of political science in 1958, he concluded that it had become unified, that the "unification has been behavioral," and that it should continue to move forward, albeit modestly, in that direction. But there were distinct "worries" about the "state of the discipline," and they related "in one way or another to the place of political theory. . . . In an earlier day the place of political theory could be readily comprehended. It amounted to the history of political thought, an eminently respectable branch of intellectual history. It found an autonomous place in political science and could be pursued without influence upon, and without being influenced by, other branches of political science." Key's understanding of the actual past, which may well have reflected his educational experience at Chicago in the 1930s, was by now as dim as his attempt to see into the future. Although he believed that contemporary theorists "manifest a sharpened sophistication in their analysis and exegesis of the classics of political thought," there was still the question of "what relevance has political theory for other branches of political science." Although he believed that "among our theorists" he saw an indication that they were "bestirring themselves" and the development of "a view that a radical reorientation of their focus of attention may be in order if they are to contribute to the growth of the discipline," he confessed "bewilderment as I attempt to discern where they are leading us" and a sense of an "odd relation that prevails between theoretical and empirical work that bears in a major way upon the advance of our discipline" and that seemed to be marked by "antagonism if not hostility."[82]

By this point the debate had become abstracted and transformed into formulae that disguised the underlying tensions. What was criticized as the traditional study of political theory was not really traditional at all but quite foreign to political science, while the so-called scientific revolution was, at least in conception, hardly an innovation.

American practitioners of historical and normative theory may have found themselves pushed, or slipping, into one side of the increasingly bifurcated field, just as many of those who opted for behavioralism had done so by default because of their commitments to empirical research. But the division within political theory was not simply intellectual. It was disciplinary and professional. By this point, the idea of political theory as a field of study separate from political science, or even a "vocation," had not emerged. Yet all the talk about the identity and death of political theory was, ironically, creating and shaping the very field that was supposedly endangered.

Whatever the motives that lay behind the conflict, which on both sides were still ostensibly concerns largely about making political theory politically meaningful, the irony was that the result was essentially professional differentiation and specialization. By the early 1960s, the conflict was not simply one between individuals such as Easton and Strauss. It had been passed to a new generation of scholars who had been trained in the new ways of political theory, defined both by the émigrés and by the founders of the behavioral movement, and who had already begun to lose sight of the roots of the conflict between the paradigms into which they had been initiated.

11

Exodus

Political Theory and Philosophy: Historical, Normative, and Empirical.
Biographical Directory, APSA, 1968

When William Anderson reviewed Brecht's *Political Theory,* he noted that much of the material was unfamiliar. The issues confronted had "seemed relatively unimportant in American political science" and had never been directly discussed before the 1940s.[1] Although political scientists were beginning to adopt more explicitly the language of logical positivism in their construction of a new scientific identity,[2] Brecht's encyclopedic volume went far beyond any earlier discussion of the philosophy of science and philosophy of social science. But he mentioned neither, for example, the term "behavioralism" nor principal members of the movement. Although the book's impact on the conversation of political theory was minimal, it symbolized the confrontation between the American and Continental traditions that had been developing over the past two decades. Brecht was nearly accurate in stating that his book was the first of this title "to appear in any country," and he was correct in his claim that it was the first of its "kind." It was entirely devoted to academic political theory defined in terms of a set of general philosophical issues. Political theory was emerging as an autonomous but politically, and somewhat disciplinarily, desituated subject.

The book reflected the Weimar conversation and projected the issues onto contemporary social science. The basic theme was relativism. Brecht claimed that the problem arose from the fact that science had come to be identified with the investigation of "reality" rather than the proclamation of "dogma" such as natural law. Because there had been a broad value consensus in the early part of the century, the problem had not been apparent, but with the appearance of totalitarianism, relativists not only "weakened the defense" against its development but "were among the first victims." For Brecht, however, the real crisis of modernity was less totalitarianism than "the rise of the theoretical opinion that no scientific choice between ultimate values can be made." This, he claimed, was the "tragedy of twentieth-century political science."[3] Social scientists were paralyzed in the face of this dilemma and, instead of confronting it directly, turned to denial, religion, existential resignation, a search for a naturalistic basis of values, or "asylum in the history of ideas." Some, he noted, *even turned to practice*, but Brecht, the man who was driven from politics to science, saw this as another form of escape which failed to see that theories were embodied in practice. "The apocalyptic Armageddon will be, in the first place, a battle of theories."[4]

In Brecht's work, the underlying problem was not really the collapse of standards of practical judgment but the relationship of scientific authority to that judgment. The problem of "scientific value relativism" remained a surrogate for the practical problem of the relationship between theory and practice, between academic and political discourse. It represented the dilemma of the Weimar intellectuals and Brecht's notion of the continuing paradox facing social science at mid-century, but now it was presented as a logical problem. What distinguished his analysis from those of many who came after him was that, while he transformed the practical issue into a logical and epistemic one, he recognized that there was no resolution at that level—that there was no theoretical answer to the problem of theory and practice. He suggested, somewhat as had Easton, that scientific research might overcome the gulf between fact and value or science and politics by seeking "universal and invariant" elements in ethical practice. "Here then, in the ocean of relativity, is an island where we can take foot." But how such putative knowledge might have practical meaning was not explored. He also once again suggested that more attention should be given to "divine alternatives in scientific thinking."[5] Modern science, he claimed, was as much about the unseen as the seen, and therefore the divine need not be outside its scope.

The beliefs that the problem of the relationship between social science and politics was basically an epistemological issue, that the crisis of the modern age was at bottom a failure of philosophy, and that the future of politics was to be decided on the battlefield of political theory were part of an academic fantasy, but it was one which would increasingly come to define the conversation. In the case of both the émigrés and many traditional American political scientists, there was historical poignancy attached to this fantasy. They had seriously entertained the idea that science or epistemic authority might be translated into political authority. For the next generation of political theorists, however, the problem of the philosophical grounds of practical judgment was little more than a discursive artifact.

The émigré literature began to define the agenda of political theory by the late 1950s. Among the pivotal works were the first volume of

Voegelin's extended study of *Order and History*, Arendt's *The Human Condition*, and Strauss's *What is Political Philosophy?*[6] Despite ideological, philosophical, and professional differences, these works solidified and elaborated the image of political theory, as both an activity and an object of inquiry, intimated in their earlier contributions and in Hallowell's text. Although most broadly oriented toward a critique of modernity, this literature was also, in an important and intentional sense, a critique of political science—and the vision of the history of political theory that had been the property of the discipline. It addressed what was characterized as the crisis of the West defined in terms of a crisis of politics grounded, in turn, in the decline of political thought and the exhaustion of the great tradition of political philosophy that had begun in ancient Greece. The decline was represented by the values of modern liberalism and positivistic social science as well as by totalitarianism, but the modern crisis was viewed as more than a particular political and philosophical problem. It was a crisis involving, as Arendt's work so pointedly emphasized, the demise or distortion of the political dimension of human existence, a dimension essential to the constitution and realization of human being.

The explanation of the present, as well as direction for the future, was to be found in the exegesis, deconstruction, and reconstruction of the tradition. The study of the tradition was not, they claimed, an antiquarian enterprise but a historico-philosophical exercise in therapeutic reflection that was demanded by the modern predicament and which itself constituted the remnant of the tradition. The goal was to seek the decisive point at which the tradition had been derailed and recover what had been lost. What emerged in this literature was a world-historical drama in which politics appeared as reflections of the movement of political thought. The tradition was represented as an organic whole which had a definite beginning and a decisive end and to which could be imputed a synoptic meaning. Within this story of fall and, maybe, redemption, the classic authors such as Plato, Machiavelli, Hobbes, and Marx played distinctive and crucial roles. Closely related to this genre was Wolin's *Politics and Vision*.

Although this book reflected the American tradition of writing about the history of political theory, it was not offered as a successor to Dunning and Sabine. It was a distinctly more selective and interpretative exercise and was informed by the idea—exemplified by Karl Popper's critique of Plato, what Popper later referred to as his "war effort," as well as the general perspective to which Wolin had been exposed at Harvard—that contemporary issues could be addressed through a discussion of the history of ideas and the classic texts.[7] The work was, more specifically, a pointed response to the now widely voiced behavioral depreciation of the relevance of the study of the history of political theory, and it spoke, in an extended analysis of the universal nature of political philosophy, directly to political theorists seeking a positive self-image separate from mainstream political science. It also offered an alternative for those who could not accept the tenets of the Straussian persuasion which was emerging as the most visible and articulate institutional opponent of behavioral political theory.

The subject was distinctly the history of political theory, and more literally than any previous writer, Wolin advanced the idea that the canon of classic texts represented "a special tradition of discourse" and that political theory was a particular "intellectual enterprise" with a distinct historical career.[8] Although political philosophers had addressed the particular problems of their age, they first and foremost spoke to one another in universal terms about a set of perennial issues. The implication was, again, that there was a certain intellectual and historical connection between the tradition and those who studied it and transmitted its meaning to the present. Wolin's reconstruction of the tradition, however, was, like that of Arendt, less to recover a particular transcendental truth than to call attention to what had happened to the political realm and to reconstitute the idea of its distinctiveness and the importance of discourse about it.

Wolin claimed that modern politics and political ideas were the consequence of past thought, "a legacy accruing from the historical activity of political philosophers." His story of the tradition was less one-dimensional and dramatic than that of the émigrés, but the theme was similar. It was a story of the decline of both political theory and politics manifest in modern liberalism and in the rise of pluralism and mass society in an age of organization. It was, above all, a tale of "the erosion of the distinctly political" and of "the sublimation of the political" in other "forms of association" and, at the same time, the politicization of what had been nonpolitical. For Wolin, this historical exercise, which traced the contraction and dispersion of what he termed "the political," was essential both to rescue political philosophy and, in turn, to regenerate political life, since ultimately the political order would make the "fateful decisions about man's survival in an age haunted by the possibility of unlimited destruction." The historical study of the tradition was the key to understanding the modern predicament, and it was intended as both the content and vehicle of a "form of political education." And he pointedly offered it as an alternative at a time when there was "marked hostility towards, and even contempt for, political philosophy in its traditional form."[9]

What Wolin's book in effect contributed to, along with the work of individuals such as Strauss and Voegelin, was the development of an intellectual, and professional, patrimony and identity for academic political theory that lifted it out of the past and present of political science. Although the APSA committee on instruction maintained that "it is necessary for all graduate students to have some specialized study in the field of political theory," it was also clear, as one presidential address at the APSA recognized, that behavioralism and "the move toward scientism has made it more essential to define the role of political philosophy in the study of political science."[10] Hallowell chaired a panel in which Strauss's student and disciple Harry Jaffa engaged Easton with respect to the case "for" and "against" political theory. Jaffa, and the Straussians in general, eschewed the term "political theory," which they were willing to concede to political science in order to achieve differentiation, in favor of "political philosophy." The notion of a general theory of political behavior, such as that defended by Easton in *The Political System,* was, Jaffa argued, an impossibility and a dangerous illusion for the profession to embrace.[11]

Easton, at the same time, sought to legislate a more specific image of behavioralism and its theoretical identity. Even though he believed that by this point it had "acquired the garments of legitimacy," the "battle for acceptance" was "by no means over," and it was important to specify in detail "the nature of the creature." Easton, first of all, insisted that behavioralism, as "both an intellectual tendency and a concrete academic movement," should no longer be confused with psychological behaviorism. Yet, despite a focus on individuals and aggregate behavior such as voting, and the use of "rigorous techniques," its positive dimensions and the exact line of demarcation between "traditionalists" and the "authentic behavioralist" had remained somewhat elusive. The criterion of "membership" might be difficult to identify, but he believed that "intellectual content was more easily specified."[12] Easton's codification of the "major tenets of the behavioral credo" moved further away from his earlier emphasis on value theory and political relevance.

The essence of behavioralism, he suggested, was the quest for a "science of politics modeled after the methodological assumptions of the natural sciences" that could develop empirically verifiable generalizations. He noted that a behavioralist was "not prohibited" from "ethical evaluation," as long as the propositions were distinct from those of "empirical explanation," and that "the application of knowledge is as much a part of the scientific enterprise as theoretical understanding." But "pure science" logically preceded "efforts to utilize political knowledge in the solution of urgent practical problems of society." The reidentification of political science as behavioralism, Easton argued, was significant. It was neither simply another name for what had been pursued in the past and a more advanced application of scientific techniques nor an "ideological weapon" in the rebellion against "traditions." It signified political science joining the interdisciplinary quest for a "common underlying social theory" in the explanation of human behavior. It was a theoretical transformation exemplified in analytical "conceptual approaches" such as functionalism, communication, decision theory, the theory of action, and systems analysis, which together represented the "coming of age of theory in the social sciences" and the transcendence of the substantive and ethical orientation of "traditional theories of past political thought."[13]

It was not simply Easton's emphasis on such things as the separation of fact and value that worried the critics. Implicit in his discussion were the ideas that politics was an analytical construct and that political theory could be methodologically defined, and this position evoked old as well as contemporary concerns. The main participants in these discussions, even as late as the 1960s, had a very limited grasp of the structure and history of the dialogue in which they were joined and the direction in which it was moving. Although the polarization of political theory, and political science as a whole, was most immediately rooted in the unique developments of the past two decades, the form of the controversy, and to some extent its content, was, albeit often unconsciously, in part a legacy and residue of the debates that occurred in the 1920s in both the United States and Weimar. The participants were confined by unrecognized inherited discursive forms.

It may no longer have been the decline of the state that was at issue, but the concerns about pluralism as a definition of liberal democracy, the loss of the identity of "the political," and the threat to the autonomy of political inquiry were not merely an invention of the 1960s. The ideologies may have been different, but it was in many respects less ideology than professional and disciplinary constraints and motives that most fundamentally shaped the discourse of political theory. Although arguments such as those of Arendt and Strauss had much to do with the manner in which the issues were articulated, it would be difficult not to hear the ideas of such individuals as Elliott resonating in Wolin's insistence on the primacy of "the political" and the claim that "human existence is not to be decided at the lesser level of small associations."[14] The abstract definition of "the political system" as any relationship of "power, rule, or authority," advanced by individuals such as Dahl, seemed once again to call into question the identity of politics as well as of political theory.[15]

If those most centrally involved in the controversy were less than fully aware of its nature and heritage, students who now gravitated into the field found themselves within a paradigm, or paradigm conflict, whose origins and significance were doubly opaque. Students had little grasp of the origins of the polarization that now defined the field, and they largely became functionaries of whatever academic persuasion informed their graduate training. What was emerging was a decisive generational difference. Although professionalization had estranged both the émigrés and the founders of the behavioral movement from the immediacy of the practical concerns that had originally inspired both positions, those individuals "trained" in the 1950s and 1960s found themselves confronted with issues such as the meaning of the tradition of political thought, the nature of political theory and politics, the status of liberalism, the logic of scientific explanation, the problem of the relationship between fact and value, and the dilemma of relativism that retained only the form of their genesis. Despite the high degree of intellectual excitation and allusions to the events of the "times," these issues were increasingly determined by the internal evolution of academic discourse and the professional and institutional structures within which it resided. Characteristically, politics had found its way into the discourse of political theory even though the latter had seldom seeped out into the world of political action. Now there was little in the way of either ingress or egress.

What largely came to define the discourse of political theory, and even political science, was the dialogue, or confrontation, between what proponents on both sides accepted as "traditional" and "scientific" theory. While what Heinz Eulau called the "behavioral persuasion," or the "modern" as opposed to the "ancient" approach to political studies, represented the latter, Strauss, who also characterized the conflict as one between "ancients and moderns," became the most prominent symbol of the former.[16] One commentator, in the course of a systematic summary and critique of the emerging Straussian position and its attack on scientism, liberalism, relativism, and modernity, suggested that "no single individual has had as much impact on the discipline of political science during the past several years."[17] The point had a deeper meaning than the author intended. Not only had Strauss commanded the loyalty of many individuals who identified themselves as theorists, but his arguments continued to galvanize the behavioral movement and its own search for identity. In 1962, two books were published that represented and symbolized the division in the field: *Essays on the Behavioral Study of Politics* and *Essays on the Scientific Study of Politics*.

The former was the product of papers presented at a meeting of the

International Political Science Association that were devoted to exemplifying the character of the "behavioral approach" which, Ranney claimed, was "an approach to the study of *all* political phenomena." In an introductory essay, Evron Kirkpatrick, executive director of the APSA, who had done much to further the institutionalization of behavioralism in the discipline and profession, argued that political science had heretofore lacked "any unifying definition, unifying method, or unifying theory." Now, however, "as a result of the impact of natural sciences on the social sciences," behavioralism had moved beyond "traditional" institutional and historical studies and achieved unity and had become the "mainstream of American political science." The "war," he claimed, was "over."[18] The real war, in fact, had only begun. The Straussians, claiming a similar universality for their approach to the study of "political things," undertook a critique of the field that left little doubt about what was at issue. In successive chapters, they systematically attacked the basic premises of American political science and such iconic figures as Bentley, Lasswell, and Herbert Simon, as well as the voting studies, the most prominent and influential form of behavioral research.

The prosecution of the indictment was relentless. They claimed that despite its positivistic insistence on separating facts and values, the "new political science," which crystallized in the United States between the two world wars, was a parochial and "thoughtless universalization of the liberal democratic institutions and values of the United States." It concealed a "mysterious pre-established harmony" between its methodological commitments and a "particular version of liberal democracy," and actually embodied "a fervent commitment to a certain understanding of democratic liberalism" embodied in pluralist theory and the work of Bentley, its most "revered pioneer."[19] Second, it not only represented the "sacrifice of political relevance on the altar of methodology," as it distanced itself from the "urgency of political problems," but was fundamentally antipolitical in that it implicitly denied the existence of a distinct political dimension of life and reduced the explanation of "political things" to "sub-political" deterministic social, economic, and psychological forces and factors which depreciated human rationality and the validity of commonsense understanding. The capacity for moral judgment was ignored in favor of a focus on interests and instrumental reason as the moving forces of politics. The new science, characteristic of Lasswell, the "master-propagandist" and social psychoanalyst, pursued a vision of "positive liberalism" through scientific manipulation and social control that was distinctly antidemocratic in its implications and in a manner that should "strike terror in the hearts of free men."[20]

In the "Epilogue" to these essays, Strauss reiterated the principal themes and stressed the parallel, and historical connection, between the modern crises of the West, involving the external confrontation with totalitarianism and the internal degeneration of liberalism, and the values of the new science. Although noting that his political perspective was "conservative," Strauss cast himself professionally as on the "left" in his challenge to the present "orthodoxy" in the discipline. He argued that since the new science "wields very great authority" in the university and society, it owed an "account of itself." Instead, it concealed the problems of liberalism, provided little genuine new knowledge, accepted only a difference in "degree" between humans and "brutes" and "robots," as well as between "liberal democracy and communism," and reflected a "dogmatic atheism" in its exclusion of all things outside the realm of empirical science. It contributed to the "most dangerous proclivities of democracy" and to "the victory of the gutter" in its relativistic acceptance of the equality of all values and desires. In the end, he was not willing to accuse the new science of being intentionally "diabolical" but rather of suffering from an "almost willful blindness." Although it "fiddled while Rome burned," it was "excused by two facts: it does not know that it fiddles, and it does not know that Rome burns."[21]

It might at first seem odd that the most pointed and extended response to this attack did not come from behavioralists but from, what was becoming recognized as, the "Berkeley school."[22] These individuals, like the Straussians, were intent on criticizing what they believed had become "the authoritative voice throughout the discipline," and the two assessments, in many ways, appeared quite similar. John Schaar, Jenkin's student at UCLA, had joined Eugene Burdick, Jacobson, and Wolin at Berkeley, and the department had been awarded a large Rockefeller grant to support the development of the study of political theory. There had not, for many years, been a strong tradition of work in this subfield at the institution, and these individuals began to form a relatively unique perspective that involved both an emphasis on the autonomy of politics and political theory and a critique of scientism, as well as a concern about the implications of pluralistic liberalism. It was, for example, in this intellectual context that Crick, as a visiting scholar, formulated his historical critique of American political science. There was in many respects, and from the perspective of many political scientists, a distinct convergence between the ideas of the émigrés and the Berkeley group. Strauss was obviously surprised, and offended, by the quarter from which the review emanated, and he noted that this was "the most acrimonious critique hitherto written of what I stand for." The Straussians replied at length. Although the review was in part a response to what Schaar and Wolin described as the "hostile and destructive" Manichean tone of the Straussian polemic, which employed the "violent language" of the "fanatic," their comments equaled what they claimed was the manner in which the enemy took on a "stature of near-satanic proportions."[23] The review reflected local institutional and professional controversies about the Straussian persuasion, but there was a deeper discursive meaning.

The behavioral hegemony within the profession and the university had been achieved less by the defeat of the émigré position than by its isolation. There was little to be gained by entering into the substance of a challenge such as that of Strauss, and few political scientists had a sufficient grasp of, or interest in, these kinds of arguments and their subject matter. The émigré critique was still foreign, and sometimes bewildering, even to many in political theory. Now, however, that much of political theory was becoming something other than an appendage of mainstream political science, there was a question of its internal identity and who represented its authentic voice. This was a professional as well as an intellectual and ideological matter. Straussians, for example, did not hesitate to attack antibehavioralists whom they considered leftists, liberals, and social scientific fellow-travelers, even though the latter sometimes saw the Straussians as their allies in the study of "political things" and the search for and defense of "the political."[24] What was involved was a fight for both the soul and body of political theory, for both its intellectual and professional identity. The Straussians had achieved an unprecedented doctrinal solidarity as well as a national organized professional unity that, although smaller, more than rivaled that of the behavioralists and far outweighed any other element of the field (despite a significant group attached to Voegelin). Although there had been no systematic Straussian rendition of the history of political theory comparable to that of Sabine, or even that of Wolin, a multi-authored authoritative text interpreting the classic canon was finally produced.[25]

Schaar and Wolin, like Jacobson earlier, claimed that they did not want to see contemporary choices in political theory narrowed down to "either a morally corrupt and intellectually sterile scientism or a version of political philosophy distinguished by moral fervor and an intellectual certainty that the essential nature of all political situations has been revealed long ago." The latter's attack on political science, and individuals such as Dewey, was, they claimed, "so intemperate in tone and so often unfair to its subjects it has provoked our considerable indignation."[26] Jacobson, for example, had offered a rendition of Bentley which rescued him from both the behavioral understanding of his work and the attack of the Straussians, and Schaar's work was largely concerned with American political ideas.[27] When the chips were down, an attack so fundamental and bitter on the very essence of modernity, American political thought, and the liberal science of politics brought together, at least temporarily, those educated in that tradition in a manner that was not unlike the response of Coker and Wright in the 1940s. The Berkeley vision was still essentially an American vision. Despite the degree to which Wolin had been influenced by the émigré perspective, from Jászi to Arendt, the review reflected the residue of some congenital differences between the American and émigré philosophy and the extent to which those at Berkeley were still linked to a search for a theoretical core to political science.

There were, and would be, consistent attempts to find complementarity between political science and the increasingly exclusive subfield of political theory.[28] These intellectual exercises often reflected more a search for compromise rooted in concrete professional concerns and circumstances than the development of distinct intellectual positions, and they not only failed to please protagonists on either side but, as before, tended to accentuate the fact and problem of the division. Although political theorists were now the ones who often cast themselves as a beleaguered and revolutionary minority, it was hardly the case that political theory was institutionally ostracized from political science. Political theory panels attracted large audiences at association meetings, the subject was popular in the curriculum, and articles and books on political theory proliferated even if often residing somewhat anomalously among the contributions of mainstream political science. For some, the growing distinctiveness of the émigré literature itself represented the "revival of political theory."[29] What was taking place was the professional differentiation of the field with "empirical" theory becoming the property of behavioralism and the increasingly distinct but internally diverse remainder designated as "traditional" or normative and historical.

The exact terms of such divisions were primarily a legislative act of the disciplinary establishment and reflected its assumption about the distinction between fact and value and between empirical and normative claims, but the grudging acceptance by political theorists was both a recognition of the de facto situation and a reflection of a wish for greater institutional autonomy. Part of the growth and differentiation of political theory was, however, a function of its participation in a broader critique of the intellectual and professional establishment in political science. The mid-1960s was the zenith of the behavioral image of theorizing as the construction of conceptual or analytical frameworks, but there was the emergence of a variety of arguments to the effect that behavioralism represented the study of a kind of "pseudopolitics" and that the "behavioral syndrome" consisted of *"conservatism, fear of popular democracy, and avoidance of vital political issues."*[30]

Although a significant dimension of political science clung to the notion that empirical theories would arise from inductive efforts of empirical research and the formulation of narrow-gauge theory,[31] the dominant vision, represented most paradigmatically by the work of Easton, was that these constructs—these "models," "approaches," "orientations," or "strategies"—were, at least, prototypes of an emerging "general theory" based on a single concept, as physics is based on "mass." What would emerge, they claimed, would be a universal predictive causal theory of politics consisting of "a deductive system of thought so that a limited number of postulates, as assumptions and axioms, a whole body of empirically valid generalizations might be deduced in descending order of specificity."[32] This language indicated the degree to which both the philosophical identity and theoretical program of behavioralism was specified and visualized in terms of the language of logical positivism. Before the critical implications of Kuhn's work were perceived, this search for a stronger sense of philosophical legitimacy also drew upon his image of scientific change.

In his APSA presidential address, Truman cast the history of political science in terms of a paradigmatic transformation from a long period of "non-theoretical empiricism," or "almost total neglect of theory in any meaningful sense," lasting through the 1930s, to "a new disciplinary consensus" based on the idea of the "political system." He noted that despite the emergence of this paradigm and the "recommitment to the goal of science," the "theory chorus" was still "less polyphonus than cacophonus" and that it might not be possible to create fully "hypothetico-deductive theories" in the near future. Also there would likely remain in the field for some time "a less or non-scientific component" that could best be represented by the study of the history of political thought.[33] Another, more detailed and extensive, survey of political theory co-authored by Deutsch, from the behavioral perspective, was less generous. It defined theory as a concern for "what 'is' or exists in politics" and particularly as a "search for a coherent image of the political system." As did the Straussians, it argued that normative, exegetical, and historical matters should be called "political philosophy" and pursued elsewhere.[34] Almond's presidential address, once more drawing on Kuhn, affirmed the appearance of a new theoretical consensus and "a more surely scientific paradigm" revolving around the concept of the political system.[35]

The new "paradigm," however, was for many an orthodoxy that exhibited exactly the attributes of "normal" science that Kuhn had described. It was intellectually conservative in terms of both methodological commitments and its view of political reality at a time when "anomalies" were increasing, and strong and growing voices for theoretical and ideological diversity were emerging. Its eschewal of values and its emphasis on the authority of facts concealed the manner in which values were, "in fact," embedded in both the form—that is, the conceptual frameworks and method—and the substance—or the interpretation of politics and political reality—embraced by mainstream political science.[36] Furthermore, many argued, the discipline seemed to have forsaken the very purpose for which it had historically pursued science, that is, social change, and instead had become an apologist for the status quo and for the contemporary character and practice of domestic and international politics.[37] Waldo, in a survey of American political science a decade earlier, had already noted that the basic structure and values of the American political order had been largely accepted and endorsed by political science in a manner that allowed political theory to be transformed into methodology.[38]

It was at this point, however, that divergence between mainstream political science and politics became dramatically apparent. At the very historical moment that events such as the civil rights movement, the urban crisis, the Vietnam War, and upheavals on university campuses such as Berkeley and Columbia were taking place, political science research seemed to ignore these matters in favor of the study of such things as voting. It had, paradoxically given the historical context, tended to endorse Daniel Bell's argument about "the end of ideology" as a conscious affirmation of the values that marked the unreflective complacency, conformity, and chauvinism of the previous decade.[39] Social and political scientists such as Seymour Martin Lipset defended Western liberal democracy and pluralist politics not as the "way" toward the good society but as "the good society in operation," and political scientists studying comparative politics adopted this as both a description of and prescription for politics in other countries.[40] While the critics were focusing on the loss of the idea of "the political" and worrying about the corresponding decline of political theory, behavioralism seemed to be celebrating both. The idea that in the United States theory was embodied in practice was hardly a new theme, but now "realism" was no longer a critical stance. The comparison of American political practice with democratic ideals led to suggestions, by pluralists such as Dahl and students of voting behavior, for bringing the latter into conformance with the former.[41] Robert Lane (Yale) suggested that there was, and should be, a "decline of politics in a knowledgeable society" and that the contemporary "age of affluence" had produced "a growing state of confidence between men and government" which rendered both an "acrimonious political style" and ideology, in general, obsolete.[42]

This kind of official endorsement of cognitive dissonance persisted until Easton's presidential address, and it was often linked to both worries about and hopes for the death or decline of normative political theory. While individuals such as Morgenthau continued to press the case for political theory as social criticism and condemned political science's silence with respect to such issues as Vietnam, most seemed embarrassed by this kind of moralism as well as by the lack of seemliness and the intolerance of methodological pluralism that characterized the "ridiculous and unproductive controversy" between the Berkeley group and the Straussians. The discipline was, in general, clearly more comfortable with Deutsch's enthusiasm for "a new kind of theory about politics" made possible by recent technologies for gathering aggregate data.[43] Crick's polemical history of the field had been countered by an account of the structure and "development" of political science which, although not simply an apology for behavioralism, tended to recapitulate the past of the field from the standpoint of the present.[44]

In an introduction to a 1968 symposium on the state of the discipline, it was noted that while "over the years the profession has been genuinely concerned with the linkage of political theory to current social concerns," there had been "a diminishing interest in political theory as the official ideologies of the 1950s became increasingly unsupportable in empirical theory and untenable in normative philosophy."[45] The symposium was also the vehicle for an extended reflection on the state of political theory as an "academic field and intellectual activity." The assessment was that the "field" had become diverse, complex, fragmented, and marked by dissatisfaction. Most political scientists, it was claimed, saw theory as a "tool" for explaining observed facts rather than the normative and prescriptive modes of "ideology" and "political philosophy" that had characterized the enterprise before the behavioral revolution. This continuing division had led to "sustained and unrestrained argumentation" which the authors believed would likely result in some form of institutional separation. As an intellectual activity in empirical political science, they saw significant developments in political theory and predicted a "previously unimaginable breakthrough because of the technological advances" in research, and even imagined the possibility of resurrecting the classic texts and "probing their theoretical content."[46] They were, at least, correct about the indications of institutional separation, even though there were still distinct but strained efforts to seek interaction across the cleavages that were developing.[47]

Political theorists more generally joined in Strauss's assessment of the blindness of the discipline to political events. One dimension of the critique of behavioralism, which involved, but was wider than, the conflict about political theory, was what must, in some measure, also be considered as a reprise of the Weimar conversation and the 1920s debate about pluralism and its adequacy both as an account of and a prescription for democratic practice. The mid-1960s marked the apotheosis of pluralism as the substance of the vision of both domestic and comparative politics accepted by behavioralism, and it was embedded in most of the conceptual schemes for political analysis.[48] But it was at the same time attacked on both empirical and normative grounds. One consistent theme, most strongly and distinctly represented by such arguments as that of C. Wright Mills, was that pluralism was a myth that masked the real, or elitist, structure of political power.[49] Less sweeping was the claim that it both was ethnocentric and failed to recognize fully the actual modes and manifestations of political power.[50] Closely related were arguments that as an account of political reality, and a more universal framework for political analysis, pluralism manifested ideological biases, which were often antidemocratic in character. Neither the pluralist account of democratic practice nor the resurrection of Schumpeter's image of plebisitary—or what Lipset termed "elitist"—democracy, and its deployment to account for the data in the voting studies and rationalize citizen apathy, were a substitute for traditional democratic theory.[51] Finally, throughout the 1960s, individuals such as Henry Kariel, C. B. Macpherson, Grant McConnell, Theodore Lowi, Marcuse, and Robert Paul Wolff argued less the unreality of the pluralist account of liberalism than the pathology of democracy inherent in its modern practice.[52]

These criticisms were complemented by an attack on the professional establishment of political science. It was charged not only with a lack of internal democracy but with organizational and individual links to certain elements of partisan politics and to such agencies as the CIA and its affiliates. This included organizations with which a number of individuals had worked. Although at the time details were not widely known, a recent study has discussed the involvement of Elliott, Kissinger,

Kirkpatrick, Talcott Parsons, and Merle Fainsod.[53] During the 1950s, the professional apparatus of the discipline, including the editorship of the *APSR,* had resisted the rise of behavioralism, but by the mid-1960s, the intellectual, professional, and, to some degree, political right wing of the behavioral movement had gained dominance. Pluralism may have been the descriptive and normative theory of external politics, but it was not widely practiced within the profession and discipline. It was in this context that the Caucus for a New Political Science was formed in 1967 and that Wolin and Easton presented their theses for the reclamation of the heritage of political theory.

The Caucus represented a more general movement in American social science associations. It challenged what its members believed was the growing internal conservatism and external irrelevance of these academic fields as well as their connection with governmental agencies which pursued dubious domestic and international policies. In political science, this involved, in particular, an attack on scientism and pluralist liberalism.[54] Theorists, particularly on the political Left, were active in the caucus which was countered by professionally conservative individuals as well as by the more moderate Committee for a Responsible Political Science. Although Easton was nominated (1967) and elected (1968) in the usual manner, by the inner circle of the APSA without any general member participation, he set out to open up the association. The 1968 annual meeting, at which Wolin had delivered his call to the vocation of political theory, had been organized in a manner designed to freeze out dissenters on all fronts. At the business meeting, Merle Fainsod resisted attempts of dissident groups representing radicals, blacks, and women to be heard. This move lost the establishment much of the support of the center, and during the next year, the Caucus developed a much broader base, as Easton worked to involve all identifiable groups in the association and provide for their participation in the 1969 meeting. It was in this context that he prepared his address on the "new revolution" which represented an attempt both to democratize the profession and to call it to its traditional practical concerns. It was also Easton's return to his original motivations which had been, in his own words, "suppressed" for a number of years by his theoretical and professional foci.

It might have seemed, given the arguments of Easton and Wolin, that there was, in the early 1970s, a basis for a rapproachment between political science and political theory. The polarized debate of the 1960s began to dissipate, and although the term "behavioralism" did not disappear, political science, in what came to be understood as a post-behavioral era, increasingly attempted to reconstitute its identity as a policy science as well as to establish an image of political science as a theoretically eclectic and pluralistic discipline and profession. Despite some of the intellectual and professional distance that separated the core of the "vocation" from that of the "new revolution," they both sprang from the same discursive past, and they both pointedly raised once more the continuing paradox of the relationship between public and academic discourse. Politics had once again found its way into the discourse of political theory, but it was as unclear as ever how the political microcosm reflected in these professional debates could speak more generally to political life. On a more personal level, it might be noted, at the very least, that Wolin and Easton belonged to the same generation, attended the same graduate school, were both trained as political theorists, and embraced similar political ideologies and social concerns. More generally, there was considerable contact between political theory and the attempt to define political science as the study of public policy in terms of both the basic concerns voiced and the specific literature.[55] And political theory and public policy analysis tended to share a common fate. Neither, any more than their predecessors a century earlier, could find an answer to the institutional barriers between the university and politics.

In his 1971 presidential address, Deutsch reversed his earlier divisive stance and argued with ecumenical fervor that, despite profound differences, the profession and discipline of political science encompassed everyone from Marcuse to Lasswell and represented every conceivable social entity while at the same time creating a bridge between "political theory and political action."[56] Even allowing for the demands of the presidential tradition of seeking professional unity, this argument was an extraordinary exercise in historical denial. The divisions within political theory and the distance between public and academic discourse had never been greater. Although the attempt to develop universal theory sharply declined during the 1970s, the "policy-turn" produced less a change in theoretical and methodological direction than an increasing acceptance of a variety of approaches. Despite some attempts to define a theoretical core organized around formal theories of public choice, political science neither established nor sought any distinct theoretical identity. There were, however, pragmatic professional reasons for theoretical and methodological tolerance.

First of all, behavioralism had, in effect, established professional dominance and could afford to be generous. Second, the profession was hardly willing to cast adrift a significant portion of its membership. Similarly, while political theory was moving in the direction of a separate interdisciplinary intellectual identity, all of the vitriolic castigation of mainstream political science as politically corrupt and intellectually sterile did not lead to any serious move to flee the institutional structure of political science, at the level of either the university or professional associations. Those who identified themselves with the "vocation" of political theory, while still seeking identity in the condemnation of scientism, increasingly stopped talking either to or about political science, but they somehow avoided sensing any hypocrisy in the fact of their continued institutional dependency. Professionalism continued to provide the grammar of motives.

During the next few years, presidential addresses to the APSA, those barometers of yearning and hope, continued to expound extravagant claims about the unity of political science and its public role in an informational society and "consultative commonwealth," its commitment to the complementarity of "scientific truth and democratic decision-making," its role as the keeper of the "divine science" of "political engineering" initiated by the founders of the American republic, and the manner in which the pursuit of its diverse forms of research would make a "massive contribution to the welfare of the nation."[57] But, even allowing for the rhetorical demands of the forensic context, there was a vast disjunction between image and practice. Never had political science offered so many, often conflicting, images of what might constitute a policy science and, in the language of Aaron Wildavsky, "speaking truth to power"—from supplying neutral information to policymakers to sending out agents to reconstitute participatory democracy.[58] But all this, like the myriad formulations of critical theory that appeared in the literature of political theory, had little to do with the actual practices and commitments of most political scientists.

The depolarization of political science had the effect of internally pluralizing not only the discipline as a whole but political theory as well. The division between "traditional" and "scientific" theory had at least given a certain identity to each and bound the discourse together in disagreement. Released from the tentative solidarity of antibehavioralism, political theory began to manifest a number of latent tensions and fractured into a number of parochial professionally and intellectually inspired discursive enclaves. And some of those enclaves, such as Straussianism, were in turn pluralized. With the breakdown of antibehavioral ideology and with their escape from the gravitational orbit of political science, the elements of political theory were pulled by the authority of cognate fields such as philosophy and history, as they sought identity and new fields of discursive action. While intense intraspecific debates emerged within some of these dispersed conversations, there was little in the way of dialogue either within or between political theory and political science.

Political theory had characteristically been the reflective and critical voice of the discipline of political science, and the discipline had been the discursive home of political theory. Political science, however, was left without a distinct reflective dimension, while the conversations of political theory floated free of their origins, and of what had been, however attenuated, their practical roots. Although the relationship between political science and politics had been a tenuous one, political theory as a distinct intellectual enterprise was even more vaguely related to political practice. While prior to the 1970s, it would have been impossible to discuss political science and political theory separately, the histories of political science and political theory subsequently became, to a great extent, different stories. Even though the character of contemporary conversations in political theory was rooted in its past, those who entered the field stepped into a discursive universe that had largely taken shape during the past two decades—and even that immediate past was dimly perceived.

One conversation between political theory and political science that did spill over into the era of the 1970s was the debate about the nature of science. Even though Easton had declared a "new revolution," this strategic surprise announcement from the top amounted in some ways to a declaration of victory and the offer of a truce before the battle was completely won, and it was explicitly not a rejection of the methodological premises of behavioralism. It was also not immediately heard either by those in the behavioral ranks who were still fighting to secure and maintain their intellectual and professional redoubts or by those who were circling their position. When Schaar and Wolin disputed the Straussian offensive, they had noted that "no genuinely philosophical critique of the new persuasion has yet appeared."[59] The Straussian position, for example, was indeed philosophical, but it was also, like much of the criticism associated with the Caucus, distinctly external. It was less an internal critique of the logical and epistemological assumptions of behavioral science, which it also tended to equate with the practice of natural science, than an attack on the very idea of a science of politics and on a very broad image of positivism. Beginning in the late 1960s, however, the full implications of Kuhn's work and other elements of postpositivism in the philosophy of science and philosophy of social science began to appear in the literature of political theory.

Political science had, at this point, in a peculiar way lost control of the dialogue about science—as it would those of so many other themes.

The issue had become the discursive property of two strands of the émigré literature—positivism and antipositivism—which in their antagonism actually reinforced one another. By the end of the 1960s, both the scientific identity of the discipline and its theoretical practice were inextricably entwined with the positivist philosophy of science. That identity and practice were challenged by an immanent critique that did not question so much the behavioral project of a scientific study of politics as its philosophical bases and even the reconstruction of natural science on which so much of the understanding of the behavioral program, by both itself and its critics, had been predicated. Since behavioralism had increasingly cast itself in the image of science elaborated by logical positivism, the critique of positivism entailed a critique of political science. This, however, was challenged by behavioralism's philosophical guardians and mercenaries who drew upon counterrevolutionary arguments in the philosophy of science.[60]

Prior to this point, the behavioral involvement in the detailed literature of the philosophy of science had been minimal. Behavioralist claims about the nature of scientific theory and scientific explanation were largely derived from secondary and tertiary sources.[61] Although these discussions engaged behavioralism on its own terms and raised general questions about the relationship between philosophy and social science, the issues tended to become submerged in a confrontation between different metatheories of scientific explanation which increasingly took on a life of its own. The discussion was tied more to the fate of the philosophical discourses to which the disputing parties attached themselves than to concrete issues about explanatory practices in political science.[62] As political science and political theory drifted further apart, issues in the philosophy of science receded from view, but the attachment of political theory to a variety of other philosophical discourses increased.

The American Society of Legal and Political Philosophy had been established in 1955 to pursue the theoretical interdisciplinary study of social science, law, and philosophy, and it began publishing its annual *Nomos* series in 1958. In 1973, the journal *Political Theory* was created and became part of the growing institutionalization of political theory represented by organizations such as the Conference for the Study of Political Thought and other groups attached to the APSA such as the Foundations of Political Theory. From the beginning, it was evident that this journal represented an agenda defined outside the world of political science, but also one generated less by reference to issues in politics than by the immanent structure of prevailing themes of various academic and interdisciplinary discourses. The growing sense of the vitality of political theory was to a large extent a function of its release, or parole, both from the professional constraints of political science and from any concrete concern with political practice. The "vocation" of political theory may have declared its independence on the basis of a platform of political relevance, but it became almost totally a world of specialized scholarly projects.

While the positivist depreciation of the cognitive meaningfulness of value judgments, and any logical distinction between modes of explanation in natural and social science, had earlier precipitated worries about the "death" of political theory, the postpositivist resuscitation of the logic of normative discourse and the autonomy of social scientific explanation provided at least a categorical basis for suggesting that the burial was premature. Political theory, chastened and more realistic after its encounter with positivism, might, it was argued, move forward cautiously with a greater sensitivity to the interdependence between normative and empirical research and facts and values. Isaiah Berlin proclaimed that since ideology—in a "pluralist society" where "ends collide"—had not in fact disappeared, political theory would not "wholly perish from the earth," and it was deemed that it was "alive again" and now deserved recognition as an autonomous enterprise.[63] In the same manner that the "value" side of inquiry was redeemed, the decline of positivism also rendered the question of the nature of *social* scientific explanation a worthy object of contemplation. Although arguments of those such as Peter Winch and Schütz about the autonomy of social scientific explanation were still predicated on a positivist account of natural science as a contrast model, they initiated a postpositivist discourse about the nature of social phenomena and the demands of social scientific investigation entailed by the "meaningful" character of human action and interpretative character of inquiry.[64] The difficulty, however, was that these issues, as in the case with the involvement in the philosophy of science, contributed, often in a quite unreflective manner, to mortgaging the discourse of political theory to that of academic philosophy.

Political theory, as a distinct intellectual activity, was at this point, then, largely functionally defined in terms of certain external philosophical criteria. Similarly, the study of the history of political theory was redefined by the "new history of political theory." Although this area of scholarship persisted, as practiced within the framework initiated by the émigrés as well as within the earlier paradigm, it, and the debates surrounding it, had limited meaning outside the structure of issues involving liberalism, scientism, and the critique of modernity, which had previously characterized discussion. It had been more a philosophical and rhetorical than a "historical" practice and consequently, if construed literally, was vulnerable to a historiographical critique. Beginning in the 1970s, much of the history of political theory was increasingly redefined in terms of broader external substantive and methodological issues in intellectual history and the history of ideas, and it retained only vestiges of the concerns that had marked its origins. Although it would develop some intense and extended internal debates about such matters as whether the foundations of the American government sprang from liberal or republican traditions, and to that degree perpetuated the debate about liberalism, the study of the history of political theory, in many respects, began to exemplify its own brand of "methodism" and to take on some of the antiquarian characteristics for which it had been chided two decades earlier.[65]

There was a great deal of convenient ambiguity attached to the optimistic claims of the 1970s about the revival of political theory. When Laslett had announced that political theory was "dead" and that the "tradition has been broken," the implication was that it was the "great tradition" celebrated in political theory textbooks. The claim that there was once again "an upswell of political and social theorizing" conveyed the message that this tradition had been reconstituted.[66] The great tradition, however, was itself an invention of academic discourse, and what was represented in the current literature was actually the growing autonomy and proliferation of that discourse rather than anything resembling the content and circumstances of works associated with the classic canon. Despite Berlin's optimism, he had noted that no "commanding work in political theory has yet appeared in the twentieth century," but by the early 1970s certain books had appeared that many believed met the messianic criteria.[67] They at least gave a distinct focus and impetus to the discourse of political theory and contributed to its further institutionalization.

Although John Rawls's *A Theory of Justice* (1971), as well as what many considered to be its ideological and philosophical counterpart, Robert Nozick's *Anarchy, State, and Utopia* (1974), could be construed as alluding to or reflecting, or in some way speaking to or about, politics, they were distinctly contextless works written by professional philosophers which lifted the perennial debates about liberalism and the ground of values to a new level of abstraction while apparently allowing academic commentators to believe that they were actually saying something about politics. The images of politics that they evoked—and to which innumerable commentaries, on reading, understanding, and realizing Rawls, responded—were distinctly disembodied, and they were disengaged from the issues that had shaped the past of political theory. Although they evoked aboriginal memories and were, to be sure, in some ethereal manner about liberalism, it was now an academic construction. The reconstitution, explication, and critique of liberalism would remain a, if not the, dominant motif in political theory. In that respect, the conversation was rooted in, and determined by, the form and content of its discursive past but in a manner that had largely become opaque to the participants. Political theory was increasingly cut loose from the constraints of its political context as it engaged in abstract debates about such matters as individualistic versus communal liberalism.[68] Similarly, the issues of relativism and of theory and practice were detached from their practical roots and transformed into philosophical, that is, epistemological, problems.

The translation of Jürgen Habermas's *Knowledge and Human Interests* was published the same year as Rawls's work and instituted a conversation, and set of paraconversations and derivative exercises, that would continue to occupy much of the discursive space of political theory. Horkheimer's essays from the 1930s on *Critical Theory* appeared the following year.[69] Critical theory and the idea of critical theory became dominant themes. Although Marcuse's work continued to represent the ideas of the Frankfurt school during the 1960s, and participate in the critique of scientism and liberalism, it was principally through Habermas that this tradition became a central influence on the literature of political theory.[70] Marcuse became something of a guru for the radical student movement, but it was a strange case, as was Kissinger's crossover into the world of political practice through the vehicle of Elliott's connection with Rockefeller, or the entrance of Straussians into Republican administrations of the 1980s. It was an exception that did not so much "prove" the rule as put into relief the more characteristic institutional distance between the academy and political life. Whatever practical political meaning and significance Habermas's reformation of the Frankfurt program and his claims about transcendental philosophical grounds for practical judgment and the constitution of a critical social science may have had in the German context, it was, in the United States, very much, in both form and substance, another replay of the Weimar conversation and the issue of relativism in a context in which it had little meaning outside the discursive parameters of academic political theory.[71]

The real issue of what would constitute a critical academically based political theory and how it would operate in the world of American politics was virtually never concretely addressed. The irony was that, as unrealistic as the strategies for bridging academic and public discourse may have been that had marked the past of political science, and as much as the discipline may have become estranged from its practical concerns, it remained in many respects more proximate to political life than the emerging conversations in political theory. The issue of theory and practice was once again repressed and displaced and took the surrogate form of the problem of seeking epistemic privilege which, detached from the practical concerns that had once inspired it, was little more than a trope in the language of political theory. Much of the conversation became indentured to and sublimated in various philosophical foundationalist epistemological projects and metatheories of social scientific explanation—and tied to the fate of those endeavors. This was a fate that became increasingly problematical as philosophical authority, through the 1980s, gravitated toward antifoundationalism and postmodernism. While the idea of a critical engagé social science and the idea of theoretical intervention were transformed into an epistemological project, postmodernism emerged as a kind of reverse epistemology. The pursuit of an image of epistemic privilege was one abstract discursive strategy for bringing theory and practice together, the declaration of the end of truth or the reduction of truth to power and solidarity was another.

This alienation of political theory, from politics and from itself, had not been the legacy that Wolin had anticipated in his call to vocation, but apart from a persistent belief that the vocation could in some way be pursued as a form of academic commentary and education, Wolin remained as unclear as many of his predecessors about how it was to provide practical wisdom and democratic political enlightenment.[72] The image of the vocation was distinctly based on his representation of classic political theory, but the actual diverse circumstances of these authors and texts held little relevance for the situation of the contemporary academic professional. Wolin's argument had, however, been more immediately inspired by his involvement with the Berkeley "free speech movement" and the attack on the "multiversity," in which for a brief moment some academicians had experienced the exaltation of what they perceived as something approaching their idealized vision of political action. This was not a situation in which the academy came to politics but one in which politics, or at least an atypical dramatic tributary and rendition of it, had come to the academy. It was a brief and anomalous visit, but here, for a time, in the view of Wolin and Schaar, "the faculty forgot its lust for research" and, in its "finest hour," joined the world of political action as it "stirred to ancestral memories of the ideal of a community of scholars."[73] The events of the Berkeley rebellion and its aftermath created a severe split within the political science department—and galvanized Wolin's image of the break between political theory and political science, which found expression in his essay on the vocation. For Wolin, the student movement and his participation in it represented the joining of academic and political issues and a sense that the relationship between theory and practice could be more than an intellectual one and that democracy could be more than an academic idea.

By the end of the next decade, however, little remained of the dream that it was possible to engage in politics by staying on campus and doing what professional academicians quintessentially did. The structural reality of the distance between academic and public discourse in America reasserted itself. The university was not a political arena, and politics seemed impervious to the academic voice except in peculiar idiosyncratic ways.[74] For Wolin, the issues were played out symbolically in the professional struggle between "methodism" and "political theory." The growing dominance of the former, however, both at Berkeley and in the profession at large, led him to pursue the idea of an independent program in political and social theory, first at Berkeley, where it ran aground, and then in the more cloistered groves of undergraduate education at the University of California at Santa Cruz, where it also foundered. It became eminently clear, however, as it had so often in the past, as in the case of Burgess and Adams, that what academic programs produced was more scholars and neither political actors nor commentators. And it was just as evident that keeping theory pure was not the answer. Wolin, in 1972, went to Princeton to head an interdisciplinary graduate program in political philosophy already in place. There was, significantly, the least support in the Department of Politics where he principally resided. In periodic forays outside the walls of Princeton, this bastion of academic professionalism, he brought into existence, in 1981, *democracy*—"A Journal of Political Renewal and Radical Change" published by the Common Good Foundation. It ceased publication in 1983.

There are many ways in which to interpret the fate of *democracy*, but surely it must be viewed as one more example of the traditional dream of American social science to find a way to bridge the gulf between academic and public discourse without fundamentally transforming the scholarly enterprise and without directly entering the distasteful and dangerous world of partisan politics. Whatever the immediate and concrete reasons for its short life, which largely involved a conflict between the more pragmatic and concrete policy goals of the journal's single financial sponsor and Wolin's more lofty concerns, *democracy*, like the *Journal of Social Philosophy* before it, symbolized the distance between the American academy and the structure of political power in the

United States as well as the manner in which academic discourse ultimately submerged the political motive and idiom.

One irony attaching to the career of the journal was, as Beard had emphasized so often, the notion that academicians might somehow contribute to the democratization of America at large and yet bypass confronting the very institutions in which they resided. The most obvious paradox, however, was the continuing disjunction between the university and the reality of American political life. The goal of the journal was to find a way in which academics could speak to a broad but still relatively elite audience. Even though they might comment on concrete political events and issues, political theorists could not really find a political voice, and the inertia of scholarly professionalism inhibited wide academic support. Like the Progressives, the project seemed to anticipate the awakening of some latent homogeneous public consciousness, but although it was relatively easy to indicate what was undemocratic about America, it was more difficult to specify concretely what would make it democratic and what role academic intellectuals would, could, or should play. While it might be salutary to point to the absence of some idealized notion of democracy in actual political life, or even to advocate, albeit outside the context of the institutional possibilities and agents of change, a vision of "strong democracy,"[75] speaking to and about politics and for democracy in concrete terms was something for which the scholar had limited competence and even less authority. Finally, it was not easy to square the prophetic urgings of an academic elite with democratic practice any more than in the case of Merriam and Lasswell.

There were some visible signs of relief when *democracy* disappeared from political theory. It was a stark reminder of the distance between the rhetoric and reality of academic political theory. The vocation no longer was forced to face concretely either the issue of the relationship between academic and public discourse nor the intractability of both profession and politics. By the mid-1980s, it was clear that the new identity of mainstream political science as a policy science did not require any fundamental dislocation of disciplinary and professional life, and political theory's concern with social relevance could be safely displaced into a range of philosophical projects. No blame could be attached to political theory as a purely academic endeavor—any more than to any scholarly discourse, but the motives of the past continued to surface discursively and engender a bad conscience. Inauthenticity resided, however, not in the pursuits of professional scholarship but in the pretension to being otherwise engaged.

Michael Walzer, maybe more than any other recent theorist, has dealt at length with the status of the social critic, and he has attempted to develop an image that avoids the idea of the theorist as a detached imperious moral rationalist. Walzer speaks of a "connected critic" who while seeking necessary "critical distance" enters the "mainstream" and pursues criticism as "interpretation" and "opposition" and seeks to mediate between "specialists and commoners" or "elite and mass."[76] What is instructive, however, is that none of Walzer's many historical examples, from the Hebrew prophets to Foucault, touch directly upon the circumstances of contemporary institutionalized academic political theory. Walzer does not attempt to blur the distinction between the authority of philosophy and its search for "objective truths" and the authority of the political community, but neither does he come to grips with the concrete relationship.

The story of political theory represents the more general history of academic intellectuals and their relationship to public life in America. By the end of the 1980s, the principal conversations in political theory ceased to speak about actual politics, let alone to it. To a large extent they became tributaries of the dominant academic persuasions such as postmodernism and reflections of debates such as that about philosophical foundationalism that permeated the humanities and social sciences. This was now less a search for philosophical grounds to underwrite theoretical intervention than a function of academic conformity. Even when an aspect of political theory had a distinct practical-issue counterpart and constituency, it was difficult to resist the attachment to the tokens of academic authority and the siren of esotericism and to speak in a manner that was not opaque to all outside the academy or even those standing outside the specialized language of subdisciplines.

From Willoughby to Wolin, the concern had been to secure the autonomy of political theory predicated on the autonomy of politics and find an answer to their articulation, but now much of political theory increasingly became a diverse world of specialized and derivative forms of scholarship in which neither inquiry nor its object had any clear identity and in which textual criticism and the presentation of self in professional circles could be construed as forms of political action. Both political theory and politics had become abstract intangible entities that rendered otoise any attempt to engage in a concrete discussion of their connection.

Max Weber noted that there are those who live for politics and those who live off it. The destiny of political theorists was toward assimilation into the latter category. The vocation that was once a calling has increasingly become merely an occupation. The idea of the great tradition of political thought had been more a projection of political theory's ideal self than an account of either its lineage or the actual influence of those antique thinkers from whose works the image of the tradition had been fashioned. Yet there was some similarity between the academic enterprise and the classic authors. The endeavors of both American political scientists and the émigrés had been characterized by a seriousness of purpose that lent a certain nobility to what in retrospect may appear a romantic and unrealistic venture. What political theory and its putative ancestors shared was the dream of knowledge dedicated to the elimination of political pathology. The vision of Plato, Aristotle, Machiavelli, Hobbes, Rousseau, and Marx resonated in the work of Lieber, Sanborn, Ely, Burgess, Willoughby, Merriam, Lasswell, Strauss, Voegelin, Marcuse, Arendt, Easton, and Wolin. In all cases, however, the dream failed in the course of a search for a vehicle of theoretical intervention. But while Plato's statesman and Machiavelli's prince, for example, were themselves the stuff of dreams, academic political theory's commitment to the university, and profession, was to something that was, ironically, ineluctably and fatefully real. Science and politics in America were, in the end, disparate and irreconcilable vocations. The challenge for political theory today may be less one of reconstituting the dream of articulating academic and public discourse than of recapturing the authentic concerns that had inspired and sustained it.

Notes

Abbreviations

AJS	*American Journal of Sociology*
APSR	*American Political Science Review*
IJE	*International Journal of Ethics*
JHI	*Journal of the History of Ideas*
JOP	*Journal of Politics*
JSP	*Journal of Social Philosophy*
JSS	*Journal of Social Science*
PSQ	*Political Science Quarterly*
ROP	*Review of Politics*

Preface

1. John G. Gunnell, "Political Theory: The Evolution of a Sub-Field," in Ada Finifter (ed.), *Political Science: The State of the Discipline* (Washington, D.C.: American Political Science Association, 1983).

2. Selected material from these oral histories has now been published in Michael Baer, Malcolm Jewell, and Lee Sigelman (eds.), *Political Science in America: Oral Histories of a Discipline* (Lexington: University of Kentucky Press, 1991). The oral history project is now located at the University of Kentucky.

Introduction

1. John G. Gunnell, *Political Theory: Tradition and Interpretation* (Cambridge, Mass.: Winthrop, 1979; Lanham: University Press of America, 1987).

2. Russell Jacoby, *The Last Intellectuals: American Culture in the Age of Academe* (New York: Basic, 1987).

3. I owe this parallel to Gene Poschman and his stimulating and informative paper, "Emerging Social Science and Political Relevance: Some Extractions from a Less than Classic Literature," presented at the annual meeting of the American Political Science Association in Denver, Sept., 1982.

4. In addition to Gunnell, "Evolution of a Sub-Field"; and Gunnell, *Tradition and Interpretation;* see John G. Gunnell, *Philosophy, Science, and Political Inquiry* (Morristown, N.J.: General Learning Press, 1975); idem, *Between Philosophy and Politics: The Alienation of Political Theory* (Amherst: University of Mas-

sachusetts Press, 1986); and idem, "Annals of Political Theory: Replies and Reflections," in John S. Nelson (ed.), *Tradition, Interpretation, and Science* (Albany: State University of New York Press, 1986).

5. For a fuller discussion of these issues, see John G. Gunnell, "The Historiogrpahy of American Political Science," in David Easton, John Gunnell, and Luigi Graziano (eds.), *The Development of Political Science: A Comparative Survey*, (London: Routledge, 1991); and the more extended treatment in John G. Gunnell, "Disciplinary History: The Case of Political Science," *Strategies* 4/5 (1991). See also John Dryzek and Stephen Leonard, "History and Discipline in Political Science," *APSR* 82 (1988) and comments by Raymond Seidelman, James Farr, and John G. Gunnell and reply by Dryzek and Leonard in "Can Political Science History by Neutral?" Symposium, *APSR* 84 (1990).

6. See Gunnell, *Tradition and Interpretation;* John G. Gunnell, "Method, Methodology, and the Search for Traditions in the History of Political Theory: A Reply to Pocock's 'Salute,'" *Annals of Scholarship* 1 (1980); idem, "Political Theory and the Theory of Action," *Western Political Quarterly* 34 (1981); idem, "Interpretation and the History of Political Theory: Apology and Epistemology," *APSR* 76 (1982); idem, "Hermeneutical Theory and Interpretative Practice: Sorting out the Arguments," in Manuel J. Pelaez and Miguel Martinez Lopez (eds.), *Essays in the History of Political Thought* (Barcelona: Promociones Publicaciones Universitarias, 1989).

7. See n. 5. Some of the works in question here include Bernard Crick's seminal study of *The American Science of Politics* (Berkeley: University of California Press, 1959); Albert Somit and Joseph Tannenhaus, *The Development of American Political Science: From Burgess to Behavioralism* (Boston: Allyn and Bacon, 1967); Raymond Seidelman (with Edward Harpham), *Disenchanted Realists: Political Science and the American Crisis, 1884–1894* (Albany: State University of New York Press, 1985); David Ricci, *The Tragedy of Political Science: Politics, Scholarship, and Democracy* (New Haven, Conn.: Yale University Press, 1984).

8. Mary O. Furner, *Advocacy and Objectivity: A Crisis in the Professionalization of Social Science, 1865–1905* (Lexington: University of Kentucky Press, 1975); Thomas Haskell, *The Emergence of Professional Social Science: The American Social Science Association and the Nineteenth Century Crisis of Authority* (Urbana: University of Illinois Press, 1977); Dorothy Ross, *The Origins of American Social Science* (New York: Cambridge University Press, 1991).

Chapter One

1. Sheldon S. Wolin, "Political Theory as a Vocation," *APSR* 63 (1969): 1062–82.

2. David Easton, "The New Revolution in Political Science," *APSR* 62 (1969): 1051–61.

3. David Easton, "Political Science, Method and Theory," in David Sills (ed.), *International Encyclopedia of the Social Sciences (IESS)*, (New York: Macmillan, 1968), 12:295–97.

4. Sheldon S. Wolin, "Political Theory: Trends and Goals," in Sills (ed.), *IESS*, 12:319, 324–25, 327–28.

5. Hermann Heller, "Political Science," in Edwin R. A. Seligman and Alvin Johnson (eds.), *Encyclopaedia of the Social Sciences (ESS)* (New York: Macmillan, 1934), 12:207.

6. Ibid., p. 220.

7. James Mill, *Analysis of the Phenomena of the Human Mind* (New York: A. M. Kelley, 1967), pp. 402–3.

8. Charles Darwin, *The Autobiography of Charles Darwin* (New York: Dover, 1958), p. 42.

9. *The Positive Philosophy of Auguste Comte,* trans. and condensed by Harriet Martineau, (London: G. Bell, 1913), 1:3, 5; ibid, 2:242.

10. John Stuart Mill, *A System of Logic* (London: Parker, 1843).

11. William Whewell, *The Philosophy of the Inductive Sciences* (Cambridge: Parker London and Deighton, 1840).

12. Richard Hildreth, *Theory of Politics: An Inquiry into the Foundation of Governments and the Causes and Progress of Political Revolutions* (New York: Harper and Brothers, 1853).

13. George Cornwall Lewis, *Treatise on the Methods of Observation and Reasoning in Politics* (New York: Arno, 1974), p. 27.

14. Ibid., p. 3.

15. John F. Lalor (ed.), *Cyclopedaedia of Political Science, Political Economy, and the Political History of the United States* (New York: Charles E. Merril, 1888), p. 257.

16. Ibid., p. 800.

17. Crick, *American Science of Politics,* pp. 81–82.

18. Richard Hofstadter and C. DeWitt Hardy, *The Development of the Scope of Higher Education in the United States* (New York: Columbia University Press, 1952); Walter P. Metzger, *Academic Freedom in the Age of the University* (New York: Columbia University Press, 1955); Laurence R. Veysey, *The Emergence of the American University* (Chicago: University of Chicago Press, 1965); Donald H. Meyer, *The Instructed Conscience* (Philadelphia: University of Pennsylvania Press, 1972); Furner, *Advocacy and Objectivity;* Haskell, *Emergence of Professional Social Science;* Dorothy J. Ross, "Professionalism and the Transformation of American Social Thought," *Journal of Economic History* 38 (1978); and idem, "The Development of the Social Sciences," in Alexandra Oleson and John Voss (eds.), *The Origins of Knowledge in Modern America, 1860–1920* (Baltimore: Johns Hopkins University Press, 1979).

19. See Albert Lepawsky, "The Politics of Epistemology," *Western Political Quarterly,* supp. (1964): 35–36.

20. George Beard, *American Nervousness: Its Causes and Consequences* [1881] (New York: Arno, 1972), p. 122.

21. Ibid.

22. Ibid., pp. 124–25.

23. Francis Lieber, *The Stranger in America* (Philadelphia: Carey, Lea and Blanchard, 1835), p. 197.

24. Ibid.

25. See Thomas Sergeant Perry (ed.), *The Life and Letters of Francis Lieber* (Boston: James R. Osgood, 1882); Lewis R. Harley, *Francis Lieber: His Life and Political Philosophy* (New York: Columbia University Press, 1899); Frank Freidel, *Francis Lieber: Nineteenth Century Liberal* (Baton Rouge: Louisiana State University Press, 1947); Bernard Edward Brown, *American Conservatives: The Political Thought of Francis Lieber and John W. Burgess* (New York: Columbia University Press, 1951); James Farr, "Francis Lieber and the Interpretation of American Political Science," *JOP* 52 (1990).

26. Nathaniel Chipman, *Sketches of the Principles of Government* (Rutland, Vt.: J. Lyons, 1843).

27. Francis Lieber (ed.), *Encyclopedia Americana* (Philadelphia: Thomas Desilver, 1835), vol. 10.

28. Ibid., 11:568.

29. Ibid., 10:225.

30. William Paley, *The Principles of Moral and Political Philosophy* (Philadelphia: Thomas Dobson, 1788).

31. Francis Lieber, *Manual of Political Ethics* (Philadelphia: J. B. Lippincott, 1885), 1:162.

32. Ibid., chap. 12.

33. Francis Lieber, *Civil Liberty and Self-Government* (Philadelphia: J. B. Lippincott, [1853] 1959), p. 39.

34. Ibid., p. v.

35. Francis Lieber, *Miscellaneous Writings* (Philadelphia: J. B. Lippincott, 1881), 1:217.

36. Ibid., pp. 330–34.

37. Ibid., pp. 367–68.

38. Ibid., pp. 351–52.

39. Ibid., p. 353.

40. Ibid., pp. 358–59.

41. Ibid., p. 374.

42. Ibid., pp. 378, 385.

43. Ibid., p. 381.

44. Lieber, *Miscellaneous Writings*, 2:99.

45. Ibid., p. 13.

46. Daniel Coit Gilman, *Bluntschli, Lieber, and Laboulaye* (Baltimore: privately printed, 1884), p. 32.

47. Johann Caspar Bluntschli, *The Theory of the State* (Oxford: Clarendon, 1885).

48. Ibid., p. 7.

49. Ibid., p. 69.

50. Ibid., p. 10.

51. Ibid., p. 12.

52. Ibid., p. 15.

53. Ibid., p. 54.

54. Ibid., pp. 167–68.

55. Ibid., p. 235.

56. Anna Haddow, *Political Science in American Colleges and Universities: 1636–1900* (New York: D. Appleton-Century, 1939).

57. See Gladys Bryson, "The Emergence of the Social Sciences from Moral Philosophy," *IJE* 42 (1932): 17. See also idem, "The Comparable Interests of the Old Moral Philosophy and the Modern Social Sciences," *Social Forces* 11 (1932).

58. Herbert B. Adams, *The Study of History in American Colleges and Universities* (Washington, D.C.: Bureau of Education, 1887), p. 55.

59. Theodore Woolsey, *Political Science or the State Theoretically and Practically Considered* (New York: Scribner, Armstrong, 1878).

60. William W. Crane and Bernard Moses, *Politics: An Introduction to the Study of Comparative Constitutional Law* (New York: Putnam, 1884).

61. Haddow, *Political Science in American Colleges*, p. 219.

Chapter Two

1. See Andrew D. White, *Education in Political Science* (Baltimore: John Murphy, 1879). See also Glenn C. Altschuler, *Andrew D. White—Educator, Historian, Diplomat* (Ithaca, N.Y.: Cornell University Press, 1979).

2. Laurens Hickok, *A System of Moral Science* (Schenectady, N.Y.: G. Y. Van Debogert, 1853).

3. For a more general discussion of Adams, see John Martin Vincent, "Herbert Baxter Adams," in Howard Odum (ed.), *American Masters of Social Science* (New York: Holt, 1927).

4. See, for example, Herbert B. Adams, *The German Origins of New England Towns* (Baltimore: Johns Hopkins University Press, 1882).

5. Herbert B. Adams, *Methods of Historical Study* (Baltimore: Freeman, 1884), p. 21.

6. Adams, *Study of History in American Colleges*, p. 171. See Carl Diehl, *Americans and German Scholarship, 1770–1870* (New Haven, Conn.: Yale University Press, 1978).

7. Adams, *Study of History in American Colleges*, p. 194.

8. This continues to be the basic interpretation in Dorothy Ross's *Origins of American Social Science* (see intro., n. 8).

9. For comprehensive discussions of the development of the German university, see Frederick Lilge, *The Abuse of Learning* (New York: Macmillan, 1948); and Charles E. McLelland, *State, Society, and University in Germany, 1700–1914* (Cambridge: Cambridge University Press, 1980).

10. See Fritz Ringer, *The Decline of the German Mandarins: The German Academic Community, 1890–1933* (Cambridge: Harvard University Press, 1969).

11. See Charles F. Thwing, *The American and German University: One Hundred Years of History* (New York: Macmillan, 1928).

12. Haskell, *Emergence of Professional Social Science* (see intro., n. 8); Furner,

Advocacy and Objectivity (see intro., n. 8); L. L. and Jessie Bernard, *The Origins of American Sociology: The Social Science Movement in the United States* (New York: Russell and Russell, 1943), p. 559; and idem, "A Century of Progress in the Social Sciences," *Social Forces,* 11 (1933).

13. See *JSS* 5 (1873): 137.

14. See, for example, George M. Marsden, *Fundamentalism and American Culture* (New York: Oxford Press, 1980).

15. *JSS* 3(1871): 68.

16. See Peter R. Senn, "The Earliest Use of the Term 'Social Science,'" *JHI* 19 (1958); Fred R. Shapiro, "A Note on the Origin of the Term Social Science," *Journal of the History of the Behavioral Sciences* 20 (1984).

17. Frank Sanborn, "The Three-fold Aspect of Social Science in America," *JSS* 14 (1881): 27.

18. *JSS* 1 (1869): 1.

19. George William Curtis, *JSS* 6 (1874): 34.

20. Frank Sanborn, *JSS* 8 (1876): 24.

21. F. B. Sanborn, "Social Science in Theory and Practice," *JSS* 9 (1878): 1, 7, 8.

22. *JSS* 46 (1909).

23. Frank Sanborn, "Past and Present of Social Science," *JSS* 43 (1905): 3, 15, 21.

24. See Andrew D. White, *The Warfare of Science* (New York: Appleton, 1876).

25. Quoted in Haskell, *Emergence of Professional Social Science* (see intro., n. 8), p. 195.

26. Daniel Coit Gilman, *JSS* 12 (1880): xxii–xxiii.

27. For Ely's own account of his life, see *The Ground Under Our Feet* (New York: Macmillan, 1938). For another perspective, see Benjamin Rader, *The Academic Mind and Reform: The Influence of Richard T. Ely in American Life* (Lexington: University of Kentucky Press, 1966).

28. Richard Ely, "Recent American Socialism," *Johns Hopkins University Studies in History and Political Science* 4 (1885): 72–74.

29. Ely, *Ground Under Our Feet,* pp. 146, 154.

30. Ibid., pp. 132, 140.

31. Richard Ely, "Past and Present of Political Economy," *Johns Hopkins Studies in History and Political Science* 3 (1884): 64.

32. Ely, *Ground Under Our Feet,* p. 187.

33. Ibid., p. 145.

34. See Jürgen Herbst, *The German Historical School in American Scholarship* (Ithaca, N.Y.: Cornell University Press, 1965).

35. For a history of the association, see Franz Boese, *Geschichte des Vereins für Sozialpolitik, 1872–1932* (Duncker und Humboldt, 1939). Also Dieter Lindenlaub, *Richtungskampfe im Verein für Sozialpolitik* (Westbaden: Steiner, 1967).

36. Quoted in Ralph Gordon Hoxie et al., *A History of the Faculty of Political Science, Columbia University* (New York: Columbia University Press, 1955), p. 51.

37. Sheldon Amos, *The Science of Politics* (New York: Appleton, 1883).

38. John Burgess, *Reminiscences of an American Scholar* (New York: Columbia University Press, 1934), pp. 254–55. Idem, *Political Science and Comparative Constitutional Law*, vols. 1, 2 (Boston: Ginn, 1890–91). An abridged version of this work was published as *Foundations of Political Science* (New York: Columbia University Press, 1933).

39. John Burgess, *The Civil War and the Constitution, 1859–1865*, vols. 1, 2 (New York: Scribner's, 1901).

40. For an analysis of the development of German historical scholarship, see George Iggers, *The German Conception of History* (Middletown, Conn.: Wesleyan University Press, 1969). For a more detailed account of Burgess's view of history, see Bert James Loewenberg, "John William Burgess, the Scientific Method, and the Hegelian Philosophy of History," *Mississippi Valley Historical Review* 42 (1955). Also W. Stull Holt, "The Idea of Scientific History in America," *JHI* 1 (1940).

41. Burgess, *Reminiscences of an American Scholar*, pp. 109, 124.

42. Ibid., p. 131.

43. Ibid., pp. 202–3.

44. Ibid., p. 139.

45. In addition to Burgess, the original faculty consisted of Clifford Bateman (political scientist) and Richard Mayo-Smith (statistician and economist) but within a few years were joined by a dozen others who included Frank Goodnow (political scientist), E. R. A. Seligman (economist), Franklin Giddings (sociologist), and William Archibald Dunning (historian). These individuals, as well as others such as the philosopher Archibald Alexander and the historian James Harvey Robinson, were also involved with the *Quarterly*.

46. See Haddow, *Political Science in American Colleges*, p. 180.

47. Burgess, *Reminiscences of an American Scholar*, p. 244.

48. John Burgess, "The Study of the Political Sciences in Columbia College," *International Review* 12 (1882): 346.

49. Ibid., p. 347.

50. Ibid., p. 348.

51. Ibid., p. 350.

52. Adams, *Study of History in American Colleges*, p. 67.

53. Ibid., pp. 83–84.

54. John Burgess, "Germany, Great Britain, and the United States," *PSQ* 19 (1904): 19.

55. Burgess, *Reminiscences of an American Scholar*, p. 397.

56. Ibid., p. 213.

57. John W. Burgess, "The American Commonwealth. Changes in Its Relation to the Nation," *PSQ* 1 (1886): 12–13.

58. Ibid., p. 34.

59. John W. Burgess, "Ideal of American Commonwealth," *PSQ* 10 (1896): 407.

60. Burgess, *Reminiscences of an American Scholar*, p. 358.

61. John Burgess, "Political Science and History," *American Historical Review* 2 (1897): 403–4.

62. Burgess, *Political Science and Comparative Constitutional Law*, vol. 1, p. v.

63. Burgess, "Political Science and History," pp. 404, 407–8.

64. Munroe Smith, "Introduction: The Domain of Political Science," *PSQ* 1 (1886).

65. Frederick Pollock, *An Introduction to the History of the Science of Politics* (London: Macmillan, 1890), pp. 1–5.

66. Ibid., pp. 93, 3.

67. See Stefan Collini, Donald Winch, and John Burrow, *That Noble Science of Politics* (Cambridge: Cambridge University Press, 1983).

68. Frank Sargent Hoffman, *The Sphere of the State or the People as a Body-Politic* (New York: Putnam's, 1894), pp. 1–6, 17.

69. Woodrow Wilson, *The State: Elements of Historical and Practical Politics* (Boston: Heath, 1889).

70. Westel Woodbury Willoughby, *An Examination of the Nature of the State* (New York: Macmillan, 1896), p. 5.

71. Ibid., p. 338.

Chapter Three

1. See Richard Ashcraft, "German Historicism and the History of Political Theory," *History of Political Thought* 8 (1987).

2. Crick, *American Science of Politics* (see intro., n. 7), p. 97.

3. Ross, *Origins of American Social Science* (see intro., n. 8), represents the latest version of this claim.

4. Charles Edward Merriam and Harry Elmer Barnes, *A History of Political Theories: Recent Times* (New York: Macmillan, 1924), p. vi.

5. Charles Merriam, "William Archibald Dunning," in Odum (ed.), *American Masters of Social Science*, p. 134.

6. *Truth in History and Other Essays by William A. Dunning*, ed. J. G. de Roulhac Hamilton (Port Washington, N.Y.: Kennikat, 1937), p. xvii.

7. Merriam, "William Archibald Dunning," p. 136.

8. Alvin Johnson, *Pioneer's Progress* (New York: Viking, 1952), p. 124.

9. Dunning, *Truth in History*, pp. 139–42.

10. William Dunning, "A Century of Politics," *North American Review* 179 (1904): 803, 813.

11. William A. Dunning, review of Harold Laski's *Studies in the Problem of Sovereignty*, *PSQ* 32 (1917).

12. Dunning, *Truth in History*, pp. 163, 36.

13. Ibid., pp. 5, 20.

14. Ibid., pp. 17, 20.

15. William Dunning, *A History of Political Theories, Ancient and Mediaeval* (New York: Macmillan, 1902), pp. vii–viii, xxii.

16. Paul Janet, *Histoire de la Science politique dan ses rapports avec la morale*

(1887): Robert von Mohl, *Des Geschichte und Literatur der Staatswissenschaften* (1855–58); Karl Hildenbrand, *Gechichte und System der Rechts—und Staatsphilosophie* (1860). There were also other works that he did not note such as Gustav Strive, *Kritische Geschicte des Allgemeinen Staatsrechts* (1847); and Adolphe Franck, *Reformateurs et Publicistes de L'Europe: Moyen Age–Renaissance* (1864).

17. Hugh Seymour Tremenheere, *The Political Experience of the Ancients and Its Bearing on Modern Times* (London: Kegan Paul, Trench, 1851, 1882), p. v.

18. Robert Blakey, *The History of Political Literature* (London: Richard Bentley, 1855), pp. i, vi.

19. Dunning, *History of Political Theories* (1902), pp. xxii–xxiv.

20. Ibid., p. xiv.

21. Ibid., pp. 8, xxv.

22. Ibid., pp. viii, xix, 1–2.

23. Ibid., pp. xv–xvii.

24. Ibid., pp. xix–xx.

25. Ibid., pp. xviii–xxx.

26. Merriam and Barnes, *History of Political Theories*, p. vi.

27. William A. Dunning, *A History of Political Theories, from Rousseau to Spencer* (New York: Macmillan, 1920), p. 423.

28. Dunning, *History of Political Theories* (1902), p. 1.

29. Dunning, *History of Political Theories* (1920), pp. 393, 407, 409.

30. Ibid., pp. 412, 414.

31. William A. Dunning, "Current Political Theory," *PSQ* 22 (1907): 693.

32. Charles Beard, "Politics," Columbia University Lecture, Columbia University Library, 1908.

33. Albert Bushnell Hart, "The Growth of American Theories of Popular Government," *APSR* 1 (1907).

34. W. W. Willoughy, "The Value of Political Philosophy," *PSQ* 15 (1900).

35. Frank J. Goodnow, *Politics and Administration* (New York: Macmillan, 1900).

36. W. W. Willoughby, "The American Political Science Association," *PSQ* 19 (1904): 110.

37. Ibid., p. 107.

38. Henry Jones Ford, "The Scope of Political Science," *Proceedings of the APSA* (1906): 203–6. See also idem, *The Rise and Growth of American Politics* (New York: Macmillan, 1898).

39. Frank J. Goodnow, "The Work of the APSA," *Proceedings of the APSA* (1905): 37–38. Idem, *Social Reform and the Constitution* (New York: Macmillan, 1911).

40. Westel Woodbury Willoughby, *Political Theories of the Ancient World* (New York: Longmans, Green, 1903), pp. vi–vii.

41. Ibid., pp. ix–x.

42. Ibid., pp. xi–xii.

43. Willoughby, "The American Political Science Association," pp. 108, 111.

44. Westel Woodbury Willoughby, "Political Philosophy," in Howard J.

Rodgers (ed.), *Congress of Arts and Science,* (Boston: Houghton Mifflin, 1906), 7:310. See also W. W. Willoughby, "Political Philosophy," *South Atlantic Quarterly* 5 (1906).

45. Willoughby, "Political Philosophy," in Rodgers (ed.), pp. 312–13.

46. Ibid., p. 312.

47. Ibid., p. 325.

48. George Grafton Wilson, "Problems of Political Theory," in Rodgers (ed.), *Congress of Arts and Science,* 7:337.

49. W. W. Willoughby, "Political Science as a University Study," *Sewanee Review* 14 (1906): 257–58.

50. Ibid., p. 261.

51. Ibid., pp. 264–65.

52. W. W. Willoughby, "The Political Theory of John W. Burgess," *Yale Review* 17 (1908): 68, 59, 64, 71.

53. Charles Merriam, "The Political Philosophy of John C. Calhoun," in James Garner (ed.), *Studies in Southern History and Politics* (Port Washington, N.Y.: Kennikat, 1964), p. 319.

54. Otto Gierke, *Political Theories of the Middle Ages* (Cambridge: Cambridge University Press, 1900).

55. R. W. Carlyle and A. J. Carlyle, *A History of Medieval Political Theory in the West* (New York: Putnam's, 1903), pp. vi, 1–21.

56. John Neville Figgis, *Studies of Political Thought from Gerson to Grotius, 1414–1625* (Cambridge: Cambridge University Press, 1907), pp. 1–3, 29–30.

57. James Bryce, "Relations of Political Science to History and to Practice," *APSR* 3 (1909).

58. A. Lawrence Lowell, "The Physiology of Politics," *APSR* 4 (1910): 15.

59. James Wilford Garner, *Introduction to Political Science* (New York: American Book, 1910).

60. George H. Sabine, "Descriptive and Normative Sciences," *Philosophical Review* 21 (1912): 449–50; idem, "Liberty and the Social System," *Philosophical Review* 25 (1916): 668.

61. Henry Jones Ford, *The Natural History of the State* (Princeton, N.J.: Princeton University Press, 1915), pp. 1, 175.

62. See, for example, James Quayle Dealy, *The Development of the State* (New York: Silver, Burdett, 1909).

63. Raymond Garfield Gettell, "Nature and Scope of Present Political Theory," *Proceedings of the APSA* (1914): 49–50.

64. Ibid., pp. 52–54.

65. "Report of Committee of Seven on Instruction in Colleges and Universities," *APSR* 9 (1915).

66. Ernest Barker, *Nietzsche and Treitschke: The Worship of Power* (Oxford: Oxford University Press, 1914); idem, "The Discredited State," *Political Quarterly,* 2 (1915); idem, "The Superstition of the State," *Times Literary Supplement,* July 1918.

67. William Dunning, "The German Idealists," *PSQ* 28 (1913): 493–94.

68. John Dewey, *German Philosophy and Politics* (New York: Henry Holt, 1915), pp. 123–25.

69. Westel Woodbury Willoughby, *Prussian Political Philosophy* (New York: Appleton, 1918), pp. vii–viii.

70. Franklin Giddings, *The Responsible State* (Cambridge, Mass.: Riverside, 1918), pp. 48, 46.

71. Harold J. Laski, *Studies in the Problem of Sovereignty* (New Haven, Conn.: Yale University Press, 1917); idem, *Authority in the Modern State* (New Haven, Conn.: Yale University Press, 1919); Leon Duguit, *Law in the Modern State,* trans. Frida and Harold Laski (New York: R. W. Huebsch, 1919); Harold J. Laski, *Foundations of Sovereignty and Other Essays* (New York: Harcourt, Brace, 1921).

72. For a full discussion of Laski's life and work, see Herbert A. Deane, *The Political Ideas of Harold J. Laski* (New York: Columbia University Press, 1955).

Chapter Four

1. Woodrow Wilson, *Congressional Government* (Boston: Houghton Mifflin, 1885).

2. Woodrow Wilson, "The Character of Democracy in the United States," *Atlantic Monthly* 64 (1889); idem, "The Study of Administration," *PSQ* 2 (1887).

3. Woodrow Wilson, "A Literary Politician," in *Mere Literature and Other Essays* (Boston: Houghton Mifflin, 1897).

4. Woodrow Wilson, "The Law and the Facts," *APSR* 9 (1911): 8, 10, 11.

5. Ibid., pp. 2, 8, 11.

6. For a full discussion of Wilson, see Niels Aage Thorsen, *The Political Thought of Woodrow Wilson* (Princeton, N.J.: Princeton University, 1988).

7. For extended discussions of Bentley's life and work, see Paul Kress, *Social Science and the Idea of Process: The Ambiguous Legacy of Arthur F. Bentley* (Urbana: University of Illinois Press, 1973); and James F. Ward, *Language, Form, and Inquiry: Arthur F. Bentley's Philosophy of Social Science* (Amherst: University of Massachusetts Press, 1984).

8. Charles Beard, "The Study and Teaching of Politics," *Columbia University Quarterly* 12 (1909–10).

9. Charles Beard, *An Economic Interpretation of the Constitution of the United States* (New York: Macmillan, 1913).

10. E. R. A. Seligman, "Economic Interpretation of History," *PSQ* 16 (1901). This work was published in book form the following year by Macmillan.

11. For a fuller discussion of Beard's career, see Ellen Nore, *Charles A. Beard: An Intellectual Portrait* (Carbondale: Southern Illinois University Press, 1983); and Howard K. Beale (ed.), *Charles A. Beard: An Appraisal* (Lexington: University of Kentucky Press, 1954).

12. For an extended discussion of this issue, see John G. Gunnell, "Continuity and Innovation in the History of Political Science: The Case of Charles

Merriam," *Journal of the History of the Behavioral Sciences* 28 (1992). For a general account of Merriam's career, see Barry Karl, *Charles Merriam and the Study of Politics* (Chicago: University of Chicago Press, 1974).

13. Charles Merriam, *New Aspects of Politics* (Chicago: University of Chicago Press, 1925).

14. Charles Merriam, *History of the Theory of Sovereignty since Rousseau* (New York: Columbia University Press, 1900), p. 179; idem, *A History of American Political Theories* (New York: Macmillan, 1903), pp. 347–48.

15. Merriam and Barnes, *History of Political Theories,* p. vi.

16. Charles Merriam, "William Archibald Dunning," p. 143.

17. For a discussion of problems of academic freedom and the situation of the university after 1917, see Clyde Barrow, *Universities and the Capitalist State* (Madison: University of Wisconsin Press, 1990).

18. Charles Merriam, "The Education of Charles Merriam," in Leonard D. White (ed.), *The Future of Government in the United States: Essays in Honor of Charles E. Merriam* (Chicago: University of Chicago Press, 1942), p. 4.

19. Merriam, *History of Sovereignty since Rousseau,* p. v.

20. See Merriam, "The Education of Charles Merriam."

21. Letter from Dunning to Merriam, Merriam Papers, box VII, folder 12, University of Chicago Library.

22. Merriam, *History of American Political Theories,* pp. vii–viii, 334, 336, 305.

23. Ibid., pp. 306, 337.

24. Ibid., pp. 343–48.

25. Merriam, "The Education of Charles E. Merriam," p. 5. The experience of this political period was represented in *Chicago: A More Intimate View of Urban Politics* (New York: Macmillan, 1929).

26. Charles Merriam, *American Political Ideas: Studies in the Development of American Political Thought, 1865–1917.* (New York: Macmillan, 1920), pp. 466, 357.

27. Ibid., p. 405.

28. Ibid., p. 472.

29. Charles Merriam, "The Present State of the Study of Politics," *APSR* 15 (1921): 174.

30. Ibid., pp. 176, 178.

31. Ibid., pp. 175, 179, 183–85.

32. Harry Elmer Barnes, "Some Contributions of Sociology to Modern Political Theory," *APSR* 15 (1921): 530–33.

33. Harry Elmer Barnes, "The Historian and the History of Science," *Scientific Monthly* 11 (1920): 113.

34. William Kay Wallace, *The Passing of Politics* (New York: Macmillan, 1921), pp. 5–7, 123, 289.

35. Barnes, "Some Contributions of Sociology to Modern Political Theory," pp. 491, 502, 530.

36. A. Gordon Dewey, "On Methods in the Study of Politics," *PSQ* 38 (1923): 636.

37. Raymond G. Gettell, "The Nature of Political Thought," *APSR* 17 (1923): 214–15.

38. "Progress Report of the Committee on Political Research," *APSR* 17 (1923): 275, 281–83.

39. Ibid., p. 286.

40. Ibid., p. 295.

41. Charles Merriam, "The Significance of the Study of Psychology for the Study of Politics," *APSR* 18 (1924): 488.

42. Horace M. Kallen, "Political Science as Psychology," *APSR* 17 (1923): 203.

43. "Report of the First National Conference on the Science of Politics," *APSR* 18 (1924): 120.

44. Ibid., p. 119.

45. Ibid., p. 121.

46. Arnold Bennett Hall, "Report of the Second National Conference on the Science of Politics," *APSR* 19 (1925): 104.

47. Ibid., pp. 105–7, 110.

48. Arnold Bennett Hall, review of Walter Lippman's *The Phantom Public*, *APSR* 20 (1926): 199.

49. Merriam and Barnes, *History of Political Theories*, p. 1.

50. Ibid., pp. 11, 15–19.

51. Ibid., pp. 20–21, 44–45.

52. Merriam, *New Aspects of Politics*, p. 237.

53. Ibid., p. 18.

54. Ibid., p. 330.

55. Charles Merriam, "The Progress of Political Research," *APSR* 20 (1926): 3, 11.

56. Charles Merriam, "Recent Developments in Political Science," in Charles A. Ellwood, Clark Wissler, Robert H. Gault, et al. *Recent Developments in the Social Sciences* (Philadelphia: J. B. Lippincott, 1927), pp. 326–27.

57. See, for example, C. E. M. Joad, *Introduction to Modern Political Theory* (Oxford: Clarendon, 1924); C. R. and Mary Morris, *History of Political Ideas* (London: Cristopohers, 1924); Harold Laski, *Political Thought in England from Locke to Bentham* (Oxford: Oxford University Press, 1920).

58. Eric Voegelin, "Political Theory and the General Pattern of History," *APSR* 38 (1944): 746.

59. A. R. Lord, *The Principles of Politics: An Introduction to the Study of the Evolution of Political Ideas* (Oxford: Clarendon, 1921), pp. 11, 13, 42.

60. C. E. Vaughn, *Studies in the History of Political Philosophy before and after Rousseau* (Manchester: University of Manchester Press, 1925), pp. 1–2.

61. Raymond G. Gettell, *History of Political Thought* (New York: Century, 1924), p. v.

62. Ibid., pp. 17, 19.

63. Ibid., pp. 4–5, 6, 16.

64. Ludwig Gumplowicz, *Geschichte der Staatstheorien* (Innsbruck: Verlag

Wagner, 1926). Gaetano Mosca, *Short History of Political Philosophy*, trans. Sondra Koff (New York: Thomas Y. Crowell, 1972), first published in 1933 and revised in 1937. Robert H. Murray, *The History of Political Science from Plato to the Present* (Cambridge: W. Heffer, 1926), p. v. Francis William Coker, *Readings in Political Philosophy* (New York: Macmillan, 1926), p. vii.

65. F. J. C. Hearnshaw, *The Development of Political Ideas* (New York: Thomas Nelson and Sons, 1927), p. 7.

66. Ernest Barker, "Medieval Political Thought," in F. J. C. Hearnshaw (ed.), *The Social and Political Ideas of Some Great Medieval Thinkers* (New York: Barnes and Noble, 1928), p. 10.

67. J. W. Allen, *A History of Political Thought in the Sixteenth Century* (New York: Dial, 1928).

68. Roger Chance, *Until Philosophers Are Kings*, foreword by Harold Laski (New York: Oxford University Press, 1929), p. vi.

69. Gesa Engelmann, *Political Philosophy: From Plato to Jeremy Bentham* (New York: Harper and Bro., 1927), pp. xi–xiii.

70. Ibid., pp. xv–xviii.

71. See Charles Merriam, *Civic Education in the United States* (New York: Scribner's, 1934).

Chapter Five

1. Jesse Macy, "The Scientific Spirit in Politics," *APSR* 11 (1917).

2. Walter Shepard, review of Laski's *Authority in the Modern State, APSR* 13 (1919).

3. Graham Wallas, *Human Nature in Politics* (London: Archibald Constable, 1908); A. Lawrence Lowell, *Public Opinion and Popular Government* (New York: Longmans, Green, 1913); Walter Lippmann, *A Preface to Politics* (New York: Mitchell Kennerley, 1914); idem, *The Phantom Public* (New York: Harcourt, Brace, 1925); Frank Kent, *The Great Game of Politics* (New York: Doubleday, Page, 1924); Charles E. Merriam and Harold F. Gosnell, *Non-Voting: Causes and Methods of Control* (Chicago: University of Chicago Press, 1924); and Charles E. Merriam, *The American Party System* (New York: Macmillan, 1922).

4. M. P. Follett, *The New State: Group Organizations, the Solution of Popular Government* (New York: Longmans, Green, 1918).

5. For a detailed discussion of this debate, and particularly the work of Laski and W. Y. Elliott, see John G. Gunnell, "The Declaration of the State and the Origins of American Pluralism," Manuscript.

6. See Raymond G. Gettell, "Pluralistic Theories of Sovereignty," in *History of Political Thought* (New York: Century, 1924); and Kung Chuan Hsiao, *Political Pluralism: A Study in Contemporary Political Theory* (New York: Harcourt, Brace, 1927).

7. Ellen Deborah Ellis, "The Pluralistic State," *APSR* 14 (1920): 394.

8. Ibid., pp. 405–7. See also idem, "Guild Socialism and Pluralism," *APSR* 17 (1923).

9. See George H. Sabine, "The Concept of the State as Power," *Philosophical Review* 29 (1920): 301. Idem, "Pluralism: A Point of View," *APSR* 17 (1923).

10. George H. Sabine in Hugo Krabbe, *The Modern Idea of the State*, trans. George H. Sabine and Walter J. Shepard (New York: D. Appleton, 1922), pp. xii–xiii.

11. F. W. Coker, "Pluralistic Theories and the Attack on State Sovereignty," in Merriam and Barnes (eds.), *History of Political Theories* (see chap. 3, no. 4). Also idem, "The Technique of the Pluralist State," *APSR* 15 (1921).

12. W. Y. Elliott, "The Pragmatic Politics of Mr. H. J. Laski," *APSR* 18 (1924): 251. Also idem, "Sovereign State or Sovereign Group?" *APSR* 19 (1925).

13. Elliott, "Mr. H. J. Laski," p. 275.

14. William Yandell Elliott, review of Merriam and Barnes (eds.), *History of Political Theories, APSR* 19 (1925): 178–179.

15. William Ernest Hocking, *Man and the State* (New Haven, Conn.: Yale University Press, 1926).

16. R. M. MacIver, *The Modern State* (London: Oxford University Press, 1926). W. Y. Elliott, review of MacIver's *The Modern State, APSR* 21 (1927): 432–34.

17. Ellen Deborah Ellis, "Political Science at the Crossroads," *APSR* 21 (1927): 773, 784.

18. See George H. Sabine, "Political Science and the Juristic Point of View," *APSR* 22 (1928). W. W. Willoughby, "The Juristic Theories of Krabbe," *APSR* 20 (1926).

19. Johnson, *Pioneer's Progress* (see chap. 3, n. 8), p. 240.

20. Charles Beard, "Some Aspects of Regional Planning," *APSR* 20 (1926): 278.

21. Charles A. Beard, "Time, Technology, and the Creative Spirit in Political Science," *APSR* 21 (1927): 7–8.

22. G. E. G. Catlin, "The Delimitation and Measurability of Political Phenomena," *APSR* 21 (1927): 255.

23. Floyd H. Allport, "Notes on Political Definition and Method," *APSR* 21 (1927): 64.

24. William B. Munro, "Physics and Politics—An Old Analogy Revised," *APSR* 22 (1928): 3, 5, 10.

25. G. E. G. Catlin, *The Science and Method of Politics* (New York: Knopf, 1927), pp. x–xi, 284, 295.

26. Ibid., pp. 75, 81, 84–85.

27. Ibid., pp. 93, 200–205.

28. Ibid., p. 143.

29. Raymond G. Gettell, *History of American Political Thought* (New York: Century, 1928), p. 3.

30. Oral history of R. Taylor Cole, APSA.

31. W. Y. Elliott, *The Pragmatic Revolt in Politics: Syndicalism, Fascism, and the Constitutional State* (New York: Macmillan, 1928), p. vii.

32. Ibid., p. 7.

33. Ibid., pp. viii, 250, 354, 464.

34. See John Dewey, *The Public and Its Problems* (New York: Henry Holt, 1927).

35. Elliott, *The Pragmatic Revolt in Politics,* p. 107.

36. Ibid., pp. 4, 8, 84–85, 217.

37. G. E. G. Catlin, review of Elliott's *The Pragmatic Revolt in Politics, PSQ* 44 (1929): 259.

38. Harold Lasswell, review of Elliott's *The Pragmatic Revolt in Politics, AJS* 35 (1929–30): 134–35.

39. Catlin, review of Elliott, pp. 260, 261, 263, 265.

40. Howard W. Odum and Katherine Jocker, *An Introduction to Social Research* (New York: Henry Holt, 1929), pp. v–vi.

41. Charles Austin Beard, "Political Science," in Wilson Gee (ed.), *Research in the Social Sciences* (New York: Macmillan, 1929), pp. 270–71, 286.

42. Ibid., pp. 289–90.

43. Charles A. Beard, "Conditions Favorable to Creative Work in Political Science," *APSR* 24, supp. (1930): 30, 26.

44. Charles A. Beard, *The Nature of the Social Sciences* (New York: Scribner's, 1934), pp. 47, 77.

45. Edward S. Corwin, "The Democratic Dogma and the Future of Political Science," *APSR* 23 (1929): 569–70.

46. George H. Sabine, "The Pragmatic Approach to Politics," *APSR* 24 (1930): 867, 884–85.

47. W. W. Willoughby, *The Ethical Basis of Political Authority* (New York: Macmillan, 1930).

48. George E. G. Catlin, *A Study of the Principles of Politics* (New York: Russell and Russell, 1930), p. 22.

49. Ibid., pp. 22–23, 38.

50. Ibid., pp. 24, 51, 54.

51. Ibid., pp. 119, 132.

52. Stuart Rice (ed.), *Methods in Social Science: A Case Book* (Chicago: University of Chicago Press, 1931), pp. 731–35.

53. Ibid., p. 7.

54. Ibid., pp. 9–10.

55. W. Y. Elliott, "The Possibility of a Science of Politics: With Special Attention to Methods Suggested by William B. Munro and George E. G. Catlin," in Rice (ed.), *Methods in Social Science,* pp. 72, 78.

56. Ibid., pp. 79, 80–81, 86.

57. Ibid., p. 94.

58. Karl Mannheim, review of Rice (ed.), *Methods in Social Science, AJS* 37 (1932): 273–82.

59. "Report of the Committee on Policy," *APSR* 24, app. (1930): pp. 1–199.

60. See, for example, William F. Willoughby, "A Program for Research in Political Science," *APSR* 27 (1933).

61. *Recent Social Trends in the United States,* Report of the President's Re-

search Committee on Social Trends (New York: Whittlesey House, 1934).

62. Ibid., p. lxxi.

63. Ibid., pp. 1530–31.

64. Ibid., p. 1534.

65. See, for example, Charles H. Titus, "A Nomenclature in Political Science," *APSR* 25 (1931); and Henry S. Dennison, "The Need for the Development of Political Science Engineering," *APSR* 26 (1932).

66. See oral histories of David Truman and Herman Pritchett, APSA.

67. For a full discussion of Lasswell's notion of context, see Douglas Torgerson, "Contextual Orientation in Policy Analysis: The contribution of Harold D. Lasswell," *Policy Sciences* 18 (1985).

68. Willard E. Atkins and Harold D. Lasswell, *Labor Attitudes and Problems* (New York: Prentice-Hall, 1924).

69. For a full discussion of Lasswell's intellectual development, see Bruce Lannes Smith, "The Mystifying Intellectual History of Harold D. Lasswell," as well as other essays, in Arnold Rogow (ed.), *Politics, Personality, and Social Science in the Twentieth Century: Essays in Honor of Harold D. Lasswell* (Chicago: University of Chicago Press, 1969).

70. Harold Lasswell, letter to Charles Merriam, August 10, 1923, Merriam Papers, University of Chicago Library. For a full discussion and analysis of Lasswell's letters during this period with respect to this theme as well as others, see Douglas Torgerson, "Political Vision and the Policy Orientation: Lasswell's Early Letters," paper delivered at the 1987 annual meeting of the APSA, Chicago, September 1987.

71. (New York: Knopf, 1927).

72. Harold Lasswell, review of Lippmann's *The Phantom Public, AJS* 31 (1925–26): 533–35.

73. See his early discussion of "Personality Studies" in T. V. Smith and Leonard White (eds.), *Chicago: An Experiment in Social Science Research* (Chicago: University of Chicago Press, 1929).

74. (Chicago: University of Chicago Press, 1930).

75. Ibid., pp. 49–46.

76. See Harold D. Lasswell, "The Strategy of Revolutionary and War Propaganda," in Quincy Wright (ed.), *Public Opinion and World Politics* (Chicago: University of Chicago Press, 1933).

77. Harold D. Lasswell, "Self-Analysis and Judicial Thinking," *IJE* 40 (1929–30); idem, "The Problem of World-Unity: In Quest of a Myth," *IJE* 44 (1933); idem, "The Moral Vocation of the Middle-Income Skill Group," *IJE* 45 (1935).

78. Charles E. Merriam, *Political Power: Its Composition and Incidence* (New York: McGraw-Hill, 1934), p. 3

79. Merriam, "The Education of Charles E. Merriam," p. 13.

80. Merriam, *Political Power,* pp. 4, 14, 327. See also Charles E. Merriam, *The Role of Politics in Social Change* (New York: New York University Press, 1936); and idem, *Prologue to Politics* (Chicago: University of Chicago Press, 1939).

81. T. V. Smith, "Social Intelligence and the Communistic Experiment," *IJE* 42 (1932): 113; idem, "Philosophy and Democracy," *IJE* 47 (1937): 423.

82. T. V. Smith, *Power and Conscience: Beyond Conscience* (New York: McGraw-Hill, 1934), pp. ix–x. See also idem, *The Democratic Way of Life* (Chicago: University of Chicago Press, 1926); and idem, *Creative Skeptics: In Defense of the Liberal Temper* (Chicago: Wilett, Clark, 1934).

83. Harold Lasswell, *World Politics and Personal Insecurity* (New York: McGraw-Hill, 1934).

84. Ibid., p. 3.

85. Ibid., p. 20.

86. Ibid., pp. 21, 26; Lasswell, "The Problem of World-Unity."

87. Lasswell, *World Politics and Personal Insecurity*, pp. 23–25.

88. Harold D. Lasswell, *Politics: Who Gets What, When, How* (New York: McGraw-Hill, 1936), pp. v, 3.

89. Ibid., p. vii; T. V. Smith, *The Promise of American Politics* (Chicago: University of Chicago Press, 1936), p. 207.

90. See, for example, Smith, *Democratic Way of Life*.

Chapter Six

1. J. Mark Jacobson, *The Development of American Political Thought* (New York: Appleton-Century-Crofts, 1932), p. vii.

2. Ibid., pp. viii–ix. Also see George Sabine, "Hegel's Political Philosophy," *Philosophical Review* 41 (1932): 261.

3. Oral history of R. Taylor Cole, APSA.

4. Charles Howard McIlwain, *The Growth of Political Thought in the West* (New York: Macmillan, 1932), pp. v, 3, 201, 390–92.

5. Francis W. Coker, *Recent Political Thought* (New York: Appleton-Century, 1934), pp. v, 1–2, 4.

6. Edward Westermarck, *Ethical Relativity* (London: Kegan Paul, Trench, Trubner, 1932), p. 289.

7. See, for example, Phyllis Doyle, *A History of Political Thought* (London: Jonathan Cape, 1933); Chester C. Maxey, *Political Philosophies* (New York: Macmillan, 1938).

8. Thomas I. Cook, *History of Political Philosophy, from Plato to Burke* (New York: Prentice-Hall), pp. vi, 3, 13.

9. Edward R. Lewis, *A History of American Political Thought* (New York: Macmillan, 1937).

10. David Easton, *The Political System: An Inquiry into the State of Political Science* (New York: Knopf, 1953), p. 249.

11. George H. Sabine, *A History of Political Theory* (New York: Holt, Rinehart and Winston, 1937), pp. iii, v, 8.

12. Ibid., p. vi.

13. Ibid., pp. 924–25.

14. Henry Jansen, review of Sabine's *History of Political Theory, APSR* 31 (1937): 959–60.

15. Arthur N. Holcombe, "The Political Interpretation of History," *APSR* 31 (1937): 1, 11.

16. J. P. Mayer et al., *Political Thought: The European Tradition* (New York: Viking, 1939), pp. v, vii, 1, 3. See also Paul Ward, *A Short History of Political Thinking* (Chapel Hill: University of North Carolina Press, 1939).

17. R. H. S. Crossman, *Government and the Governed: A History of Political Ideas and Practice* (New York: Putnam's, 1940).

18. George Catlin, *The Story of the Political Philosophers* (New York: McGraw-Hill, 1939), p. x.

19. William Y. Elliott and Neil A. McDonald, *The Western Political Heritage* (New York: Prentice-Hall, 1949), pp. vii–xi.

20. For a general discussion of this period, see Edward A. Purcell, Jr., *The Crisis of Democratic Theory: Scientific Naturalism and the Problem of Value* (Lexington: University of Kentucky Press, 1973).

21. Robert Maynard Hutchins, *The Higher Learning in America* (New Haven, Conn.: Yale University Press, 1936), pp. 99, 101, 104, 110.

22. John Dewey, *Liberalism and Social Action* (New York: Putnam's, 1938), pp. 72–73.

23. Richard McKeon, "Education and the Disciplines," *IJE* 47 (1937): 370–81. Charles E. Clark, "The Higher Learning in a Democracy," *IJE* 47 (1937): 317–35. For some contrasting accounts of these years at Chicago, see Mortimer J. Adler, *Philosopher at Large: An Intellectual Autobiography* (New York: Macmillan, 1977); and William H. McNeill, *Hutchins' University: A Memoir of the University of Chicago, 1929–50* (Chicago: University of Chicago Press, 1991).

24. Smith, *Promise of American Politics.*

25. See, for example, John Dickinson, "Democratic Realities and Democratic Dogma," *APSR* 24 (1930); Walter J. Shepard, "Democracy in Transition," *APSR* 29 (1935).

26. E. Pendelton Herring, *Group Representation before Congress* (Baltimore: Johns Hopkins University Press, 1929): idem, "Special Interests and the Interstate Commerce Commission," *APSR* 27 (1933); idem, *The Politics of Democracy: American Parties in Action* (New York: Norton, 1940).

27. Thurman Arnold, *Symbols of Government* (New Haven, Conn.: Yale University Press, 1935); Walter Lippmann, *An Inquiry into the Principles of a Good Society* (Boston: Little, Brown, 1937).

28. Reinhold Niebuhr, *Moral Man and Immoral Society* (New York: Scribner's, 1932); idem, *Beyond Tragedy: Essays on the Christian Interpretation of History* (New York: Scribner's, 1937).

29. Charner M. Perry, "Bases, Arbitrary and Otherwise, for Morality: A Critique Criticized," *IJE* 43 (1933); idem, "Knowledge as a Basis for Social Reform," *IJE* 45 (1935); idem, "The Relation between Ethics and Politics and Political Science," *IJE* 47 (1937).

30. Benjamin Wright, *American Interpretations of Natural Law* (Cambridge: Harvard University Press, 1931).

31. Pitirim A. Sorokin, *Social and Cultural Dynamics* (New York: American Book, 1937).

32. Aurel Kolnai, *Psychoanalysis and Society* (London: Allen and Unwin, 1921); and idem, *The War Against the West* (New York: Viking, 1938). Kolnai, originally a Hungarian but with a degree from the University of Vienna, was an émigré and eventually professor of political philosophy at Laval, Quebec.

33. Rauschning had been appointed president of the German senate by Hitler, but, disillusioned with National Socialism after two years, resigned, fled the country, and emigrated to the United States and became a bitter critic of the Nazi regime. *The Revolution of Nihilism* (New York: Longmans, Green, 1939); idem, *The Redemption of Democracy* (New York: Alliance Book, 1940).

34. See, for example, Carl Mayer, "On the Intellectual Origins of National Socialism," *Social Research* 9 (1942).

35. Carl Becker, "New Liberties for Old," *JSP* 1 (1936): 121.

36. Oscar Jászi, "The Good Society," *JSP* 3 (1938): 154–57.

37. Albert G. A. Balz, "The Challenge of Metaphysics to Social Science," *JSP* 3 (1938).

38. Marten Ten Hoor, "Medievalism in Contemporary Political Thought," *JSP* 3 (1938): 348–49.

39. C. J. Friedrich, "Some Thoughts on the Politics of Government Control," *JSP* 1 (1936). See also Alexander Goldweiser, "Nature and Task of the Social Sciences," *JSP* 2 (1936).

40. Horace S. Fries, "Science, Ethics, and Democracy," *JSP* 6 (1941): 302.

41. Alpheus T. Mason, "The Dilemma of Liberalism," *JSP* 3 (1938).

42. Francis G. Wilson, "Prelude to Authority," *APSR* 31 (1937): 13, 25; idem, *The Elements of Modern Politics* (New York: McGraw-Hill, 1936).

43. Karl Lowenstein, "Militant Democracy and Fundamental Rights," *APSR* 31 (1937).

44. Leslie M. Page, "Liberalism, Dogma, and Negativism," *JSP* 5 (1940): 346.

45. *Theory and Practice in Historical Study: A Report of the Committee on Historiography*, Bulletin 54 (New York: Social Science Research Council, 1946). For a full discussion of these issues in the discourse of American history writing, see Peter Novick, *That Noble Dream: The "Objectivity Question" and the American Historical Profession* (Cambridge: Cambridge University Press, 1988).

46. Carl Becker, *Everyman His Own Historian* (New York: F. S. Crofts, 1935).

47. Charles A. Beard, "Written History as an Act of Faith," *American Historical Review* 39 (1934); idem, "That Noble Dream," *American Historical Review* 41 (1935).

48. Charles A. Beard and Alfred Vagts, "Currents of Thought in Historiography," *American Historical Review* 42 (1937): 481, 483.

49. See, for example, Maurice Mandelbaum, *The Problem of Historical Knowledge: An Answer to Relativism* (New York: Liveright, 1938).

50. Charles A. Beard, review of Mandelbaum's *The Problem of Historical Knowledge, American Historical Review* 44 (1939): 571–72.

51. Marshall E. Dimock, "Scientific Method and the Future of Political Science," in John Mabry and Janice Hunt (eds.), *Essays in Political Science, in Honor of Westel Woodbury Willoughby* (Baltimore: Johns Hopkins University Press, 1937), p. 183.

52. Charles E. Merriam, "Public Administration and Political Theory," *JSP* 5 (1940).

53. Carl J. Friedrich, *Constitutional Government and Politics: Nature and Development* (New York: Harper and Bros., 1937), p. 4.

54. See, for example, Carl J. Friedrich, "The Deification of the State," *ROP* 1 (1939); and the 1941 edition of idem, *Constitutional Government and Democracy* (Boston: Little, Brown, 1941).

55. Friedrich, *Constitutional Government and Politics,* p. xvi.

56. C. J. Friedrich, "Thomas Hobbes: Myth Builder of the Modern World," *JSP* 3 (1938): 251, 256.

57. George H. Sabine, "What is Political Theory?" *JOP* 1 (1939): 2.

58. Ibid., pp. 2–3.

59. Ibid., pp. 6–7.

60. Ibid., p. 15.

61. George H. Sabine, "The Historical Position of Liberalism," *American Scholar* 10 (1940–41): 49.

62. Frank O'Malley, "The Image of Man: Ten Years of the *Review of Politics*," *ROP* 4 (1948):395.

63. See M. A. Fitzsimmons, "Die Deutschen Briefe: Gurian and the German Crisis," *ROP* 17 (1955): 50.

64. Jacques Maritain, "Integral Humanism and the Crisis of Modern Times," *ROP* 1 (1939): 7–9, 16.

65. W. Y. Elliott, "The Pragmatic Revolt in Politics: Twenty Years in Retrospect," *ROP* 2 (1940).

66. John Nef, *The United States and Civilization* (Chicago: University of Chicago Press, 1942).

67. Mortimer J. Adler, "God and the Professors," in *Science, Philosophy and Religion* (New York: Conference on Science, Philosophy and Religion in Their Relation to the Democratic Way of Life, 1941); Nef, *United States and Civilization;* Nathaniel Micklem, *The Theology of Politics* (Oxford: Oxford University Press, 1941); W. T. Stace, *The Concept of Morals* (New York: Macmillan, 1937). See also Goetz A. Briefs, "The Crisis of an Age," *ROP* 4 (1942); and idem, "The Crisis of Democracy," *ROP* 2 (1940).

68. See Robert M. Hutchins, "Toward a Durable Society," *Fortune* 27 (1943): 160.

69. John Dewey, "Challenge to Liberal Thought," *Fortune* 30 (1944): 190.

70. Charles E. Merriam, "Government and Intelligence," *Ethics* 54 (1944); Harold D. Lasswell, "Toward a Science of Democracy," in *Science, Philosophy and Religion,* p. 239; T. V. Smith, "Compromise: Its Context and Limits," *Ethics* 53

(1942); and idem, *The Compromise Principle in Politics* (Urbana: University of Illinois Press, 1941).

71. Sidney Hook, "The Philosophical Presuppositions of Democracy," *Ethics* 52 (1942); and idem, *Reason, Social Myths, and Democracy* (New York: John Day, 1941).

72. Philipp Frank, "Science and Democracy," in *Science, Philosophy and Religion;* and idem, "The Relativity of Truth and the Objectivity of Values," in *Science, Philosophy and Religion,* Third Symposium (Conference on Science, Philosophy and Religion in Their Relation to the Democratic Way of Life, 1943), pp. 12–13. Frank received his Ph.D. from the University of Vienna and left his position at the University of Prague to emigrate to the United States in 1938.

73. George H. Sabine, *Social Studies and Objectivity* (Berkeley: University of California Press, 1941), pp. 131–33, 142.

74. George H. Sabine, *Democracy and Pre-Conceived Ideas* (Columbus: Ohio State University Press, 1945). For a fuller discussion of Sabine, see Milton R. Konvitz and Arthur E. Murphy (eds.), *Essays in Political Theory: Essays Presented to George H. Sabine* (Ithaca, N.Y.: Cornell University Press, 1948).

75. Crick, *American Science of Politics* (see intro., n. 7), pp. 232–34.

Chapter Seven

1. See Henry M. Pachter, "The Intellectuals and the State of Weimar," *Social Research* 39 (1972).

2. Dagmar Barnouw, *Weimar Intellectuals and the Threat of Modernity* (Bloomington: University of Indiana Press, 1988), p. 12.

3. Works that I have found most helpful include Arthur Mitzman, *The Iron Cage: An Historical Interpretation of Max Weber* (New York: Knopf, 1970); Wolfgang Mommsen, *Max Weber and German Politics* (Chicago: University of Chicago Press, 1984); David Beetham, *Max Weber and the Theory of Modern Politics* (London: Allen and Unwin, 1974); Reinhard Bendix and Guenther Roth, *Scholarship and Partisanship* (Berkeley: University of California Press, 1971); Stephen P. Turner and Regis A. Factor, *Max Weber and the Dispute over Reason and Value* (London: Routledge and Kegan Paul, 1984); Dirk Kasler, *Max Weber: An Introduction to His Life and Work* (Chicago: University of Chicago Press, 1988); Edward Bryan Portis, *Max Weber and Political Commitment: Science, Politics, and Personality* (Philadelphia: Temple University Press, 1986); Lawrence Scaff, *Fleeing the Iron Cage: Culture, Politics, and Modernity in the Thought of Max Weber* (Berkeley: University of California Press, 1989).

4. See G. L. Ulmer, "The Sociology of the State: Carl Schmitt and Max Weber," *State, Culture, and Society* 1 (1985); Max Weber, letter to Marianne Weber, May 30, 1919, quoted by Wolfgang Mommsen in "Introduction," *Max Weber Gesamtausgabe* (Tübingen: Mohr, 1988), 16:34.

5. Max Weber, "Science as a Vocation," in *From Max Weber,* ed. H. H. Gerth and C. Wright Mills (New York: Oxford University Press, 1946), pp. 137–39.

6. Ibid., p. 152.

7. .Ibid., pp. 145–46.

8. Ibid., pp. 146–47.

9. Ibid., pp. 149–50.

10. Ibid., pp. 152–53.

11. Ibid., pp. 115–16.

12. See Max Weber, *Roscher and Knies: The Logical Problems of Historical Economics,* trans. Guy Oakes (New York: Free Press, 1975).

13. Max Weber, *The Methodology of the Social Sciences,* trans. and ed. Edward A. Shils and Henry A. Finch (Glencoe, Ill.: Free Press, 1949). For a discussion of the history of the *Archiv,* see Regis A. Factor, *Guide to the Archiv für Sozialwissenschaft und Sozialpolitik Group, 1904–1933* (New York: Greenwood, 1988).

14. Max Weber, *On the Universities: The Power of the State and the Dignity of the Academic Calling in Imperial Germany,* trans. Edward Shils (Chicago: University of Chicago Press, 1974), p. 17.

15. Ibid., p. 47. Emphasis added.

16. Ibid., p. 49.

17. See Gustav Radbruch, "Anglo-American Jurisprudence through Continental Eyes," *Law Quarterly Review* 208 (1936).

18. Weber, *From Max Weber,* p. 128.

19. See Gerd Schroeter, "Max Weber as an Outsider: His Nominal Influence on German Sociology in the Twenties," *Journal of the History of the Behavioral Sciences* 16 (1980); Kasler, *Max Weber,* chap. 7.

20. See, for example, Max Horkheimer, discussion of *"Value Freedom and Objectivity,"* in Otto Stammer (ed.), *Max Weber and Sociology Today* (New York: Harper and Row, 1971), pp. 51–53.

21. Edmund Husserl, "Philosophy as Rigorous Science," in Peter McCormick and Frederick A. Elliston (eds.), *Husserl: Shorter Works* (Notre Dame, Ind.: University of Notre Dame Press, 1981).

22. Edmund Husserl, *The Crisis of European Sciences and Transcendental Phenomenology* (Evanston, Ill.: Northwestern University Press, 1970).

23. Heinrich Rickert, "Max Weber's View of Science," in Peter Lassman and Irving Velody (eds.), *Max Weber's "Science as a Vocation"* (London: Unwin Hyman, 1989), p. 86.

24. Ernst Robert Curtius, "Max.Weber on Science as a Vocation," in Lassman and Velody (eds.), *Weber's "Science as Vocation,"* p. 74.

25. Kahler, a Social Democrat and Czechoslovakian Jew, received a doctorate from Vienna but studied at several German universities including Heidelberg. A cultural critic and friend of Thomas Mann, he eventually emigrated to the United States—teaching first at the New School for Social Research and eventually at Cornell. He continued his critique of modernity as representing a distortion of human consciousness caused by the forces of "scientification and collectivization" and the decline of values in the face of positivism, historicism, and relativism. See Erich Kahler, *The Tower and the Abyss* (New York: George Braziller, 1957); and idem, *The Meaning of History* (New York: George Braziller, 1964).

26. Erich von Kahler, "The Vocation of Science," in Lassman and Velody (eds.), *Weber's "Science as Vocation,"* pp. 42, 44.

27. Ibid., p. 40.

28. Arthur Salz, "For Science: Against the Intellectuals," in Lassman and Velody (eds.), *Weber's "Science as Vocation,"* p. 57. Salz, a member of Weber's circle, was a political economist and sociologist who emigrated to the United States (Ohio State) in 1934.

29. Ernst Troeltsch, "The Revolution in Science," in Lassman and Velody (eds.), *Weber's "Science as Vocation,"* pp. 60, 67.

30. This extended to the Nazis, but it is important not to attribute to George the position of all those who drew upon his ideas. See Michael M. and Erika A. Metzger, *Stefan George* (New York: Twayne, 1972). See also Peter Gay, *Weimar Culture: The Insider as Outsider* (New York: Harper and Row, 1968).

31. See Max Scheler, *Problems of a Sociology of Knowledge* (London: Routledge and Kegan Paul, 1980).

32. Max Scheler, "Sociology and the Study and Formulation of *Weltanschauung*," and "Max Weber's Exclusion of Philosophy," in Lassman and Velody (eds.), *Weber's "Science as Vocation,"* p. 90.

33. Ibid. See also Max Scheler, *Formalism in Ethics and Non-Formal Ethics of Values: A New Attempt toward the Foundation of an Ethical Personalism* (Evanston, Ill.: Northwestern University Press, 1973); and Stephen Frederick Schneck, *Person and Polis: Max Scheler's Personalism as Political Theory* (Albany: State University of New York Press, 1987).

34. See the work of David Kettler, Volker Meja, and Nico Stehr which includes *Karl Mannheim* (New York: Tavistock, 1984); *Conservatism: A Contribution to the Sociology of Knowledge* (London: Routledge and Kegan Paul, 1986); "The Reconstitution of Political Life: The Contemporary Relevance of Karl Mannheim's Political Project," *Polity* 20 (1986). Also Kettler and Meja, "Settling with Mannheim," *State, Culture, and Society* 1 (1985); and the paper "Rationalizing the Irrational: Learning from Karl Mannheim," by Kettler, Meja, and Stehr. Two other valuable studies are Calvin Loader's *The Intellectual Development of Karl Mannheim* (Cambridge: Cambridge University Press, 1985); and Henk E. S. Woldrung's *Karl Mannheim: The Development of His Thought* (Assen: Van Gorcum, 1986).

35. Karl Mannheim, *Ideology and Utopia* (New York: Harcourt, Brace, 1936), pp. 33, 37.

36. Ibid., p. 38.

37. Ibid., p. 79.

38. Ibid., pp. 80, 85.

39. Ibid., p. 98.

40. Ibid., p. 112.

41. Ibid., p. 149.

42. Ibid., pp. 154–55.

43. Ibid., p. 162.

44. Ibid., p. 173.

45. Ibid., p. 191.

46. For a full discussion of the *Streit um die Wissenssoziologie* occasioned by Mannheim's work and a selection of responses, see Volker Meja and Nico Stehr (eds.), *Knowledge and Politics: The Sociology of Knowledge Dispute* (London: Routledge, 1990). Also David Frisby, *The Alienated Mind: The Sociology of Knowledge in Germany 1918–33* (Atlantic Highlands, N.J.: Humanities Press, 1983).

47. Meja and Stehr (eds.), *Knowledge and Politics,* pp. 87, 91–92.

48. Ibid., pp. 113–20.

49. Ibid., pp. 107–12, 129–57.

50. Ibid., pp. 196–208.

51. See Karl Mannheim, "Problems of Sociology in Germany," in Kurt Wolff (ed.), *From Karl Mannheim* (New York: Oxford University Press, 1971).

52. One of the first to make this criticism was Alexander von Schelting, once a managing editor of the *Archiv* who emigrated to the United States in 1933 and who had written one of the first major works on Weber (*Max Weber's Wissenschaftslehre,* 1934). See his review of Mannheim in the *American Sociological Review* 1 (1936).

53. Hans Speier, "Karl Mannheim's *Ideology and Utopia,*" *AJS* 43 (1937): 183–97. For further discussion of this issue, see Kettler and Meja, "Settling with Mannheim." The wives of Speier and Strauss had been lifelong friends, but Speier became intellectually involved with Strauss only after emigration. See "Autobiographical Notes" in the Speier Collection at SUNY at Albany.

54. Karl Mannheim, *Man and Society in an Age of Reconstruction* (London: Routledge and Kegan Paul, 1940). Originally *Mensch und Gesellschaft im Zeitalter des Umbaus* (1935).

55. Oscar Jászi, *APSR* 35 (1941): 551–52.

56. For comprehensive accounts of Schmitt's career and work, see George Schwab, *The Challenge to the Exception: An Introduction to the Ideas of Carl Schmitt* (Westport, Conn.: Greenwood, 1969); Joseph Bendersky, *Carl Schmitt, Theorist for the Reich* (Princeton, N.J.: Princeton University Press, 1983); Paul Edward Gottfried, *Carl Schmitt: Politics and Theory* (New York: Greenwood, 1990); Richard Wolin, *The Terms of Cultural Criticism* (New York: Columbia University Press, 1992), chap. 4. For further discussions of Schmitt's influence, see Stephen Holmes, "The Scourge of Liberalism," *New Republic,* August 1988; Ellen Kennedy, "Carl Schmitt in the West German Perspective," *West European Politics* 7 (1984); idem, "Carl Schmitt and the Frankfurt School," *Telos* 71 (1987); Alfons Sollner, "Leftist Students of the Conservative Revolution," *Telos* 61 (1984). Also *Telos* 72 (1987) for an extensive discussion of Schmitt and his influence, and *Telos* 73 (1987) for Kennedy's reply to her critics.

57. For a discussion of this institution in relation to the history of political science in Germany, see Rainer Eisfeld, *Ausgeburgert und doch Angebraunt: deutsche Politikwissenschaft 1920–1945* (Baden-Baden: Nomos, 1991); Hans Kastendieck, *Die Entwicklung der westdeutschen Politikwissenschaft* (Frankfurt: Campus, 1977).

58. Carl Schmitt, *Political Theology* (Cambridge, MIT Press, 1985), pp. 5, 17.

59. Ibid., p. 53.

60. Ibid., p. 65.

61. Carl Schmitt, *The Concept of the Political,* trans. George Schwab and including Leo Strauss's "Comments on Carl Schmitt's *Der Begriff des Politischen,*" (New Brunswick, N.J.: Rutgers University Press, 1976), pp. 19, 26.

62. Ibid., p. 27.

63. Ibid., pp. 53, 78.

64. See Paul Bookbinder, "Hermann Heller versus Carl Schmitt," *International Social Science Review* 62 (1987).

65. Bendersky, *Carl Schmitt,* p. 203.

66. See, for example, Walter Benjamin, *The Origin of German Tragic Drama* (London: NLB, 1977).

67. See Keith Tribe, "Introduction to Neumann: Law and Socialist Political Theory," *Economy and Society* 10 (1981).

68. See Frank Peter Wagner, "Rudolf Hilferding and the Rise and Fall of the State," Paper delivered at the 1990 annual meeting of the Western Political Science Association, Newport Beach, California, March 22–24.

69. Otto Kirchheimer, *Politics, Law, and Social Change* (New York: Columbia University Press, 1969), pp. 40–41.

70. Ibid., pp. 73–74.

71. Karl Jaspers, *Max Weber: Politiker, Forscher, Philosoph* (Tübingen: Mohr, 1926).

72. Karl Jaspers, *Man in the Modern Age* (Garden City, N.Y.: Doubleday, 1951), p. 85.

73. Ibid., p. 14.

74. Ibid., pp. 87–89, 209.

75. Ibid., p. 95.

76. Ibid., pp. 148–49, 154, 216.

77. See Bendersky, *Carl Schmitt,* p. 203.

78. See, for example, Victor Farais, *Heidegger and Nazism* (Philadelphia: Temple University Press, 1989); and Luc Ferry and Alain Renaut, *Heidegger and Modernity* (Chicago: University of Chicago Press, 1990). Also Jacques Derrida, *Of Spirit: Heidegger and the Question* (Chicago: University of Chicago Press, 1989); Jean-Francois Lyotard, *Heidegger and the Jews* (Minneapolis: University of Minnesota Press, 1990); Istvan M. Feher, "Fundamental Ontology and the Political Interlude: Heidegger as the Rector of the University of Freiburg," in Marcelo Dascal and Ora Gruengard (eds.), *Knowledge and Politics: Case Studies in the Relationship between Knowledge and Politics* (Boulder, Colo.: Westview, 1989); Richard Wolin, *The Politics of Being: The Political Thought of Martin Heidegger* (New York: Columbia University Press, 1990); and Wolin (ed.), *The Heidegger Controversy: A Critical Reader* (New York: Columbia University Press, 1991).

79. H.-G. Gadamer, *Philosophical Apprenticeships* (Cambridge: MIT Press, 1985). Review by Sheldon Wolin, *New York Times,* 28 July 1985, Book Review section. For a detailed discussion of this period in Gadamer's life, see Robert Sullivan, *Political Hermeneutics: The Early Thinking of Hans-Georg Gadamer* (University Park: Pennsylvania State University Press, 1989).

80. For some sense of Heidegger's influence, see Hannah Arendt, "Martin Heidegger at Eighty," in Michael Murray (ed.), *Heidegger and Modern Philosophy* (New Haven, Conn.: Yale University Press, 1987); "Heidegger's Politics: An Interview with Herbert Marcuse by Frederick Olafson," *Graduate Faculty Philosophy Journal* 6 (1977); Leo Strauss, *The Rebirth of Classical Political Rationalism* (Chicago: University of Chicago Press, 1989).

81. See Kettler, Meja, and Stehr, "Rationalizing the Irrational: Learning from Karl Mannheim," for a discussion of this group.

82. Fritz Stern, *The Failure of Illiberalism* (New York: Knopf, 1972), p. 97. For further discussion of Riezler, who came to the New School for Social Research in 1938, see Leo Strauss, *What is Political Philosophy?* (Glencoe, Ill.: Free Press, 1959), pp. 233–60; and Wayne C. Thompson, *In the Eye of the Storm* (Iowa City: University of Iowa Press, 1980).

83. See Susan Buck-Morss, *The Origins of Negative Dialectics: Theodor W. Adorno, Walter Benjamin and the Frankfurt Institute* (New York: Macmillan, 1977); idem, *The Dialectics of Seeing* (Cambridge: MIT Press, 1989); Richard Wolin, *Walter Benjamin: An Aesthetic of Redemption* (New York: Columbia University Press, 1982).

Chapter Eight

1. See oral history of Herman Prichett, APSA.

2. See Leo Strauss, *Spinoza's Critique of Religion* (New York: Schocken, 1965), and *Philosophy and Law* (New York: Jewish Publication Society, 1987).

3. Leo Strauss, "Comments on Carl Schmitt's *Der Begriff des Politischen*," in Schmitt, *The Concept of the Political*, pp. 89–90. For a fuller discussion of Strauss's early work, see John G. Gunnell, "Strauss before Straussianism: Reason, Revelation, and Nature," *ROP* 53 (1991). For broader appraisals of Strauss's work, see Kenneth Deutsch and Walter Soffer (eds.), *The Crisis of Liberal Democracy: A Straussian Perspective* (Albany: State University of New York Press, 1987); and Shadia B. Drury, *The Political Ideas of Leo Strauss* (New York: St. Martin's, 1988).

4. Erich Hula, "Memorial to Leo Strauss," October 18, 1974, oral history tape, German Émigré Collection, SUNY at Albany.

5. See Robert Boyers (ed.), *The Legacy of the German Refugee Intellectuals* (New York: Schocken, 1972); William Rex Crawford (ed.), *The Cultural Migration: The European Scholars in America* (Philadelphia: University of Pennsylvania Press, 1953); Lewis A. Coser, *Refugee Scholars in America* (New Haven, Conn.: Yale University Press, 1984); Claus-Dieter Krohn, *Wissenschaft im Exil. Deutsche Sozial und Wirtschaftswissenschaftler in den USA und die New School for Social Research* (Frankfurt: Campus, 1987); Laura Fermi, *Illustrious Immigrants: The Intellectual Migration from Europe, 1930–41* (Chicago: University of Chicago Press, 1968); Daniel Fleming and Bernard Bailyn (eds.), *The Intellectual Migration* (Cambridge: Harvard University Press, 1969); Anthony Heilbut, *Exiled in Paradise* (New York: Viking, 1983); H. Stuart Hughes, *The Great Sea Change* (New York: Harper and Row, 1975); Jarrell C. Jackman and Carla Borden (eds.), *The Muses*

Flee Hitler (Washington, D.C.: Smithsonian Institute Press, 1983); Martin Jay, *The Dialectical Imagination* (Boston: Little, Brown, 1973); idem, *Permanent Exiles: Essays on the Intellectual Migration from Germany to America* (New York: Columbia University Press, 1985); Donald Paterson Kent, *The Refugee Intellectual: The Americanization of the Immigrants, 1933–1941* (New York: Columbia University Press, 1953); Karl Löwith, *My Life in Germany before and after 1933* (New York: Columbia University Press, 1992); Helge Pross, *Die Deutschen Akademische emigration nach den Vereinigten Staaten, 1933–45* (Berlin: Duncker und Humboldt, 1955); Peter M. Rutkoff and William B. Scott, *The New School: A History of the New School for Social Research* (New York: Free Press, 1986); Herbert A. Strauss (ed.), *Jewish Immigrants of the Nazi Period in the USA* (Detroit: K. G. Sau, 1991); idem, *Biographisches Handbuch der deutschsprachigen Emigration nach 1933* (New York: K. G. Saur, 1980); Alfons Söllner (ed.), *Zur Archaologie der Demokratie in Deutschland: Analysen politischer Emigranten im amerikanischen Gebeimdienst 1933–1945* (Frankfurt: Fischer Verlag, 1986).

6. Leo Lowenthal, *An Unmastered Past* (Berkeley: University of California Press, 1987), p. 158.

7. John Herz, oral history tape, German Intellectual Émigré Collection, SUNY at Albany.

8. Henry Ehrmann, notes for a personal memoir, Ehrmann Papers, German Intellectual Émigré Collection, SUNY at Albany.

9. Hannah Arendt, *The Origins of Totalitarianism* (New York: Harcourt, Brace and World, 1951); idem, *Eichmann in Jerusalem* (New York: Viking, 1963).

10. Quoted in Elizabeth Young-Bruehl, *Hannah Arendt: For the Love of the World* (New Haven, Conn.: Yale University Press, 1982), p. 327.

11. Hannah Arendt, Address at reception of Sonning Prize, 1975, Arendt Papers, Library of Congress; Lotte Kohler and Hans Saner (eds.), *Hannah Arendt–Karl Jaspers Correspondence 1926–1969* (New York: Harcourt Brace Jovanovich, 1992), p. 29.

12. Lowenthal, *An Unmastered Past*, p. 156.

13. John Heartfield, "German Natural History," *Photomontages of the Nazi Period* (New York: Universal, 1977).

14. Quoted in Ronald Beiner, review of George Kateb's *Hannah Arendt: Politics, Conscience and Evil, Political Theory* 13 (1985): 628.

15. Johnson, *Pioneer's Progress* (see chap. 3, n. 8), pp. 273–4, 278.

16. Ibid., pp. 305, 336.

17. Alvin Johnson, "Foreward," *Social Research* 1 (1934): 1–2.

18. See, for example, Emil Lederer, "Freedom and Science," *Social Research* 1 (1934); Paul Kecskemeti, "Ethics and the 'Single Theory,'" *Social Research* 2 (1935); Max Wertheimer, "Some Problems in the Theory of Ethics," *Social Research* 2 (1935); Gerhard Leibholz, "The Nature and Various Forms of Democracy," *Social Research* 5 (1938).

19. Johnson, *Pioneer's Progress* (see chap. 3., n. 8), p. 347.

20. For a discussion of Parsons's education, see Talcott Parsons, *The Early Essays*, ed. Charles Camic (Chicago: University of Chicago Press, 1991).

21. Theodor Adorno, *Minima Moralia: Reflections from Damaged Life* (London: NLB, 1974), p. 33.

22. Hans Speier, *Social Order and the Risks of War* (New York: George W. Stewart, 1952), p. 93.

23. In Speier's papers, a personal statement of political views as part of the Rand application stressed how he came to reject any negative assessment of capitalism. It also depreciated his involvement with Marx's ideas and disavowed any connection or sympathy with communism. His "Autobiographical Notes" mention how his appointment was held up because the wife of a friend had once made a ten dollar purchase from a bookstore without knowing that it sold communist literature.

24. Hannah Arendt, "We Refugees," *The Jew as Pariah,* ed. Ron Feldman (New York: Grove, 1978), p. 55.

25. Hans Morgenthau, in Kenneth W. Thompson and Robert J. Myers (eds.), *Truth and Tragedy: A Tribute to Hans J. Morgenthau* (New Brunswick, N.J.: Transaction, 1984), p. 385. Similar sentiments were expressed by the sociologist Reinhard Bendix, *From Berlin to Berkeley: German-Jewish Identities* (New Brunswick, N.J.: Transaction, 1986).

26. Henry Pachter, "On Being an Exile," in Boyers (ed.), *Legacy of German Refugee Intellectuals,* pp. 18, 25, 30; Kohler and Saner (eds.), *Arendt–Jaspers Correspondence,* pp. 30–31.

27. Fleming and Bailyn (eds.), *intellectual Migration,* pp. 270–71.

28. See Allan Janek and Stephen Toulmin, *Wittgenstein's Vienna* (New York: Simon and Schuster, 1973); Carl Schorske, *Fin-De-Siècle Vienna, Politics and Culture* (New York: Knopf, 1980); Mark Francis (ed.), *The Viennese Enlightenment* (New York: St. Martin's, 1985).

29. See Hans Kelsen, *Staatsform und Weltanschauung* (Tübingen: Mohr, 1933); and idem, "The Pure Theory of Law," *Law Quarterly Review* 50 (1934).

30. Heilbut, *Exiled in Paradise,* p. 160.

31. Fleming and Bailyn (eds.), *Intellectual Migration,* p. 339.

32. Ibid., p. 370.

33. Lowenthal, *An Unmastered Past,* p. 140.

34. Fleming and Bailyn (eds.), *Intellectual Migration,* p. 368.

35. See, for example, Fermi, *Illustrious Immigrants.*

36. Franz Neumann, "The Social Sciences," in Rex Crawford (ed.), *Cultural Migration,* pp. 19, 24.

37. Ibid., p. 9.

38. Franz Neumann, *The Democratic and Authoritarian State* (Glencoe, Ill.: Free Press, 1957), p. 162.

39. Franz Neumann, *Behemoth: The Structure and Practice of National Socialism* (Oxford: Oxford University Press, 1942), p. 463.

40. H. Stuart Hughes in Jackman and Borden (eds.), *Muses Flee Hitler,* p. 120.

41. Hans Kohn, *The Mind of Germany* (New York: Scribner's, 1960).

42. See Emil Lederer, "Social Control versus Economic Law," *Social Research* 1 (1934); and idem, "Freedom and Science," ibid.

43. Hans Speier, "The Salaried Employee in Modern Society," *Social Research* 6 (1939); Emil Lederer, *The State of the Masses: The Threat of a Classless Society* (New York: Norton, 1940).

44. Arnold Brecht, *The Political Education of Arnold Brecht: An Autobiography, 1884–1970* (Princeton, N.J.: Princeton University Press, 1970), p. 444.

45. Exchange of letters contained in the Brecht Papers, Box I, A-19, German Intellectual Émigré Collection, SUNY at Albany.

46. Brecht, *The Political Education of Arnold Brecht*, pp. 447, 445–46.

47. Ibid., p. 484.

48. Lowenthal, *An Unmastered Past*, p. 89.

49. Quoted in Jay, *The Dialectical Imagination*, p. xi.

50. Lowenthal, *An Unmastered Past*, p. 156.

51. Max Horkheimer, *Studies in Philosophy and Social Science* 8 (1939).

52. Barry Katz, *Foreign Intelligence* (Cambridge: Harvard University Press, 1989), p. 29. Also Alfons Söllner, "The Political Dissent to Intellectual Integration: The Frankfurt School in American Government, 1942–49," in Bruce Robbins (ed.), *Intellectuals* (Minneapolis: University of Minnesota Press, 1990).

53. John Herz, oral history tape, German Intellectual Émigré Collection, SUNY at Albany.

54. Herbert Marcuse, review of Dewey's theory of valuation, *Studies in Philosophy and Social Science* 9 (1941): 144–48.

55. See Helmut R. Wagner, *Alfred Schütz: An Intellectual Biography* (Chicago: University of Chicago Press, 1970).

56. Guido de Ruggerio, "Postivisim," in Seligman and Johnson (eds.), *ESS* (see chap. 1, n. 5), 12:235.

57. Herbert Feigl, "The Wiener Kreis in America," in Bailyn and Fleming (eds.), *Intellectual Migration*, p. 630.

58. Charles W. Morris, *Logical Positivism, Pragmatism, and Scientific Empiricism* (Paris: Hermann et Cie, 1937).

59. Otto Neurath, Rudolf Carnap, and Charles Morris, *Foundations of the Unity of Science: Toward an International Encyclopedia of Unified Sciences* (Chicago: University of Chicago Press, 1939), p. 1.

60. Rudolf Carnap, "Intellectual Biography," in Paul A. Schlipp (ed.), *The Philosophy of Rudolf Carnap* (La Salle, Ill.: Open Court, 1963), p. 36.

61. Ibid., pp. 40–42.

62. Morris Cohen, "Method, Scientific," in Seligman and Johnson (eds.), *ESS* (see chap. 1, n. 5), 10:389, 395.

63. See Morris Cohen, *Reason and Nature: An Essay on the Meaning of Scientific Method* (New York: Harcourt, Brace, 1931). For a full discussion of Cohen's work, see David A. Hollinger, *Morris Cohen and the Scientific Ideal* (Cambridge: MIT Press, 1975).

64. Felix Kaufmann, *Methodology of the Social Sciences* (New York: Humanities Press, 1944), pp. 15, 42.

65. Quoted in Vukan Kuic, "The Contribution of Yves R. Simon to Political Science," *Political Science Reviewer* 4 (1974): 60.

66. For a full discussion of Morgenthau's work and intellectual development, see Thompson and Myers (eds.), *Truth and Tragedy;* Hans J. Morgenthau, "An Intellectual Biography," *Society* 15 (1978); and Greg Russell, *Hans J. Morgenthau and the Ethics of American Statecraft* (Baton Rouge: Louisiana State University Press, 1990).

67. In addition to works already cited, see, for example, Dagmar Barnouw, *Visible Spaces* (Baltimore: Johns Hopkins University Press, 1990); George Kateb, *Hannah Arendt: Politics, Conscience and Evil* (Totowa, N.J.: Towman and Allenheld, 1983); Melvyn Hill (ed.), *Hannah Arendt: Recovery of the Public World* (New York: St. Martin's, 1979); Margaret Canovan, *The Political Thought of Hannah Arendt* (New York: Harcourt Brace Jovanovich, 1974); Hans Jonas, "Hannah Arendt," *Social Research* 42 (1976).

68. Hannah Arendt, *Rahel Varnhagen: The Life of a Jewish Woman* (New York: Harcourt Brace Jovanovich, 1974).

69. See James M. Rhodes, "Philosophy, Revelation, and Political Theory: Leo Strauss and Eric Voegelin," *JOP* 49 (1987).

70. Kohler and Saner (eds.), *Arendt–Jaspers Correspondence,* pp. 244, 593, 644; Young-Bruehl, *Hannah Arendt,* p. 98.

71. For autobiographical and biographical discussions of Voegelin, see Eric Voegelin, *Anamnesis* (Notre Dame, Ind.: University of Notre Dame Press, 1978); idem, *Autobiographical Reflections* (Baton Rouge: Louisiana State University Press, 1989); Ellis Sandoz, *The Voegelinian Revolution* (Baton Rouge: Louisiana State University Press, 1981); and idem, *Eric Voegelin's Thought: A Critical Appraisal* (Durham, N.C.: Duke University Press, 1982).

72. Eric Voegelin, *Über die Form des amerikanischen Geistes* (Tübingen: J. C. B. Mohr, 1928).

73. Eric Voegelin, *Rasse und Staat* (Tübingen: J. C. B. Mohr, 1933); idem, *Die Rassenidee in der Geistesgeschichte von Ray bis Carus* (Berlin: Junker und Duennhaupt, 1933). For a full discussion of these works, see Thomas W. Heilke, *Voegelin on the Idea of Race* (Baton Rouge: Louisiana State University Press, 1990).

74. Eric Voegelin, *Der authoritaere Staat* (Vienna: Springer, 1936).

75. Eric Voegelin, *Die politischen Religionen* (Vienna: Berman-Fischer, 1938).

76. Voegelin, *Autobiographical Reflections,* p. 42.

77. Ibid., p. 58.

78. Voegelin, *Anamnesis,* pp. 7, 213.

Chapter Nine

1. Robert S. Lynd, *Knowledge for What?* (Princeton, N.J.: Princeton University Press, 1940), pp. 1, 115.

2. Ibid., pp. 118, 140.

3. Related in the oral history of Manning Dauer, APSA.

4. Leo Strauss, *Social Research* 8 (1941); and ibid., 10 (1943).

5. Herbert Marcuse, *Reason and Revolution* (New York: Humanities Press, 1941), pp. viii, 326.

6. Benjamin Lippincott, *APSR* 36 (1942): 387. George Sabine, *AJS* 48 (1942): 259.

7. Benjamin Lippincott, "The Bias of American Political Science," *JOP* 2 (1940): 130.

8. Whyte received his Ph.D. in sociology from the University of Chicago in the same year (1943) that he published *Street Corner Society* and was appointed to the faculty.

9. William F. Whyte, "A Challenge to Political Scientists," *APSR* 37 (1943): 692–93, 697.

10. John H. Hallowell, "Political and Ethics," *APSR* 38 (1944): 642.

11. John H. Hallowell, "The Decline of Liberalism," *Ethics* 52 (1942); idem, *The Decline of Liberalism as an Ideology with Particular Reference to German Politico-Legal Theorists* (Berkeley: University of California Press, 1943).

12. See, for example, Micklem, *The Theory of Politics* (see chap. 6, n. 67); and Helmut Kuhn, *Freedom Forgotten and Remembered* (Chapel Hill: University of North Carolina Press, 1943).

13. Cole first met Hallowell while the former was a tutor at Harvard and the latter a senior. See R. Taylor Cole's oral history, APSA.

14. Jacques Maritain, *Scholasticism and Politics* (New York: Macmillan, 1940).

15. Niemeyer, now an Episcopalian priest and retired from Notre Dame, is the author of *Between Nothingness and Paradise* (Baton Rouge: Louisiana State University Press, 1971) in which he sees the modern age, from Marx to Mark Rudd, as characterized by the rise of a "total critique of society" based on a revolt against traditional metaphysics and issuing in "creative destruction" and totalitarianism. See also essays in *Aftersight and Foresight* (Lanham, Md.: University Press of America, 1988).

16. Hallowell is now deceased. This account of his career is largely derived from an interview conducted in the summer of 1989 at his home in Amherst, New Hampshire.

17. Hallowell, *The Decline of Liberalism,* pp. vii–viii.

18. Ibid., p. 122.

19. Eric Voegelin, *From Enlightenment to Revolution,* ed. John Hallowell (Durham, N.C.: Duke University Press, 1975).

20. Reinhold Niebuhr, *The Children of Light and the Children of Darkness: A Vindication of Democracy and a Critique of Its Traditional Defense* (New York: Scribner's, 1944). See Hallowell's review, *APSR* 34 (1945).

21. J. Roland Pennock, "Reason, Value Theory, and the Theory of Democracy," *APSR* 38 (1944): 873–84. See also his *Liberal Democracy: Its Merits and Its Prospects* (New York: Rinehart, 1950).

22. Frederich A. Hayek, *The Road to Serfdom* (Chicago: University of Chicago Press, 1944); T. V. Smith's review, *Ethics* 55 (1945): 224.

23. For a general discussion of the evolution of pluralist theory, see G. David

Garson, *Group Theories of Politics* (Beverly Hills, Calif.: Sage, 1978).

24. Otto Kirchheimer, "In Quest of Sovereignty," *JOP* 3 (1944).

25. John H. Hallowell, "Compromise as a Political Ideal," *Ethics* 54 (1944).

26. F. G. Wilson, "The Ethics of Political Conservatism," *Ethics* 53 (1942). See also, idem, *The American Political Mind* (New York: McGraw-Hill, 1949); and idem, *The Case for Conservatism* (Seattle: University of Washington Press, 1951).

27. Francis G. Wilson, Benjamin F. Wright, Ernest S. Griffith, and Eric Voegelin, "Research in Political Theory: A Symposium," *APSR* 38 (1944): 726, 729.

28. Ibid., pp. 727, 730.

29. Ibid., pp. 727–28.

30. Ibid., pp. 730–31.

31. Ibid., pp. 739–40.

32. Ibid., pp. 740–42.

33. Ibid., pp. 746–51.

34. John Hallowell, review of Arnold Brecht's *Prelude to Silence* (New York: Oxford University Press, 1944), *JOP* 6 (1944): 466–69.

35. John Hallowell, "Modern Liberalism: An Invitation to Suicide," *South Atlantic Quarterly* 46 (1947).

36. Charles Merriam, review of Herman Rauschning's *Times of Delirium* (New York: D. Appleton-Century, 1946), *APSR* 41 (1947): 1207–8.

37. Herman Finer, "Towards a Democratic Theory," *APSR* 49 (1945): 239.

38. Gabriel Almond, Lewis Dexter, William Whyte, and John Hallowell, "Politics and Ethics—A Symposium," *APSR* 40 (1946): 283–312.

39. Ibid., pp. 291–92.

40. Ibid., p. 297.

41. Ibid., pp. 305–307.

42. Hans J. Morgenthau, *Scientific Man and Power Politics* (Chicago: University of Chicago Press, 1946), pp. v, vi, 7.

43. Ernst Cassirer, *The Myth of the State* (New Haven, Conn.: Yale University Press, 1946).

44. Max Horkheimer, *The Eclipse of Reason* (New York: Oxford University Press, 1947), pp. v, vi.

45. Ibid., pp. 23–24.

46. Ibid., pp. 122–23.

47. Ibid., pp. 138–39, 149, 174.

48. Leo Lowenthal and Norbert Guterman, *Prophets of Deceit: A Study of the Technique of the American Agitator* (New York: Harper and Bros., 1949).

49. See Arnold Brecht, *The Political Philosophy of Arnold Brecht*, ed. Morris D. Forkosch (New York: Exposition Press, 1954).

50. Arnold Brecht, review of Maritain's *Scholasticism and Politics*, *APSR* 35 (1941): 545.

51. Arnold Brecht, review of Voegelin's *The New Science of Politics*, *Social Research* 20 (1953): 230–33.

52. Arnold Brecht, *The Political Education of Arnold Brecht*, pp. 434, 457, 490,

494; idem, "The Latent Place of God in Twentieth-Century Political Theory," in *The Political Philosophy of Arnold Brecht*, p. 155.

53. Arnold Brecht, "The Rise of Relativism in Legal and Political Philosophy," *Social Research* 6 (1939); idem, "Relative and Absolute Justice," ibid; and idem, "The Search for Absolutes in Legal and Political Philosophy," *Social Research* 7 (1940).

54. Arnold Brecht, "Democracy: Challenge to Theory," *Social Research* 13 (1946).

55. See Rene De Visme Williamson, "The Challenge of Political Relativism," *JOP* 9 (1947); Hans Kelsen, "Absolutism and Relativism in Philosophy and Politics," *APSR* 42 (1948); and idem, "Science and Politics," *APSR* 45 (1951). For a similar position to that of Kelsen, see Felix Oppenheim, "Relativism, Absolutism, and Democracy," *APSR* 44 (1950).

56. Arnold Brecht, "Beyond Relativism in Political Theory: A Symposium," *APSR* 41 (1947): 470–73.

57. Ibid., pp. 474–82.

58. Ibid., p. 485.

59. Eric Voegelin, "The Origins of Scientism," *Social Research* 15 (1948): 494.

60. Frederick Watkins, *The Political Tradition of the West: A Study of the Development of Modern Liberalism* (Cambridge: Harvard University Press, 1948), p. ix.

61. See William Anderson, *Man's Search for Political Knowledge* (Minneapolis: University of Minnesota Press, 1964).

62. William Anderson, "Political Science North and South," *JOP* 11 (1949): 309.

63. John Hallowell, *Main Currents of Modern Political Thought* (New York: Holt, Rinehart and Winston, 1950), p. 110.

64. Ibid., p. 289.

65. Frederick M. Watkins, review of Hallowell's *Main Currents of Modern Political Thought, APSR* 45 (1951): 607–8.

66. Benjamin Lippincott, "Political Theory in the United States," in William Ebenstein (ed.), *Contemporary Political Science* (Paris: UNESCO, 1950), pp. 208–16.

67. Ibid., pp. 218–23.

68. Leonard D. White, "Political Science, Mid-Century," *JOP* 12 (1950): 18.

69. See, for example, Ellen Schrecker, *No Ivory Tower: McCarthyism and the Universities* (New York: Oxford University Press, 1988).

70. James G. Miller, in Leonard D. White (ed.), *The State of the Social Sciences* (Chicago: University of Chicago Press, 1956), p. 290. This volume consisted of papers presented at the 25th anniversary of the Social Science Building at the University of Chicago.

71. Karl Löwith, *Meaning in History: The Theological Implications of the Philosophy of History* (Chicago: University of Chicago Press, 1949), p. 3.

Chapter Ten

1. Robert Dahl, "The Behavioral Approach in Political Science: An Epitaph for a Monument to a Successful Protest," *APSR* 55 (1961): 763–72.

2. See, for example, Alfred de Grazia, "What is Political Behavior?" *PROD* I (1958).

3. David Truman, "The Implications of Political Behavior Research," *Items* (Social Science Research Council) 5 (1951), pp. 37–39.

4. David B. Truman, "The Impact on Political Science of the Revolution in the Behavioral Sciences," in *Research Frontiers in Politics and Government* (Washington, D.C.: Brookings Institution, 1957), pp. 215–230.

5. Oral history of Robert Dahl in Baer, Jewell, and Sigelman (eds.), *Political Science: Oral Histories of a Discipline* (see preface, n. 2). See also Ian Shapiro and Grant Reeher (eds.), *Power, Epistemology, and Democratic Politics: Essays in Honor of Robert A. Dahl* (Boulder, Colo.: Westview, 1988).

6. Charner Perry, "The Semantics of Social Science," *APSR* 44 (1950): 397–99, 401.

7. Ibid., pp. 399–400.

8. Ibid., pp. 411, 421, 423. This discussion is based in part on personal correspondence with Herbert Simon in March 1984.

9. Harold D. Lasswell and Abraham Kaplan, *Power and Society: A Framework for Political Inquiry* (New Haven, Conn.: Yale University Press, 1950), pp. ix–x.

10. Ibid., pp. xi–xiii.

11. Ibid., pp. xiv, xxiv. For a similar argument, see Harold Lasswell, "The Immediate Future of Research Policy and Method in Political Science," *APSR* 45 (1951).

12. Harold D. Lasswell, "The Political Science of Science," *APSR* 50 (1956). See also Daniel Lerner and Harold Lasswell (eds.), *The Policy Sciences* (Stanford, Calif.: Stanford University Press, 1951); and Harold D. Lasswell, "The Normative Impact of the Behavioral Sciences," *Ethics* 67 (1957).

13. Harold Lasswell in Richard Christie and Marie Jahoda (eds.), *Studies in the Scope and Method of the Authoritarian Personality* (Glencoe, Ill.: Free Press, 1954), pp. 195–96.

14. Hans Morgenthau, review of Lasswell and Kaplan's *Power and Society, APSR* 46 (1952): 234. See also idem, *Dilemmas of Politics* (Chicago: University of Chicago Press, 1958), pp. 17–24.

15. See, for example, G. Lowell Field, "Hypotheses for a Theory of Political Power," *APSR* 45 (1951).

16. J. J. Spengler, "Generalists versus Specialists in Social Science: An Economist's View," with comments by T. I. Cook, Stuart Rice, and Francis Wilson, *APSR* 44 (1950): 375, 386, 388.

17. Paul Appleby, "Political Science: The Next Twenty-Five Years," *APSR* 44 (1950); Oliver Garceau, "Research in the Political Process," *APSR* 45 (1951).

18. *Goals for Political Science,* Report of the Committee for the Advancement of Teaching, American Political Science Association (New York: William Sloane

Associates, 1951), pp. 126–27. See discussion in *APSR* 45 (1951): 996–1024 and *APSR* 46 (1952).

19. Leonard D. White, "Political Science, Mid-Century," *JOP* 12 (1950): 18.

20. This discussion of Easton is based on personal interviews and on the APSA oral history.

21. David Easton, "Walter Bagehot and Liberal Realism," *APSR* 43 (1949): 17–37.

22. David Easton, "Harold Lasswell: Policy Scientist for a Democratic Society," *JOP* 13 (1951): 450–55.

23. Ibid., pp. 455–58.

24. Ibid., pp. 467–77.

25. Alfred de Grazia, "Preface, Four Essays on the Relation of Political Theory to Research," *JOP* 13 (1951): 35.

26. Donald W. Smithburg, "Political Theory and Public Administration," ibid., pp. 61, 68.

27. Samuel T. Eldersveld, "Theory and Method in Voting Behavior Research," ibid., p. 87.

28. Alfred de Grazia, "The Process of Theory-Research Interaction," ibid., pp. 88, 99.

29. David Easton, "The Decline of Modern Political Theory," ibid., pp. 36–40.

30. Ibid., pp. 41–46.

31. Ibid., pp. 41–50.

32. Ibid., pp. 51–58.·

33. Gertrude Himmelfarb, "Political Thought: Ancients vs. Moderns, the New Battle of the Books," *Commentary* 12 (1951).

34. Francis W. Coker, "Some Present-Day Critics of Liberalism," *APSR* 47 (1953).

35. Dwight Waldo, "The Development of the Theory of Democratic Administration," *APSR* 46 (1952): 81, 97.

36. Herbert Simon, "The Development of Democratic Administration: Replies and Comments," *APSR* 46 (1952): 494, 496.

37. Ibid., p. 492.

38. See his development of this framework in "An Approach to the Analysis of Political Systems," *World Politics* 9 (1957).

39. William Anderson, *APSR* 47 (1953): 862–65.

40. David Easton, *The Political System: An Inquiry into the State of Political Science* (New York: Knopf, 1953), p. ix. George E. G. Catlin, "Political Theory, What Is It?" *PSQ* 72 (1957).

41. Hannah Arendt, "Ideology and Terror: A Novel Form of Government," *ROP* 15 (1953): 304.

42. "Journalism and Joachim's Children," *Time* 61 (March 1953), pp. 57–61.

43. Georg Lukács, *The Destruction of Reason* (London: Merlin, 1980).

44. Eric Voegelin, review of Arendt's *The Origins of Totalitarianism*, and "Reply," by Hannah Arendt, *ROP* 15 (1953): 68–85.

45. Eric Voegelin, *The New Science of Politics* (Chicago: University of Chicago Press, 1952).

46. Francis G. Wilson, review of Voegelin's *New Science of Politics, APSR* 47 (1953): 542–43.

47. Leo Strauss, *Natural Right and History* (Chicago: University of Chicago Press, 1953).

48. David Easton, *The Political System*, pp. ix, 5–6.

49. Ibid., pp. 17–22, 31, 36.

50. See, for example, Arnold S. Kaufman, "The Nature and Function of Political Theory," *JOP* 5 (1954).

51. George H. Sabine, review of Strauss's *Persecution and the Art of Writing, Ethics* 63 (1953): 220–22. Also idem, "Two Democratic Traditions," *Philosophical Review* 61 (1952).

52. See Kaufman, "The Nature and Function of Political Theory."

53. Robert Dahl, "The Science of Politics: Old and New," *World Politics* 7 (1954–55).

54. John H. Hallowell, *The Moral Foundations of Democracy* (Chicago: University of Chicago Press, 1954), p. v.

55. See the volume dedicated to Hallowell, Francis Canavan (ed.), *The Ethical Dimension of Political Life* (Durham, N.C.: Duke University Press, 1983).

56. Walter Lippmann, *Essays in the Public Philosophy* (Boston: Little, Brown, 1955), pp. 178–79.

57. Daniel Boorstin, *The Genius of American Politics* (Chicago: University of Chicago Press, 1953).

58. Louis Hartz, *The Liberal Tradition in America: An Interpretation of American Political Thought since the Revolution* (New York: Harcourt, Brace, 1955).

59. Robert Dahl, *Who Governs?* (New Haven, Conn.: Yale University Press, 1961).

60. David B. Truman, *The Governmental Process* (New York: Knopf, 1951). See also Earl Latham, *The Group Basis of Politics* (Ithaca, N.Y.: Cornell University Press, 1952); and Bertram M. Gross, *The Legislative Struggle: A Study in Social Combat* (New York: McGraw-Hill, 1955).

61. Robert Dahl, *Preface to Democratic Theory* (New Haven, Conn.: Yale University Press, 1956).

62. Hans Morgenthau, "Reflections on the State of Political Science," *ROP* 17 (1955): 444–46, 448, 450, 452–60.

63. Harry Eckstein, "Political Theory and the Study of Politics: A Report of a Conference," *APSR* 50 (1956). Among those attending were Easton, Friedrich, Herring, Norman Jacobson, Thomas Jenkin, Evron Kirkpatrick, Roy Macridis, Robert McCloskey, Ranney, Mulford Q. Sibley, David Smith, Kenneth Thompson, Watkins, and Wolin.

64. Dwight Waldo, "'Values' in the Political Science Curriculum," in Roland Young (ed.), *Approaches to the Study of Politics* (Evanston, Ill.: Northwestern Uni-

versity Press, 1958). Louis Hartz, "The Problem of Political Ideas," in ibid., pp. 78–79, 83–85.

65. Frederick M. Watkins, "Political Theory as a Datum of Political Science," in Young (ed.), *Study of Politics,* pp. 148–54. Robert G. McCloskey, "American Political thought and the Study of Politics," in ibid., p. 160. Carl J. Friedrich, "Political Philosophy and the Science of Politics," in ibid., pp. 172–73.

66. Norman Jacobson, "The Unity of Political Theory: Science, Morals, and Politics," in Young (ed.), *Study of Politics,* pp. 117–19, 122–24.

67. Jean M. Driscoll and Charles S. Hyneman, "Methodology for Political Scientists: Perspectives for Study," *APSR* 49 (1955): 192–93, 207.

68. Thomas P. Jenkin, *The Study of Political Theory* (Garden City, N.Y.: Doubleday, 1955).

69. Alfred Cobban, "The Decline of Political Theory," *PSQ* 68 (1953): 333, 335.

70. See, for example, A. J. Ayer, *Language, Truth and Logic* (New York: Dover, 1936).

71. T. D. Weldon, *The Vocabulary of Politics* (London: Penguin, 1953); and idem, "Political Principles," in Peter Laslett (ed.), *Philosophy, Politics and Society,* 1st ser. (New York: Macmillan, 1956). See also Margaret McDonald, "The Logic of Political Theory," in A. G. N. Flew (ed.), *Logic and Language* (Oxford: Blackwell, 1951); and J. C. Rees, "The Limitations of Political Theory," *Political Studies* 1 (1953).

72. Peter Laslett, in *Philosophy, Politics and Society,* 1st ser., pp. vii, ix.

73. See William A. Glaser, "The Types and Uses of Political Theory," *Social Research* 22 (1955); Andrew Hacker, "Capital and Carbuncles: The 'Great Books' Reappraised," *APSR* 48 (1954); idem, "Dostoevsky's Disciples: Man and Sheep in Political Theory," *JOP* 16 (1955); C. Northcote Parkinson, *The Evolution of Political Thought* (Boston: Houghton Mifflin, 1958); Thomas I. Cook, "The Prospects of Political Science," *JOP* 16 (1955); Bibliography on Politics and Values, *APSR* 49 (1955).

74. George E. G. Catlin, "Political Theory: What Is It?" *PSQ* 72 (1957); also idem, "The Function of Political Science," *Western Political Quarterly* 9 (1956).

75. David Easton, "An Approach to the Analysis of Political Systems," *World Politics* 9 (1956–57); idem, "Traditional and Behavioral Research in American Political Science," *Administrative Science Quarterly* 2 (1957–58): 112.

76. Leo Strauss, "What is Political Philosophy?" *JOP* 19 (1957).

77. Judith N. Shklar, *After Utopia* (Princeton, N.J.: Princeton University Press, 1957), pp. vii–ix, 271–73.

78. Sheldon S. Wolin, review of Shklar's *After Utopia, Natural Law Forum* 5 (1960): 172.

79. Robert Dahl, "Political Theory: Truth and Consequences," *World Politics* 11 (1958): 89, 95, 98.

80. David G. Smith, "Political Science and Political Theory," *APSR* 51 (1957): 734, 743, 745–46. David E. Apter, "Theory and the Study of Politics,"

ibid., pp. 757–59, 761. Arnold A. Rogow, "Whatever Happened to the Great Issues?" ibid.

81. See Young (ed.), *Study of Politics*.

82. V. O. Key, "The State of the Discipline," *APSR* 52 (1958): 964–65, 967–68.

Chapter Eleven

1. William Anderson, review of Arnold Brecht's *Political Theory: The Foundations of Twentieth-Century Political Thought, APSR* 54 (1960): 205.

2. See, for example, Anatol Rapaport, "Various Meanings of Theory," *APSR* 52 (1958).

3. Arnold Brecht, *Political Theory: The Foundations of Twentieth-Century Political Thought* (Princeton, N.J.: Princeton University Press, 1959), pp. 5, 8–9.

4. Ibid., pp. 11, 19. Emphasis added.

5. Ibid., pp. 401, 415, 479.

6. Eric Voegelin, *Israel and Revelation*, vol. 1 of *Order and History* (Baton Rouge: Louisiana State University Press, 1956); Hannah Arendt, *The Human Condition* (New York: Doubleday, 1958); Strauss, *What Is Political Philosophy?* (see chap. 7, n. 82).

7. Karl Popper, *The Open Society and Its Enemies* (London: Routledge and Kegan Paul, 1945). See Karl Popper, *Unended Quest: An Intellectual Autobiography* (LaSalle, Ill.: Open Court, 1976), p. 115.

8. Sheldon Wolin, *Politics and Vision: Continuity and Innovation in Western Political Thought* (Boston: Little, Brown, 1961), pp. v, 1–2.

9. Ibid., pp. 3, 5, 27, 288–90, 429, 434.

10. Emmette S. Redford, "Reflections on a Discipline," *APSR* 55 (1961): 758.

11. Harry Jaffa, "The Case against Political Theory," *JOP* 22 (1960).

12. David Easton, "The Current Meaning of 'Behavioralism,'" in James C. Charlesworth (ed.), *The Limits of Behavioralism in Political Science* (Philadelphia: Academy of Political and Social Science, 1962), pp. 1–7.

13. Ibid., pp. 8–25.

14. Wolin, *Politics and Vision*, p. 434.

15. Robert Dahl, *Modern Political Analysis* (Englewood Cliffs, N.J.: Prentice-Hall, 1963), p. 6.

16. Heinz Eulau, *The Behavioral Persuasion in Politics* (New York: Random House, 1963); idem, "Tradition and Innovation: On the Tension Between Ancient and Modern Ways of Studying Politics," in Heinz Eulau (ed.), *Behavioralism in Political Science* (New York: Atherton, 1969).

17. Stanley Rothman, "The Revival of Classical Political Philosophy: A Critique," *APSR* 56 (1962): 341.

18. Evron M. Kirkpatrick, "The Impact of the Behavioral Approach on Traditional Political Science," in Austin Ranney (ed.), *Essays on the Behavioral Study of Politics* (Urbana: University of Illinois Press, 1962), pp. 5, 14, 16, 27.

19. Herbert J. Storing (ed.), *Essays on the Scientific Study of Politics* (New York: Holt, Rinehart and Winston, 1962), pp. 103, 153, 230, 326.

20. Ibid., pp. 55, 57, 301, 318.

21. Ibid., pp. 307, 317, 322, 326–27.

22. The sense that Sheldon Wolin, John Schaar, and Norman Jacobson, and some of their students such as Hanna Pitkin constituted an identifiable persuasion within the field was recognized by individuals such as the editor of the *APSR*. See oral history of Austin Ranney, APSA.

23. John H. Schaar and Sheldon S. Wolin, "Essays on the Scientific Study of Politics: A Critique," review of Storing (ed.), *APSR* 57 (1960): 125, 126–7, 132.

24. See, for example, Walter Berns, "The Behavioral Sciences and the Study of Political Theory: The Case against Christian Bay's *The Structure of Freedom*," *APSR* 53 (1961); and Mulford Q. Sibley, "The Limitations of Behavioralism," in Charlesworth (ed.), *Limits of Behavioralism*.

25. Leo Strauss and Joseph Cropsey (eds.), *History of Political Philosophy* (Chicago; Rand McNally, 1963).

26. Schaar and Wolin, review of Storing (ed.), p. 150.

27. Norman Jacobson, "Causality and Time in Political Process: A Speculation," *APSR* 58 (1964); John H. Schaar, *Loyalty in America* (Berkeley: University of California Press, 1957).

28. See, for example, Thomas Landon Thorson, "Political Values and Analytic Philosophy," *JOP* 23 (1961); William T. Bluhm, *Theories of the Political System: Classics of Political Thought and Modern Political Analysis* (Englewood Cliffs, N.J.: Prentice-Hall, 1978).

29. Dante L. Germino, *Beyond Ideology: The Revival of Political Theory* (New York: Harper and Row, 1967).

30. Christian Bay, "Politics and Pseudo-Politics: A Critical Evaluation of Some Behavioral Literature," *APSR* 59 (1965); Charles A. McCoy and John Playford (eds.), *Apolitical Politics: A Critique of Behavioralism* (New York: Thomas Y. Crowell, 1967), p. 10.

31. Bernard Berelson and Gary Steiner, *Human Behavior: An Inventory of Scientific Findings* (New York: Harcourt, Brace and World, 1964).

32. David Easton, *A Framework for Political Analysis* (Englewood Cliffs, N.J.: Prentice-Hall, 1965), p. 9; see also idem, *A Systems Analysis of Political Life* (New York: Wiley, 1965); David Easton (ed.), *Varieties of Political Theory* (Englewood Cliffs, N.J.: Prentice-Hall, 1966); Karl Deutsch, *Nerves of Government* (New York: Free Press, 1963); Ithiel de Sola Pool (ed.), *Contemporary Political Science: Toward Empirical Theory* (New York: McGraw-Hill, 1967); Gordon J. Direnzo (ed.), *Concepts, Theory, and Explanation in the Behavioral Sciences* (New York: Random House, 1966).

33. David B. Truman, "Disillusion and Regeneration: The Quest for a Discipline," *APSR* 59 (1965): 867, 870–72, 874.

34. Karl W. Deutsch and Leroy N. Rieselbach, "Recent Trends in Political Theory and Political Philsophy," *Annals of the American Academy of Political and Social Science* 360 (1965): 139, 162.

35. Gabriel Almond, "Political Theory and Political Science," *APSR* 60 (1966): 869.

36. One of the outstanding examples was Gabriel Almond and Sidney Verba, *The Civic Culture* (Princeton, N.J.: Princeton University Press, 1963).

37. See Barrington Moore, Jr., *Political Power and Social Theory: Six Studies* (Cambridge: Harvard University Press, 1958).

38. Dwight Waldo, *Political Science in the United States of America* (Paris: UNESCO, 1956).

39. Daniel Bell, *The End of Ideology: The Exhaustion of Ideas in the Fifties* (Glencoe, Ill.: Free Press, 1960). See Stephen W. Rousseas and James Farganis, "American Politics and the End of Ideology," *British Journal of Sociology* 14 (1963); and Chaim Isaac Waxman (ed.), *The-End-of-Ideology Debate* (New York: Simon and Schuster, 1969).

40. Seymour Martin Lipset, *Political Man: The Social Bases of Politics* (Garden City, N.Y.: Doubleday, 1960), p. 403. See also Joseph LaPalombara, "Decline of Ideology: A Dissent and an Interpretation," *APSR* 60 (1965); and Seymour Martin Lipset, "Some Further Comments on 'The End of Ideology,'" ibid.

41. See, for example, Angus Campbell, *The American Voter* (New York: Wiley, 1960).

42. Robert E. Lane, "The Politics of Consensus in an Age of Affluence," *APSR* 59 (1965): 895; and idem, "The Decline of Politics and Ideology in a Knowledgeable Society," *American Sociological Review* 31 (1966).

43. See James C. Charlesworth (ed.), *A Design for Political Science: Scope, Objectives, and Methods* (Philadelphia: American Academy of Political and Social Science, 1966). Hans Morgenthau, "The Purpose of Political Science," ibid; Karl Deutsch, "Recent Trends in Research Methods in Political Science," ibid; Heinz Eulau, comments on Deutsch's paper, ibid.

44. Somit and Tannenhaus, *Development of American Political Science* (see intro., n. 7).

45. Marian D. Irish, "Introduction: Advance of the Discipline?" *JOP* 30 (1968): 293, 298.

46. Neil A. McDonald and James N. Rosenau, "Political Theory as Academic Field and Intellectual Activity," *JOP* 30 (1968): 317, 320–21, 323, 334, 337.

47. See David Spitz (ed.), *Political Theory and Social Change* (New York: Atherton, 1967); and Oliver Garceau (ed.), *Political Research and Political Theory* (Cambridge: Harvard University Press, 1968).

48. See, for example, William Kornhauser, *The Politics of Mass Society* (New York: Free Press, 1959); Gabriel Almond and James Coleman, *The Politics of the Developing Areas* (Princeton, N.J.: Princeton University Press, 1960); Charles Lindblom, *The Intelligence of Democracy: Decision-Making through Mutual Adjustment* (New York: Free Press, 1965); Bertrand de Jouvenal, *The Pure Theory of Politics* (Cambridge: Cambridge University Press, 1963); Mancur Olson, *The Logic of Collective Action: Public Goods and the Theory of Groups* (Cambridge: Harvard University Press, 1965); Don Price, *The Scientific Estate* (Cambridge, Mass.:

Belknap, 1965). John Galbraith, *The New Industrial State* (Boston: Houghton Mifflin, 1967); Robert Dahl, *Pluralist Democracy in the United States: Conflict and Consent* (Chicago: Rand McNally, 1967).

49. C. Wright Mills, *The Power Elite* (New York: Oxford University Press, 1956); and Irving Louis Horowitz (ed.), *Power, Politics and People: The Collected Essays of C. Wright Mills* (New York: Ballantine, 1963).

50. Peter Bachrach and Morton S. Baratz, "Two Faces of Power," *APSR* 56 (1962).

51. William Connolly (ed.), *The Biases of Pluralism* (New York: Atherton, 1969); Peter Bachrach, *The Theory of Democratic Elitism: A Critique* (Boston: Little, Brown, 1967); Jack L. Walker, "A Critique of the Elitist Theory of Democracy," *APSR* 60 (1966); Lane Davis, "The Cost of Realism: Contemporary Restatements of Democracy," *Western Political Quarterly* 17 (1964); Graeme Duncan and Steven Lukes, "The New Democracy," *Political Studies* 11 (1963).

52. Henry Kariel, *The Decline of American Pluralism* (Stanford, Calif.: Stanford University Press, 1961); C. B. Macpherson, *The Political Theory of Possessive Individualism* (Oxford: Clarendon, 1962); Herbert Marcuse, "Repressive Tolerance," in Robert Paul Wolff, Barrington Moore, Jr., and Marcuse (eds.), *A Critique of Pure Tolerance* (Boston: Beacon, 1969); Grant McConnell, *Private Power and American Democracy* (New York: Knopf, 1966); Theodore Lowi, *The End of Liberalism* (New York: Norton, 1969); Robert Paul Wolff, *The Poverty of Liberalism* (Boston: Beacon, 1968). See also J. Roland Pennock and John W. Chapman (eds.), *Voluntary Associations*, Nomos 11 (New York: Atherton, 1969).

53. See Sigmund Diamond, *Compromised Campus: The Collaboration of Universities with the Intelligence Community, 1945–55* (New York: Oxford University Press, (1992).

54. See Marvin Surkin and Alan Wolfe (eds.), *An End to Political Science: The Cancus Papers* (New York: Basic, 1970); and Theodore Roszak (ed.), *The Dissenting Academy* (New York: Pantheon, 1968). Also Theodore J. Lowi, "The Politics of Higher Education: PoliticalScience as a Case Study," in George J. Graham and George W. Carey (eds.), *The Post-Behavioral Era: Perspectives on Political Science* (New York: David McKay, 1972).

55. For a comprehensive discussion, see Edward Bryan Portis and Michael B. Levy (eds.), *Handbook of Political Theory and Public Policy* (New York: Greenwood, 1988); and James Dunn and Rita Mae Kelley (eds.), *Advances in Policy Studies since 1950* (New Brunswick, N.J.: Transaction, 1992).

56. See Karl Deutsch, "On Political Theory and Political Action," *APSR* 65 (1971).

57. Heinz Eulau, "The Skill Revolution and the Consultative Commonwealth," *APSR* 67 (1973); Avery Leiserson, "Charles Merriam, Max Weber, and the Search for Synthesis in Political Science," *APSR* 69 (1975); Austin Ranney, "The Divine Science of Politics: Political Engineering in American Culture," *APSR* 70 (1976); Warren E. Miller, "The Role of Research in the Unification of a Discipline," *APSR* 75 (1981).

58. Aaron B. Wildavsky, *Speaking Truth to Power: The Art and Craft of Policy Analysis* (Boston: Little, Brown, 1979).

59. Schaar and Wolin, review of Storing (ed.), p. 125.

60. See John G. Gunnell, "Deduction, Explanation, and Social Scientific Inquiry," *APSR* 63 (1969); Arthur S. Goldberg, "On the Need for Contextualist Criteria: A Reply to Professor Gunnell," ibid.; A. James Gregor, "Gunnell on 'Deduction,' the 'Logic' of Science and Scientific Explanation: A Riposte," ibid.; and Gunnell, "Science and the Philosophy of Science: A Rejoinder to Professors Goldberg and Gregor," ibid.

61. See, for example, Vernon van Dyke, *Political Science: A Philosophical Analysis* (Stanford, Calif.: Stanford University Press, 1960). One book which carried considerable authority was Abraham Kaplan's *Conduct of Inquiry* (San Francisco: Chandler, 1964), which was a kind of synthesis of positivist and American perspectives.

62. See A. James Gregor, *An Introduction to Metapolitics* (New York: Free Press, 1971); Eugene F. Miller, "Positivism, Historicism, and Political Inquiry," *ASPR* 66 (1972); David Braybrooke and Alexander Rosenberg, "Getting the War News Straight: The Actual Situation in the Philosophy of Science," ibid.; Richard S. Rudner, "On Evolving Standard Views in Philosophy of Science," ibid.; Martin Landau, "On Objectivity," ibid.; and Miller, "Rejoinder," ibid.; Gunnell, *Philosophy, Science, and Political Inquiry* (see intro., n. 4); Donald J. Moon, "The Logic of Political Inquiry," in Fred I. Greenstein and Nelson W. Polsby (eds.), *Handbook of Political Science*, vol. 1 (Reading, Pa.: Addison-Wesley, 1975).

63. Peter Laslett and W. G. Runciman (eds.), *Philosophy, Politics and Society* (New York: Barnes and Noble, 2d ser., 1962; 3d ser., 1967). Isaiah Berlin, "Does Political Theory Still Exist?" in ibid. (1962). W. G. Runciman, *Social Science and Political Theory* (Cambridge: Cambridge University Press, 1963).

64. Peter Winch, *The Idea of a Social Science and its Relation to Philosophy* (London: Routledge and Kegan Paul, 1958); Alfred Schütz, *The Phenomenology of the Social World* (Evanston, Ill.: Northwestern University Press, 1967); John G. Gunnell, "Social Science and Political Reality: The Problem of Explanation," *Social Research* 35 (1968); Charles Taylor, *The Explanation of Behavior* (New York: Humanities Press, 1964); and idem, "Interpretation and the Sciences of Man," *Review of Metaphysics* 25 (1971).

65. Quentin Skinner, "Meaning and Understanding in the History of Ideas," *History and Theory* 8 (1969); J. G. A. Pocock, *Politics, Language, and Time* (New York: Antheum, 1971).

66. Peter Laslett and James Fishkin (eds.), *Philosophy, Politics and Society*, 5th ser., (New Haven, Conn.: Yale University Press, 1979), p. 2.

67. See, for example, comments about the state of the field in Robert Freeman and David Robertson (eds.), *The Frontiers of Political Theory* (New York: St. Martin's, 1980); and David Miller and Larry Seidentop (eds.), *The Nature of Political Theory* (Oxford: Clarendon, 1983).

68. Michael J. Sandel, *Liberalism and the Limits of Justice* (New York: Cam-

bridge University Press, 1982); and Sandel (ed.), *Liberalism and Its Critics* (New York: New York University Press, 1984).

69. Max Horkheimer, *Critical Theory* (New York: Herder and Herder, 1972).

70. See, for example, Herbert Marcuse, *One-Dimensional Man* (Boston: Beacon, 1964); idem, *An Essay on Liberation* (Boston: Beacon, 1969).

71. Jürgen Habermas, *The Theory of Communicative Action*, 2 vol. (Boston: Beacon Press, 1984, 1987).

72. See Sheldon S. Wolin, "Political Theory and Political Commentary," in Melvin Richter (ed.), *Political Theory and Political Education* (Princeton, N.J.: Princeton University Press, 1980). See also Bill Moyers's television interview with Wolin on the *World of Ideas*. For a more detailed and comprehensive critical discussion of Wolin's work, see Gunnell, *Between Philosophy and Politics* (see intro., n. 4).

73. Sheldon S. Wolin and John H. Schaar, "The Abuses of the Multiversity," in Seymour Martin Lipset and Sheldon S. Wolin (eds.), *The Berkeley Student Revolt* (Garden City, N.Y.: Anchor, 1965), p. 356.

74. Note, for example, Tom Hayden's indication of the influence of Wolin's notion of political vision in the Port Huron statement discussed by James Miller, *Democracy Is in the Streets: From Port Huron to the Seige of Chicago* (New York: Simon and Schuster, 1987), p. 94.

75. For example, Benjamin Barber, *Strong Democracy* (Berkeley: University of California Press, 1984).

76. Michael Walzer, *Interpretation and Social Criticism* (Cambridge: Cambridge University Press, 1987), pp. 39, 60; idem, *The Company of Critics* (New York: Basic, 1988), pp. 4, 11.

Index

pluralism vs. monism, 106–7; on political theory, 139–40; on pragmatism, 116, 144; on sciences, 77

Salz, Arthur, on Weber, 156–57

Sanborn, Frank B.: academia and, 44–45; ASSA and, 42–44

Schaar, John H., 261; at Berkeley, 259

Scheler, Max: on philosophy, 158; on Weber, 157–58

Schlick, Moritz, 193

Schmitt, Carl: Heller on, 169; *Legality and Legitimacy* of, 169; on modernity, 167–68; Nazi movement and, 169–70; *Prussia vs the Reich* of, 169; on sovereignty, 166–68; on "the political," 165–66, 167–68

Schumpeter, Joseph, *Capitalism, Socialism, and Democracy* of, 183

Schütz, Alfred: background of, 191–92; criticism of, 192; on social scientific explanation, 271

Science: debate over nature of, 269–70; method of, 194–95

Scientific method of philosophy, 194

Scientism, 214; Beard on, 115; Corwin on, 116; decline of, 137–38

Seelye, Julius, 37–38

Seligman, E. R. A., influence on Beard, 85

Shklar, Judith, on demise of political theory, 247

Simon, Herbert: on language of political science; on redefinition of political theory, 224; on Waldo, 235

Simon, Yves, 237

Smith, David, on political theory, 248

Smith, T. V., 133; on compromise, 143; on ethic of conscience, 124; on Hayek, 204

Smithburg, Donald, on political theory and research, 231

Social Research, 180

Social science: dimensions of, 41; religion and, 42–44

Social Science Research Council (SSRC), 117

Sombart on Mannheim, 163

Sorokin, Pitirim A., on positivism, 134

Speier, Hans: on Mannheim, 163, 164–65; on plight of emigrant, 181–82; on totalitarianism, 187

Spengler, J. J., on political science as social science, 227

Spengler, Oswald, *Decline of the West* of, 155

State: Bluntschli on, 33–34; "concept" vs. "idea" of, 55; government and, 53–55; Jaspers on, 171–72; Lieber on, 28–29; natural history of, 77; university and, 37–59; Willoughby on, 58; Wilson on, 57; World War I and, 79–81

Staudinger, Hans, on Nazi success, 187

Strauss, Leo, 138; on behavioralism, 259; Berkeley group and, 260; on decline of political thought, 246; on experimental method, 199; Friedrich on, 138–39; on Hobbes, 175–76; *Natural Right and History* of, 237; on relativism, 238–39

Theoretical intervention, 146–47

Theory: concept of, 21–22; institutionalization of, 60–81; Merriam on, 93; political (*see* Political theory); science and, 219–20; of state, 22–23

Totalitarianism, émigrés on, 187–88

Tremenheere, H. S., 63

Troeltsch, Ernst, on Kahler, 157

Truman, David B., on history of political science, 262

University: politics and, 47–53; state and, 37–59; study of ethics in, 34

Value theory, Easton on, 232–34

Vaughan, C. E., 101

Verein für Sozialpolitik, 47–49; general differences in, 152

Vienna group in U.S., 193

Voegelin, Eric, 100, 197–98; on Arendt, 237–38; assimilation of, 183; Brecht on, 211; on Hallowell, 204; on modernity, 213; *The New Science of Politics* of, 237, 238; on research in political theory, 207

Waldo, Dwight: on American political order, 263; on political theory and public administration, 235; on practical role of political science, 242; on Simon, 235–36

Walzer, Michael, on social critic, 276–77